The Defence of
the Undefended Border

The Defence of the Undefended Border

Planning for War
in North America
1867–1939

Richard A. Preston

McGill–Queen's University Press
Montreal and London   1977

© McGill-Queen's University Press
International Standard Book Number 0-7735-0291-2
Legal Deposit fourth quarter 1977
Bibliothèque nationale du Québec

Design by Hjordis Petersen Wills
Printed in Canada by
John Deyell Company

This book has been published with the help
of a grant from the Social Science Federation of Canada using funds provided by the
Canada Council

CONTENTS

ILLUSTRATIONS

PREFACE

The late Robin Strachan, whose premature death was a tragic loss for scholarly publishing in Canada, suggested that I should write a book on the military factor in Canadian-American relations. The validity of the mythology of the well-publicized "longest undefended border in the world" had, of course, already been thoroughly examined by Colonel Stacey, who had also written the classic study of the British army in Canada down to the end of the Confederation period. Stacey had demonstrated the relation of defence problems to the development of responsible government in Canada and had shown that, despite the agreement on naval limitation on the Great Lakes, fortification building had continued on both sides of the line. Defence against the United States figured largely in his story. Later books by J. M. Hitsman, Kenneth Bourne, and Robin Winks have given more details of British defence planning which continued vigorously until 1870 and even after. However, in course of preparation of my *Canada and 'Imperial Defense'* it had become clear to me that there still remained grave deficiencies in our knowledge of the history of Canadian military policy and of the militia after Confederation because other historians of the later period had been content to repeat traditional versions. In particular, although it was obvious that the frequently stated rationale for a militia—fear of an American attack—declined in relevance after 1870, it could not be assumed that all thought of the possibility of war had been as quickly dismissed. This was the problem that Robin Strachan proposed I should explore.

Dr. James Eayrs's provocative account of Canadian war planning in the 1920s, in the first volume of his *In Defence of Canada*, called my attention to the persistence of that practice north of the border, and to the need to set it in its proper context by relating it to American planning and the reality of the danger of war. In view of the growth of Canadian-American amity in the past century, the relation between war planning and policy making seemed obscure. When writing *Canada and 'Imperial Defense'* I had studied British planning after the withdrawal of the garrison, and its relation to British imperial interests. It now merited reexamination for the light that it might throw on the question of a possible war in North America.

On the American side, a State Department ruling prohibited access to all records relating to American plans for wars with presently friendly or neutral countries, even those prepared in the nineteenth century. This ruling had severely limited knowledge of the development of war planning in the United States. However, published articles and U.S. Army War College records suggested that there had been more American planning than was generally known. Fortunately, before I completed the research for this book the removal of the State Department prohibition enabled me to provide a fuller and more satisfactory account of American activities than would have been otherwise possible. My study confirms that American planning for a war in North America steadily increased—right down to the eve of the Second World War—even while closer and more friendly relations were developing.

The present book is therefore a study of war planning in all three countries. It is designed to provide a better understanding of the nature and extent of the work of the planners on all sides. It does not claim to give a definitive answer concerning the importance of the military factor in Canadian-American relations.

While the development of modern military and naval staffs meant a natural growth of war-planning activities, these were undertaken primarily for training purposes and secondarily for preliminary preparation for a contingency that was deemed unlikely to materialize. Plans devised in the United States for war with Britain and Canada were of a broad general nature, being appraisals of an unexpected military situation and of the possible course of operations if the unlikely happened, rather than the detailed plans for deployment which hostilities would have required.

The reason why the U.S. Army was particularly active in the sphere of planning for a war in North America was because the navy monopolized planning for a Pacific war; and army planning for participation in a war overseas would have aroused a storm of public protest. American plans for war in North America were much less detailed than those for war with potential enemies like Japan, and for the local defence of places of strategic significance.

As all planning for war in North America was done in the strictest secrecy, often being kept from the knowledge of the responsible civil authorities, it appears to have had little effect on public opinion. But some information about it may have leaked. In the United States warnings about the difficulties that would be experienced in a war with Britain, and therefore with

Canada, would confirm the wisdom of the popular desire to foster good relations.

British and Canadian military leaders were similarly aware of the great difficulties that a war in North America would bring; and their political masters had even less confidence in the outcome. The Canadian public was conscious also of the consequences of a strategy which would inevitably be based on a withdrawal to strong points. Professional war planning, therefore, may not have contributed to an increase in the possibility of war, as is often assumed, but rather to a more solid foundation for peace.

In the course of writing a book of this kind an author becomes indebted to many institutions and many people. Initial stimulation and encouragement came from Col. C. P. Stacey, Robin Winks, the late J. M. Hitsman, H. P. Gundy, and Gerald M. Craig. The Commonwealth Studies Center, the Duke University Research Council, the John Simon Guggenheim Memorial Foundation, and Duke University provided financial assistance in the form of study leave, travel expenses, and typing grants, without which the task could not have been completed.

The staffs of various libraries gave aid enthusiastically in many obscure searches. At the expense of risking discriminatory reference, some individuals must be mentioned by name. Ernest Swiger, a research assistant, did some preliminary investigation of printed U.S. government sources. At the Perkins Library of Duke University, the Reference Librarians, Florence Blakeley and Mary Canada, and their assistants, Mattie Russell and William Erwin in Manuscripts, and Gertrude Merritt, the Assistant University Librarian, have given me much help. During summers in Kingston, the staff of the Massey Library of the Royal Military College, including the Chief Librarian, John W. Spurr, Cliff Watt, and Jean Malach, were always willing to interrupt other duties to help me. The

Directorate of Military History of the Canadian Armed Forces College in Ottawa, and especially Sydney Wise and Alec Douglas, were unfailing in their support. At the Douglas Library of Queen's University, Kingston, Ontario, Ian Wilson and William Morley have earned my special thanks.

Others to whom I am indebted include the librarians and archivists at the Public Archives of Canada, the Public Record Office in London and at Ashbridge Park, the British Museum, the Public Record Office of Northern Ireland, the British War Office Library, the Commonwealth Relations Office Library, the India Office Library, the Foreign Office Library, the U.S. National Archives (especially John E. Taylor and William H. Cunliffe), the Library of Congress (especially the Manuscripts Division and Paul T. Heffron), and the Office of the Chief of Military History of the U.S. Army in Washington D.C. (especially Marice Matloff). The U.S. Army Military History Collection at Carlisle Barracks was a source of invaluable information, and George S. Pappas and Franklin B. Cooling helped to make it so. Howard Moon, John Weaver, Richard Pierce, and Peter Kasurak provided specific items.

Access to private papers in Britain was facilitated by the National Register of Archives of the Historical Manuscripts Commission which also made it possible for me to see the Palmerston papers by permission of Viscount Mountbatten. Other useful British archives included dissertations at the Institute of Historical Research of the University of London, and papers at Christ Church College and the Bodley Library, Oxford, Nottingham University, Birmingham University, Durham University, the National Archives of Scotland, the National Archives of Wales, the Gloucester County Record Office (where they were seen by permission of Earl St. Aldwyn), and the Royal Archives, Windsor (where the papers of the duke of Cambridge were seen by

gracious permission of Her Majesty the Queen).
Maldwin Drummond permitted me to see a diary
in the Cadland Mss; and Anthony S. Nicolosi of
the Naval War College, and P. A. Kennedy of
the Devon County Record Office, at two archives
I did not visit, forwarded extremely valuable
materials in photographic form.

All or portions of the manuscript have been
read by Desmond Morton of Erindale College, by
Barry Gough of Sir Wilfrid Laurier University,
and by Steve Harris. I am grateful to them for
suggestions, as also to three anonymous readers. All offered valuable criticism which I accepted gratefully and incorporated in the test.
Marion Salinger, of Duke University International Studies Center, made many constructive
editorial suggestions. Nevertheless, what now
emerges is solely on my own responsibility.

At various stages a series of typists have
laboured with drafts that were often difficult to
decipher. I wish to make special mention of
Penelope Maunsell, Suzanne Cusick, Colleen
Evans, and Sara Watts. I am also indebted to
K. B. Ames for her skilful redrawing of the "invasion plan" that appears in this volume.

RICHARD A. PRESTON
Duke University

The Military Factor in Canadian-American Relations

It is popularly believed that a state's military policy should be framed to provide sufficient force to carry out its foreign policy; but the objectives of foreign policy are not easy to define for this purpose, and the nature and degree of the military preparations required are difficult to determine and even more difficult to develop. Middle and small powers are often especially hard put to maintain military force sufficient to implement their foreign policy goals. Furthermore, in all countries short-term problems and political issues intervene to distort or divert planning. In some cases foreign policy is in fact determined by the existing military capabilities and so is not the basic reason for requiring them; nevertheless the armed forces that are available may not conform with the real needs of the state. For very many reasons, therefore, the relation between foreign policy and military policy is complex rather than simple and clearly does not coincide with the popular image premised above.[1] A satisfactory relationship is frequently not achieved.

Professor Denis Stairs has expressed the view that Canada's foreign policy, during the Cold War and its aftermath, came to be increasingly concerned with organization maintenance, including the establishment of diplomatic credit, particularly with the United States.[2] Thus it can be seen that military force may function not so much to oppose a potential enemy as to impress a friend. If one isolates (for closer consideration) Canada's relations with the United States, now the most important aspect of Canadian foreign policy, then the relation of military strength to foreign policy is revealed as actually quite different from the simple popular image of building defence strength in preparation for direct confrontation.

One or two illustrations will serve. When pressed by newsmen to reveal the nature of the Canadian government's protests to Washington against the testing of a nuclear device on Amchitka Island in the fall of 1971, Prime Minister Pierre Trudeau is said to have replied in exasperation, "The only further thing we can do is declare war." If this story is true, his irritable or sarcastic reaction did not make many headlines. The idea of war with the United States and of the critical maintenance of armed forces to protect Canada against the United States was so inconceivable that Trudeau's ironic comment was not even newsworthy. Few Canadians thought that war potential was a factor in Canadian-American relations.

Earlier in the same year, a Canadian newspaper published what it said was an article reprinted "from *The Examiner*, an American journal," in which President Richard Nixon was alleged to have approved a policy for obtaining water and other resources from Canada, by force if necessary.[3] The newspaper editor responsible had not taken the precaution of verifying the source of his information. If he had done so he would have learned that no such American periodical had ever existed. When challenged, the editor privately explained that he, personally, felt the opinions in the article "reflect by exaggeration a point of view held by at least some segments in the United States."[4] Although a few of his readers were alarmed, the majority apparently regarded the alleged reprinting as a spoof or a fraud since there was little reaction beyond a few enquiries addressed to American and Canadian government officials. The fact that an allegation of this kind had had to be manufactured in an attempt to provide sensational support for what a few Canadians feared suggests that no hard evidence in the form of official American statements, or of American journalistic output, was available at that time. Threats of a Canadian-American war were not regarded as credible.

A Canadian graduate student, writing a dissertation in the 1960s about British Imperial naval bases in North America at the end of the nineteenth century, described contingency plans for a counter-invasion of the United States in the event of a war as "airy nonsense" and, following J. A. S. Grenville's *Salisbury*, as "the lunatic fringe of official documents." Grenville had also called the same plans "bizarre."[5] The opinions of these historians reflect the sentiments of our own age rather than those of the time of which they were writing when, in fact, British sea power was still considered to be a deterrent force, and when planning to exploit it, in case of need, was a natural concomitant. Examples like these could be multiplied many times. Collectively they serve to illustrate the present-day popular belief that a military solution for Canadian-American problems has become unthinkable.

Such dismissal of the feasibility of military confrontation between two nations is not unique. In other cases close contact, protection by a balance-of-power system, common fear of a third party, satellite status, or other factors have created not dissimilar situations in which conflict is accepted as improbable. Cases in point are the relations between Britain and France and among the three Scandinavian countries, the Russo-Finnish tie, Russia's relations with members of the Warsaw Pact, relations among most NATO countries, the relations of the United States with many countries that seek American protection, and the relations between India and some of the states on her northern border. But what makes Canada's relationship with the United States different from most of these examples—and indeed virtually unique—is that it displays much less possibility of outside interference, very many more points of contact and of social and economic association and even integration, and many more instances of friendship and harmony. Most important of all, this special relationship is not a direct result of a past demonstration or potential threat of superior force.

The commonly-held belief that American military force will never again be used to threaten Canada or to override Canadian wishes is, however, fairly recent. It has not always been, and is perhaps still not, universally accepted. During the early days of the Second World War a group of Canadian intellectuals (some of whom came at a later date to be much exercised about the presence of American troops on Canadian soil) urged the Canadian government to make a diplomatic approach to secure the protection of the United States. Something more than the Hyde Park and Ogdensburg agreements seems to have been implied. These Canadians apparently assumed that if the Northern American continent were threatened, the United States would take whatever measures it deemed necessary without consulting Canada. They therefore thought it wise to come to terms in advance.[6]

Events in recent years have served to nurture still more unease about what the United States might do if its vital interests were threatened by Canadian action or inaction. There have been many incidents—President Kennedy's approval of the Bay-of-Pigs invasion and President Johnson's war without congressional approval in Viet Nam; Congress's Tonkin Bay resolution based on dubious information; the illegal activity of members of the White House staff in the name of national security; the invasion of Cambodia and the bombing of North Viet Nam and mining of Hanoi Harbor, and the CIA's move to "de-stabilize" the Allende government in Chile which President Ford excused in retrospect as an effort to defend democratic forms of government. President Ford warned oil-producing states that nations have often gone to war to obtain vital natural resources (a pronouncement that was, incidentally, made in Detroit close to the Canadian border); Henry Kissinger stated that force could not be ruled out if the industrial states were being strangled; and the CIA revealed past plans to assassinate heads of state. All these things suggest that irresponsibility within the American system of govern, or a ruthless president, might cause the engulfment of Canada in some future crisis. It would be interesting to know what plans American government departments or agencies prepared and held in readiness during the October 1970 crisis in Quebec, and to know further what is envisaged for the protection of American interests if Quebec separatism again leads to turmoil.

Nevertheless, by a kind of latter-day extension of the unilateral Monroe Doctrine, the United States is still widely regarded as Canada's primary guarantor of freedom from external threat. Up to a century ago Britain was Canada's guarantor, chiefly against the United States. Clearly a gradual strategic evolution has occurred. Fear of an Anglo-American military clash, and therefore of a possible invasion of Canada, declined after the British withdrew their military forces from the interior of the continent in 1870–71. This decline was accompanied by a withering of the need for the British military support which had been freely offered to Canada during the first three-quarters of the century, an assurance that had been repeated when withdrawal was announced.

If the principles of stark *Realpolitik* and a simplistic view of the relations of foreign policy to military strength had applied after Britain's withdrawal, Canada's increasing loneliness in North America would have left her a victim of American military blackmail, or perhaps of invasion. Instead Canadian-American confrontation has become diplomatic, economic, and cultural, rather than military. Although this confrontation is often charged with emotion, the military factor seems to be taken into account only in estimating the degree of cooperation or of detachment that will secure greater American respect for Canada's interests—or in efforts to show that American help is relatively unnecessary. Canadian armed forces thus may protect Canada not only against other foreign, but also American, encroachment—not so much by direct confrontation in defence, but indirectly, by building diplomatic credit, by bearing the fullest possible responsibility for Canada's defence against other powers, and by "surveillance and control."[7]

How did it come about that Canada, despite lack of protection, survived after the British withdrawal? What has made possible this present non-violent Canadian-American relationship and this paradoxically inverted connection between foreign and military policies? One explanation could be that an enduring amicable relationship was based upon growing mutual awareness of real political and social similarities. There is, and always was, an underlying feeling of kinship and of social and cultural homogeneity among English-speaking North Americans despite the heritage of the American Revolution and later threats of war, and despite Canadian suspicion, disparagement, and dislike of American *mores* and institutions. But kinship and similarity are not always forces for harmony between peoples, any more than they are between individuals, and of course these harmonizing factors have not much affected French Canadians.

Another possibility is that the Canadian-American entente was greatly facilitated by common geographic isolation and by the preoccupation of both peoples with the more engrossing problems of occupying and developing a continent. Because governments and electors in both Canada and the United States were loath to spend money on warlike preparations in times of peace, and since there was a healthy suspicion of standing armies in both countries, they were slow to develop those military institutions which are normally assumed to be essential for the preservation of national sovereignty. Consequently they were never prepared for war with each other. Furthermore, although Canadians often pointed to the long history of aggressive American expansion, it gradually became clear on both sides of the border that "manifest destiny," as applied to Canada, usually meant to most Americans some form of continental union that was natural and inevitable and therefore not worth a fight. American and Canadian interests clashed at many points, but there were large areas of mutual concern, developed especially in face of pressure from potential enemies. Finally, in the twentieth century, confidence in non-military solutions for specific disputes increased as appropriate machinery for settlement was developed and as both countries gained experience in its use. The familiar popular myth of the long undefended border has also served to reduce the possibility of a resort to arms.

This consolidation of pacific relations with the United States coincided with the ripening of Canadian autonomy into independence. Military institutions eventually came to be needed by both countries and were belatedly developed, but for purposes other than war with each other. Dangers arising outside North America, thought to be more important, eventually led to military cooperation in war and even to alliance in peacetime. The trust that some Canadians and their governments placed, rather hesitantly, in the pacific intentions of the United States, almost from the birth of the Dominion, had been justified by events. This trust stemmed in part from an instinctive Canadian understanding of American psychology, and in its turn may have fostered American restraint. It correctly depreciated the significance of the military factor in Canadian-American relations.

What is not clear, however, is to what extent a sound appreciation of the nature of the military prospect had been a cause of its elimination. Some light was shed on this question in the studies made by C. P. Stacey, J. M. Hitsman, Robin Winks, and Kenneth Bourne; but these books, with one partial exception, carried the investigation down only to 1871.[8] The exception, Bourne's *Britain and the Balance of Power in North America*, was primarily concerned with the relation of the Canadian defence question to Britain's global position rather than to the balance within North America which the title suggests. He had little to say about what happened between the time of Britain's withdrawal of the garrison and the Venezuela crisis of 1895–96, although this is the period when the strategic revolution was developing.[9] Desmond Morton in his *Ministers and Generals* covered that crucial period in detail, but he was concerned with the domestic political forces that conditioned Canadian military development and he touched only incidentally the evolution of strategic thought.[10] James Eayrs's *In Defence of Canada* picked up the story after the First World War, but by that time the emphasis and interest had switched to whether Canada's forces were adequate to meet world-wide responsibilities. Eayrs's caustic comments about one Canadian soldier's contingency planning for war with the United States were not matched by a parallel reference to the much more extensive contemporary American planning for the same, by then unlikely, possibility.[11]

The aim of the present book is to study official and unofficial thought in Canada and the United States about the problem of fighting a war in North America, especially from the British withdrawal up to the consummation of alliance in 1939. The growth of the American capacity for planning war is an especially important element in this story. Canada did not make much progress in developing the same kind of capacity until after the Second World War when the idea that war between

Canada and the United States was no longer feasible had fully captured popular opinion. However, Britain, although no longer primarily
responsible for the defence of Canada, had improved her own
defence-planning capability after the withdrawal from North America,
and had made a more effective study of the Canadian problem than was
possible earlier. Some British officers continued for longer than has
been realized to be concerned about the security of Canada. Study of
war planning in Britain, as well as in Canada and the United States, is
therefore necessary.

Light may be thrown on the nature of the influence of the military
factor in the evolution of Canadian-American relations by studying
opinion in Canada and the United States about Canadian-American relations. This does not mean a reiteration of the frequent expressions of
good will and harmony or the occasional blustering threats made by
politicians. These were undoubtedly important in their own way, but if
a head-on military confrontation had developed, such rhetoric would
probably have proved either ephemeral or misleading. Rather what is
intended is a study of the opinions of soldiers and civilians with military interest and knowledge who speculated, privately or publicly,
about the possible course and outcome of a war in North America.
What perhaps may not be discovered is how far the secret planning of
experts influenced public opinion—through leakage and deliberate dis-
semination. Public discussion in the military press of the uncertain
outcome of possible operations shows what politicians and their con-
stituents could have learned from the professionals about the technical
problems of defence, although such lessons would certainly not have
been the only causes of the neglect of preparations for the possibility of
war.

What is especially interesting is that improved war-planning capability, before and after the introduction of the General Staff system in
both Britain and the United States, produced increased planning for
war in North America when the likelihood of such a war was declining.
Increased capacity for war-planning activity on both sides did not
make war more possible or more likely. On the contrary, it seems to
have served as a brake on resort to the use of force, because it showed
that even after the British limited their commitments in North
America an American victory would not have been easy—particularly
if domestic friction was an impediment to a prolonged campaign, especially one which might advance some interests in the United States but
prejudice others.

It will be shown that there was for a long time no real unanimity on a
strategy to be followed or on its likely success. Either side might have

achieved a decisive advantage at the outset by secret preparations and a preemptive strike in the vital Great Lakes area. But it was realized that public opinion at home might be revolted by such an initiative and disavow it. Or, on the other hand, the public might prove to have no stomach for a long war. Considerations of this kind probably suggested to thoughtful people in both countries that war would be a very uncertain means of achieving political objectives; such awareness must undoubtedly have had some effect on the course of events.

It is impossible to pinpoint now the precise time when the idea that non-military solutions were the only feasible ones became generally accepted. However, a study of this neglected saga of the consideration of a possible war in North America may help to throw more light on the development of one of the most remarkable features of the modern international scene: a relationship between two close neighbors in which it is, and one hopes always will be, mutually accepted that issues must be resolved peaceably, whatever the apparent provocation or need.

1

Anglo-American Confrontation
(1775–1870)

For almost a century after the American Revolution, the British possessions in North
America which eventually became the Dominion
of Canada played a relatively minor role in the
international power struggle that would decide
their destiny. For much of that period their
weaknesses were very apparent. Their population was usually less than one-tenth of that of the
United States,[1] their only likely enemy; and
their resources were much less developed. They
also suffered from the chronic difficulties of
pioneer settlements: they were short of specie,
their taxation was unproductive, and they lacked
sufficient capital for essential public works and
private economic development. Britain had conceded representative institutions to them at an
early date; but until the middle of the nineteenth
century executive and administrative control
was wielded by British-appointed governors,
councils, and officials. As a result there were de-
bilitating internal political struggles much like
those that had preceded the American revolt.
Although British control suggested the possibility of effective prosecution of military operations
inasmuch as centralized civil and military power
could be established by fiat over all the provinces, commanders would have had to deal with
several different legislatures. To complicate the

problem further, a large part of the population of Lower Canada was French in origin and could not be expected to have the same loyalties and attitudes as the rest. In these circumstances a vital element in the relations between Britain and the United States in North America was that the colonial contribution to security was uncertain, weak, and liable to be unavailable in times of crisis.

A second important element in an assessment of those relations is the appraisal of American intentions and capabilities. Dr. Hitsman, who discussed defence strategy in his *Safeguarding Canada*, had a personal conviction that the United States had very little in the way of plans for invasion or conquest before the British left in 1870. He therefore did not look "at the other side of the hill," as Dr. Bourne had done.[2] That American planning for war in peacetime was minimal, as Bourne discovered, could, however, have been due as much to the rudimentary nature of American military and naval organization as to a lack of aggressive intention. What was important was that Canadians continued to fear that the Americans would overcome this disability and might again resort to force as in 1812.

There was some justification for this state of mind. From colonial times American colonial charters had assumed a right to occupy the continent from sea to sea. Americans were afraid that other powers would forestall them in their inheritance: the Monroe Doctrine was a warning to Europe, including Britain, to keep out. It was an easy step from that to the belief in Manifest Destiny which was forcibly demonstrated by the admission of Texas, by the threatened annexation of what is now British Columbia, and by the acquisition of New Mexico and California.[3] Furthermore, American democracy was notoriously hostile to Britain's aristocracy; and it was despised and feared in return.[4] Little wonder, then, that many British and Canadian observers were convinced that American menaces, periodically voiced by sensational demagogues and journalists, must inevitably lead one day to an invasion. Long after that invasion had become very unlikely, Canadian patriotic orators made a practice of recalling the history of past incursions as well as of the favorable boundary settlements that the United States had won by aggressive diplomacy.[5]

Partly to offset these fears, the Mother Country not only accepted ultimate responsibility for the defence of the colonies in the event of a major crisis but also undertook military preparation in peacetime. British soldiers were prone to assert, as had the duke of Wellington, that the defence of all the Queen's dominions was a point of honour;[6] but there were actually more pragmatic motives. Britain's role in all the Americas, her worldwide prestige and trade, and her competence to maintain on a global scale the pre-eminence that has been described as the Pax Britannica, would have been seriously compromised by the loss of Canada. Furthermore, until the demise of the wooden sailing man-of-war was dramatically demonstrated by the decisive Russian victory over the Turks at Sinope (1853) and by the course of other naval operations during the Crimean War, North American timber and naval stores were considered vital for the preservation of Britain's ocean hegemony because East European supplies might not always be available.[7] The dominating theme of the North American international scene was, therefore, the Anglo-American confrontation; and Britain's concern with the military aspect of relations with the United States across the Canadian border was motivated by important British interests.

This Anglo-American confrontation was the more sensitive because the land border of British possessions in North America was the longest in the British Empire, longer and less protected naturally than the heavily defended frontier of British India. It was the only one in which Britain directly faced a modern Western country of great potential strength. The defence of the Canadian border was the Empire's most difficult, and could become its most dangerous, problem on land. One reason for this was that Britain was the United States' most powerful neighbour and rival and the only possible obstacle to the fullest realization of the great American dream. Although Canada has sometimes been described as a hostage held by the United States as bond for Britain's good behaviour,[8] it was also true that Canada gave Britain a foothold to exert leverage on the United States in international diplomatic negotiations and politics. Without that point of vantage in North America Britain would have had little scope to deploy full force in the event of a show-down.

The fact that there can be two such contradictory analyses of Canada's role in British relations with the United States in the nineteenth century shows how difficult it is to arrive at a convincing estimate of the strategic balance then prevailing in North America. It was at least as difficult at the time. The Anglo-American confrontation, a question of great import for both countries as well as for the people in the colonies, was fraught with uncertainty. Much depended on American intentions, on American capacity to back them up, on correct British appraisal of these factors, and on Canadian attitudes, all of which were difficult to gauge and all of which were changeable.

Nineteenth-century Britain, with its long military and naval tradition, its worldwide commitments, and its larger service establishments (although these lagged behind contemporaries in Europe in some respects), was better equipped than the United States to evaluate the complications and implications of this strategic confrontation.[9] The responses of British professional soldiers to every nuance of each new development in North America were recorded in a long series of strategic appraisals. The extent to which they resulted in strategic adjustments during the days of the garrison has been examined in detail by Hitsman. Bourne covered the same ground and also considered British military developments at home and the role of British sea power. These historians have shown conclusively and effectively that no satisfactory solution was found for the difficult problem that Britain faced in North America. There was too much uncertainty.[10] As many of the same problems and the same factors continued to operate after the British left Canada, a preliminary recapitulation and analysis of the strategic issues in the Anglo-American confrontation down to 1870 can be helpful for the study of later Canadian-American military relations by showing the origin of certain permanently operating forces and certain concepts.

In the early nineteenth century, and later, British territory in North America was, as Wellington once said, "all frontier and nothing else."[11] There was no depth for manoeuvre for defence, the most populous areas could be attacked from more than one direction; and for a long time lateral communications were poor. In winter the St. Lawrence was closed by ice and shipborne supplies and reinforcements could not get to Quebec. Adequate routes from Halifax to St. John through the empty wilderness that separated the Atlantic provinces and the Canadas were constructed only belatedly and would always be vulnerable.[12] The direct river route to the lakes and the upper province was impeded by some of the world's greatest rapids which were only slowly by-passed during the century by means of successively deeper canals and by railroads; and for nearly a hundred miles the south bank of the river was American. The alternative route to the interior by the Ottawa River was also much impeded by quick water, and although it did lead directly to the upper lakes, that was only by canoe.

For a quarter of a century after the War of 1812 these geographic problems were not even partially eased. Effective Canadian settlement did not reach out beyond the lakes to the West until after Confederation. Throughout this period it stretched from Quebec to Lake Huron. The big change was therefore in its density. But in the same period the Americans extended the settlement of areas that in 1812 had only recently been occupied, developed the Ohio valley where industrial growth had already given them an advantage during the war,[13] and moved in increasing numbers into Michigan and even into Minnesota. British America was in danger of being not only outnumbered but also outflanked.[14]

The most important lesson of the War of 1812 was the significance of British sea power; and it was not properly understood. The two wars fought after the American revolt should have impressed both sides that geography made total victory in North America difficult, if not impossible, for either side. Sea power could enable the British to blockade and invade the United States, but the country was too big to conquer by occupation. On the other hand, American cruiser victories in both wars had misled many Americans into thinking that the Royal Navy had an Achilles' heel and could be held in check.[15]

Both contenders had been made fully aware that Canada would be the prize in any future contest. The crucial strategic question was whether the country could be overrun before it was reinforced. It was known that American officers after the War of 1812 freely admitted that their strategy in that war had been faulty, in that it had not given primacy to the cutting of the St. Lawrence communications at Montreal and the seizure of Quebec.[16] Henceforward all strategic thought on both sides started from the premise that the critical struggle would be at that point and that it might be decided by grasping an early advantage on the Great Lakes.

Faced with these complicated problems, British service officers who were charged from time to time with the defence of Canada held widely different views about the best strategy to adopt in war and the best military and naval preparations to make in peacetime. In the first half of the century they usually assumed that British North America could be defended, but some realized that a major offensive on the Canadian front was virtually impossible. This view had the prestigious support of the Iron Duke.[17] In 1845 Governor Metcalfe estimated that an offensive would require 50,000 men;[18] and the great distances involved would have made cooperation between separate commands very difficult even for defensive purposes. Therefore aggressive strategists leaned only to limited opportunist offensive moves in an offensive-defensive strategy.

Speaking about the critical point, the St. Lawrence–Great Lakes system, Wellington had advised during the War of 1812 that if defeat in North America was to be avoided the lakes must be held at all costs.[19] After the war naval experts feared that it might be impossible to command the inland seas in a future conflict because of the insecurity of their link with the ocean. To get this budget passed in 1816, Lord Castlereagh, the British foreign minister, expressed concern about the need to maintain strength on the lakes;[20] but after the estimates were safely through the House of Commons, in his concern to avoid a crippling arms race in a theatre of war that did not seem as critical as the European, he decided that moderation would be the best approach to security. He therefore approved the negotiation of the epoch-making Rush-Bagot agreement for inland naval limitation.[21]

However, naval limitation did not mean an entente. It merely diverted attention to an alternative means of defending British North America, fortification.[22] It was clearly impossible to cover the whole length of the land frontier; but there were only three possible lines of approach for an American attack. The first was the historic invasion path up the Richelieu towards Montreal, and then on to Quebec to the east and Kingston to the west. The second was across the Niagara frontier. The third was across the Detroit River. In 1819 Wellington had assumed that two army corps, each 5,000 strong, would be needed to meet these invasions effectively. One should be based on the Rideau River, a tributary of the Ottawa, and the second near the Grand River that flows into Lake Erie.[23] But armies of that size were unlikely at that time in North America. Therefore, to facilitate the rapid deployment and greater effectiveness of smaller forces, Wellington had advocated the construction of what came to be known as the Rideau Waterway to link the Ottawa and the lower end of Lake Ontario at Kingston. This work would by-pass the American dominated section of the St. Lawrence. He also suggested the need for a second water passage to connect Lake Ontario with the Upper Lakes by way of Lake Simcoe and Georgia Bay. This would by-pass Lake Erie which had been lost in 1813.[24] At about the same time as Wellington proposed these improved lines of lateral communication, the governor-in-chief in Canada, the duke of Cumberland, began to repair the fortifications and barracks at Quebec and Kingston, to build a new fort at Ile-aux-Noix on the Richelieu, and to relocate the supply depot at Montreal on St. Helen's Island.[25]

All these measures and proposals seemed to have been justified when relations with the United States became strained in the 1820s. As a result, in 1825 Wellington sent a commission of engineers under Col. Sir James Carmichael Smyth, RE, to review the defences of British North America. Smyth and his colleagues secretly discussed the possibility of a pre-emptive invasion of the United States; but they concluded that it would be unwise. They then recommended extensive permanent defence works for Halifax, Montreal, Kingston, and the Niagara frontier, the completion of a winter road from New Brunswick to Quebec, and the construction of the Rideau Waterway. They added that in the event of war Britain should seize Long Island and Staten Island and blockade the American coast.[26]

Smyth's strategic analysis anticipated all future discussion of the problem of the defence of Canada. He proposed to concentrate on a few strong points: Quebec, Montreal, Kingston, Niagara, with smaller outlying posts. This program of fortification was so extensive that it was never completed. However, in the course of the next fifteen years some of the works that he recommended were built at the expense of the British taxpayer, notably the citadels at Quebec and Kingston, the Rideau Waterway, and the defences at the Ile-aux-Noix. But the debate about concentration as against dispersion continued into the 1850s and afterwards.[27]

Meanwhile, the renewed policy of fortification, even though restricted in scope, had been used immediately to rationalize a reduction of the inland dockyard establishments which the Rush-Bagot agreement had not forbidden and which might be a means for quickly restoring British naval strength on the lakes. In the early 1830s the economy-minded Whig government in Britain closed the yards down.[28] The rebellions in Upper and Lower Canada in 1837 soon compelled reconsideration. The fortification program was resuscitated, reform of the militia was attempted, and a regiment of old soldiers in British pay, the Royal Canadian Rifles, was raised for the specific purpose of the defence of North America, to reinforce the few regular battalions sent out for routine garrison duty.[29] More important still, the dockyard at Kingston was partially reactivated. Small steamers were built or hired to patrol the river and the Great Lakes. Maintained in service during the 1840s, these ships, built of iron, exceeded the limitations imposed by the agreement with the United States; but in view of the need to prevent possible border incursions by raiders this circumstance was overlooked.

Sir George Arthur, lieutenant-governor of Upper Canada, saw that technological advance had affected the stability introduced in 1817. Iron ships might be built in sections, stored at a distance, and rushed to the lakes in emergency.[30] The Americans had in fact responded to the British ships by building a much bigger iron vessel, the *Michigan*, on Lake Erie. Allegedly for revenue service, she carried a heavier gun than the small British warships. Similar American vessels on the other lakes were planned, but were not built.[31] Nevertheless, Lt.-Gen. Sir George Murray, master general of the Ordnance, a former lieutenant-governor of Canada and colonial secretary, who had always thought that Carmichael Smyth's proposals were too extravagant and that Wellington was a scaremonger, rejected proposals for the planning of an offensive strategy and approved only a limited defensive strategy and limited defensive construction.[32]

Other technical changes had also begun to disturb the precarious balance. As the Rideau Waterway was too shallow to permit the passage of naval vessels of any size, it had not overcome the old reliance on local resources for building and therefore had not altered the crucial naval situation on Lake Ontario. Moreover it had been partially offset by the Erie Canal built about the same time. The construction of the St. Lawrence canals in the 1840s, to permit the passage of bigger vessels, did for a time swing the balance on Lake Ontario towards Britain's advantage; and the railways that followed improved Canada's lateral communications still further. But American railroads reached the frontier at several different places and increased the number of possible routes of attack. Furthermore, like the St. Lawrence canals, and the Welland Canal that gave access to Lake Erie, the Canadian railways could be fairly easily cut or destroyed. The strategic situation remained uncertain.

Two British naval officers, Captains Frederick Warden and Edward Boxer, who were sent separately to survey different aspects of the problem in the 1850s, thought that steamships should be exploited to adjust the balance which they believed would swing more against Canada with the growth of American shipping on the lakes. Boxer thought that an offensive, rather than a defensive, campaign should be planned.[33] He believed that it would be possible to seize control of Lake Ontario as soon as trouble developed because the volume of Canadian shipping was greater there.[34] The situation was actually still difficult to assess, but it was clear that in the long run the development of steam and iron ships must ultimately benefit the United States and that therefore it must be forestalled. The British government's only immediate answer was to rush improvement of water communications and revive the militia.[35] Further construction of inland defence works was limited to additional fortifications to supplement the works built at Kingston in the 1820s.[36]

Crises kept these strategic problems alive and menacing. Popular support in the United States for the Patriots who had invaded Canada in 1838, and the American trial of Alexander MacLeod, a British citizen who was alleged to have taken part in the burning of the Patriot vessel *Caroline* in American waters,[37] inflamed opinion on both sides of the border. War seemed imminent during disputes about the Maine-New Brunswick border and the possession of the Hudson's Bay Company's Oregon holdings. James Polk, seeking election to the presidency, spoke of the acquisition of disputed territories, and the American claim was later expressed in the slogan, "Fifty-four forty, or fight!".[38]

Two closely connected restraints averted the resort to force in these developing disputes: many Americans still believed, as their ancestors had done in 1775 and 1812, that Canadians would eventually seek to join the United States of their own free will; and as a result American military preparations in peacetime were inadequate for the prosecution of a war against a superior force-in-being. But the events of 1837–38 had shown that a voluntary union was unlikely. In the 1840s and 1850s therefore, some Americans began to think that war might be the best way to win a favorable solution in disputes.[39] The trend of American thinking about this problem must be examined in a little more detail.

Since the War of 1812 the American army had remained much too small for such a war. Furthermore it was scattered along the Indian frontier and therefore not immediately available; nor was it trained for either offence or defence on the northern frontier. War had not come during the crisis of 1837–38 because cooler heads were well aware that the United States was ill-prepared militarily to take on the British army in Canada: the American army was clearly not in a condition to fight a major European power; and the American militia, efficient in only a few states, was useless for an offensive. American officers feared that, even if they were permitted to operate free from other distractions, they might not be able to defeat the British garrison before the arrival of such reinforcements as the British could send freely across the Atlantic. Meanwhile, British sea power could attack American coastal cities and American shipping.

After the war, American defensive construction to meet these dangers had at first been mainly limited to the Atlantic ports and had adjusted slowly to the technical development of weapons.[40] As a consequence of the events of 1837–38 a relatively small amount of new construction was also undertaken along the northern border. This included Fort Montgomery at Rouse's Point on Lake Champlain, where a minor boundary adjustment had been made because earlier building had been found to be on British territory and had had to be halted. Atlantic coast building could be purely a defensive precaution against a possible British attack; but construction of northern border forts seemed to suggest a greater American readiness to go to war. Significantly, fort construction in the north in the 1840s and 1850s, though still hesitant and incomplete, had come when Americans had begun to realize that Canada might, after all, not join the United States voluntarily.

General Totten, chief engineer of the U.S. Army, who reported on defence works in 1840 and 1851 in order to justify their retention, said Canada could easily be overrun, but only at a cost "beyond all calculation in life and treasure." He added that it would be "unnecessary and fruitless"; it would not bring a "real conquest" of Canada and would lead to war with England. Yet he continued to discuss strategies for an effective invasion.[41] Joel Poinsett, secretary for war, who began Fort Montgomery on the Lake Champlain route in 1851, had declared ten years earlier that a fort there could serve as the base for an invasion. But it long remained only two-thirds completed.[42] The United States was thus slow to take offence, but its intentions remained uncertain.

Turning back to the Canadian side, it is clear that British officials in Canada (Governor Metcalfe for example) were inclined to believe that whatever the cost "effective protection [by Britain was] . . . the condition on which the allegiance of British North America was held, and on that peace must depend."[43] But it was also understood in Britain that an effective defence of Canada would only be possible if it were adequately backed by the Canadians. The defence policy of Lord Stanley, the colonial secretary, was therefore contingent upon provincial cooperation.[44] In principle Canadians accepted the obligation to help in defence; but in practice they were disposed to seek British protection on the grounds that they did not have the resources and the organization to protect themselves. British North American legislatures were always reluctant to vote money for preparation for war when there was no emergency. Their electorates were interested in local military arrangements almost solely for the preservation of law and order within the colonies, to keep them safe for the protection of life, business, and trade.

As a consequence, although one of the lessons that Canadians believed they had learned from the War of 1812 was that it had been won by the heroism of their militia, that force had been allowed to decline after the war. It was assumed that the intrinsic qualities of patriotic citizens needed little or no peacetime training. Periodic muster days were, as in the American colonies in an earlier century, not much more than a holiday from work for a short parade for the purpose of registration—followed by a drinking session. Furthermore, a few selected militia units, organized like the voluntary flank companies of 1812, expected, if called out, to be taken on British pay.

While they wanted Britain to defend them and disliked taxation and military preparation when relations with the Americans were harmonious, at the same time Canadians disliked the British concept of sound defensive strategy which, by a withdrawal to defend strong points, would leave their homes and families exposed to an invading army. When British soldiers became impatient with this attitude, and argued that a colony that would not defend itself was not worth help-ing, some colonial governors and Colonial Office officials pointed to the paradox that Canadians were expected to take military steps to obtain security which they could obtain more easily by joining the United States.[45]

At mid-century, the introduction of responsible government in British North America greatly increased the significance of powerful political factors.[46] Henceforward colonial governments had much more opportunity for initiative in preparation for defence. Opinion in Britain began to stress that colonies that governed themselves (and which were soon to tax British imports) should contribute more to the costs of their defence. Lord Grey, the colonial secretary, was pressed by radical supporters who argued that concessions of colonial self-government ought to be coupled with self-defence; and he was deter-mined to cut government spending. Lord Elgin, the governor general of Canada, agreed with him that responsibility should have the moral effect of stimulating Canadian willingness to carry the burden; but he warned that British economic policies had been received with distaste and that Canadians could get security by joining the United States. To require a province to assume more of the costs of its defence might cause it to prefer separation.[47]

Responsible government, in fact, had been conferred without requir-ing defence precautions. Indeed, both the British and the Canadian governments had shown more concern for such financial details as canal tolls than for the solution of strategic problems. Although the British had handed over ordnance property on condition that it be kept in repair and readily available for use if required in a future crisis, these agreements were not always carried out.[48] When, for reasons of economy, Britain began to withdraw the garrison shortly after the concession of responsible government, Canadians did not replace the departing regulars. They were too preoccupied with economic prob-lems. Except at times of periodic crises, friendly relations with the United States made defence seem unnecessary.

Yet, although Britain and the United States were the principals in the confrontation, Canada was the likely victim in case of war. De-terioration of relations in the 1850s therefore brought the whole prob-lem of the defence of British North America and the likely fate of Canada into sharp relief. Weakness caused by withdrawal of troops for the Crimean War had left Britain liable to embarrassment if the Americans wished to capitalize on their advantage. The British ships built a decade earlier had been laid up or had become obsolete but, although no longer a very efficient fighting ship, the USS *Michigan* still dominated Lake Erie.[49] The Americans protested that she was maintained only for revenue purposes, and to rescue vessels in distress, including Canadian ships.[50] However, by controlling Lake Erie, the United States could prevent communication with the West and the Upper Lakes and could dismember Canada.

The international crises of the 1850s, and a growing sense of vulnerability, led the British North American provinces to introduce what were called "unequivocally successful" volunteer systems to build up their militia.[51] Some of these volunteers may have joined in the hope of seeing action overseas or of getting a commission in the regular army; but the evidence seemed to show, nonetheless, that, at least in the event of a great imperial crisis, Canadians would enlist to defend their country. Furthermore, when the Crimean War ended, and an angry controversy about British wartime recruiting disturbed relations in the United States, the policy of troop withdrawal was slowed. Troops were returned from the Crimea directly to North America—although not in the numbers that had been garrisoned there before the war.

Greater reliance on the militia for defence renewed the old debate about the best strategy for protection against the United States. Militia, less well trained than regulars, were considered unsuitable for field operations and had greater need of fixed defences.[52] Concentration in a few heavily defended strong points did not appeal to them, however. They preferred many scattered minor defence works, of the blockhouse type, to protect their homes. Such a deployment would have strengthened Canadian military and civil morale. But British military engineers had set their faces against outlying posts, which provided opportunities for desertion to the United States, could be mopped up one by one, and were vulnerable to modern artillery.[53] Moreover, not only was Montreal still not fortified but its outposts had not yet been completed because of differences of opinion as to what was preferable—to build far in advance of, or closer to, the city. The western part of the province (apart from Kingston, which guarded the entrance to the Rideau Canal) was quite unprotected.

The defence of Canada on land thus still depended on the British garrison. Hitherto this had usually been maintained at a strength about equal to that of the American army. An early advantage was expected because the Americans were scattered along the Indian frontier. The British, although likewise not properly concentrated for operations, could converge and deploy more quickly. When the policy of garrison withdrawal was renewed again in the 1850s, the regulars who remained were clearly too few to fight a war but were more than were needed to guarantee the British commitment to the defence of Canada. In effect, the British garrison now, more than ever, was a token insurance against an American attempt to seize advantage by surprise. The defence of Canada thus ultimately rested, as always, on the deterrent effect of British sea power. However, much would depend on how the circumstances that brought on a war and the course of early operations affected morale and war spirit in both Canada and the United States. More important still was the question whether Britain would be diverted by other international problems.

For half a century, then, there had been not so much a balance of power as an equilibrium of weakness—with the British garrison standing as a cautionary force in Canada and the Royal Navy posing a threat in the background. At times peace had been precariously maintained only because British statesmen like Lord Aberdeen preferred to make concessions, conveniently at Canadian expense, rather than precipitate a major conflict, the consequences of which were uncertain; also because in the United States people were more concerned with developing what they possessed than with seizing territory from Canada. Finally, constitutional government on both sides had acted as a brake on pure adventure. In the United States the separation of powers and lack of a military planning system, and in the British Empire the division of responsibility and power between the metropolitan and colonial governments and civil control of military policy, had served to prevent minor, and even more serious, incidents from becoming full-blown war. Wellington had said in 1841 that it was "not easy to separate political from military considerations" in considering the defence of British North America.[54] Where defence problems persisted and military solutions could not be confidently anticipated, political factors prevailed by default.

An enthusiastic reception for the Prince of Wales in the United States in 1860, and the subsequent amicable postponement of the sensitive territorial dispute in Puget Sound, suggested that mutual tolerance and possible future harmony had been fostered during the long period in which Britain controlled the seas and maintained a counterpoise in North America with a small garrison of regular troops.[55] However, as C. P. Stacey has shown, the British assumption that representative government would lead colonials to put more into defence had been unrealized.[56] In his study of Canadian-American relations during the Civil War years, Robin Winks has suggested that it had become clear even before the war began that the British attempt to retain a land base in North America had failed.[57] If this was so, the equilibrium of weakness on that continent had already become seriously distorted and the Civil War merely confirmed the obvious. But Winks agreed with Stacey that the American Civil War crisis warned the colonies that they must seek safety in union. He added that henceforward the United States, even when its army was allowed to decline, would never again be challengeable in the northern half of the continent. Britain and Canada had now to learn new techniques for dealing with a colossus. Winks concluded that this task was eased because the Northern victory, by ensuring the triumph of bourgeois Republican capitalism and middle-class ethics, turned the United States towards economic rather than military, conquests, "except as an emotional crusade."[58]

A changeable course of opinion and policy in all three countries in *ad hoc* response to Civil War situations had led to this new form of confrontation. This development has been fully examined by other scholars, as well as by Stacey and Winks. However, before investigating the extent to which military factors continued to affect relations after the British withdrew, it is necessary to analyse the strategic problems that the Civil War brought to a head.

Britain accepted the idea of American military supremacy in North America only reluctantly. The growth of the Army of the United States to 700,000 men within a few months[59] showed how quickly the British attempt to maintain either a meaningful proportionate relationship to the American army, or even only a significant token force, could be upset. The British garrison of five thousand would soon be outnumbered a hundred-fold; and Canadian manpower could never make up this startling deficit.

Nevertheless, the government in London had reacted automatically at the first signs of a serious tipping of the balance. Within a few weeks of Lincoln's call to arms a battalion of British infantry was quietly sent to Canada. Shortly afterwards, in what was unmistakeably a deliberate warning, two more battalions followed on the largest passenger ship afloat, the *Great Eastern*.[60] Britain thus acted to fulfil its historic obligation to defend the colonies. But contemporaries realized that these moves could not guarantee security in North America.[61] They were only deterrent gestures. For, quite apart from the increasing disparity in numbers, infantry without field artillery or cavalry, and without supply services, would have been of little use against large-scale American aggression. The governor general, Sir Edmund Head, was of the opinion that, as war would be the result of British policy,

British artillery should also have come;[62] but artillery officers were sent to Canada only to organize militia artillery.[63]

There were some signs that an invasion might soon occur. Lincoln's secretary of state, W. H. Seward, was an avowed annexationist; and in the first months of the war citizens in the border states were annoyed that their Canadian neighbours, after preaching piously against slavery, refused to supply them with much-needed arms.[64] Britain had approved Monck's policy of neutrality partly in Canadian interest—to avoid external menaces and internal conflicts of opinion in British North America. The governor general's proclamation was accepted in the colonies largely because of the confusion caused by the fact that war had been declared for the preservation of the Union, not the abolition of slavery.

But a declared neutrality did not eliminate the external threat: Northern newspapers talked of punishing Canada when the South was defeated. Furthermore, Gen. Fenwick Williams, the New Brunswick-born commander-in-chief in North America, feared that if the North lost the war, as he thought quite likely, it would seek compensation by the acquisition of British territory.[65] Some people also believed it to be not impossible that the warring parties might attempt to heal the breach by joining in a national crusade against a foreign power.[66] In that event British North America was the most likely objective. Speculations of this kind were unrealistic: the Union and the Confederacy were too evenly balanced to allow the North to undertake secondary adventures and the crack in the American polity was too wide to paper over; but flying rumours caused deep concern in both Britain and Canada early in the war and made for anxious consideration of defence against possible United States aggression.

A wide variety of circumstances, some new and some old, helped to keep apprehension high. Although the North's disgrace at Bull Run gave the British temporary comfort, the swelling Union Army would soon gain more battle experience. Furthermore it was no longer scattered in widespread frontier posts but it was available for operational service north as well as south. The seven railroads that now ran towards Canada made possible a many-pronged assault.[67] Lateral communications in the British provinces were still poor and vulnerable: one part of the lateral defence-communications line, the Beauharnois Canal, passed close to American territory, and other canals, especially the Welland, and railways were also close to the border. Connections between the Maritimes and the Province of Canada were still uncertain and exposed;[68] and as telegraphic communication was in the hands of an American company, it was suspected that the American government got copies of all important defence messages sent between the provinces.[69] To crown all, the United States, hitherto virtually powerless at sea, began to rebuild its navy. This did not yet present a serious challenge to British world sea power, but it created a potential threat which could not be ignored. Preoccupation with its war with the Confederacy might deter the Union from turning north for a considerable time, but it was obvious that at any moment an incident might produce a crisis.

Gen. Fenwick Williams, ostentatiously attempting to shore up feeble defences and put on a bold front, was distressed because the Canadians at first showed little enthusiasm for militia training.[70] Unlike the British ruling classes, not many of them were moved by the idea that there could be advantage in weakening the United States. Therefore, even though they did nothing to promote it, they were more inclined than the British government to accept a Northern victory; and they did not prepare to defend themselves against the consequences of British policies.

As it happened, the first crises did come over non-Canadian issues. The Union's seizure of Mason and Slidell from the British packet-boat *Trent* in 1861 caused Britain to send out more infantry, bringing the number of regulars in the garrison to about 18,000 men. With them went a supply train.[71] This extra reinforcement showed that Britain was continuing to take its responsibility, and the threat of war, very seriously and was apparently preparing to meet it in arms. Yet even now cavalry and field artillery were not sent. They were to go only when war really became imminent. Clearly the new reinforcements were still just a gesture to back diplomacy—notice to the Americans that Britain would not climb down easily.

But what was really significant about the *Trent* crisis was that for the first time Canadians responded by enlisting in considerable numbers for militia training.[72] This has been seen as a "decision for nationhood," an assertion of Canadian determination to prepare to resist an American effort to eliminate the British provinces.[73] It certainly proves that, even though a war at that point still might have been brought about by British imperial, rather than colonial, issues, many Canadians were prepared as of old to help Britain defend their country. But events soon showed that Lincoln had no intention of getting involved in more than one war at a time and that the danger to Canada was therefore not as great as appeared. Winks holds that in all three countries public opinion had greatly magnified crises in these early years when a war, and an invasion of Canada, would have resulted only from a British *casus belli*.[74] However, in October 1862, T. E. Elliot, colonial under-secretary, minuted a dispatch from the governor general about the defence problem with the claim that if war came it would be a war for Canadian independence vis-à-vis the United States.[75] Thus in British eyes it would be fought for Canadian interests. Yet in 1862 the legislature of the United Province of the Canadas rejected John A. Macdonald's Militia Bill that would have introduced a form of compulsory service to fulfil colonial responsibilities in defence. Although the defeat of the bill was actually due to an unrelated factor (the unpopularity of a government that had grown corrupt in power) it suggested incidentally that the majority in the Canadian Legislature was not yet convinced of the need to prepare to resist the United States, especially when Britain could be held responsible and when things seemed to have quietened down.

Friction arising from British failure to prevent a breach of neutrality by Confederate cruisers on the high seas (the case in point being the *Alabama*) soon pointed again to the possibility of a war brought on by British error. The provincial government of John Sandfield Macdonald, which had replaced that of his namesake, now succeeded in passing a revised Militia Bill to provide support for voluntary training. In effect this committed the Province of Canada to take up arms alongside the British army if the Americans attacked. However, this preliminary step was taken only half-heartedly. Reluctance to do anything more immediately may have been due to lack of conviction that there was any real danger of invasion. As Lord Lyons, the British ambassador in Washington reported, "the weather is threatening but the storm may not improbably blow over"[76]—which indeed it did for a time. The conclusion to be drawn is that, although many Canadians were ready to fight to defend their country, even if an invasion were caused by imperial issues, most were still unconvinced that one was likely.

A new face was put on the problem when the South, growing desperate after Gettysburg and Vicksburg, belatedly began to attempt to embroil Britain by the devious plan of inspiring attacks on the North from Canadian soil.[77] War now seemed to come closer, especially when Confederates who had robbed banks in St. Albans, Vermont, fled to Canada and after being arrested there, were freed on doubtful technical grounds by a Canadian magistrate. It now seemed that invasion might result from Canadian rather than British actions.[78]

Meanwhile, the British, irritated by the defeat of the first Militia Bill, wearying of maintaining a garrison that might fail to deter, and faced with European complications, were seeking to shift the burden of defence to the colonial taxpayers. The United States possessed armies of great size that had had operational experience with new military technology. Military weakness in face of Prussian aggression in Denmark had made Britain seem to be only a "stuffed lion"[79] and therefore less able to face the American eagle now soaring confidently.

It was now Canada's turn to fear that the British might not live up to the contract to defend the Queen's domains. The provincial government therefore sought a renewed British promise of commitment.[80] The fact that Canadian negotiators in 1864 and 1865 asserted even more vigorously than before that a war would be a result of British policy should not be taken too seriously. They were undoubtedly aware that the colonies could no longer limit their involvement by alleging imperial responsibility.

Until late in the Civil War there had continued to be considerable lack of agreement about the strategy to be adopted in British North America if the conflagration spread. But it had long been realized in Britain that a victory over the United States by invasion was not possible. An officer who had served in Canada during the border troubles in the 1830s and 1840s, writing to his son in the Canadian garrison in 1862, put the situation plainly. He said, "Of all the generals who talked of war in North America only two had sensible views on the subject, Sir George Murray and Sir James Kempt. . . ." The views of these men were that no aggressive campaign should be undertaken in such a country "if it can be avoided." The writer went on to explain in detail why an offensive was bound to fail.[81]

This view apparently circulated also at the policy-making level. In 1861 Gen. John F. Burgoyne, inspector-general of fortifications, although admitting that it would be injudicious for him to try to lay down the details of a campaign when thousands of miles from the seat of war, stated as a principle that "the party that acts on the defensive will have great advantages." He believed this would be so because the forces employed by both sides would essentially be militia and volunteers who would receive support at home and could fight better on prepared battlefields. "With regard to Canada . . . there would be little to be gained by us assuming the offensive there."[82]

Nevertheless, the advisability of seizing the initiative inevitably came up for further discussion because from the naval point of view such a move was essential. Capt. William Hatt Noble of the Royal Engineers reported on harbours in the Great Lakes to Capt. Richard Collinson, RN, who had been instructed to recommend to the Admiralty what assistance the navy could give the Province of Canada in the event of war. Noble wrote, "Should war arise between the United States and Great Britain, it will be absolutely necessary to seize the following American forts at the very outset," and he listed "Champlain" (Montgomery?) at Rouse's Point, Niagara, and Mackinac between Lakes Huron and Michigan. Noble also said that British or Canadian military and naval forces should defend the Beauharnois Canal (which is south of the river system), and the Welland Canal.[83]

Those actions were, however, undoubtedly intended to be in the context of a defensive-offensive strategy and not part of a major offensive movement. Burgoyne had stated in 1861, "The general there will have to watch the demonstrations of the enemy's preparations, and to form the best judgment he can of the course they will pursue. Should they take liberties, by the formation of depots of troops or other preparations near the frontier without a sufficient guard, he will naturally make an incursion and break them up." He concluded, "The *defensive* policy here advocated supposes the enemy to be firm, united, energetic and moderately prudent in their proceedings; should however weaknesses be discovered in these respects, we may have opportunities, by bold measures, with our well organised forces, of striking some offensive blows with good effect."[84]

A year later, in 1862, Burgoyne admitted that when he took this stand, "the neighbouring United States . . . were in an all-powerful condition and could have rapidly brought to bear upon this, our weak point [Canada], such a force as we could hardly expect to withstand." He now advocated that, while Federal lodgements on the Confederate coasts should be swept away, no attempt should be made at invasion from that direction either, because such an attempt would eventually be overwhelmed by superior numbers. He was adamant that no operations should be undertaken in combination with the Confederates. The only exception to this essentially defensive strategy that Burgoyne would contemplate was a possible advance from bases in New Brunswick into Maine to cover Halifax more effectively. Official policy, which was not made public at this time, was thus strictly defensive; and this posture was maintained even after more reinforcements arrived in Canada following the *Trent* incident.[85]

But wars can rarely be won by purely defensive strategies. The idea of an offensive therefore continued to attract military strategists. The area where it seemed useful and necessary to strike first, as well as practicable, was on the Great Lakes. Command of the lakes was imperative for the defence of the western part of the province. Therefore it was tempting to suggest that either before a war commenced, or at the very outset, a quick move should be made there. In his report on naval assistance to the province, Captain Collinson had written, "In the face of exposure to fire throughout 100 miles of navigation against the stream, it is scarcely possible to expect that the communication with Lake Ontario can be maintained by the River St. Lawrence, even if the canals escape destruction during the war. It will therefore be necessary to send vessels to Kingston with the least possible delay. . . ." He added, "After the declaration of war it will be almost impossible for any vessel to reach Lake Huron from the sea. It will be, however, of great importance that there should be a squadron upon it."[86] This idea of anticipating the outbreak of war by organizing a naval force on the Great Lakes, which the Rush–Bagot agreement had outlawed in time of peace, or of evading the treaty restrictions by opening up new communications or by making preparations at a distance to rush ships up at the outbreak, was to persist until the end of the decade and even later. But Collinson's own words had revealed its fundamental weakness. If communication with the lakes could be cut off in wartime, no sane strategist would place a force there to be isolated and mopped up unless he was quite certain that that force would be an effective deterrent or would determine the course of operations elsewhere and win the war.

Not only was there no consensus on the proper strategy to be adopted, there was also no clear policy on troop deployment while the garrison awaited events. Gladstone, when colonial secretary, noted that Colonel Jervois, reporting on fortifications in 1864, had stated that until 1863 troops were to be found in six stations, and that 700 men were scattered in smaller outposts.[87] When Gladstone persisted with his criticisms of planning and deployment, Palmerston accused him of playing up such strategic errors to support his case that Canada was not defensible. The prime minister declared that it was not necessary to go into the details of deployment until such time as an attack was imminent.[88]

In consequence of this policy, at no time during the Civil War were the British regulars in Canada deployed to withstand an attack in anything like the manner that Wellington had indicated. Concentration in readiness for defensive manoeuvre, or to defend essential strong points, was delayed not only because it might provoke the Americans, but also because it would alarm Canadians who would feel exposed if local defence units were withdrawn. There were also problems about housing the troops, especially in winter. And there was the old problem of desertion from outlying posts close to the border. Furthermore local communities wanted garrisons for social and economic reasons, as well as because they gave a sense of security.

Actual deployment was therefore based on other than strategic need. In 1860 and 1861, before the Civil War had begun, when the provincial government claimed remission of the cost of repairs to barracks at out-stations that had been handed over to the province three years earlier but were still occupied by British troops, the War Office refused to allow it. It also threatened to withdraw troops from those stations unless the province paid £150 that was owed for repairs. The Colonial Office was horrified that the location of troops should be decided by disputes about the payment of so paltry a sum. It complained that Canadian willingness to pay, rather than what would be effective, was apparently the deciding factor in strategic deployment.[89]

There were other instances of disagreement on deployment. In his report on Canadian defence, Collinson suggested that the defence of Quebec, and the fleet's base there, should be left to militia in order to permit the regulars in the city's garrison to move up country where they would be in a position to operate in the field.[90] However, the regulars were not yet properly organized for field operations; and it also seemed dangerous to leave the main link with Britain in the care of militia troops. On the other hand, when the *Trent* crisis occurred the mayor of Windsor asked for a garrison for that border city. He was not heeded.[91] In addition to garrisons in Quebec, Halifax, and St. John's, which were the ports of disembarkation, there were troops at Montreal, Kingston, and Toronto, with detachments in Hamilton, Guelph, and London, and some other outlying places, although not everywhere on the border.

When the provincial government failed to pass the Militia Bill in 1862, Monck recommended the concentration of the British garrison in Quebec, Montreal, and Kingston on the grounds that the government, by not providing a militia, had deliberately determined to run the risk of leaving the west exposed. Their rash action, he said, should not be allowed to endanger British troops.[92] But Fenwick Williams noted that it was the west that had voted for the Militia Bill and that that part also paid most of the taxes. It would be unjust to leave that loyal part exposed so that the Americans could occupy the most productive section of the country at will.[93] Edward Cardwell, the new colonial secretary, countered that it would be "deceptive" to leave the troops in the west in peacetime when the plan was to concentrate them when a war began.[94]

The British had in fact kept troops in the west partly as an encouragement to secure the passage of a Militia Bill. When the second bill became law it was felt that they could be withdrawn. Concentration of the British garrison was partially carried out in 1864 as a consequence of the reduction of the garrison when a part of the reinforcements of 1862, the Guards battalions, was sent home. The provincial government then complained that there would be no troops to train the militia in the west. It offered to pay for a detachment in Toronto for this purpose.[95] Thus only towards the end of the war did the Province of Canada begin to show some willingness to pay for the bad strategic deployment that was maintained largely to meet political, more than strategic, needs.

Another strategic problem concerning fortification was related to this debate about deployment and showed the same forces at work. It was to have even more influence on public opinion in Canada. Before the Civil War economic stringency and apathy about defence works had slowed building efforts on both sides of the border. Citadels had been built on the British side at Halifax, Quebec, and Kingston; elsewhere a few out-of-date works were still used. On the American side there were fairly new forts at Detroit (Wayne) and Buffalo (Porter), but Fort Montgomery on the Champlain invasion route was still incomplete.[96]

Early in the war representatives of American border states, contending that the suggestion was made in the cause of peace, urged Congress to appropriate money for the construction of forts along the Canadian border on the grounds that this was the American territory that was closest to a potential enemy and that the British had a military advantage there. Such arguments had little immediate effect, partly because they were aborted by rivalry between various areas.[97] The first concern of the U.S. Army Engineers was for the Atlantic coast where some new fortifications were built. At the same time proposals for canals to improve American defence communication in the north made little progress, because they were clearly intended principally for private profit.[98] In 1862 British intelligence agents and other visitors saw little sign of precautions along the northern frontier of the United States either in fortification building or troop movements. Existing forts, some of them obsolescent, were being used as recruiting depots. They were manned by prisoners of war who had been paroled by the Confederacy on condition that they not take up arms against it again.[99]

By 1864, however, the U.S. Engineers were satisfied that the coastal forts, and also the old forts along the north border which had now been repaired and improved, were prepared for any eventuality.[100] But, as Bourne has noted, these precautions on the northern frontier were not extensive and should not have alarmed the

British.[101] On the Canadian side, Gen. Fenwick Williams had failed in 1861 to persuade the imperial government to build works to protect the Welland canal, but a blockhouse was erected by the province. When tension increased at the beginning of 1862, Lord Monck, to reassure the provincial government that its small appropriation for defence was being well spent, appointed a commission of soldiers—along with one sailor and a civilian engineer—to survey the frontier.[102] General Burgoyne warned the commissioners against recommending expensive construction because it was doubtful whether the money would be forthcoming from either imperial or colonial resources. After a thorough survey, the commissioners recommended works which they declared would cost $1,611,000, probably a gross underestimate. They argued that these defences, scattered across the province, would provide adequate protection if backed by an army of 150,000 regulars and militia. The commissioners also recommended that as Quebec was an imperial fortress (which agreed with a decision made by the British cabinet committee that same year), it should be the responsibility of the home government.[103]

Construction on such a scale was, however, far beyond the bounds of political, and perhaps economic, possibility. Furthermore, the whole question of fortification was in a state of flux because of the development of new weapons. Finally, the scattering of defences piecemeal, which meant they could be mopped up by an enemy at will, was strategically unsound. Burgoyne therefore sent Lt.-Col. W. F. D. Jervois, the deputy director of fortifications, to Bermuda and Canada in 1864 to report what defences should be constructed.[104]

In his first report Jervois argued that, since they were building temporary defence works on the coast, the Americans must be expecting war soon. It took him only a few days to decide that, as command of the Great Lakes could not be maintained, Canada was not defensible west of Montreal. A copy of the 1862 commission's report now in the Canadian archives is annotated by him as follows, "What is the good of these little posts. They can delay the enemy but a short time, must eventually fall—why waste troops to defend them or money to build them." He recommended that only Halifax, Quebec, and Montreal should be fortified to enable the British to keep a foothold in North America.[105]

After he had submitted his report in London, Jervois was immediately sent back to advise the Canadian government.[106] The British hoped to get Canada to shoulder some or all of the costs of fortification. By this time, as a result of the 1863 Militia Bill, the Province of Canada seemed at last to be putting its military house in order. A letter of the duke of Cambridge reveals that, whereas Jervois's first mission had been undertaken specifically in the imperial interest, on his second trip he was instructed to take colonial interests into consideration.[107]

The provincial government delayed the implementation of its defence policy until it could hear Jervois's advice. It put a series of questions to him that appear to have been designed to find out whether it was his professional opinion that Canada could be defended.[108] Hence the tenor of Jervois's second report was, in certain important respects, quite different from the first. He still believed that Canada West could not be held indefinitely; but he now suggested that with a militia, and with temporary fortifications as far west as Hamilton, a strategic withdrawal could be fought (plates 1 and 2).[109] He added that if Kingston were fortified and a naval force put on Lake Ontario, this defensive strategy would be strengthened.[110]

Jervois's second report thus presented a somewhat less dismal prospect for the province if war came; and it offered a rationale for the militia program. But John A. Macdonald was annoyed at what he termed the "indiscreet" release of the Jervois reports in England. This had caused a near panic in western Canada.[111] The reports had probably been released in an attempt to frighten Canadians into making military preparations; but they had an opposite effect in some quarters since they made clear that much of the west would not be defended at all, and that the heart of the upper province would be occupied or would become a battleground where delaying actions would be fought.

Jervois probably expected that a war with the United States would be won on the Atlantic. He had recommended fortifications for West Indies bases; but it was not within his terms of reference to discuss the strategy of an offensive at sea. Hence in laying out a defensive strategy for Canada he failed to take any account of the fact that the United States was growing stronger on the ocean, that the American coast defences were no longer negligible, and that it would not be easy now to use British sea power to cow the Americans into surrender. Furthermore he relied on the shortness of the campaigning season to ensure that an American occupation of British North America would not be completed before the navy's operations could be effective; but inland Canadians had little understanding of the relation of seapower to their predicament. Finally, Jervois had, in fact, skirted the whole question of what would happen to Canada if the province was unsuccessful in resisting an American attack.

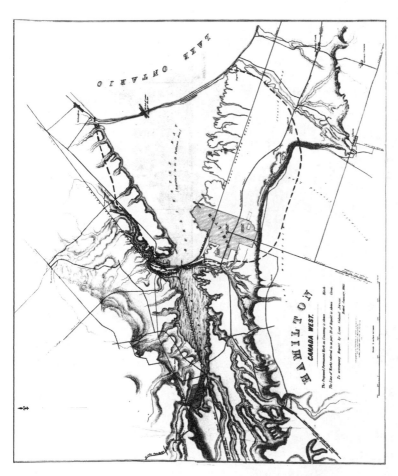

1. Lt.-Col. W. H. D. Jervois' map of defences for Hamilton, January 1865. Permanent defences were to be constructed on the causeway and temporary earthworks (dotted line) around the town and harbour.

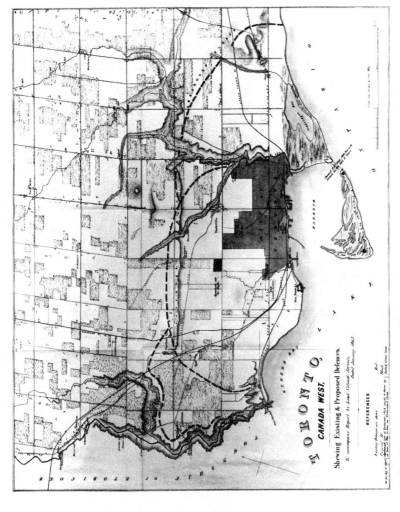

2. Lt.-Col. W. H. D. Jervois' map of defences for Toronto, January 1865. Proposed earthworks are indicated by the dotted line, batteries by round dots.

When Jervois's report was considered, the British cabinet could not agree on the policy to be adopted. Gladstone questioned whether even Quebec citadel could be held if American cruisers threatened communications in the lower St. Lawrence. He also alleged that the reason it was being retained as a fortress was because it was supposed to be an imperial interest; but he argued that that was in fact not true. He declared that, on the contrary, the British tie was the cause of American hostility to Canada and if the British commitment were reduced, that danger would be decreased also.[112] Gladstone's primary object in all this was to reduce British defence spending and taxes; but much of his argument in fact made military and political sense and would have been understood in Canada if it had been known there.

Gladstone declared that the adoption of Jervois's plan would throw Western Canada into the arms of the United States. Provincial ministers used similar arguments about devastation to rationalize doing as little as possible for defence. Richard Cartwright, a future opponent of Macdonald's, published a book on the militia in which he said that there could be no Canadian "national" policy while there was doubt whether Great Britain would defend Canada as a whole.[113]

This brings up the basic strategic question. Was Canada defensible? The famous British war correspondent, William Howard Russell, hinted that it was not when he said that if Canada was not defensible it could not be used as a base against the United States. He added that the Americans would invade Canada only to humiliate Britain.[114] The people of Canada had been reluctant to support spending more on the militia, not only because war would be a result of British policy, but probably also because they believed a defence might be hopeless.[115] While the earlier professional defence discussions had not been made public, the Jervois reports had brought military doubts to public notice. Colonel Stacey has pointed out that during the war British professional opinion was coming around to the conclusion that it would be extremely difficult to defend Canada.[116] Although he also claimed that provincial ministers failed to act because they did not realize the military needs of the moment, he had noted earlier that defence policy would have to have Canadian support, otherwise Britain would have to pay for it.[117] In an attempt to reassure Macdonald, Newcastle, the colonial secretary, told the governor general that Canada's defence would be possible because the war would be fought not only in Canada, but "everywhere."[118] But this must have been cold comfort. In Canada "everywhere" meant where Canadians lived. They feared that the British redcoats and the Canadian militia would be unable to resist the blue-clad hordes if they came north. They disliked a strategy that would leave them to American mercies after they had made a show of force in an impossible defence.[119]

As the Civil War drew to a close, events appeared to confirm Canada's historic exposure to invasion as a consequence either of American expansionism,[120] or of British policy, or of a combination of both. Confederate-inspired border disturbances, a presidential announcement of intention to terminate the Rush-Bagot agreement, American introduction of passport regulations, and a proposal to end reciprocity, all seemed to forebode ill. Because of the possibility that the huge American armies might turn north when the war ended, the provincial government was anxious to obtain a firm guarantee of future British protection. In 1864 its envoys to London talked of an expenditure of eight or ten million dollars for defence.[121] But they expected Britain to put up much of that money. In November 1864, when the Canadian government offered to ask its legislature for a million dollars for the militia and for a measure to finance defences for Montreal, Britain decided to refortify Quebec without waiting for implementation of these promises.[122]

Britain's motive in this was to provide a more secure refuge for the small garrison of British regulars. Although the Canadian government did not so interpret the decision, sceptical Canadians feared that "the dangers to which Her Majesty's [Canadian] subjects would be subjected in the event of war would not be fully and to the last moment shared by Her regular troops here."[123] Canadian and British views on what should be done about preparation for the defence of Canada against the United States were obviously still far apart. The War Office continued to assume that Quebec could become a Torres Vedras if the United States invaded.[124] But many Canadians wanted an assurance of protection for all of their country.

Details of the steps that led to the compromise in the defence agreement of 1865 have been fully related by Stacey and Hitsman.[125] The prime minister, Lord Palmerston, and a majority in his cabinet, while professing a desire to avoid provoking the United States, adopted Jervois's strategy.[126] This meant the construction of defence works to enable the army to fight a delaying action until the guns of the navy could be brought to bear, an elaboration of the traditional approach to the problem of defending British North America. Bourne, Stacey, and Hitsman have remarked on the influence of "Little Englanders" and of Gladstone in the formation of this British policy.[127] Two of these historians have also suggested that the colonial government failed to assume a sufficient share of the defence burden.[128] As chancellor of the exchequer in the British cabinet, Gladstone, although primarily concerned with reducing expenditures, and without being fully informed of professional opinion on the strategic issue, had followed a course closer to that opinion than he probably realized, when he argued that Britain should not act without "unequivocal proof that it is the desire and intention of the Canadian people."[129]

For, as Kenneth Bourne has shown, the Admiralty, while believing that in essentials the Royal Navy was still superior to the new American fleet, had come to the conclusion that the rise of United States sea power had seriously diminished the possibility of a successful British strategic offensive by invasion, or even against ports and shipping in the Western Atlantic.[130] The foundations of the traditional strategy for the defence of Canada had thus been undermined. What use would a delaying action be if help could never come? The traditional strategy was, of course, aimed at deterrence; but to succeed a deterrent must be credible, that is backed by certain and sufficient force.

Although Canada had promised to spend a million dollars a year on the militia, and even to build the fortifications west of Montreal that Jervois had suggested, this would still leave Britain to carry the heaviest part of future peacetime defence costs. Lord Monck calculated that, of Jervois's estimate of £1,754,000 for the defence of Canada, Britain would pay £300,000 for Quebec fortifications and armament and £400,000 for armed gunboats; and he did not include in this account the cost of the troops in the garrison, perhaps because it could be argued that Britain would need to have those troops anyway and it was cheaper to keep them in Canada, now only within two weeks steaming time of Europe. Monck said that for the fortifications west of Quebec, Canada would borrow £1,054,000 at a cost of £60,000 per annum in interest. With the $1,000,000 per annum Canada would pay for the militia, this would be an expenditure of $2,300,000 as against Britain's $3,500,000 (£700,000).[131] His Canadian ministers pointed to the high costs of public works in a new country and to the fact that Britain enjoyed the profits of worldwide empire.[132] Britain's military role in Canada, which would now be effective only if the United States permitted, was part of international power politics. If it was successful Britain and the empire, including Canada, would gain. If it failed, Canada would be lost, and perhaps laid waste.

The effect of the deterrent could be strengthened, however, by building Canada politically and economically. This was clear to both British and Canadian statesmen. Hence the Canadian delegation in London in 1865 secured a promise of British support for Confederation as a contribution to defence measures. It also obtained a clear affirmation of British military aid in future crises and a guarantee for the loan for western fortifications that would enable the Dominion to borrow at a low rate of interest and so reduce the cost. But it did not carry home with it a promise of British naval support on the Great Lakes.[133] The Canadian delegates may not have realized that this aid for the inland sea power without which even a delaying operation, let alone an effective defence of Canada, would be weakened, would never be forthcoming on a permanent basis if the Admiralty got its way. The agreement had other specific deficiencies, notably no adequate provision for the timing and degree of British aid in an emergency and for the coordination of the Canadian militia with the garrison for training and operations; but its vague generality made it acceptable to Canadian ministers who wanted to avoid domestic political controversy.

As it happened, disbandment of the American armies, which were the chief cause of Canadian unease at this time, quickly removed the immediate potential threat. Four months after Appomattox, two-thirds of the Union army was demobilized. Three months later four-fifths had gone home.[134] In 1866 it was known in Canada that the size of the American forces had been reduced to 54,000, a reassuring figure.[135] George Brown's *Globe*, which had always scoffed at the idea that the end of the war would bring an attack on Canada, and which had called war talk in Congress "buncombe," reported with smug satisfaction that many American generals were already in civilian jobs.[136] Lt.-Gen. Sir John Michel, GOC in North America, reported that the United States was fully occupied with Reconstruction.

But Michel added that; if present Canadian weakness continued and a dispute with Britain arose, American troops could occupy Montreal within ten days. Michel's disturbing revelation was not made public.[137] Yet unfortunately for Canadian peace of mind, just when the possibility of a major American invasion seemed to have declined, Fenian disturbances increased on the border and continued for several years. Unofficial, instead of official, forces were being organized on American soil to attack Canada. They caused what Macdonald described at this date as "astonishing panic of the people on the frontier [although] there were no Fenians of any account."[138]

The Fenian problem was in part a consequence of the rapid disbandment of the American armies. Unemployed veterans of Irish descent were persuaded by wild oratory that Ireland's historical grievances could be righted by a blow struck at Canada. Irish servant girls in the United States were induced to contribute their meagre savings. Later, when the first attempt failed and nothing much more seemed likely, British officials began to suspect that the Fenian leaders were more interested in money than in invasion. But the possibility of invasion or raids had caused volunteers to report for the Canadian militia in greater numbers than were called out, evidence that in spirit, if not in efficiency and training, many were ready to defend their country. The provincial government's professed intention to strengthen the militia was thus confirmed and reinforced. At the same time the British rebuilt the garrison almost to what it had been at the time of the *Trent* crisis. Furthermore this time the War Office sent cavalry, an indication that it believed operations more likely. What was even more immediately useful was that the Admiralty provided naval personnel and some ships to patrol the St. Lawrence and the Great Lakes.[139] These things concealed the fact that British determination to reduce its commitment to Canadian defence still prevailed. And the War Office insisted that the province should live up to an earlier agreement to provide barracks and that it should repay money already spent on fitting them out, otherwise the troops would be withdrawn.[140] This showed that the Fenian problem had not changed the imperial government's assumption that Canada should pay for its own defence.

When the lives and homes of its readers seemed endangered by the Fenians, and after George Brown had joined the cabinet, the Toronto newspaper, the *Globe*, normally continentalist and anti-militarist, changed its tune.[141] It reported late in 1866 that Congress was considering an increase of the peacetime strength of the American army to 166,000.[142] If this was for the purpose of controlling the Fenians it meant well for Canada; but Canadians did not have much confidence in American goodwill. The crucial question was how the United States would see its responsibilities and what role it would play. In England the foreign secretary, Lord Clarendon, declared that the American government's toleration of the Fenians was "evidence of unfriendliness as great as the escape of the *Alabama*."[143] Canadians too believed that Washington was suspiciously dilatory in taking action to control its borders.

Fear of the Fenians lasted into the 1870s. There were, however, compensatory signs that gradually restored self-confidence. The defence agreement in 1865, the almost simultaneous disbandment of the Union army, and the failure of the Fenian raid in 1866 despite the poor showing of the Canadian militia in its first solo action, were good morale boosters. Without waiting to cooperate with British regulars who were in the vicinity, the Canadians had blundered into the Fenian force at Ridgeway. Lack of training and experience had led to their withdrawal from the field in confusion; but fortunately the Fenians were even more demoralized and withdrew simultaneously. The invaders had then been arrested by American officials as they crossed back into the United States. By enemy default the militia of Canada West had won their spurs in defence of their country.[144] Confederation a year later promised a larger militia and a new comradeship of the formerly separate provincial forces. The inspiration of a common patriotism might help to offset deficiency in numbers as against the United States.[145]

The possible military effects of Confederation were noted across the border where their significance was exaggerated. The governor of Maine, the state most exposed to a British-Canadian attack, saw Confederation as a threat.[146] But the *Portland Argus* retorted that the Republicans had brought this on themselves by ending reciprocity with Canada; and they praised the new Dominion. They said that the admission of a "free" Canada to the Union would be welcome but they added that this was a decision for Canadians.[147] The possibility of Canadian expansion beyond the Great Lakes by the acquisition of Prince Rupert's Land, which might have been taken to be an over-extension of the strength of the Confederation, was also seen by some Americans as an increase in potential Canadian strength, a last desperate British effort to redress the balance of power in North America. Alaska was purchased in part as an attempt to offset it, and to bring pressure on Canada for annexation.[148]

Reinforcement for Canadian morale followed quickly. At the time of Confederation the *Globe* forecast that there would soon be 655,567 Canadians capable of bearing arms and that 59,379 of these could make a first-class militia.[149] Carrying out its promise to contribute to defence, the new Dominion government's first major legislation was its Militia Bill to amalgamate the militia of three provinces. George Cartier, the minister who introduced it, described it as a measure to give the new state an essential element, the power of the sword.[150] The 1868 act provided for a voluntary part-time force of 40,000 men organized similarly to that of the pre-Confederation Province of Canada. The volunteer principle in the bill was essential to the survival of a Canadian military force in peacetime.[151]

Although it was not a regular army, the militia was a force large enough for one of the customary functions of military power, the preservation of internal order. For defence against the United States it had certain deficiencies, in addition to its inevitable comparative weakness in numbers if the Americans mobilized fully. It consisted almost entirely of infantry, with only relatively small numbers of artillery and cavalry; it was deficient in engineers; and it had no support services at all. Desmond Morton has said that Canada was "taking advantage of her limited liability status in the defence of British North America."[152] Cartier obviously assumed that Canada would continue to depend on a British garrison to provide essential services and possibly also the nucleus of a striking force. In addition the British regulars would supply the all-important instructors needed to train the militia.

The Militia Act showed that up to this point Canada was endeavouring within certain limits to live up to the defence agreement of 1865. Britain had also done its part so far by the construction program at Quebec and by putting pressure on the Maritime provinces to join the Confederation. But there was no evidence of progress in building fortifications west of Quebec.[153] When Britain gave a guarantee for the loan, Canada stalled. Further progress was problematical because western fortifications were clearly dependent on the unsettled question of responsibility for naval forces on the Great Lakes. So, despite the Militia Act and other steps towards the provision of guarantees and protection for Canada, the defence problem was not eased. Colonel Stacey has said in another connection, "colonies were far more ready to assume the rights of free communities than to take up the responsibilities of such communities."[154]

Undoubtedly one reason for this was that in the "perilous position" in which Canada stood, preparation for defence was not the only possible course. As Gen. Sir John Michel, the British GOC, told Macdonald on August 19, 1867, "The worst that could happen to Canada would be the annexation to a free and prosperous country. To England pecuniary ruin and loss of prestige."[155] A former adjutant-general of the militia, Gen. P. L. Macdougall, admitted in an anonymous article in *Blackwood's Magazine* that Canada could not be called on to do more than provide "her 40,000 excellent militia men." She could not be asked to pay for fortifications "of which the object is altogether Imperial."[156] Canadians did not want to join the United States, but they apparently did not feel it their responsibility to risk provoking violent annexation by activity in support of Britain's worldwide strategic power.

A few months after the Militia Act was passed, the premise on which defence measures were based was completely destroyed by Cardwell's intimation that the British garrison would be removed from the interior of the continent. Withdrawal was in line with the long-standing British effort to reduce the expense of all overseas military commitments.[157] Expedited at this time by Gladstone's appointment as prime minister, it was a part of Cardwell's plans for reforming the British army to fit it for possible European conflicts. Although withdrawal was not brought about solely by the logic of the strategic situation in North

America, Canada's vulnerability was a contributing cause. More important still was the possibility that a small British garrison might become a hostage within reach of American power.

The GOC of British troops in North America, General Windham, had suggested that in the event of war his small force should concentrate at Quebec so that "it would be ready to embark for England . . . for in such an eventuality its insignificance would invite attack which could only lead to disastrous results."[158]

The colonial secretary, Lord Granville, had suggested that the presence of the redcoats was an irritation to the Fenians and to the United States, and also a provocation for an attack on Canada. Cartier and MacDougall, to whom this was said, did not agree. They protested that the opposite was the case: the troops were a deterrent to American aggression.[159] But British policy could not be reversed. The fact that Canada had not yet lived up to its agreement to match British construction at Quebec with fortifications west of that point was used to justify, rather than to delay, withdrawal.[160]

So amidst scenes of emotion the troops departed from Quebec, where, it had recently been claimed, new defences had made the citadel safe. The British commander-in-chief wanted to keep the citadel until Canada provided regulars to ensure that this strong point was adequately defended.[161] In December 1869 Cardwell said the defences of the city were nearly completed.[162] But Quebec's defences were not adequate. The city was undefended on the north side and the Lévis forts on the south bank, which commanded the river in order to defend Quebec from attack by land or sea, had not yet been armed. A British military engineer had declared that the city's defences were deplorable and that an army would not be safe in it. Cardwell rationalized lamely that it had never been intended to defend Quebec from the direction of Montreal.[163] Yet that was the historic line of attack. The colonial secretary, Kimberley, seeking to delay final withdrawal, contended that Canada would be able to say that Britain had not lived up to its agreement because it had failed to provide properly for the defence of the main base in North America.[164] That failure would appear to be justification for the Dominion's failure to undertake fortification elsewhere.

The duke of Cambridge argued that colonial garrisons gave the British army valuable experience,[165] and that withdrawal would inevitably lead to the loss of all overseas possessions;[166] but the Liberal government in London would not be dissuaded. Although the withdrawal from Canada was part of a general withdrawal from overseas colonies which had responsible government, the strategic impossibility of defending Canada, though not universally accepted, had been an important factor in the decision. The British garrison was withdrawn from Canada partly because of a realization that American strength could now not be resisted.

In 1868 and 1869 there had been increasing public confidence in Canada that the Fenian menace would not amount to much. In the latter year, seeking to retain a British garrison at Prescott, Macdonald had said that people not behind the scenes were unaware of the need for preparations against what they considered an "imaginary enemy" because "the cry of wolf has been raised so often."[167] Macdonald had his own spies in the United States under Gilbert McMicken of Windsor; the Americans watched the Fenians with Pinkerton's agency and with troops on the border; and Ambassador Thornton, who had kept a close watch, thanked the United States government and reported home and to Canada signs that the danger was decreasing.[168] Sir John A. Macdonald said he thought it imperative that vigilance should be maintained;[169] but although he may have wished to persuade the British to make a slow withdrawal because the situation was not yet completely safe, he was no longer alarmed about a major threat to the country. With minor irritations declining, with few signs of American hostility or of preparation or even capability for major aggression, and with the certainty that in the long run Canada was bound to be overrun if war came, withdrawal was probably the wisest, as well as the cheapest, policy for Britain and for Canada. Much would depend on Canada's future adjustment to the problems caused by the potential disparity of military forces on the continent.

2

"Left without Home Protection"[1] (1870–1878)

It is usually assumed that Canadian defence policies in the late nineteenth century demonstrate a failure on the part of politicians to give leadership to an unmilitary people. The Liberal government of Alexander Mackenzie has been blamed for inaugurating this trend.[2] This interpretation whitewashes Macdonald and maligns Mackenzie. What is more serious, it ignores the complexity of Canada's defence problems.

Two years after the confederation of the British North American provinces, the new Dominion found itself facing a situation that had not been anticipated. An American attack might be provoked by Canada's ties with Britain; yet the announced withdrawal of the garrison from the interior would leave two provinces, Ontario and Quebec, without the British troops who had formed their first line of defence since Wolfe captured Quebec. For almost a decade, when there appeared to be no urgency, successive Canadian governments took inadequate steps to cope with this problem. In so doing they and many unofficial critics debated questions that were to persist for at least another half century. The basic problem that contemporaries had to resolve was whether Canada could be defended if attacked, and how it could be done. Bearing on this issue were questions that were even more difficult. Was the United States likely to resort to war? Would war be precipitated by American differences with Canada or with Britain? If war should result from British differences with the United States, was the alternative to fighting a fate that was entirely unacceptable? The fact that these questions were unanswerable made it difficult for Canadian politicians to do much to fashion a more effective military force, even if they were so inclined, which many were not. The latter believed that Canada's risk was small, and that the insurance premium should be proportionate.

In advising the governor general, Sir John Young, that Britain planned to withdraw the garrison from Canada, Lord Granville, the colonial secretary, said that he agreed with the secretary of war, Edward Cardwell, that it would soon be unnecessary to maintain a British force there, except to train the militia. The ostensible reason he gave for commencing the repatriation of the troops at this time was that Fenianism in the United States was "fast disappearing." Granville added that he was "by no means inclined to press [this opinion] too far."[3] His caution was justified. A year later the embarkation at Quebec had to be suspended because of Fenian incursions across the border.[4]

There were several other grounds on which Canada could protest that the British withdrawal was premature or too precipitous. Although the militia had been organized, Canada had not built the fortifications west of Quebec that had been proposed in the defence agreement of 1865; and Canada had not agreed to take over the naval force on the border lakes that was still partly maintained with British help. Furthermore, since the abrogation of the Reciprocity Treaty with the United States, American fishing in Canadian waters had once again become an irritant. Finally there was strong pressure in some quarters in the United States for the acquisition of Canada, or at least of the Hudson's Bay Company territories transferred to Canada in 1869 where Canadian authority was not yet established.[5] These were all Canadian, rather than British, problems.

In April 1869 negotiations for the settlement of American *Alabama* claims had run into trouble. The Senate refused to ratify the Johnson-Clarendon Convention for an adjustment, thus souring the brief post-Civil War Anglo-American honeymoon and reviving President Grant's bitter recollections of British toleration of Confederate raiders. Grant said impatiently that he was restrained from resorting to war only by the size of the American national debt.[6] Knowing of American antipathy to England and appetite for Canada, Canadians feared that the proposal to withdraw the garrison was a sign that the mother country wished to cut the umbilical cord and to leave Canada to fend for herself. This might mean at least the loss of the West and the stifling of Canadian prospects there; it might also lead to annexation by the United States. Many were dismayed because the withdrawal would leave Canada exposed to an American threat that might develop precisely because it was part of the empire; some looked forward to independence as a way out of the dilemma, and these included a few recent pro-annexationists, particularly Nova Scotians, who turned that way because they saw it as a step towards continental union.[7]

Of all these perplexing problems, it was the Fenian raids, a source of panic in 1866, which were still uppermost in Canadian minds in 1870. Colonel Stacey has pointed out that the Fenian danger inspired more militia recruiting and greater defence appropriations than had wartime threats from "the greatest military power in the world."[8] Canadians either regarded the Fenians as the greater danger or else thought they posed a problem with which they could cope without aid. The effective fashion in which the militia mustered and deployed to meet "General" O'Neill's raid south of Montreal in 1870 showed that there was some truth in the latter belief.[9] Canada's ability to handle minor border filibustering raids had obviously improved since the fiasco at Ridgeway in 1866. Success in facing the Fenians did not prove that the Canadian defences were capable of meeting greater emergencies. Nevertheless it tended to entrench Canada's questionable faith in part-time soldiers as against regulars, and to enhance belief in voluntary, as against compulsory, military training for all males, even though the Canadian voluntary part-time militia lacked the departmental support corps previously obtained from the British garrison.[10]

A second problem was as much a source of concern to Macdonald as were the Fenian raids when, towards the end of 1869, after a series of personal troubles and a long bout of drinking, he turned his attention again to public affairs. Canadian acquisition of the Hudson's Bay Company's lands was opposed by some of the inhabitants. Lieutenant-Governor William McDougall and his designated chief of police and commandant of militia, D. R. Cameron, sent to establish Canadian authority, had been unceremoniously hustled out by armed Métis.[11] Americans in the Northwest openly talked of acquiring Prince Rupert's Land. Interference by the United States might end Macdonald's hopes for a Canada from sea to sea. Although President Grant and his secretary of state, Hamilton Fish, had prevented Hudson's Bay Company arms stored on American soil from falling into the hands of the Métis, Fish told the British ambassador, Sir Edward Thornton, that the western problem could best be solved by the removal of the

British flag from Manitoba. Fish also urged that forcible reconquest of the Red River territory should not be attempted.[12] The secretary of war, William Belknap, then ordered that British vessels carrying military stores must not be permitted to pass through the American canal at Sault Ste. Marie into Lake Superior.[13]

A force organized by the Canadian government under the command of Col. Garnet Wolseley pushed west. As a result of a delay in the transmission of a U.S. Army telegram, and also because General Sherman had ordered that instructions concerning restricted use of the canal must be kept secret,[14] the vessel *Algoma* got through the canal unladen. She was then available to ferry the expedition on to the head of Lake Superior; but another unladen supply ship, *Chicora*, and also the gunboat *Prince Alfred*, were refused passage even though the latter's captain offered to dismount his guns. However, an American ship was then permitted through when her captain stated, falsely, that he had not been hired by the British for the expedition.[15] With two supply ships on Lake Superior, Wolseley, although delayed, could proceed.[16] He moved from Port Arthur by the "Dawson route," a series of lake passages and portages built to link Ontario with Manitoba. Three hundred and seventy officers and men of the 60th Rifles, with detachments of Royal Engineers, Royal Artillery, and other ancillary services, had been lent by the withdrawing British garrison; but the expedition also included two battalions of Canadian militia with a strength of 770.[17] This was a major contribution and a demonstration that Canada would not lightly let the West go. It also gave the militia more experience and more prestige.

The significance of the military factor in this incident was, however, equivocal. The British government had urged Canada to come to terms with delegates sent by residents in the territory; and diplomatic representations in Washington, which quickly secured passage through the canal for other ships not carrying warlike stores, had stressed the peaceful objectives of the expedition.[18] Wolseley achieved his objective without fighting because Riel and his supporters fled when the troops approached Fort Garry. Although the militia stayed on after the British troops left, within a year Macdonald cut the Fort Garry garrison down to two companies to save money. It seemed that the West might be held with relatively little military effort.

Some Canadians thought that looser ties with Britain might lead to the absorption of Canada by the United States. Canada's defence problem was how to develop strength to stand up against American pressures without the support of the British military presence. The garrison's departure would remove an important demonstration of British commitment to aid Canada against the United States. Primarily for this reason Macdonald and Cartier, having ignored British suggestions that the Royal Canadian Rifles and the lake gunboats be taken over, sought to retain a permanent British garrison in Quebec. They succeeded only in obtaining a temporary postponement of the departure of one battalion of infantry and one battery of artillery over the winter of 1870–71. Announced on February 12, 1870, this British concession was probably made to give the Canadian government time to reverse its refusal to create a force of Canadian regulars in place of the Royal Canadian Rifles which the British were disbanding.[19] But the decision was not reversed.

Macdonald's desire to keep a British garrison in Quebec as a symbol of the imperial connection conformed with a prevailing Canadian belief that, "however independent, [Canada] must lean for support on either Great Britain or the United States" for a long time to come. One Canadian view was that annexation to the United States would bring "a prohibitory tariff, a whole heritage of wrongs. Irish and American, [and would be] aggravated by a sense of loyalty repulsed with scorn, and of love requited not." "Under its present constitution," proclaimed an exponent of this thesis, an anonymous self-proclaimed admirer of Cartier who was possibly a militia officer, Canada enjoyed "all the independence it desires," and with it a prosperous relationship with Britain.[20] The postmaster-general, Alexander Campbell, told the colonial secretary, Lord Kimberley, that the retention of a garrison in Quebec, even though small, would reassure the Canadian people that Britain intended to maintain the imperial connection.[21] In his biography of the American secretary of state, Hamilton Fish, Allan Nevins expressed the view that in 1870 Canada still enjoyed "full British protection."[22] But if war had broken out in 1870–71, the small force in Quebec could have done little to defend Canada. It was the continued token of a British commitment to give aid, such as had been given in 1861 in the *Trent* incident, that was important.

Whether Canada could actually be defended against the United States was another question altogether. Ten years later, admitting that he was not a military expert, Macdonald was to tell the Carnarvon Commission that he had always understood that leading military men believed that "the Americans, from their immense power and superiority, could go where they liked and do what they pleased in the country," and that only a few places could be held.[23] Macdonald had undoubtedly formed this stark opinion from the findings of the Defence Commission of 1862, from the Jervois Reports, and from information supplied him by senior British officers serving in Canada. He may not have known that other military appreciations made around 1870 had confirmed his pessimism.

In connection with a Canadian request for an imperial guarantee for a fortifications loan, which was about to be put before the British Parliament, Colonel Jervois, author of the two Civil War reports that had largely determined the future shape of British military policy in Canada, had been asked in 1869 for his opinion about the possibility of defending the Dominion. Jervois repeated the gist of his earlier reports, but he added categorically what had been veiled before, that in view of the disparity of population and resources, and the lack of a prepared basis of defence, it was "out of the question" for Canadians "to protect themselves against attacks of an American Army." Canada could be defended, he said, "only by the aid of fortifications, combined with an effective organization of local forces, properly disciplined and supported by military and naval forces from this country." He went on to say that, even with British support, the whole of the border could probably not be protected. Yet he was still reluctant to abandon the idea of a resort to some form of offensive action. He thought that British troops were probably superior in quality to American and that they might be able to capture the fort at Rouse's Point and push up the St. John's River. He said that it might be worth keeping small 12-ton vessels at Quebec in readiness for this kind of operation.[24]

A second professional appraisal had been made by Capt. Lindesay Brine, a British naval officer who travelled in the United States in 1869 and 1870. Brine thought that the temper of American feeling against England was such that war was inevitable within a few years. He declared that "it is evident that Canada, even if aided by Great Britain, could never contemplate any successful resistance to a military invasion from the States." She could resist for a short time and could always hold Quebec when the forts at Lévis on the south side of the river were armed, "but the rest of the country would have to be ultimately left to the mercy of the invaders." Brine argued that both banks of the St. Lawrence could be made practically untenable by the navy as far up as the river was navigable (a somewhat optimistic view of the effectiveness of sea power inland) but that above the canals Upper Canada was "endangered."

However, Brine believed that conditions had changed since Wellington's time. Wellington had pronounced that possession of command of the lakes was essential to the defence of Canada and had argued that geography obstructed a counter-attack. Brine said that roads and railways now provided alternative means of communication. After presenting a detailed survey of the frontier, he too suggested that the best form of defence was a gunboat attack on exposed American lake cities. He added that it was "unreasonable to suppose that Upper Canada, however supported by Great Britain, could long maintain a war with America; and therefore she has only to study how far it is in her power [so] to menace the lake ports as to make an invasion inexpedient."[25] These British officers thus thought Canada vulnerable, but both urged that preparation for offensive action could forestall or blunt an American attack.

Before the militia accomplishments of 1870, some unofficial strategists had painted rosier pictures of the possibilities of Canadian defence provided certain measures were taken in time. A correspondent, possibly a Canadian, who wrote to *The Times* of London early in 1870, argued that the United States would never attack Canada merely to conquer it, but that aggression would be incidental to a great war of exhaustion with Britain. His three unsigned letters, probably intended to check British withdrawal, challenged the prevailing belief that Canada was indefensible. He said that because Canada had several strong fortresses separated by great distances, an American invasion would require several separate great armies. Canada had 500,000 men capable of bearing arms. This, he said, was as many as the Confederacy had been able to put into the field during the late war; and Canada's winter climate would be an advantage. Because this enemy had always observed the rules of civilized warfare, Canadians would accept an American occupation of part of their country "as the price of their loyalty." The United States could not easily win control of the Great Lakes, and especially of Lake Ontario, because American tonnage on Ontario was not greatly superior, and because good harbours on the south shore were few. If Canada seized the advantage at the outset, all the conditions favoured her. The potential drain on American resources, reminiscent of what the Union had suffered when it fought against the South, would be a strong deterrent.[26]

A very similar contention that Canada was secure without a British garrison was presented by the anonymous author of *Thoughts on Defence*, "A Canadian," who was quoted earlier. He argued that much of the long frontier was "invulnerable" and that the possible approaches could be defended by the militia, provided the British held the tidal waters and navigable reaches of the St. Lawrence, and provided also that Canada made preparations to seize the lakes and attack American cities there while the British attacked those on the coast.[27] But he admitted that these conditions had not yet been met.

This critic concluded by saying that the "philosophy" for the defence of Canada was to "give no offence" and to engage in "friendly rivalries in the arts of peace. . . . If we are compelled to appeal to the arts of war, we will hold on our own as best we may, . . . until England casts her mighty buckler before us." He did not show how that shield, primarily a naval force, could be pushed into the interior of the continent. Nevertheless, he had indicated suggestively that, if preparations for defence and an early offensive were not made, future Canadian policy would have to stress peaceful cooperation with the United States.[28]

Another self-appointed expert was much more confident that the militia could defend Canada. Capt. Francis Duncan, RA, author of *Our Garrisons in the West* (1864), when lecturing in London in 1871, declared that British withdrawal had excited the hopes of Canada's "republican neighbours" but had also "compelled Canadians to look matters in the face, and learn to trust themselves. . . . It may be said that an army of 40,000 men would be but a mouthful to the Americans" but, he added (as if he thought it an advantage), these men were "changing annually." Their camp at Niagara ("whose sole *raison d'être*" was, he said, "a protest against annexation") was "seen by invitation by American officers from the neighbouring garrison" who must have learned "an unwelcome truth, [with] the dispersion of some cherished illusions."[29]

What these various appreciations of the military situation indicated had long been clear to informed experts: Canada could probably not be defended by the militia, certainly not in a long war, but effective Canadian preparation and a promise of British support might possibly deter United States aggression. "A Canadian" argued that "the purse is the true arbiter of war" and said that if "the enemy" could be made to realize the cost of conquest, there would be no war.[30] Jervois believed there would be less enthusiasm in the United States for war with Great Britain than there had been for war with the South and that the need for a huge army to keep the South down and to defend the coasts would influence American policy.[31] Brine believed that the United States Congress would not place naval establishments on the lakes in peacetime and would hesitate at taking any action that might lead to the annexation of two large disaffected states.

Officials in the Admiralty found Brine's paper "very interesting," especially his information about the academies at Annapolis and West Point. But one of those who read it noted an important inconsistency and wrote a minute pointing out that "The paper is written in the assumption that before many years a war with the United States is inevitable. It shows, however, that no preparations are being made [by the Americans] with this object and that their navy is reduced to the lowest possible point in respect of men, ships and votes, etc."[32] It was thus becoming clear that the real security of Canada would rest ultimately on American lack of aggressive intention. It was therefore tempting for Canadians who disliked military expenditures and were faced by many domestic problems, to believe or hope that the United States would always be benevolent, to rely on distant British support as a deterrent, and furthermore to seek to avoid provocation.

Trends in Anglo-American relations converted this belief into a course of action, or rather of inaction. The Admiralty minute quoted above was written five days before the British and American commissioners signed the Treaty of Washington. If ratifications could be secured, this would greatly reduce the possibility of an armed clash between Britain and the United States and therefore the need for defence preparations.[33]

Six months earlier, Anglo-American relations had been so bad that Lord Tenterden, a Foreign Office specialist in American affairs, had declared that relations with the United States "without being absolutely unfriendly" were "unsatisfactory." "If such a state of things existed between any two European countries, war would be inevitable." In an epoch-making memorandum Tenterden had detailed sources of friction and had noted Grant's readiness to "give vent" to ill-humour against England. Tenterden had proposed the International Commission that was set up in 1870 to seek an understanding which would, among other things, remove the possibility that, in an Anglo-Russian war that seemed imminent, United States ports might become refuges for Russian *Alabamas*. Tenterden had also noted that disputes about the *Alabama* claims, the San Juan boundary, reciprocity, fisheries, and the Fenian raids were not likely to lead to war; but he knew that some of these things hung like a cloud over Canada. He had therefore suggested that the Dominion should be represented at the negotiations in Washington.[34]

In the course of the ensuing negotiations a military factor may have been all-important. It had recently been noted in the War Office that the new works at Quebec, hardly yet completed, were "unfit to receive the armaments necessary for their defence." The easy destruction of French masonry fortifications by Prussian rifled guns had led to a realization that against the new rifled guns an even wider outer ring of forts was needed.[35] The regulars in Canada had been like pawns in jeopardy. So if retention of the small British garrison had been intended to "strengthen Macdonald's hand" in the bargaining at Washington, as has been suggested,[36] this concession had been singularly unsuccessful. On the contrary, the retention of the British garrison at Quebec had weakened Canada's negotiating position because the British became anxious to settle outstanding issues and remove from a weak fortress, within easy reach of American attack, a small force that was, more than ever before, a hostage.

However, the negotiations at Washington amply demonstrated in another way that there is a relationship between lack of military strength and diplomatic failure. Macdonald, the weakest participant militarily, had come away with practically nothing of what he worked for, neither compensation for losses during the Fenian raids nor a favorable settlement in the dispute about fishing rights. The San Juan boundary dispute which seemed strategically important to Britain, in which the United States had displayed a tendency to use force, and which now concerned the Dominion because British Columbia had joined confederation, was left to arbitration.[37] At Washington, as in the struggle to keep a British garrison in the interior of Canada, the Canadian government had been forced, as Macdonald informed a correspondent about the latter problem, "to yield to the paramount power."[38]

Yet the Canadian prime minister did not deduce from these experiences of dealing from weakness at Washington that what Canada needed was greater military force at her own disposal. On the contrary he was unwilling to strengthen the militia by the introduction of a ballot for compulsory service, and he agreed only to encourage volunteering. His rationalization was, "There is not much chance of a war with the Yankees at present and we need fear no other foe." He was therefore undisturbed by the fact that the militia volunteer companies were not up to strength.[39] Macdonald had realized that Canada could benefit greatly from the most important result of the Washington negotiations, namely the achievement of an entente between Britain and the United States, and that this advantage overrode more superficial lessons about the relation between military power and untrammelled national sovereignty. At the same time the negotiations at Washington had left a degree of Canadian rancour toward both the United States and Britain that helped to undercut what was left of the annexation movement in Canada. Canadians were thereby encouraged to depend on their own resources.

There was still no immediate incentive to do anything about defence. Americans in Minnesota were increasingly expansionist in mood. In 1871, after the Washington accord, Fenians attempted to exploit dissatisfaction in Manitoba by an invasion from Pembina. The incident amply demonstrated that the official American attitude had now been modified, or perhaps clarified. A year earlier, as we have seen, American authorities, although not as negligent or hostile as in 1866, had deliberately attempted to obstruct Wolseley's passage west. In 1871 Canada sent reinforcements over the Dawson route without British aid (further evidence of the Dominion's military potential), but by the time the militia arrived the trouble was nearly ended.[40] An American captain at Pembina, carrying out orders from Washington to keep the peace on the border, had anticipated Canada's moves and had arrested the Fenian leaders. He had taken advantage of the fact that the Hudson's Bay Company store, which they had seized, was on territory still claimed by both sides.[41] Thus it was American, rather than Canadian, military strength that snuffed out the raid.

Later the captain who had made these arrests was incensed by reports from Manitoba that American citizens seized in the disputed territory where he had acted were being prosecuted in Canada. He complained that this undermined the legality of his action,[42] but his superiors did not take the matter up. On the contrary they criticized a federal commissioner who released Fenian prisoners in response to local pressures. It was apparent that, presumably as a consequence of the Treaty of Washington, the United States was now not likely to challenge Canada's hold on the West. Therefore it seemed to follow that only a minimal military force would be needed to hold it. Canadian confidence in peaceful national development had been vindicated.

While emphasizing that he "was no believer in the eternal friendship of nations," Sir John A. Macdonald repeated in 1873 what he had stated two years earlier: "Thanks to the Washington Treaty there is not the slightest chance of a row between the United States and England"; and he added, "We ought to take advantage of this to keep down our Militia estimates." Macdonald declared that militia camps did little good in comparison with their enormous cost and "the injury they do to young men's morals."[43] The year 1873–74 therefore saw the militia training in company and battalion headquarters instead of in camp.[44]

Early in 1872, without cabinet approval, Sir Francis Hincks, the Canadian minister of finance, had approached the British through Sir John Rose, Canada's representative in London, about arranging the surrender of the British guarantee for the loan for fortifications in exchange for a guarantee for a loan for a Pacific railway. Macdonald reacted with a show of anger. He said he thought that the cabinet would not want to lose the defence pledge. He was even more concerned that "such a proposition emanating from Canada would have been held as a formal declaration of our resolve not to fight in case of a war between England and the United States." However his reaction was really determined by fear that at the next election this diversion of effort from military to civil channels might bring charges of disloyalty to Britain. He had in fact already decided that the western fortifications would not be built in the near future;[45] and before the year was out he was negotiating the substitution.[46] He had decided against relying on military strength to counter future American policies.

The following year Col. Robertson Ross, the British officer who was adjutant general of the Canadian militia, crossed British territory to the Pacific to report what would be needed to establish Canada's authority. Ross argued that a civil police force unbacked by military force would not be able to cope with a major crisis in an area which was still in a "primitive" state of society, where strong political party feeling existed, where there were restless and reckless characters among whites and Indians on both sides of the border, and where smugglers, illicit whisky traders, and Indian horse thieves and raiding parties freely crossed the international border. He therefore proposed that a regiment 550 strong should be distributed in companies of about fifty men in posts scattered across the prairies.[47]

Macdonald did not agree. No military force that Canada could at that time have provided would have been able to withstand a determined American attack on the Canadian West. Since the United States had apparently now accepted the idea of Canadian ownership, Macdonald regarded the matter as a civil responsibility and not (as across the line where a hostile Indian frontier was patrolled by cavalry) as a military problem.[48] He decided to establish the North West Mounted Police to control the plains. Although this was to be a paramilitary force, organized and trained rather like soldiers, and even uniformed in the red coats of the British soldiers of that day—with which the Indians were supposedly familiar—the NWMP was a civilian, rather than a military, means of extending Canadian authority and of asserting Canadian sovereignty. This arrangement for policing the West and the border had been adopted because of Canadian military weakness and dislike of military force; but it would have been impossible without American forbearance. It was an important indication of the future significance, or rather insignificance, of the military factor in Canadian–American relations.

Macdonald believed it unnecessary to spend money on defence against the United States until such time as the political situation deteriorated to the point where the Americans began to prepare for war. He said that the volunteer Canadian militia battalions, drilled at their headquarters until they were "tolerably efficient," could, "in case of the first cloud of war . . . be brought into camp, and a short mingling with the Regular troops would be sufficient for all purposes."[49] But this naïve opinion did not show how "mingling" could occur when there were no regular troops in Canada, nor how it would help to deter the United States from contemplating a future resort to war.

There was, however, plenty of evidence to support Macdonald's trust in American non-aggression. During the annexation movement in Nova Scotia in 1868–69 the United States had made it quite clear that it would not support the Canadian annexationists by force of arms.[50] By 1870 the concept of "political gravitation," or inevitable continental union, had taken root in the United States and had further reduced Canada's fear of American use of force.[51] The American army was indeed inadequately prepared for invasion. Dr. Weigley has pointed out that for more than a decade after the Civil War the American army had perhaps "less of a directing brain than at any other time in its history," because clashes between the secretary of war and the commanding general had eroded the latter's office "to the verge of nullity."[52] Although the Canadian government had no military intelligence service (the British army's Intelligence Department at the War Office was established only in 1874), and there may no longer have been Canadian secret agents or spies in the United States, such as McMicken had used to watch the Fenians, official publications told of the decline of American strength. From the peak reached in 1865, when the Union's active army numbered more than a million, the U.S. Army had been cut to 57,072 in 1866. By the early 1870s that figure had been further reduced to less than 30,000, i.e. less than the Canadian volunteer militia. For ten years after the war, a large part of the American army was employed on reconstruction duties in the South and on the Mexican border. The remainder had returned to its old task of "pacifying" Indians. In 1869 twenty-five one-company regiments were scattered among 255 military posts, and only a few of these were on the Canadian border.[53]

During the Crimean War there had been evidence that rifled artillery, steam, and armour had given ships greater effectiveness against land fortifications. Henceforward these must be sunk into the ground. By the end of the Civil War the American Atlantic coast defences, which in 1861 had been "unsurpassed anywhere in the world," were dangerously out-of-date. European governments were hastily applying the lessons of the Civil War to their coastal defences; but American investigators sent to Europe, and experiments to test the new guns against defences, could not produce a conclusive solution for the United States. The cost of rebuilding with steel, which seemed the most likely proposal, was prohibitive. As a result of these and other circumstances, the United States had quickly dropped a fort rebuilding program that it began in 1870, "the most short-lived of all American harbor defense efforts."[54]

Figures for Congressional appropriations for fortifications on the coast and the northern border were fully available to the Canadian government and people. They told an encouraging story. In 1866 and 1867 more than a million dollars had been spent annually on the construction and maintenance of the forts, finishing off works begun during the war. But in each of the years 1868 and 1869 only $200,000 for "contingencies" was appropriated. Between 1870 and 1875 the appropriations rose from $1,311,500 to $2,037,000 but then fell back to $719,000. Thereafter, until 1885, there was an annual allocation of a mere $100,000 (increased to $175,000 from 1881 to 1884), for maintenance only.[55] American foundries had not produced cannon since 1867. In 1875 President Grant decided to stock-pile guns, because it would take much time to cast them when they were needed. He said that fortress construction, on the other hand, could be done "very speedily for temporary purposes when needed."[56] The United States was obviously ill-prepared, and was also apparently not preparing, for war with a naval power like Great Britain. It therefore could not possibly undertake an early invasion of Canada.

American plans for the defence of the northern border were even less impressive than those on the coast. Most of the Northern forts dated from the early part of the century. Although some had been rebuilt during the Civil War, they were already obsolescent. They had exposed masonry or stone ramparts. From time to time after the war requests for money for the northern forts emphasized their "strategic importance . . . for the defence of the northern frontier";[57] but there was considerable opposition in Congress to the spending of money on forts which, it was said, "would be no earthly use."[58] One of the smaller forts, Wilkins, which had been established on the south side of Lake Superior in 1844, was abandoned soon after the war "under changed conditions on part of the Lake Superior frontier."[59] At Forts Niagara and Ontario strong batteries were completed on the landward side, but the waterfront was left "to that future in which the general public look for a change of frontier, which shall render these forts more curious than useful."[60] Fort Wayne had barbettes from which it was said that the Detroit River could be controlled; but in 1873 these had not yet been completed.[61] Everywhere little more than the most essential repair was undertaken, to protect a shoreline against erosion, or to build or turf a glacis.[62] Mackinac was described as a good place to station troops for the Upper Lakes area, but useless to control the Sault Straits.[63]

Canadians could read American official publications, or go to see the forts. They concluded that the United States had no thought of the invasion of Canada. A published report on Sackets Harbor, where there was an unfortified garrison, showed a factor that shaped American military policy about northern defence. In 1871 the general commanding the Department of the Lakes recommended that the Sackets garrison would be more conveniently located at Ogdensburg which commanded the St. Lawrence. From there field guns could bombard the Grand Trunk Railway. But this apparently offensive move was not intended to secure a better starting point for an invasion of Canada. It was proposed only in order to make troops more readily available for the prevention of Fenian raids.[64]

American lack of either military capability or hostile intention made possible Macdonald's dream of building a nation by rails rather than with arms. The Canadian Pacific Railway was his instrument. Although Macdonald was aware that the CPR could be of military value, making it possible to rush troops out west in the event of another rising like that in 1869, for him the railway was more a means of binding the country together peaceably than a contribution to defence. Macdonald's purpose was to strengthen Canada. He therefore rejected proposals to run the line south of Lake Superior because to do so would have helped to produce one nation instead of two in North America. Later decisions about the route through the Rockies and about the Pacific terminus also involved military considerations; but as alternatives more vulnerable to attack were eventually chosen, it is clear that the danger was never taken very seriously.[65] Like the Intercolonial and other Canadian railways, the CPR could easily be cut by American forces in case of war. Macdonald was gambling on permanent peace.

Macdonald's concentration on railway building, and on the political machinations to bring it about, led to the fall of his government in 1873, when it was found that financial interests seeking to build the railway (including some Americans) had financed his party. Meanwhile, as a result of attention to peaceful developments, he had let military preparedness deteriorate. His was not the sole responsibility. The electorate, since it did not call him to account on this score, must bear its share.

A major cause of the qualitative decline in Canadian military preparedness was the departure of the British military instructors with the garrison. Thereafter it proved to be more difficult to maintain discipline and efficiency in a volunteer force, especially in one that was inadequately equipped. The British adjutant-general, Robertson Ross, was not equal to all the demands of his job, and Cartier, the minister, who was more interested in politics than defence, was not an efficient administrator. Furthermore, as a result of illness he had let things slide.[66] But the chief responsibility was Macdonald's. He thought of military preparations in Canada almost solely in terms of the need for defence against the United States; and he believed that nothing need be done when relations were harmonious. As a result the militia, and also the forts left vacant by the garrison, soon began to decay.[67] Within three years there were signs that the minimal Canadian military force that Macdonald had declared could be expanded in time of emergency might soon entirely cease to exist.[68]

From the time of the withdrawal of the garrison, defence-minded critics in the British Parliament had questioned whether Canada was now adequately defended.[69] In answer to a War Office request in 1874, the adjutant-general, Col. Walker Powell, described the militia organization and reported it to have a strength of 42,169. This was more than the authorized establishment of 40,000. But Powell did not reveal that many militiamen were not carrying out the three-year enlistment necessary to bring them to a reasonable degree of efficiency. Furthermore his reference to the vulnerability of the Canadian railway system to American attack noted rather anxiously, "It will be unnecessary [sic] to attempt to foreshadow where such interruption to railway traffic is most likely to occur . . . [because an army might land anywhere on shores and boundaries] used in common." The Americans had railway facilities for massing hostile armies at many points of the frontier east of Huron. Walker Powell knew that Canada was dangerously vulnerable to an American attack if one came.[70]

Canadian opinion was divided and still uncertain on the defence question. Some urged military preparedness but no longer related it to defence against the United States.[71] Others were sure that American invaders could be driven back as they had been in 1812.[72] One view took note of the length of the frontier and advocated that "defence not defiance" should be the motto;[73] yet others prophesied that the Americans would not attempt forcible annexation and that reciprocity would lead to "absorption."[74] There were some who warned that American malevolence must be taken for granted, that Canada could not defend itself against a people ten times more numerous and "equally brave and civilized," and that Canada's only security lay in Imperial Federation.[75] What was perhaps of most significance amidst this welter of conflicting opinion was that George Brown's influential Liberal newspaper, the *Toronto Globe*, in an editorial published on April 28, 1874, under the heading "Our fortifications," professed friendly feelings towards the Americans, but maintained that the militia, and the fortifications on which it must rely, must be kept up.[76] But all the advocates of militia expansion and fortification building for defence against a possible American attack complained that the Canadian ministers did not heed them.[77]

Canada First, a most revealing political development of this time, showed something of the intellectual confusion about the defence problem that was to be found among politically-minded Canadians. In 1868 Canada First's five founders wanted Canada to dominate the northern half of North America and, inspired by George Denison, they saw the Red River Expedition in 1870 as a military operation leading to that end. They thought of Canada as Britain's partner in the Empire. In the aftermath of the overthrow of Riel, when Canada First became a party with political ambitions, it took in new members. Among these was Goldwin Smith, who was already suspect for his pro-American sentiments during the Civil War. Canada First thus became tainted by the charge that it sought independence as a step towards continental union.[78] On the defence question Smith wrote in 1877, "Canadian nationality being a lost cause, the ultimate union of Canada with the United States appears now to be morally certain." He attacked expenditure on "military and political railways . . . armaments and defences" as "flagrant improvidence."[79] Denison and other founding members of Canada First, on the other hand, were sturdy nationalists who, while rejecting subordination to Britain, believed that Canada's security and future lay in avoiding American absorption by maintaining the imperial tie and by gaining a voice in imperial and foreign policy. Denison and Smith later became bitter opponents. Two completely opposite political and military concepts of Canada's future and her defence posture thus sprang from Canada First. The movement met its political Waterloo, however, in the election of 1873, when it failed to make its mark as Macdonald's government fell and the Liberals came to power.

In 1871 Macdonald had described the Liberal party to the governor general, Lord Lisgar, as a "peace at any price party who look upon all monies expended for military purposes as thrown away." He declared that if it came to power there would be a virtual, if not an explicit, breach of the Canadian promise to maintain the militia. This would be brought about by a decrease in appropriations and drill.[80] These views seemed to be confirmed by Liberal attacks on the militia estimates made when in opposition, and by Liberal efforts to reach an accommodation with the United States through a new reciprocity treaty.

Lord Dufferin, governor general from 1872, was therefore pleasantly surprised to find his new ministers "more liberally disposed" on the defence issue than were their predecessors.[81] The reason for this was that the prime minister, Alexander Mackenzie, who had been a major in the Lambton County Militia and had advocated militia reform in 1874, had a loftier, though perhaps more naïve, sense of duty than Macdonald [82] and so was more receptive to the governor general's persuasion. Dufferin's secretary, Lt.-Col. Henry C. Fletcher of the Scots Fusilier Guards, furnished the new prime minister with information about the state of the militia and supplied a rationale for its improvement.

In a lecture delivered to militia officers and later published, Fletcher admitted that American military capacity was low and this might seem to justify spending money on "developing the resources of the country" rather than on the militia. But he argued that history showed that "periods of peace have never continued for any length of time, and clear as the political horizon now is, there are still clouds no larger than a man's hand which may be seen by those who are not dazzled by its brilliancy." Fletcher said that because the American army was small Canada needed only the nucleus of a larger force "to defend the country against external foes . . . to act as a last resource in maintaining the power of the law . . . [and] far in the background to be a symbol of the state which pertains to all nations aspiring to rank as such among their compeers." [83] Two years later, in a second lecture on the "Defence of Canada," he reiterated that, although the United States was not a present threat, he feared that if it were to break up, "sections of men," or even separate states, might be a "present danger to Canada." Fletcher also noted that the United States could quickly arm merchant vessels in Chicago to threaten Ontario and that a military force stationed to defend the province would be in danger of being cut off unless the command of Lake Ontario was secured. He warned that Montreal, only thirty miles from the American frontier, must be garrisoned at the time of any threat of hostilities. Finally he argued that as long as Quebec held out, Canada would be unconquered because she could be resupplied each summer from Britain. [84]

Although when he was in Canada Fletcher talked of a possible American threat in the future, the defence of Canada against the United States was probably not his primary concern. After his return to England he lectured at the Royal United Services Institution on the need for colonial volunteers to defend the empire in the event of a major war and he then suggested that the Canadian Military College might provide staff officers for a Canadian expeditionary force. [85]

Imperial and Canadian officers, following Fletcher's lead, had been surprised to find Mackenzie receptive to suggestions that Canada ought to improve her defence capability. [86] Col. Walker Powell, the Canadian acting adjutant-general, had criticized Macdonald's plan for training the militia at local headquarters instead of in camps. He wrote, "A small force, carefully trained and well paid and cared for, is much more desirable from every point of view than a numerically large force without these requisites to efficiency."[87] Mackenzie restored brigade camps for the militia in 1874–75, but only for 30,000 out of the 43,750 authorized strength. The reduction in numbers was made by cutting down the size of units.[88]

The extent to which Dufferin and Fletcher succeeded in arousing Mackenzie to take a personal interest in defence is illustrated by the fact that the prime minister personally inspected the citadels at Quebec and Kingston to see for himself their state of repair and their suitability for use as a military college. He then allocated money for repairs.[89] Mackenzie established the Royal Military College at Kingston to produce officers; and he appointed a British general officer, Selby Smyth, to command the militia. His defence policy was directed towards long-term development of a Canadian military capacity. But his further plans had already been frustrated by the onset of economic depression in 1873. In 1876, the year RMC opened, the cutting of the militia estimates was cheered by both sides of the House of Commons.[90] Militia brigade camps were once again dropped. They were not to be restored for the city corps for nearly two decades; and the reduction in strength of the militia made in 1875 was continued.

Mackenzie had in fact adopted Macdonald's pacific policies, for instance for the civil development of the West, including the construction of the CPR as a nation-building agent. He horrified Dufferin by suggesting that it would be cheaper to let the Americans cross the border to deal with whisky smugglers than for Canada to take action,[91] but he accepted the police as the necessary prop for Canadian sovereignty. There was even a suggestion that the Americans should send a cavalry force along their side of the border to accompany the NWMP's first move in the West and to intercept the runaways that it flushed out.[92] This does not appear to have been done, but the fact that it was discussed officially suggests that the Canadian government believed that its sovereignty in the West was now fully accepted by the Americans and would be unlikely to be challenged. In future, problems would arise only from the activities of outlaws, wandering Indians, and other malcontents, or from rebellion.

A year later the American secretary of war still hesitated to arrange police and military cooperation across the border to deal with criminals; but the American cavalry aided Gen. Selby Smyth when he toured the West. The American army post band at Walla Walla played "God Save the Queen" for him (or was it "My Country 'tis of thee"?).[93]

There was now cooperation between Canada and the United States in the arrest and return of deserters who crossed the border. When an American patrol crossed into Canada to arrest one of its army musicians who had deserted, diplomatic protests quickly secured his release at the Canadian border.[94] This was noteworthy recognition of Canada's sovereignty.

The most serious problem in the West in the first years of the mounted police was the presence of American Sioux Indians, hereditary enemies of the Canadian Blackfeet and therefore a most disturbing element. Large numbers had crossed to Canada in 1873 to escape United States control.[95] After the defeat of Custer in 1876 eight thousand more fled American vengeance. The American authorities pointed out that by international law it was Canada's duty to disarm the warriors. But this was beyond the power of the NWMP. It would also have deprived the Indians of hunting weapons on which they depended for subsistence. Canada therefore invited an American commission to come to negotiate with the Indians for their return to the United States.[96] Canada's sovereignty in the prairies was thus not yet complete, but there was no evidence of an American disposition to move in.

From 1873 American entry to Canadian fishing grounds had been matched by reciprocal access for Canadians to American markets. Although there was grumbling by the Americans about the cost of licenses and about Canadian competition in the domestic market, for about ten years incidents in the fishing grounds no longer seemed a threat to peace.[97] By the middle of the 1870s economic depression in the United States had begun to reduce still further any concern Americans still had about the growth of the Dominion which they had watched a decade earlier with suspicion and cupidity. In 1876 the British ambassador in Washington, Sir Edward Thornton, dismissed reports about American naval building, which was allegedly connected with fisheries disputes, as newspaper hysteria.[98] Furthermore, the annexation movement was apparently dead.[99] A convention held in Buffalo to discuss continental union to mark the centenary of American independence was described by Thornton as a "moderate affair" which would probably receive no support and no delegates from Canada.[100]

Despite the failure of the politically powerful George Brown, joint plenipotentiary for negotiating a fisheries agreement, to secure ratification of his reciprocity treaty with the United States in 1874, harmony continued to increase and fear of a resort to arms to diminish. Americans were more concerned about their own economic recovery than about Canada. Canadians, experiencing the blight a little later than their neighbours, were also tightening their belts and striving to recover prosperity.[101] On neither side was there thought of resort to foreign adventure as a means of diverting public attention from domestic problems, as sometimes occurred in Europe. Canadian appropriations for militia drill, cut in 1876, were only slightly increased in the following years.[102] The practice of comparing the size of the Canadian militia with that of the American regular army, which had been followed in the Militia Report for 1871,[103] had not been repeated. An increase in the American army in 1876, the year in which the Canadian militia was reduced by about half, had been noted calmly by Ambassador Thornton, who saw it as a problem for Canada only inasmuch as the Sioux, against whom it was directed, would probably flee to that country,[104] as indeed they did. Gen. Selby Smyth, struggling in hard times to foster military efficiency and spirit in the militia, emphasized the need for reform in wordy reports to the Canadian Parliament and complained privately to the duke of Cambridge about the Dominion government's lack of concern;[105] but the militia's most frequent duty was in fact to give aid to the civil power to maintain public order in strikes and riots. With no enemy in sight Smyth had to resort to vague rhetorical hyperbole in order to rationalize the need for a militia to deter what seemed to be an increasingly improbable aggression. In 1877 he declared that the danger was the spread of "communism." A year later he admitted that aggression by American Fenian or Communist forces was unlikely.[106]

On the American side, opinion about Canada's military potential as a danger to the United States assessed the problem much in the same way. *Colburn's United Service Magazine* in 1875, after stating that Canadians neither wanted nor anticipated a war with the United States, went on to discuss Canada's military capability. The long frontier was weakly defended and could easily be cut. However, if Canadians took "more than a barrack-yard view of the situation," they would not be content with dependence on Quebec, ice-bound for seven months of the year, as their only base. In the event of war they could take the initiative, occupy Portland and part of Maine, and make contact with the British fleet. That course was, however, only possible for a country "which always stands prepared." The article went on to show that Canada's military potential for such an initative had not yet been developed.[107]

American military critics were sometimes impressed by Canada's experiment with voluntary part-time service, contrasting it favourably with the militias of their own states. The editor of the *Army and Navy Journal* believed that the *Canadian Volunteer Gazette* [sic] had "spitefully" distorted the activities of honest American traders (the whisky smugglers) in the West in order to gain support for militia development.[108] He warned that Smyth's first *Militia Report* showed that Canada was "not so helpless as we imagine" because successive generations of men were going to be trained quickly on the Prussian model.[109] A year later the same journal quoted Macdonald as saying that to attack Britain was to attack half-a-dozen nations because of the growth of military strength in the colonies.[110] In 1878 the *Journal* declared that the American army would quickly suppress Fenianism if it was revived;[111] yet it also quoted an American officer who had noted that some Americans still wanted a war with Britain to "gobble up Canada," and it gave its opinion that "Canada would gobble us, or at least a very considerable part of us."[112] These statements, though misinformed and erroneous as regards the military capability of Canada, support the view that American appetite for northern expansion had declined considerably since the 1860s.

Declining fear of American military aggression continued to encourage relaxation in Canadian defence policy until 1878 when there was a threat of an Anglo-Russian war. Mackenzie's ideas about a defence policy for Canada were set forth in a letter to Dufferin written after the Russian crisis when he was fighting the election which drove him from power. They were expressed in answer to questions that Dufferin had raised in a talk at Quebec. The prime minister had not been able to consult other members of his cabinet who were electioneering, and the opinions were therefore entirely his own.

Mackenzie said that it was a popular belief in Canada that all that was needed was a volunteer force to keep domestic order and protect the frontier against Fenians. Personally he was aware of the need for a more effective form of military organization, but he claimed that he must recommend only what Canada could afford for the purpose of advancing a sense of unity in the Empire. He noted that he had already provided a means of training officers. But if war with Russia had come in the 1878 crisis, no graduates of RMC would have been ready. Mackenzie said he recognized a need for training noncommissioned officers. He was considering the selection of one of three plans, infantry schools for the militia, temporary call-outs for militia regiments, or the integration of Canadian regiments with British regiments as proposed by Selby Smyth. Although he thought that the last of these proposals might lead to friction with Britain and to expense that Canada could not afford, he was prepared to have it examined in Britain.[113]

Mackenzie professed to be willing to do more than Macdonald had done to improve Canada's general military capacity. However, even though the recent Anglo-Russian crisis of 1878 had drawn attention to a possible need for protection against the United States, he showed little concern about such an eventuality. His more conscientious approach had made little, if any, better provision for defence against the United States than had Macdonald's bland assumption that no such defence was needed.

Canadian military historians, seeking for signs of efforts to give Canada a military potential, have overlooked Mackenzie's intentions and achievements. Despite the lower degree of imperial interest in his party, his efforts were directed elsewhere than against the United States even after his schemes for reciprocity had failed. Macdonald, in many ways more imperially-minded, was in agreement that war with the United States was something for which Canada need not prepare; but he was also slow to build Canada's general military strength. History has shown that the American threat did not materialize. But history cannot tell whether Canada's interests would have been better served in future Anglo-American negotiations if Canada had adopted Mackenzie's proposal to build military strength to make a contribution to imperial defence. What is clear is that Canada was learning to live with the United States without leaning on a British garrison.

3

Imperial Defence
(1878–1885)

On the Queen's birthday, May 24, 1878, Lord Dufferin, governor general of Canada, addressed a banquet of the Montreal Brigade of the militia. He expressed confidence in Canada's security. During the preceding months fear of renewed Fenian activity in the United States, which had been described by the GOC, Selby Smyth, as "communistic,"[1] had led to the issue of arms to militia units along the border. But Dufferin claimed that he did not take "rumours of a certain amount of Celtic effervescence" very seriously; and he pointed to Canada's "indissoluble friendship" with the United States. He told Sir Michael Hicks Beach, who had been appointed colonial secretary earlier in the year, that on this occasion amicable American-Canadian relations had been marked by the presence of "a company of Yankees from Vermont with a flag which covered more ground than their entire body." Invited by a Canadian regiment, the Americans had been permitted to fall in with the parade and to join in firing the *feu-de-joie*.[2] Privately Dufferin thought it good for Americans to become aware of Canada's military strength. In public, he declaimed, "Today we have witnessed how soldier-like and martial is the array of our Southern neighbours (Loud Cheers). But if they have forced the bulwarks of our land, if they have penetrated to the heart of our richest city, it has only been to give fresh proof of the kindly feelings entertained for us by themselves and their fellow countrymen in the States, and perhaps to lay siege to the hearts of our young ladies (Laughter)." He invited the Americans to come back again and he offered free land above the Arctic Circle to any who would take the oath of allegiance.[3] Humorous sallies of that kind suggest that there was little serious thought of war.

A year later the Brooklyn Battalion of the New York National Guard, led by its distinguished chaplain, Henry Ward Beecher, on a white horse, took part in the Birthday Review and *feu-de-joie* at Montreal. Gen. Selby Smyth informed the visitors that they were "the first American battalion . . . that had been under the orders of a British general officer for full one hundred years."[4] This second more formal American visit was the more noteworthy because, a few days before the previous one in 1878, the cabinet in Ottawa had been jolted from its usual apathy about defence. Reports had been received that a Russian ship, *Cimbria*, had arrived from the Baltic at the port of Ellsworth, Maine, carrying a cargo of rifled guns. Its supposed purpose was to arm cruisers to prey upon shipping and to bombard colonial ports in the event of a Russian war with Britain.[5] Mackenzie and his cabinet had cabled the Admiralty to ask for protection for transatlantic shipping. The Canadian ministers had also discussed the installation of guns for the defence of Atlantic ports and the establishment of defences for the Pacific naval base at Esquimalt.[6] Before these measures could be implemented, the Berlin Conference had brought relaxation of tension; but this crisis in 1878 had stimulated a new interest throughout the Empire in a military concept that came to be called Imperial Defence.

Strategists and historians have stressed that the new British interest in Imperial Defence, which began in 1878, was primarily a reemphasis on sea power in line with the teachings of Capt. J. C. R. Colomb, RMA, who had anticipated the work of the American Admiral Mahan. It had many other elements. Although the new strategic concept in Britain was in part a reaction against an obsessive concern about the defence of the British Isles that had marked the 1860s, the defence of Britain as the heart of the Empire remained a principal objective in all Imperial Defence strategy. Defence of the frontiers of India, the most valued inperial possession, was also an essential element.

An equally important aspect of Imperial Defence (and one which like sea power received new attention after 1878) was colonial participation. Lord Carnarvon, who presided over the Royal Commission that sat from 1880 to 1883 and "set [before the British government] definite aims and distinct objects" for the defence of the Empire, reasoned that "people who are desirous of enjoying the privileges of constitutional freedom must be prepared to make some sacrifices in return for that inestimable boon." Maj. G. S. Clarke, secretary of the Colonial Defence Committee, declared that that sentence went "to the very root of the great question of Imperial Defence."[7]

Imperial Defence strategists stressed that colonies must make preparation for their own defence in peacetime. But much of the argument that poured from their pens was also a plea for colonial aid, including manpower, not only for the Royal Navy, as sought by Lord Brassey,[8] but also on land. Col. H. C. Fletcher's article in 1877, mentioned in the preceding chapter, had been prologue to these pleas.[9] Colonial land forces were needed for the protection of imperial naval bases. This recommendation of the Carnarvon Commission was echoed by Maj. Gen. J. W. Laurie, deputy adjutant-general of the Nova Scotia Militia, who had resided in Canada since coming there with British reinforcements during the Civil War and who twice tried to raise Canadian militia for imperial campaigns. Laurie, who commanded the militia in British Columbia briefly, urged the application of the Carnarvon thesis to Esquimalt.[10] The British advocate of Imperial Defence mentioned above, Captain Colomb, asked for much more. In an article on "The Naval and Military Resources of the Colonies" in 1879, he spoke of colonials as "a raw material of war resources."[11] Imperial Defence was thus in part an effort to make up for Britain's growing inferiority in manpower at a time when European armies, fed by conscription, were expanding rapidly. Canada, the most populous of British colonies, was the best source of colonial "raw material."

The long debate about Canada's role in Imperial Defence, which was to run on until 1914 and even after, has been dealt with elsewhere.[12] Suffice it to say here that Imperial Defence strategy required that a colony prepare to defend itself against possible dangers as far as its means would allow. At the same time it should also prepare to contribute to the defence of the Empire as a whole because a colony obviously benefited from the continued existence of the Empire. These two assumptions were closely entwined—preparation for the one could be diverted to serve the purposes of the other. But where there was responsible government, colonial populations, their political leaders, and their military advisers had to be convinced that defence measures were related to the colony's interests. As it was often difficult to assess whether imperial wars would be fought primarily in British or in Empire-wide interest, the need for self-defence was by far the most compelling argument by which colonial participation in Imperial Defence could be secured. But the reasonable contribution that could be expected from a colony on those grounds was not easily estimated. In addition to an assessment of the intentions and offensive capacity of each colony's potential enemies, it was necessary to appraise the colony's capability for defence and also its deterrent effect in the whole balance of international power. For Canada, this meant not only an assessment of American intentions and capability for attack but also of the effect that American actions might have on Britain's worldwide security and therefore on Canada's well-being.

The idea of providing men to defend the Empire had many supporters in Canada. This was a less complicated concept than other aspects of Imperial Defence; and it could be correlated with capability for defence against the United States since trained men could serve for either purpose. In 1878 and later, although neither Mackenzie nor Macdonald gave official encouragement except for the recruiting of boatmen for Wolseley's Nile expedition, many Canadians offered their services to the War Office and some offered militia units as well. Lt.-Col. T. C. Scoble, an engineer and militia officer who wrote in Canadian periodicals under the pen-name "Centurion" in support of "Canada First" and later edited a Winnipeg newspaper, *The Nor'-Wester*, said that colonies could not afford monetary contributions because of their need for development; but he declared that they could supply men. Scoble, who believed in the British connection but not in the British view of Imperial Defence, thought that Britain should pay Canada's troops.[13]

Others preferred to base proposals for troops for Imperial Defence on Canada's own needs including Canadian relations with the United States. Lt.-Col. Salter M. Jarvis, who retired from the Queen's Own Rifles in 1881, argued a year later that Canada would receive deference from the United States as an integral part of the British Empire if there was a system of Imperial Defence that provided the force to restrain the hostility of foreign powers. He declared that until the forces of the Empire were properly organized it could not be said that Canada's "ability to repel attack is the best guarantee of her immunity from it." After deploring the state of Canada's fixed defences, he alleged that the Canadian government had maintained a defence policy for twenty years merely "out of deference to the Old World prejudice of the British government" but that she had spent as little as possible on it. He admitted that the cost of building the CPR precluded spending more on the militia. To make the militia more efficient with the means available, Jarvis thought its numbers should be reduced.[14]

Another article similarly discussed the question of militia reform for

Imperial Defence in terms of relations with the United States. The author, probably a militia officer, noting that only the United States could attack Canada by land, held that an attack was unlikely and would come only as a consequence of an Anglo-American war. He was, however, of the opinion that a determined American attack would be irresistible and that Britain would be unable to help. The only consolation was that war was unlikely because both nations would suffer commercially. This writer, who has not been identified, then went on to say that the militia had great value for preserving public order and ceremonial duties, an emphasis on functions which virtually ignored the militia's historic role—defence against the United States.[15]

Such arguments for the development or reform of the militia, which were often inspired by Imperial Defence propaganda, may have been motivated by the ambitions of men who enjoyed part-time soldiering; yet they were also indicative that opinion in the Canadian militia ranged from belief that Canada could be defended against the Americans to fear that an attack could not be resisted. Furthermore, despite the diversionary panic created by the *Cimbria* that had focused attention on the coasts and the oceans, it is clear that for many Canadians the most important element of Imperial Defence, namely self-protection, meant resistance to the United States. Even though many outstanding Anglo-American issues had been settled at Washington in 1871, and American hostility had cooled and might not now postulate the seizure of Canada by force, there was always the possibility that—in the event of Britain being involved elsewhere—Canada might be a pawn which American politicians could exploit to gain some other advantage. Canadian capacity for self-defence would therefore be a contribution to Imperial Defence strategy if it offset that possibility.

On the other hand, as Col. Walker Powell, the Canadian adjutant-general, wrote in 1882, the creation of a Canadian regular force for defence against the United States might draw American attention to Canada's "want of organization."[16] Furthermore Americans might regard Canadian military development, whether for self-protection or to aid Britain in imperial wars, as an unfriendly gesture. Canadian military expansion might precipitate the invasion that it was designed to prevent. Powell's argument may have been advanced to justify present reliance on the militia, but it shows that British pressure for participation in Imperial Defence preparations placed Canada in a difficult dilemma.

Proposals for the use of Canadian manpower for Imperial Defence inspired much more than militia reform and expansion. They led to agitation for the creation of an Imperial Reserve in the colonies. In addition they gave renewed strength to older arguments for the arrangement of exchanges of British and Canadian troops to further the development of a Canadian regular army. Sir John A. Macdonald claimed in 1882 that he had been in favour of a Canadian permanent force since 1866, but that he was not sure that his political associates would accept it.[17] On the eve of the election that returned him to power in 1878, he had told Sir Stafford Northcote, the British chancellor of the exchequer, and also Lord Dufferin, that this was his personal inclination.[18] But Macdonald made no move in that direction until 1883 when he set up the Militia Infantry Schools with permanent staffs. These infantry schools graduated 154 officers and NCOs in the first year of operation, 1874.[19]

Although this step went some little distance towards compensating for the loss of the instructional staffs that had been drawn from the British garrison up to 1871, it was far short of providing an effective military force for immediate service. Since Macdonald had told the Carnarvon Commission two years earlier that in peacetime Canada would not provide troops for imperial purposes, he presumably had some other purpose in mind in setting up the schools. No doubt one reason for improving the Canadian militia, which he could not advertise, was a desire to make it more efficient for aiding the civil power, its most frequent duty. Since Macdonald had told the Carnarvon Commission that in his opinion the defence of Canada against the United States was impossible, it may be confidently assumed that he did not establish the militia schools primarily to resist American aggression.

The impact of Imperial Defence propaganda on Canadian politicians and on the Canadian government was thus quite different from its effect on British, and on many Canadian, soldiers. General Luard, who succeeded Smyth as GOC, told the British commander-in-chief, the duke of Cambridge, on more than one occasion that the Canadian government only acted when it got a sudden scare.[20] The *Cimbria* sensation had passed quickly. It had as quickly ceased to impress Canadian politicians with the need to spend money on defence, especially for defence against the United States.

It has been suggested by a recent historian that the 1878 crisis, which had made Britain think seriously about Imperial Defence, caused the Canadian government to "turn inwards." Furthermore, it has been said that Gen. Selby Smyth, who was aware of political realities in Canada, leaned in the same direction.[21] This interesting theory needs closer examination. For some time previous to the crisis of 1878 Smyth and his political masters had been gravely concerned about the infiltration of radical ideas from the United States and also about Fenian raids. It was not the *Cimbria* incident, that made them "turn inwards" in the sense of seeking to preserve domestic order or prevent minor incursions from across the border. They were already fully concerned about these things. Furthermore, although the *Cimbria* must have reminded many Canadians of the *Alabama*, and must also have suggested to them that sea-raiders operating from American ports might bring on a war with the United States, there is no firm evidence that Smyth believed that the imperial crisis made a war in North America more likely.

On the contrary, Smyth's reports from 1878 on show that, like other British soldiers at home and in the colonies, he was concerned about the need for Canadian support for Imperial Defence measures generally, rather than to defend Canada itself. This is supported by both the detail and the general conclusions of Smyth's annual reports. His 1878 report repeated earlier warnings that the interior fortresses were deteriorating and emphasized that military force was needed to aid the civil power. Its new stresses were on the defence of the seaboard, on the need for an Imperial Reserve, and on the question of naval reserves for imperial purposes—and not on defence against the United States. Smyth referred to the Pacific railway as a means of sending reinforcements to Esquimalt, which was an imperial naval base—one of his few references to the United States was to their ability to interfere with the approaches to that base. However, he regarded Esquimalt's weakness as essentially unimportant because in any event the American demeanour was pacific. Speaking of possible Indian unrest as a result of the decimation of the buffalo, Smyth referred only to a peaceful return of the American Sioux to reservations in the United States—apparently he did not contemplate a military resolution of the problem.

Smyth, in fact, admitted that he placed great emphasis on securing direct Canadian contributions to the defence of the Empire. He stated flatly that his report was "intended to include not only plans for defence and military development of Canada, but also the means of utilizing her strength for Imperial purposes, as well as finding a place for the voluntary aid which Canada has so chivalrously proffered in the event of any considerable expedition beyond the British seas."[22]

Thus, although managing to establish a good rapport with Canadian government leaders, Smyth actually gave priority to Britain's overseas needs on the grounds that these served Canada's interests best. He therefore did not "turn inwards" in the sense of putting emphasis on defence against the United States, except in so far as that might be necessary as part of a general Imperial Defence strategy.

As for the Canadian government, it did not, as a consequence of 1878, "turn inwards" to become more apprehensive about the security of the border or about internal order. What is meant by "turning inwards" is that some members of the cabinet were becoming more afraid of involvement in imperial wars. They therefore became more hesitant about undertaking military development of any kind, and especially against the United States. Macdonald's military changes in 1883 were so minimal that it is clear that he actually had been "turned off," rather than "turned inwards," by the Imperial Defence crisis. His militia schools, merely an attempt to gratify the militia colonels in Parliament, had remote rather than immediate value.

There was, however, an appendix in Smyth's report that did "turn inwards" in the sense of showing more concern about defence against the United States. This was Lt.-Col. T. B. Strange's lecture on "The Military Aspect of Canada," which was delivered at the Royal Service Institution in London on May 2 and 7, 1879. The lecture was published by the Institute in a separate volume on defence as well as in its *Journal*, and also appeared as an appendix to Smyth's annual *Militia Report*.[23] The following paragraphs are derived from it.

After dealing with the problem of the defence of the Atlantic and Pacific Coasts and of the all-important base at Quebec, Strange turned to the "Frontier" on the South and to the way in which "an enemy" would operate there. He hastened to explain that this question was "treated merely in a military and, it is hoped, philosophic spirit, such as cannot give offence to our kinsmen of the great Anglo-Saxon Republic with whom the most friendly relations exist."

Strange went on to discuss in detail the probable strategy of a war across the Canadian-American border. After describing the 4,000-mile Canadian-American frontier, he said that even though Canada had a much smaller population and could be attacked at all points, its defence would not be as difficult as was sometimes thought, provided there was proper forethought and organization, because the Americans would have to establish themselves securely at several vital points in order to obtain any decided military advantage. Garrisoned by a small force of regulars, such places could be held against the Americans for the five months of the northern campaigning season. If Quebec could be held securely, British gunboats could dominate the St. Lawrence, which was a defensive "fosse." Road and rail communications running behind the frontier would permit Canadian operation on interior lines. The Rideau Waterway, and the larger canals now contemplated for commercial purposes, would permit the passage of gunboats to the Great Lakes at the outset of a war. Strange quoted Fletcher on the importance of Lake Ontario. He also noted that an attack from the West, while a good political move, would be bad military strategy for the Americans because it would be an attempt to roll up the defence along its line of communications instead of cutting those strategic arteries.

Strange then examined the probable lines of American invasion strategy. He said that an attack would be based on Albany and directed against Montreal. This pointed to St. John's, P.Q., as a base comparable in importance with Montreal, Quebec, and Kingston. Finally he declared that the arrangement proposed by Canada in 1872 to replace the guarantee for the loan for building fortifications by one for building the CPR had weakened Canada's security.

Strange was an independent-minded British officer, with long service in Canada, whose character bordered on the eccentric. He was unorthodox in his behaviour and in the methods by which he achieved his objectives. He often surmounted obstacles by drastic methods: for instance, he drove gun-carriages over rough ground to break those that were weak; and he fired guns in Quebec after midnight to demonstrate that in conditions of severe frost it took a long time to prepare them for action.[24] If he thought it would serve a good purpose, such a man was not to be deterred by diplomatic nicety from publishing military appraisals which had hitherto only appeared in confidential reports. He declared that without further military preparation Canada was dangerously vulnerable—the only consolation being that the cultivated classes in the United States were friendly, and that Canadian loyalty "could at any time be rendered active in the defence of the country provided the principal expense and direction was taken by Great Britain, or the Council of the federated Empire."

Strange thus reiterated the theme of all his contemporary military colleagues, the need for a reorganized system of Imperial Defence. But with his customary lack of finesse he added to it an elaboration of the idea that Imperial Defence was necessary for the security of Canada against the United States even though Americans were at present not hostile—the argument used earlier by Colonel Fletcher.

The final paragraph of Strange's examination of the lines of a future Canadian-American war, one headed "Offence," was innovative and explosive. Strange argued that, although Canada as a colony did not have the initiative, its militia system and interior lines of communication could facilitate an attack on the United States that might succeed in surprising 40,000,000 unarmed people "who have hitherto relied upon their successful diplomacy." Parliamentary government and the sharing of political control between the Imperial and Dominion governments would render the making of a colonial offensive "perilous if not impossible." However, "a combined military force starting from Canada at the first declaration of hostilities might, by giving up their communications to the rear" and emulating Sherman, seize Atlantic bases for use by the British fleet while an expedition from India landed British and Sikh troops on the Pacific seaboard.

As we have seen, Colonel Fletcher had talked to militia officers in 1873 about the possibility that the United States might not always be friendly; and references to a preemptive strike had appeared from time to time in secret British military appreciations since 1815. But Strange went further than this. He implied that Britain could use Canada against the United States; and this idea was not only published for all to read but was also given official approval by being appended to the GOC's report and especially mentioned in it. Although the author was actually quite pessimistic about the sources of Canada's defence against the United States, because of her lack of preparedness, and although he thought an offensive was beyond her present capability, these qualifications came to be ignored. Strange's lecture did much to persuade Canadian military opinion to accept the need for preparation for defence against the United States as a contribution to Imperial Defence. It had no immediate impact, however, on Canadian government thinking or policies. Like many another British soldier who talked about Canada's military problems, the man who was later to write a book significantly entitled *Gunner Jingo's Jubilee*[25] was known to be an ardent imperialist. Canadian political leaders undoubtedly saw his lecture as merely an attempt to strengthen his case for Canadian participation in Imperial Defence by relating it to the security of Canada.

The Canadian government was therefore not stirred to further action. It responded only belatedly to British requests for a study of Canada's defence problems which would apply the new concepts of Imperial Defence to the Canadian situation. When the minister of militia, Adolphe Caron, set up a defence commission in 1884 under the chairmanship of the governor general's military secretary, Lord Melgund, he wanted to include the defence of the Canadian border in its scope. But Colin Campbell, the commission's secretary, contended that this subject was too big and the danger remote. Campbell was influenced by the British government's greater concern about the safety of the imperial bases on each coast and its desire to have Canada protect them. The GOC, Maj. Gen. Frederick Middleton, followed the same line. He proposed that the commission should restrict its investigation to what he called "the flanks," meaning the defence of the Atlantic and Pacific ports. This terminology implicitly though inadvertently pointed to the fact that defence against the United States, which

Campbell had excluded, was the central question for Canada. But Caron accepted Middleton's limitation.[26]

Presumably, in accord with the neglected line of thought in Strange's article, Caron did not fear an American attack in the fore-seeable future. Even though Imperial Defence strategy required Canadians to prepare to defend themselves lest future British involve-ment elsewhere give the United States an opportunity to embarrass Britain by threatening, or even invading, Canada, Prime Minister Macdonald also showed no concern. Macdonald may have been still convinced that Canadian resistance would be incapable of saving most of Canada. Hence he may have believed that, as defeat seemed certain, the Canadian taxpayer could not be induced to bear heavy defence costs in peacetime. The idea of a contribution to a general imperial de-terrent would be even harder to sell.

A typically simplistic Canadian reaction to proposals that Imperial Defence required more effective Canadian preparation against the United States was advanced by Macdonald's finance minister, Sir Francis Hincks. He asserted that Canada cost Britain nothing for de-fence because the only British troops in the country were in Halifax, an imperial base "kept up not for us but for English objects." Hincks said that Canada did not want to interfere in foreign policy and would take her chance on war. She would defend herself (presumably by means of her militia) but would not pay any share of imperial military, naval, or diplomatic costs. He went on, "If on that account England chooses to cast us off she will force us [not into independence, but] into the Ameri-can union." Hincks said that Canadians had no wish for separation. They believed, however, that Englishmen would not wish to see the United States double its territory, obtain all the fisheries, and acquire "the finest harbour in the world," Halifax. "Cyprus and Asiatic Tur-key would be a bad set off for such a loss." Hincks claimed that Duffer-in entirely concurred with these sentiments.[27] The governor general may not have been as much in agreement as Hincks alleged but he was perhaps aware that the minister's views represented a powerful strain in Canadian thinking.

Not all Canadians agreed with Hincks on one point: that a Canadian drift towards independence would mean eventual annexation. George Monro Grant, a Canadian imperialist, said that annexation was impos-sible because it would mean that Canada might eventually have to fight with the United States against Britain, which Canadian could never do.[28] When the *New York Herald*, which was frequently anglophobe, asserted that annexation sentiment in Canada had been so stimulated by British manipulation of commercial policy for her own advantage that it was now greater than when "Colonel Lyttleton [Sir Arthur Lyttleton-Amesley] stated that Canadian women presented to Princess Louise must wear low-cut dresses," the Colonial Office was not convinced. It believed the Canadian desire for annexation was feeble.[29] The Liberal Kingston newspaper, the *British Whig*, was aware that President Ulysses S. Grant and many Americans nursed a belief that "manifest destiny" meant the eventual absorption of all North America; and it believed that Fenian attacks were pointless because as far as Britain was concerned Canada could "go to the demnition bowwows." But it declared that the Americans were quite wrong in thinking that a Canadian drift towards independence meant annexation. It said American propaganda on this question was "electioneering claptrap."[30]

Those Canadians who thought that annexation was impossible, or unlikely, found their convictions reinforced by confidence that the United States would not attempt to bring it about by force. Canadian Liberals, conforming to the pattern of Liberal thinking in Britain, usually assumed that constitutional democracies by their very nature, abjured the use of force. Furthermore, they had a convenient belief that military success and prosperity were not connected. The *British Whig* contended that France's prosperity after the defeat of 1870–71 proved this point.[31] However, what is important is that, regardless of their views about annexation, many Canadians apparently thought that American aggression was unlikely and that military preparation to prevent it was therefore unnecessary.

Something of Canadian opinion in these years about the connection between Imperial Defence and relations with the United States can be deduced from consideration of a very different problem. Sitting Bull and the American Sioux Indians who had sought refuge in Canada from the U.S. Army were a continuing source of unease and difficulty. They might clash with either Canadian Indians or white American hunters. The United States government showed reluctance to take the Sioux back and tried to make Canada responsible for their good government.[32] A proposal for the re-establishment of a permanent Canadian force of about four or five hundred Métis to counter the possibility of American interference with the Sioux, or of a sudden dash by the Fenians, came to nothing.[33] The American secretary of state then tried to bring Britain into the picture. He complained that if American troops crossed the 49th parallel in pursuit of Indians the British navy would bombard New York. Therefore, he said, a British army should be sent to the prairies. This suggestion may not have been meant seriously. But the British ambassador, and on a later occasion Lord Lorne, replied to Secretary of State Evarts that Canada was the responsible agent but had only three or four hundred police in the area and therefore could not disarm the Sioux who, in any case, needed their weapons for hunting for food. They protested that American refugee Indians were living off herds on which Canadian Indians depended, and that the American cavalry were apparently trying to keep the buffalo from moving north across the border. They urged that American Indian policy should be modified to permit the return of the "hostiles."[34]

After a long series of such blunt exchanges through the British ambassador in Washington, Canadian and American authorities agreed to share intelligence to deal with the Indians who raided across the border in the West.[35] However, Canada steadfastly refused to permit American troops to cross into Canada to punish alleged Indian malefactors. On the Mexican border, where an international agreement permitted border crossings, there had been difficulty in settling Indians who had been diverted from following their traditional way of life. General Crooke, who commanded in that area, and who had not followed the U.S. War Department's "slaughter policy," had found that reservation Indians would not accept newcomers.[36] Accordingly, Canada resisted American pressure for similar arrangements and despite lack of military strength, managed to maintain Canadian sovereignty.

Canada's unwillingness to permit American troops to pursue Indians across the border did not prevent Macdonald from granting permission to that "distinguished officer," General Sherman, the commanding general of the U.S. Army, when he was inspecting American posts, to cross Canada with an armed party when it was more convenient to do so.[37] On the other hand, apprehension of an Indian attack on Fort Simpson in British Columbia led to local Canadian requests to Americans for assistance.[38] When an American mob lynched a young Indian and hanged him 500 feet north of the border, nearly causing an Indian raid in revenge, the Canadian government vigorously protested against this breach of sovereignty. It pointed out that the Fraser Indians, who were industrious and progressive, were convinced that the victim was innocent. The American minister of the interior thereupon ordered the governor of Washington Territory to make every effort to bring the lynchers to justice.[39] Yet Sir John A. Macdonald refused to intercede on behalf of some Canadian deserters from the U.S. Army who were arrested by American troops allegedly on Canadian soil; he did not wish to arouse American feeling on the basis of meagre evidence when relations between the U.S. Army and Canadian authorities in the West were cordial.[40]

The Canadian West was remote and sparsely populated. Its problems seemed of little moment to Canadians in the East. But many in Canada must have been aware that the United States was respecting Canada's sovereignty in the West even though Canada's occupation was not backed by adequate military force. This was an object lesson that could have wider application. Evarts's reference to British naval bombardment had expressed the sophisticated view that, even where prairie Indians were concerned, sea power was the decisive weapon in the background. This rationale for an Imperial Defence strategy was, however, lost on Canadians who saw that Canada's sovereign rights in the West were maintained without military force. The experience undoubtedly had great potential for shaping Canadian attitudes. Only an imperially-minded minority of Canadians preached that Imperial Defence required Canada to arm against the United States.

An intelligence branch, called the "Topographical and Statistical Department of the War Office," had been organized in Britain as long ago as the Crimean War. Its successor, the Intelligence Department set up in 1874, was concerned with the possibility of war.[41] But the idea that the United States would not, or could not, resort to force seems to have permeated British military thought. Although it was confined to secret documents, something of this belief may have been known in Canada. Hence the Carnarvon Commission on Imperial Defence in 1880–83 heard only one brief touching the question of war with the United States—that of Capt. L. M. Carmichael, DAQM, an intelligence officer who stated that American military strength was "contemptible." Carmichael's scornful estimate of American strength led him to gloss over the problem of Canada's security which he regarded as no longer primarily Britain's responsibility. Although disparity in resources and numbers between Canada and the United States would make it impossible for Canada to conquer her neighbour, Carmichael thought it possible that "Canada, by a superior naval organization on the lakes, and by the employment of a more rapidly mobilized, more homogeneous, and more efficient army, might neutralize superior numbers, capture Chicago and Buffalo and other important lake and frontier cities, cut off the Peninsula of Michigan, detach the State of Maine, and even advance by Lake Champlain upon the North-Eastern States." Carmichael believed that a rigorous blockade and the bombardment of New York and other cities would cause the United States to lose nerve.[42]

Carmichael's optimistic appraisal of the outcome of a war between Britain and the United States was probably based on information lately received from Capt. William Arthur, British naval attaché in

Washington. In 1882 Arthur had reported on the state of American port defences, many of which he was able to visit. He produced sketch maps made from memory, with distances paced out on the spot. He discovered that little work had been done on the forts since the Civil War when outer earthworks were provided for protection against shells from the new rifled guns on ironclads.[43] Like Carmichael, Arthur ignored Canada's dilemma about defence against the United States. Arthur's reports were sent to Canada, but not at the request of, or for the information of, the Department of Militia and Defence. They were wanted only for use in the instruction of gentleman-cadets at the Royal Military College.[44]

These optimistic British estimates of Canada's security were substantiated by military appraisals of the British naval bases there. In 1884 Maj. G. S. Clarke, RE, after examining the defence problems of Halifax, declared that the fortress had been overrated to offset the mushroom growth of the Union Navy during the Civil War. He said that only France and the United States were potential attackers and that France had other problems that made an attack on Halifax unlikely. If the United States inclined to aggression, Canada would be a more desirable objective than Halifax and could be attacked overland. There were no signs that the Americans had a naval building program, and therefore they could attack Halifax by land only after Canada had been conquered. Clarke said that Halifax's sole value was that it would afford some protection to British communications with Canada and to British maritime trade in the event of war with another naval power.[45] Clearly there was little basis here for giving more attention to Halifax's defences and not much reason to support an argument that as Canada was in danger she should share the responsibility and the costs of the defence of the imperial fortress.

On the other coast, Esquimalt, about the value of which the members of the Carnarvon Commission had disagreed, was said to be only locally important for Canada. The base had grown up without planning from the time of the Crimean War and was exposed to bombardment from the sea.[46] In 1878 the Canadian government erected temporary defences there and installed borrowed naval guns but then refused to pay for permanent defences for protection as it was an imperial naval base. It was willing only to send Colonel Strange to cooperate with British officers in an inspection.[47]

The question of the base's security against the United States was apparently not seriously considered at this time. However, Col. C. B. P. N. H. Nugent, RE, deputy director of works for fortification at the War Office, commented on an 1880 report by Col. John Williamson

Lovell, RE, the Commanding Royal Engineer at Halifax. He stated, "With regard to the United States, it may at once be conceded that if they are determined to obtain possession of Esquimalt, they will obtain it and nothing we can do will render the capture so costly that they will not find it worth while to undertake it."[48]

Secret British intelligence estimates in the early 1880s, which found the United States to be of little account in the world balance of power that Imperial Defence strategy was designed to stabilize (and therefore of little danger to Canada), served to confirm impressions Canadians had derived from information in the public domain. President Grant's cantankerous hostility to Britain had cooled after the signing of the Treaty of Washington, perhaps because he became more deeply involved in domestic problems. By the time he left office in 1877, Southern Reconstruction, which had absorbed a large part of the army's efforts, was ending. General Sherman succeeded in regaining much of the commanding general's authority over the army, long infringed upon by the secretary of war.[49] But the army was still scattered in small units across the Western frontier in surveillance of militant Indian tribes. Because the United States seemed very remote from European problems, American military personnel, nostalgic about their great days in the Civil War, were adjusting only slowly to the need for continuing development of technologies and tactics.

The United States had not yet been infected by the virus of far-flung imperialist ambition that was now plaguing Old World powers. Expansion to absorb Canada, a natural corollary of the belief in Manifest Destiny, was a possible exception to this general rule; but the idea that continental union might be brought about by force, which had been in the back of some American minds since the Revolution, was not heard of in Congress or elsewhere from 1870 until late in the 1880s. An explanation was offered in 1879 by Senator Ambrose E. Burnside of Rhode Island, a West Pointer who had become a major-general in the Union Army and was an ardent advocate of the absorption of Canada. He said that the United States and Canada had a natural affinity and common interests that made eventual union seem certain.[50]

In the United States it was well understood that only one European power, Britain, because of her control of the seas and possession of Canada, could present a serious threat to American security on land. But the poor condition of American fortifications in coastal ports and on the northern frontier in these years suggests that the majority of members of Congress, to whom this was pointed out,[51] did not take the threat seriously. On at least one occasion when the Senate attempted to double the small appropriation for the upkeep of the fabric of the

forts, the House of Representatives rejected the increase.[52] While
some members drew attention to the decay of the forts, others agreed
with Rep. W. S. Holman, a Democrat from Indiana, who claimed in
1884 that, because the spirit of the United States was different from
that of European states, forts were undesirable. He declared it waste-
ful to spend money on defences against a "hypothetical enemy."[53] The
president's recommendation, in that same year, to spend money on
guns because earthen forts could be quickly improvised in case of need,
was approved.[54]

In 1880 a new development announced by the secretary of war was
the abandonment of many small posts along wagon and stage routes in
order to concentrate troops "at strategic points near the national frontier or at points of railroad intersection."[55] As a result of the decay of
works and the lack of money for rebuilding or reconstruction, and in
order to put two companies in each garrison for the sake of exercising
larger formations and to inculcate better discipline,[56] the army also
considered closing less useful forts, including some on the Canadian
border. Among the forts in the North that were listed for reduction
were Mackinac, which was too far from the Sault straits, Gratiot on
Lake Huron, which was sold to a railroad company, Porter at Buffalo,
which was old and dilapidated, and Ontario at Oswego, declared to be
no longer of military value.[57]

Rumours that a border fort was to be closed down invariably
brought a loud protest in the local press. This meant that nearby
Canadians must have been fully aware of the situation. They can often
have been no more impressed by local arguments for retention that
were based on supposed strategic needs than were American military
authorities. For instance, when it was argued in the case of Fort Ontario that Kingston was well fortified and was ready to launch a fleet
that might attack Oswego,[58] Canadians were well aware that this was
nonsense. Fort Ontario was, indeed, reprieved for a time, but only because it was a good place of recuperation for troops from the Indian
frontier and not because of its defensive capability.[59]

Nevertheless, war on the northern border was not entirely ruled
out. One fort was retained for its strategic value in relation to Canada.
This was Montgomery, at the outlet of Lake Champlain, a "costly fort,
nearly if not complete, mounting 60 sea-coast guns." But Montgomery
was without adequate barrack accommodation. Quarters were required for four artillery companies.[60] Montgomery had, however, a
special value. The secretary of war reported in 1881 that "for an invasion of Canada on this line of operations it would at once be a fortified
base and store-house for the invading army."[61]

Nevertheless by the mid-1880s most of the American forts on the Canadian border were out of date and had become barracks rather than defence works. On October 16, 1882, the secretary of war had repeated that it was time for a "radical change" in the system of piecemeal work in quartering troops.[62] Troops from the West came east for rest and recuperation and the rehabilitation of depleted units. Not unnaturally the garrisons had an active social life; and they often entertained local citizens.[63] In 1884 life at Fort Ontario included lawn tennis, fashionable attire, swimming lessons for children, and boating. It was said that after falling "into decay during its ungarrisoned condition, [the fort was] fast assuming a respectable appearance."[64]

Social activities in some forts reached out across the border to embrace the neighbours whom the forts had been built to resist. Under the heading "Gaieties at Fort Niagara" there was a report of a dance in November 1883 where the beautiful decorations included stacks of muskets. Despite a blizzard, "many came from the Canada side and the city" to dance until dawn. A big sea compelled twenty-four Canadian girls to stay over in the fort for one night and one day. They had "a lively time" and found it hard to tear themselves away "from such pleasant people as are now occupying Fort Niagara."[65] Garrisoning part of the army near the Canadian border in this manner had, however, one disadvantage noted by the adjutant-general in 1883. Writing of the problem of desertion in the Army of the East, he said that it was caused by "intemperance, restlessness, and discontent; [and] marriage with Canadian women," and that it was facilitated by access to Canada.[66] A problem that had faced the British army in Canada earlier in the century was now working in reverse.

Fort Montgomery was not the only exception to a new pacific stance along the Canadian border. Despite its commitment to control aborigines, its often deadening conservatism, and the gaiety of its social life, the U.S. Army in theseyears did not completely overlook its chief responsibility, the defence of the United States. Progress in this respect was, however, hampered by bureau chiefs in the War Department, on whom the army depended. The believed that the organization which had won the Civil War could not be improved upon. Working for a small peacetime army, they had in fact forgotten how the war had been won. American military organization was now quite unfit for war with even a small foreign power. Manoeuvres of units as large as a regiment did not take place until the late 1880s. Sherman's successor as commanding general, Phil Sheridan, had been rebuffed in his attempt to consolidate his control over the bureau chiefs.

Despite the handicaps under which he worked, Sherman, a prewar college president, had been one of the most innovative of all American commanding generals. Seeds sown during his tenure of office germinated below the surface. West Point could not be budged to reform; but Sherman had found other ways to foster professionalism in the officer corps beyond the Academy level. He had established schools for postgraduate instruction, the Engineering School of Application at Willett's Point, New York, and the School of Application for Infantry and Cavalry at Fort Leavenworth, Kansas. The latter was at first restricted to infantry and cavalry tactics, but from the first it was intended to become something more, a means by which the whole army would be instructed in the science and practice of war. Sherman had also helped to found a professional association for American army officers modelled on the Royal United Services Institution in Britain. It was designed to encourage the study of military science and military history. Its *Journal of the Military Service Institution of the United States*, and other new professional publications founded at this time, became outlets for ideas from the new professional schools.[67] As a result, even though the officer corps of the United States Army lacked practical training and experience, it could compete intellectually, and even professionally, with that of other countries.[68]

Consideration of a war with Britain, and therefore with Canada, was not overlooked in these first stirrings of professional American military thought. American soldiers complained that the American people, believing erroneously that the rapid expansion achieved in 1861 could be repeated in the event of a foreign war, had not accepted the need for preparation for war during peace. An anonymous writer in the *Army and Navy Magazine* declared that the United States was at a disadvantage in face of maritime power (he could only have meant Britain) because of the "wretched condition" of its coastal defences.[69]

At about the same time *The United Service*, a periodical established for service officers in 1879, reprinted from the British magazine *Nineteenth Century* an article by an officer of the Austrian General Staff who put a more reassuring face on the possible outcome of a war with Britain than that usually seen. Capt. Alexander Kirchhammer believed that at the outset the United States would be at a disadvantage; but he noted that a naval war with Britain "is always a long business [and] the Americans would find time to create a fleet." He declared that American bases in the West Atlantic were superior to Britain's, that Halifax and Bermuda were not yet reached by cable, that British sea-borne commerce was exposed to American attack as in 1812, and that steam had diminshed the British lead based on prestige and seamanship. Though Great Britain was still absolutely the strongest naval power in the world, in other respects she was relatively weak. Although no other European power was capable of decisive influence in North America, and although the United States was incapable of action in Europe, Kirchhammer noted that Canada, Newfoundland, Prince Edward Island, the Bermudas and the Bahamas, and the British islands in the Caribbean were all within the range of American power. Britain had only nominal forces in the American colonies and could not hope to defend her continental possessions. However, she had induced Canada to do something for her own defence, and Canada was supposed to "dispose of the tremendous number of 655,000 men." Kirchhammer went on to say that since the Crimean War the "recognition of the military importance of the Empire, in attack as well as defence" had been the key to Britain's foreign policy; but he forecast that "The British Empire . . . must eventually be exclusively limited to the power of the United Kingdom." [70]

Kirchhammer's predictions cannot have been lost on American military readers. Looking at an Anglo-American war from a purely military standpoint, it seemed that Britain, the one power which could challenge the United States, could be withstood even if the latter had no allies. Furthermore, Canada could be had for the taking because the present supposed British advantage depended on a state of Canadian military preparedness that did not exist. Soldiers in North America knew that Kirchhammer was misinformed on that point.

From time to time American military periodicals considered the local problems that a war with Britain would create. They discussed the state of the Canadian militia and the situation on the Great Lakes. The development of the militia was at first noted with approval, as was an indication in Selby Smyth's fifth report in 1878 that there was no present expectation of American aggression. [71] Thus, in 1880 the *Army and Navy Journal* referred to an article on Canadian armaments in the *United Service Gazette* which claimed that Canada had ships which could be armed, well-trained officers and soldiers, a powder factory, and rifled cannon, including 64-pounder rifled guns produced by Col. T. B. Strange, RA (presumably a reference to reboring muzzle-loaders by the Palliser process). It said that twelve more rifled guns had been ordered for Montreal. There was also a small arms factory and a military college and artillery schools. "This," declared the editor, "is sound and satisfactory progress building up from the very foundations the necessary elements of military power." [72]

An article headed "Canada as a War Power" in the same issue referred to Canadian military development as a potential danger to the United States. The writer alleged that the "late Lewis C. Holton," a

Canadian member of Parliament but an American by birth, was accustomed to joke that Canada would ultimately take military control of the North American continent. The *Journal* went on to report that a Lt.-Col. Thomas M. Anderson of the 9th Infantry had outlined in a detailed letter to the *Cincinnati Enquirer* what Canada could do should she ever assume a hostile attitude. Anderson said that the Canadian militia had a potential strength of 600,000 of which 43,365 were armed and trained. Canada had 400 smooth-bore cannon, and had rolled steel in store to encase gunboats. He recalled that Colonel Strange had claimed that Canada could seize Lake Erie and he warned that the United States had no army to prevent this and that it would take a month to get one ready to resist invasion. The editor of the *Journal* commented, "The speculation is an interesting one at any rate."[73]

Belief in the possibility of a Canadian seizure of Lake Erie inspired Admiral David D. Porter, head of the Board of Inspection of the United States Navy, to suggest in his annual report that gunboats should be built on the Great Lakes. The *Army and Navy Journal* carried a retort made to this proposal by the Canadian newspaper, the *Hamilton Daily Tribune* which, it said, had been "made unhappy." The *Tribune* had editorialized:

Porter, K.C.B., of H.M.S. *Pinafore* was an ass and Admiral Porter U.S. Navy seems to be the same. The former had impossible schemes for assuring the superiority of British seamen and the latter has impossible plans for making the American navy a terror to Great Britain. One or two iron-clads are to be built on Lake Erie and some morning they are quietly to drop down to the Welland Canal entrance to destroy its gates. Naturally enough the plan, coming from an American admiral, is based upon the supposition that there will be no resistance from Canada.

History, said the *Tribune*, proved otherwise.

Canada desires to have perpetual friendship with her southern neighbour, but she is human. The cool proposal of an American admiral to build gunboats on the Lakes, whereby costly public works constructed at our national expense for the common use of commercial interests of the continent shall be destroyed, is somewhat irritating and will cause every Government shipbuilding movement on the lakes to be watched with unusual interest. The building of iron-clads on one side compels the building of them on the other. This is why we object to standing armies. . . . Instead of wasting money in preparing vessels and war materials, let both countries apply the same amount to the construction of public works likely to promote the development of our international commercial interests.[74]

Although Canadian journalists thus talked big about resisting American aggression, or considered danger unlikely in view of the prevailing state of friendship of Canada and the United States, some American military periodicals had continued to look closely at the Canadian potential for war. They became steadily less impressed by it. An opinion on this subject expressed by the British *Army and Navy Gazette* was duly noted in the United States. The *Gazette* had said that no government except that of Britain would tolerate the defenceless-ness of Canada which had been brought about because of the Canadian government's confidence in American pacific intentions; and it added, "human passions and prejudice rarely do more than slumber, and never die. With no thought of 'bunkum' or aggression, it is always well to remember the old maxim 'if thou wishest peace, be prepared for war'." [75]

One American article informed its military readers that, even though British soldiers were warning Canada that peace was not eter-nal, the Canadian militia was in no condition to fight. This article in *The United Service* was reprinted in a condensed form in *The Army and Navy Journal*. Entitled "The Soldiers of Canada," it quoted the weaknesses reported by GOC's and added that *Annual Reports* never revealed the worst. It reported that General Smyth had said that the equipment of Canadian cavalry was so bad it was likely to injure both horse and rider, that the men would not attend drill, and that the rural regiments were poor. The Canadian militia was proportionately greater than that of the United States but the Canadian military sys-tem was "all wrong" because the militia was kept unnecessarily large "owing to causes which no longer exist."

The author, M. Waters Kirwan, went on to say, "If she [Canada] wishes to go about in tinsel, it is of course her own business, but she neither deceives nor alarms any one by doing so. . . . Her destiny is one of peace, not war. Her fortunes are in timber, wheat, etc." Kirwan said that Canada did not need 39,000 men indifferently armed, poorly drilled, and badly commanded. All she needed was a force to support the civil power in case of internal commotion. For this the city corps would suffice. The rural battalions could be dispensed with and re-placed by rifle-shooting clubs. It would be much better to have a small force that commanded the respect of the people than a large one that would only succeed in war if, as Marshal Saxe once said, "it was legs and not arms that won campaigns." This caustic criticism of the state of the Canadian militia included an apt phrase later used by General Hutton and often quoted by Canadian military historians, that it was a "military Tammany." [76]

Discussing the operation of the Canadian militia in the West in 1885, and comparing this with American operations against the Indians, the *Army and Navy Journal* said that the Canadian militia was a volunteer force like the National Guard and was worth watching; but the writer regretted that its conduct and success so far did not add much to previous experience in favour of volunteer troops (meaning militia as opposed to regulars who, although not conscripted in the United States, were not referred to as "volunteers"). However, it asserted that a letter from a Canadian correspondent gave a more favourable picture than that presented by the daily press.[77]

Articles like these in the American military press about Canada and the militia were frequently written to advocate a particular rearmament policy. They represented the views of those who wanted to foster military preparedness and they often urged one or other kind of development. The *Army and Navy Magazine* said in 1881 that it believed the American people were beginning to realize the dangers of overconfidence. The establishment of the United States Army was 30,000 (less than the Canadian militia), but Congress appropriated funds for only 25,000. There was a large American militia, 200,000 strong, armed and equipped. West Point graduates provided the officer corps with a high degree of professional academic education; but the navy was "contemptible." Whereas once the United States had nearly run the British from the ocean (presumably the reference was to the War of 1812), Americans had afterwards contented themselves with complaints against England for destroying the navy while the war was in progress. It was time for active steps by Congress to aid shipbuilders to build ships which could be easily converted into vessels of war.[78]

Others who wrote of Canada wanted to reform the American militia. Brevet-Maj. William H. Powell of the 4th Infantry, who had been educated at Columbia and had served in the militia before joining the army, had taken part in stopping the Fenian raid in 1866. He was therefore probably not implacably hostile to Canada. But in 1885 he was concerned about the possibility of war with Britain. He said that an American militia force could be put on the Canadian border within five days, but any invasion of Canada would have to depend on volunteers and would take a long time to organize—meanwhile reinforcements would have come to Canada from Britain. "Canadian Militia, organized by the general government as a general armed force under central command, could be organized at any point along our frontier and pounce down upon any of our important lake cities." He declared that what the United States needed was a "national guard" under federal control instead of one that was a "mere militia."[79] About the same time yet another officer, Brig. Gen. Snowdry, of the Pennsylvania National Guard, urged that the battalion system, adopted already by the United States cavalry and artillery and by all other armies, should be introduced in the Guard to give it more operational effectiveness.[80]

Before 1885 all this speculation about the problems of a war with Canada and all these proposals for military reorganization and development in American military journals had little effect on official American military policy, partly because the United States Army lacked any kind of planning or intelligence agency. These functions lay in the province of the secretary of war and the commanding general. About 1880, however, the adjutant-general, although chiefly concerned with administrative problems, had begun to feel a need for the collection of military intelligence. On August 25, 1880, an Army General Order issued by the adjutant-general, Gen. R. C. Drum, said that officers travelling or stopping in foreign countries, whether on duty or leave of absence, *"will be required"* to avail themselves of all opportunities, properly within reach, for obtaining information of value to the military service of the United States, especially that pertaining to their own branch of the service. Written reports were to be made to the adjutant-general upon their return, if not possible earlier.[81]

This order, although of wider application, may have been partly inspired by interest in Canada. For the day before it was issued General Drum wrote to the commanding general of the Military Division of Missouri to say that it had been brought to the notice of the secretary of war and the general of the army that at some posts it was the practice to give officers "leave of absence" for hunting, but that absences beyond twenty-four hours had to be charged as leave of absence. This, said Drum, would discourage hunting which was advantageous to the service in that it helped officers to familiarize themselves with the country. In future absences for hunting were not to be charged as leave if the officer, on his return, filed with his commanding officer a certificate that his absences had been employed solely in hunting and if he furnished a report describing the country he had passed through.[82] This instruction became an army regulation in 1881.[83] In 1884 it was amended to provide that reports on hunting should be sent by commanding officers to department headquarters.[84] While the close proximity of the dates of the orders about collecting intelligence in foreign countries and about hunting may have been coincidental, U.S. army officers hunting near or across the border could furnish military intelligence about Canada.

It is perhaps also significant that among the index cards of the Army War College War Plans Division, which included intelligence reports from 1885 when an intelligence gathering service was formally established, there are only three items predating the establishment of the service that refer to Canada. They deal with the possibility of war on the northern border. The earlier of these reports is by Lt. Lowell Augustus Chamberlin of the 1st Artillery. It is dated January 14, 1878, and is entitled "The Military Resources of Canada: Plan of Invasion." It is described as "Strength of Organization of an Army Necessary to prosecute a successful invasion."[85] The second item is a copy of the British Colonel Strange's 1879 article on "The Military Aspect of Canada."[86] The third, from 1882, is another study of "The Military Resources of Canada," by First Lt. Sedgwick Pratt of the Artillery. This also includes a "Plan of Invasion."[87] The first and third of these papers were not official plans for American operations. They were probably not even contingency plans. They may have been plans prepared as training exercises by young officers in the field whose work was referred to the adjutant-general's office. They suggest, however, that some members of the United States Army were coming to believe that there was need for planning for what seemed a very unlikely possibility, a war with Britain that would require defensive or offensive operations on the Canadian border.

As we have seen, in the early years of British Imperial Defence strategy, when attempts to relate it to the need for the defence of Canada against the United States were having little political success in the Dominion, Canadian defence preparations continued to be minimal. There was still considerable differences of opinion among soldiers on each side of the border about the likely fate of Canada in the event of an Anglo-American war. It was realized that neither country was prepared to win a quick victory. But Colonel Strange's detailed public examination of the problem had had greater consequence than he had expected, and of a kind that he could not have wanted. Preparation for defence was just as politically unpopular south of the border as it was to the north of it, but those responsible for the first stirrings of American military professionalism since the Civil War had taken note of the implications of Strange's reasoning and had begun to appraise the situation in relation to its potential international and diplomatic consequences; and some military thinkers included the possibility of a war with Canada in their consideration of the problem of preparing the United States armed forces for a greater role in world affairs.

4

North American Issues (1885–1894)

In 1885 Britain faced another major imperial crisis, this time over Afghanistan. Once again war with Russia seemed imminent. Throughout the empire this new emergency stimulated further efforts to fashion an effective system of Imperial Defence. In Canada it raised again the question of Canadian participation. The debate about defence against the United States as a critical part of Canada's role in Imperial Defence strategy continued for at least another decade, but it was soon to be complicated by North American problems.

When the year 1885 opened, Colin Campbell, a retired Royal Navy officer, was secretary of a committee to report on Canada's role in Imperial Defence. This had been belatedly established by the minister of militia, Adolphe Caron, under the chairmanship of the governor general's private secretary, Lord Melgund (a future governor general as earl of Minto). While engaged in collecting papers from official files, Campbell came across a plan for defence against the United States. It was a confidential report on the protection of the border made in 1882 by Maj. G. E. Walker, RE, professor of engineering at RMC. Walker had outlined measures to be taken to prepare hasty defences if war came near.[1]

Campbell's discovery was not followed up and

no policy recommendations were made by the Melgund Committee, whose work has been discussed elsewhere.[2] The committee assembled papers about defence policy from the files of the Militia Department and prepared a printed calendar. When Campbell published the calendar,[3] the Defence Committee was already inactive, perhaps because Melgund had left Ottawa. Nothing more was done until 1888 when Caron set up a new Canadian Defence Committee. Campbell, whose primary aim had been to show that Canada was not making an adequate contribution to the defence of the Empire, was passed over in the selection of a secretary for the committee. Significantly, on the grounds that "Canada is too large and Halifax is at one end," the British GOC at the Halifax base, who expected to command all British and Canadian forces in North America in the event of war, was also not appointed to it. Macdonald and Caron, probably because they were afraid that the committee might make proposals that would call for heavy expenditures, apparently wanted to keep control of Canadian defence policy out of British military hands. They may also have felt that the American problem, which had not been the Melgund Committee's concern, but which inevitably cropped up, was too sensitive, too difficult, or not sufficiently urgent to be handled by a committee of military officers. Hence the new Defence Committee was sterile. After only one meeting, and before it had received its terms of reference, it lapsed.[4]

The earlier Melgund Committee of 1884–85 had considered that its task was to make recommendations about Canadian responsibility for some of the costs of the defence of the Canadian coasts. The problem of the Pacific coast had seemed most urgent at that time. The Admiralty had argued that Esquimalt was a valuable imperial base and should be defended but that defence of ports was not the navy's duty.[5] As the defence of British Columbia was an advantage to the peoples of that province, the Colonial Defence Committee suggested that Canada might bear the burden. The Colonial Office questioned this proposal.[6] However, the crisis of 1885 attracted attention to the West Coast and to the navy's lack of an adequately defended base there for use against Russia. The *Canadian Militia Gazette*, stating that the "recent impending cloud" in relations with the United States "most surely will burst in the not distant future," said that the "fair city of Victoria" needed defences.[7] This unofficial suggestion that defences were needed not only against Russian cruisers, but also against the United States, implied that Canada should contribute. But after the Melgund Committee proved fruitless, official discussions between Canada and the War Office about Esquimalt dragged on from year to year. By 1890, although guns had been installed, no fortifications had yet been built and arrangements for manning the guns with a Permanent Force Artillery Company backed by the local militia had proved unsatisfactory.[8] Neither could be kept at full strength because of the high cost of labour in the area.

Meanwhile, in 1889, the *San Francisco News Letter* had noted that a part of the American press was agitated about the proposed Canadian fortification of Esquimalt. As reported in the *Canadian Militia Gazette*, the newspaper went on to assure its readers that American concern was quite unwarranted because Esquimalt was designed not against the United States but to counter Russian development of Vladivostok.[9] No doubt this was substantially true, but in the 1890s the United States would begin to give greater priority to bases in the Pacific North West,[10] partly as a result of the alleged British threat. Admiral A. T. Mahan made contingency plans for war with Britain (among other countries) in 1890 and stated that the United States Navy might have to take the offensive against Britain in the Pacific. He estimated that the eight American warships on the West Coast should have no difficulty in seizing Vancouver Island and capturing and destroying the Nanaimo coal stocks.[11] In the same year Gen. Nelson Miles, commanding the United States Army, told a Senate committee that all British Columbia except Vancouver could be occupied in ten days, but that the Royal Navy would subsequently ravage American ports.[12] A year later the United States naval base at Bremerton was established and Puget Sound was upgraded in fortification planning.[13]

American naval bases and defence works in the Northwest were part of a general program of naval expansion that derived from growing American world interests and the extension of settlement in that part of the United States.[14] British-Canadian discussions about Esquimalt and its contribution to Imperial Defence and the defence of the coast against Russian cruisers undoubtedly had provided not only an example, but also an excuse, for American military development. They had posed questions about the need for the defence of American bases against Britain.[15] In turn the uncomfortable proximity of Bremerton, and even more of Port Angeles directly across the Strait of Juan de Fuca from Esquimalt, which was often visited by American warships, caused the British Admiralty to consider moving the naval base from Esquimalt.[16] The responsible authorities on both sides thus took an Anglo-American war into their calculations and were mutually spurred to build defence works, partly because stronger defences in one country might divert the Russians to the other but also because it was considered wise to plan against the possibility of an Anglo-American war.

In 1893, Gen. Ivor Herbert, GOC of the Canadian militia, succeeded in negotiating an agreement in principle between Britain and Canada to garrison Esquimalt with Royal Marines at Canada's expense. Thus Canada was brought to accept some responsibility.[17] By that time the Bering Sea sealing controversy had begun to inflame relations between Canada and the United States. New tension in the Pacific may have been a factor in helping to bring about a partial settlement of the long dispute between Britain and Canada about Esquimalt, even though it was widely realized that the base would be vulnerable to an American attack. On the other hand, there was still doubt about Esquimalt's security, and perhaps about the effect that fortification-building might have on the United States. This doubt may have helped to prevent Canada from accepting a greater share of the responsibility for another decade.

Discussion of cooperative arrangements for militia support for the defence of Halifax, which came up for consideration in 1880–90, was even more directly affected by the state of Canadian-American relations. Increased interest in Halifax coincided with, and may have been at least partly inspired by, a flare-up of the Atlantic coast fisheries dispute. This will be examined later. The strategic importance of Halifax in the event of a war with the United States was obvious. However, American naval forces were known to be too weak to attack, and an overland approach was considered highly improbable. If the fortress was already stronger than was necessary (apart from a need for modern breech-loading guns), it was because, in the eyes of the War Office and the Admiralty, Halifax could serve as a base for naval operations against the United States as well as a port through which Canada could be reinforced.

The British general who commanded the fortress feared that the naval forces of a hostile power might land large raiding parties in the vicinity. But his complaint about the inadequacy of the training of the Canadian militia made specific reference to an American attack overland. A possible involvement with the United States in the event of war in Europe was in fact the real reason for defending Halifax. The Colonial Defence Committee therefore maintained that the defences of Halifax must be correlated with the strength and development of the United States Navy. Arrangements were worked out for cooperation between the Canadian militia and the British garrison in the event of war, but without a definite commitment of the militia to serve in the fortress. Canada thus moved some way towards aiding in the defence of Halifax against the United States but was once again hesitant to make a full commitment, not merely because of fear of being dragged into an imperial war, but also because of the implications for Canada of war with the United States.[18]

All the foregoing problems about the defence of Canada against the United States stemmed from Imperial Defence strategy and the 1885 crisis; but they were quickly matched, and in Canadian eyes often overshadowed, by North American issues. A series of North American problems followed the imperial crisis of 1885: a second Métis rebellion occurred in the same year as the 1885 crisis with Russia; there was increasing acrimony over the Atlantic fisheries; there were many references to annexation in the American Congress and press; and there were disputes about sealing in the Bering Sea. All these things had military implications and focused attention on the military element in Canadian-American relations.

Although direct Canadian-American confrontation stopped far short of the critical stage, it lent support to the arguments of those individuals on both sides of the border who, because of personal conviction or professional responsibility, were already concerned about the inadequacy of defence preparations or who, in a few cases, advocated readiness for a preemptive strike. Therefore, although war between the United States and Britain and a consequent invasion of Canada did not come remotely within the bounds of possibility until the Venezuela incident ten years later, some Americans and some Canadians had long pressed for a more positive defence policy.

But the new North American issues did not point to inevitable conflict. Events in 1885 gave indication that a happier outcome was possible. A year earlier Louis Riel had returned to his people who had resettled on the Saskatchewan River, and there were fresh signs of Métis unrest. Fenians in the United States talked of seizing the opportunity to raid across the border towards Winnipeg. But John A. Macdonald's agents were on the alert. They watched every move and identified the ringleaders. The governor general's secretary, Lord Melgund, drafted detailed plans for thwarting them[19] but his work proved unnecessary. Fenian fulminations came to nothing. When the second rising in Canada's Northwest did occur some Indians expressed sympathy with their blood-relations' cause and spread unwarranted terror among scattered settlers on the prairies. There was sharp fighting with the Métis, but they were quickly suppressed by Canadian militia troops without aid. The Indians immediately capitulated. This success, though won only by a slim margin, was a sign that Canada was coming of age and could take care of its own problems.[20]

The second Riel rebellion showed the varying attitude of the United States. It also diverted Canadian attention from Imperial Defence to what was now not a primary imperial responsibility, the security of the prairie frontier. However, the American government, by dispatching army patrols to prevent the trouble from spreading,[21] had shown more promptly in 1885 than in 1870 that it would not take advantage of the situation. At the same time steps were taken to prevent the Fenians from staging a raid from American soil. The American military found, apparently to its satisfaction, that the Indians and Mixed Bloods on its side of the border did not intend to support Riel, some because they were too poor, others because they were prosperous, and all because they feared the loss of the year's crop of wheat or of free gifts of supplies. Aid was therefore not available for him from the United States.[22] The Canadian government expressed its gratitude; and a girl in London, Ontario, sent heartfelt thanks to the secretary of state on behalf of all Canadian women.[23] There could now be even greater confidence that the United States had no present intention of military interference with Canada's vulnerable occupation of the West.

Nevertheless the disturbance in the West caused some Canadians to worry about security there and to urge the need for better defences. In 1886 Lt.-Col. Alfred Wyndham of the 12th York Rangers in Aurora, Ontario, pressed for the establishment of a military colony in the prairies to offset American propaganda which, he alleged, suggested that the Canadian West might be disturbed by another rebellion. He said this diverted European immigrants to the United States.[24] There were also tentative plans for a "flying column" of militia and police to follow up the successful expedition of the previous year by "showing the flag."[25] Both of these plans came to nothing when it was learned that the Indians were no longer restive;[26] but some Canadian militia officers continued to look closely at the question of the defence of the prairies. After the completion of the Canadian Pacific Railway to the Rockies in 1885, an article in the *Canadian Military Gazette* suggested that Winnipeg, some sixty miles from the United States border behind a barrier of inhospitable countryside, was now of more military importance than Victoria because it was the base for reinforcing Western Canada and the coast in case of need.[27] This revision of defence strategy was in part due to apprehension about the United States.

If the Canadian West needed to be defended, the Canadian Pacific Railway was a new factor to be taken into account. The suppression of the Riel rebellion in 1885 had been facilitated by using the line even before it was completed, which showed its military potential. The military implications of a Canadian transcontinental railroad had received considerable attention during the debates about its proposed construction. Goldwin Smith, writing a column as "Bystander" in *The Week*, a

Toronto journal, had raised the question of its effect on Canadian-American relations. He had asserted that Edward Blake, leader of the opposition in the House of Commons, had missed the point when criticizing the transcontinental project because he had failed to show that the railway's purpose, like that of the Intercolonial, was political and military, not commercial. Smith declared, "It is the policy of a certain party in the Imperial country and here, by means of a vast connecting line of political and military railroads, to form the scattered and disjointed series of territories extending from Cape Breton to Vancouver Island into an Anti-Continental Empire antagonistic in interest and sentiment to the United States, and thus to introduce into this continent the Balance of Power, with its attendant possibility of war."[28] In a later issue of the paper he alleged that the CPR and the Intercolonial were forces by which "Imperialism hopes to vanquish nature."[29] The editor of *The Week* had previously said that there was doubt whether this purpose could either be achieved or would be "good for the people."[30]

The value of the railway for reinforcing Esquimalt and British Columbia was obvious. Although the cost by the Canadian route would be greater than by sea, some saw the CPR as an imperial line of communications to the Far East which would be safe from interference by rival European powers.[31] Its significance in commercial competition with American lines was also clear.

What was less well understood was the railway's role in a clash between Britain and the United States. As soon as the line was operating, the CPR's relation to the North American strategic question, to which Smith had pointed, received official attention. The Intelligence Department of the British War Office sent an officer to make an appraisal. Capt. Leonard Darwin, RE, confirmed some of the claims of its promoters. He said that the CPR could get troops from Liverpool to Port Moody on Burrard's Inlet in fourteen days in summer, and in fourteen and a half days in winter when the St. Lawrence was closed. Darwin noted that imperial troops would hardly be required in the interior of the Dominion, but if they were, the Canadian Pacific could get them there. He declared that the CPR was the quickest route to the Far East, including New Zealand, and, if the Suez Canal were closed, to Australia and Hong Kong as well. However, although he concluded that the CPR "should not be lost sight of," Darwin recommended only that the War Office should regard it as a "possible contingency." The reason for this less than enthusiastic endorsement was that he had noticed that for several hundreds of miles beyond Winnipeg the rails ran within a hundred miles of the American border and in one place were only fifty miles from it. Furthermore, the terminus at Port Moody, though sheltered behind the Fraser River, was within twelve miles of the United States. Darwin therefore warned, "Hence it is, I think, evident that this route would be very open to attack from the United States."[32] The CPR was, in his opinion, only a limited military asset. It would become a liability if relations with the United States deteriorated.

Back in the East, the Atlantic fisheries dispute, which may have been in part the cause of concern about Halifax, was the greatest irritant between Canada and the United States during the decade following 1885. Arrangements made in Washington in 1870 for New Englanders to fish in Canadian waters and the question of how much the United States should pay for this privilege were referred to an International Joint Commission. The assessment was so high that it was alleged that, in addition to remitting duties on Canadian fish imported into the United States, the American government would have to pay Canada about eight times the value of all the fish caught by Americans so far.[33] Opinion in the United States became inflamed. In 1879, commenting upon a statement in Gen. Selby Smyth's *Annual Report* that the danger of American aggression was not great, the American *Army and Navy Journal* retorted, "Perhaps Canada feels peculiarly well disposed towards us just now on account of that expensive codfish ball, without any bread, she lately administered to brother Jonathan. She must admit that, with a pardonable wry face, he took his codfish like a little man."[34] In 1883 Congress directed the president to terminate the fisheries clauses of the Treaty of Washington. As a result the liberty granted to Americans to fish in Canadian waters ended on July 1, 1885.[35]

An American military journalist saw the dispute about the fisheries as the first stage of a controversy that would lead to "great results" and would determine future American relations with Canada. But he expected peaceful annexation, not war. He said, "If wisely managed on our part it [the dispute] is more likely to become a means of a still further widening of the breach between different provinces of the Dominion where the idea of wholesale political changes is becoming familiarized."[36]

All three governments involved were anxious to prevent the fisheries dispute from leading to blows, and all wanted an early settlement. Joseph Chamberlain pointed out that the matter really concerned only a few fishmongers and fishermen in the Eastern States and therefore was not an insurmountable obstacle.[37] But negotiations for a settlement were impeded by Canada's desire to associate the fishing question with reciprocity in general trade, and by the intrusion of American party politics. The Republicans, while still dominating Congress, had lost the presidency for the first time since the Civil War. They tried to exploit New England fishing grievances to cripple the new administration. Meanwhile, the presence of police vessels of the Canadian Fisheries Protective Service in the fishing grounds, and the arrest and seizure of hundreds of American vessels, aroused sharp feeling in both countries. There were appeals for the dispatch of Royal Navy and United States Navy warships.[38] It looked as if the situation might take a nasty turn.

A new *modus vivendi* was worked out in 1888. But President Cleveland's statement that he would resort to retaliatory measures against Britain if this were not accepted by Congress focused attention on the possible military consequences. The *Army and Navy Journal* saw the president's *pronunciamiento* as one that if made in Europe would have brought war. The *Journal* saw it as tending, even in North America, "directly toward, if not to, war." It chided the president: "To publicly declare an intention to assume the aggressive toward a foreign nation without having the power to do so, is to humiliate us in the eyes of the world."[39] The danger passed and the temporary arrangement made in 1888 lasted until 1904.

Although the fishing dispute was correctly judged by politicians to be unlikely to lead to a breach of the peace, and although it was eased by diplomacy, it had the important effect of awakening the American military establishment to the fact that an unwanted and unexpected war with Great Britain might present them with a difficult or impossible task. The dispute therefore helped to promote interest in the need for an increase of American military strength. Other elements of that revival will be discussed later. In 1893 an official history of the development of American Army intelligence agencies revealed that the new Information Division in the War Department, which dated from the height of the fishing controversy, in addition to seeking advance knowledge of the military art in general, had the special and "different" duty of furnishing the commanding general with the information about the northern frontier that he would require "in the event of rumour of war with Canada."[40]

The fisheries dispute had thus led not only to a first step in the modernization of the American war machine, but also to consideration of the problem of a war with Canada. There were other links between Canadian-American confrontation and American military revival. The hostility provoked by Canadian transportation competition, for instance, led to warnings about the "political" railways of Canada and about alleged Canadian strategic military preparations.[41]

Corroborating evidence of the way American soldiers were reacting comes from a humble source. Lt. Thomas M. Woodruff of the 5th Infantry published a prize essay in the *Journal of the Military Service Institution of the United States*, which considered the possible military consequences of the fisheries dispute. He alleged that Britain would like to go to war with the United States because of contempt for democracy; but he thought that, as she was dependent on American trade, war was unlikely. However, since the policy of the United States was peaceful, if hostilities did unfortunately occur, England would merely have to defend Canada. Therefore, he said, the United States, after arranging for the protection of seaports, would be forced to adopt an offensive-defence strategy by invading the Dominion to seize Windsor, Fort Erie, Prescott, and the four bridges over the Niagara River. A "desperate effort" would also have to be made to destroy the Welland canal; and Winnipeg must be taken in order to sever connections with the West.

But Woodruff believed that the United States could not undertake retaliation on behalf of New England fishing interests because it would mean war with England. Accordingly he rationalized that the fisheries were only a small part of American business and that the fishermen had been too demanding. He went on to say that the United States and Canada were "connected internally," and that their relations were cordial. In his opinion Britain could not defend Canada because it was becoming more and more interwoven with the United States. Canada therefore would certainly become independent, and might seek to be annexed.[42] Woodruff thus concluded that the Canadian-American military confrontation that might arise from the fisheries dispute would be a stalemate because of mutual military weaknesses and the impossibility of either side achieving a decisive victory.

The fishing controversy was also directly responsible for stepping up consideration of Canada's future in the Canadian House of Commons and in the Canadian press. Three possibilities were envisaged: annexation (usually called by its American advocates "political" or "continental" union), Imperial Defence, and independence.[43] The debate had considerable relevance to the question of the possible course of a future war in North America. Goldwin Smith saw the fishing dispute as a step towards the peaceful realization of his continental dream. He warned that Britain's other involvements and commitments would prevent her from aiding Canada, and also that she was unlikely to go to war with a power that was "superior to her in population and probably equal in resources" when the mass of her people had not the slightest interest in the fisheries. He argued that Canada could not be too demanding because she was in no position to help. The militia was, he said, only "half-drilled", Canada had no navy, and Canadians disliked being taxed. Because of British-Canadian military unpreparedness, Smith urged moderation in the handling of the dispute.[44]

On the other hand many Canadians, like Addison Browne, the author of the article in *The Week* quoted above, thought that while annexation would mean an unwelcome involvement in American politics, Imperial Defence meant assuming British defence debts and would be a backward political step. Some Canadians were already prepared to accept Browne's conclusion that independence was the only acceptable option,[45] but many others, quite content with their national status, saw no reason for change.[46] Another contributor to *The Week* believed that Canadians might be able to maintain their interests, as in the past, by force of arms, but that such an effort would divide the country. He warned that independence would mean that a weak Canada must face a powerful United States and that Canadian interests would always suffer in disputes.[47]

Pleas for military preparedness in Canada were for the most part still advocated specifically as a contribution to Imperial Defence. *The Canadian Militia Gazette*, inspired by the publication of articles about the history of the militia, said that recent events had pointed to the militia as part of "the grand army of Great and Greater Britain . . . fighting side by side with our comrades of the Old Country for the defence of the honor and liberty of a noble empire." It added, however, that there were only two reasons for maintaining a militia force of 37,000 men at a cost of a million dollars a year: fear of attacks on the coasts and of invasion from the South.[48] The American problem was thus still a factor in the Canadian debate on defence.

George T. Denison, III, a leading voice in the campaign for militia development as well as an advocate of Imperial Defence, was disturbed by the publication in American newspapers of maps and pictures envisaging the annexation of Canada (plates 3 and 4). He told Macdonald, "Any one closely watching affairs in the States can see an intention if possible of obtaining Canada by force or fraud." For Denison even mere advocacy of commercial union was disloyalty to Canada. Denison contended that it would be useless to try to defend Canada with a small standing army. He urged that money be appropriated to train the rural militia, but he did this on the grounds that a militia was the best safeguard against continental union because "there is no such

3. "The Future Great Republic," *New York World*, Dec. 1, 1888

4. "The Annexation of Canada—the Prince of Wales Hoisting the American Flag,"
Once a Week, March 16, 1889. Among those in attendance are (l.) ex-President
Cleveland, Vice-President Morton, President Harrison and (r.) the Duke of Cam-
bridge, Parnell, Joseph Chamberlain, Prince Albert Victor, Henry Irving, Lord and
Lady Randolph Churchill, Gladstone, Bismarck, and Lord Salisbury

educator in loyalty as the Volunteer Force." He offered to work up agitation for this in the press.

Thus even Denison, an advocate of military preparedness, apparently wanted to avoid the test of war. However, he declared that if war did come every Canadian would have to fight, and Canada's policy was to prepare for this eventuality by educating the officers who would lead them. Denison claimed that RMC had been originally set up for this purpose and was "one of the finest military colleges in the world."[49]

Probably because of Canada's relative weakness, another strong opponent of annexation, Watson Griffin, editor of the *Montreal Family Herald*, advanced a less martial solution. He wrote in the *Dominion Illustrated* that the Canadian Parliament's most effective reply to President Cleveland's threat of retaliation would be to vote money to complete the canal system, to build a railway to the Maritime provinces by the shortest possible route through Canadian territory, and to improve the harbours of Montreal, Quebec, St. John, and Halifax so that no American port could compete with them for Canadian trade.[50] Some Canadians thus leaned towards non-military solutions for their differences with the United States, either because they believed that resort to force could only end in disaster or because they felt that there was plenty of room for constructive cooperation with a sharing of benefits.

A few Americans believed that war with Canada must eventually come. Benjamin Butler, a vitriolic chauvinist radical, who was nominated as a candidate for the presidency in 1884, hoped that Canada could be acquired peacefully; but he wrote that it must be acquired, "forcefully if we must." He suggested that conquest would permit the division of Canadian land among the soldiers of the victorious American army.[51] Few seem to have shared these views. Most Americans believed that union with Canada was just a matter of time and was therefore not worth fighting or preparing to fight for. Furthermore they assumed that the initiative must, and would, come from Canada.[52] A Washington correspondent of *The Week* reported in 1885 that there had never been any official discussion of annexation in the United States, only passing allusions to the benefits that Canada would receive. The general attitude was, "If she should knock, our door would be open."[53]

The Canadian retort was that this expectation of continental union had been generated by the reckless and mischievous utterances of a few American newspaper editors, by a number of resolutions introduced in Congress, and by Goldwin Smith. The chief clerk of the Canadian House of Commons declared that Canadians did not want to be annexed.[54] Cleveland's threat of retaliation against Britain in 1888 changed these positions very little. Most Americans, not contemplating the use of force, were puzzled by Canadian reactions. The *Army and Navy Journal*, under the heading, "Canada's Present Attitude," illustrated this bewilderment by relating an anecdote. *"Uncle Sam*: 'Oh! Miss Canada, Glad we met. I am thinking of annexing you.' *Miss Canada*: 'Oh! You are, you baldheaded toothless old bachelor. I'll fight first.' *Uncle Sam*: 'I was only joking. I wouldn't think of annexing you.' *Miss Canada*: 'Oh! You, you (boo hoo), mean thing you'."[55]

However, many Americans were aware that Canadians would probably resist an attempt at forcible annexation. A foreign correspondent reported to the *Journal of the Military Service Institution* that they would fight, and fight well, whatever the disparity of numbers; but he added that it would be "of little avail."[56] In March 1893 Lt. Arthur L. Wagner, an instructor in the art of war at Fort Leavenworth, quoted this opinion in an article on "The Military Geography of Canada." He said that it would take several months to raise the 81,900 men available to defend the border from Quebec to Detroit. Wagner also referred to another correspondent who had declared that the Canadian militia was "not one whit superior to our National Guard."[57]

Opinions like this may have influenced some in the United States to lean towards direct action. Thus, an anonymous American author of "The Canadian Question: A Military Glance at it," who called himself *Terrae Filius*, reported views in the United States about continental union that were based on Canada's alleged instability and on Britain's international preoccupation. Americans who talked like that envisaged that in certain circumstances the use of force might be inescapable.[58] In reply to *Terrae Filius* a Canadian imperialist protested that this article was written "from the point of view of a possible invader."[59]

Articles about a possible Canadian-American conflict that were published in American military periodicals were the surface manifestation, and an indication of the substance of, the first stages in the development of the U.S. Army's capacity for war planning. In the navy the Office of Naval Intelligence of the Bureau of Navigation had been set up in 1882 and the Naval War College in 1884.[60] Similar organization in the army dated from the time of the fisheries dispute with Canada and was undoubtedly inspired by the realization at that time that the army must be ready for a war it did not expect and did not want, but which the politicians might provoke.

The development of professional intelligence sources in the United States had a relevance to possible war with Canada that has hitherto been entirely overlooked. Brig.-Gen. Richard C. Drum, the adjutant-general, established the Military Information Division in 1885. This was the army's first peacetime organization for the collection of military intelligence. It was headed by Maj. William J. Volkman, an assistant adjutant-general and the chief of the Reservations Division of the Miscellaneous Branch. On November 23, 1886, the Bureaux of the War Department and division commanders were requested to supply information to it. Intelligence was also to be collected from American legations in foreign countries; and military and naval attachés were appointed to the principal capitals. By 1889 the flow of information of all kinds was so great that a special division of the adjutant-general's office was set up to receive it. In 1891 the Division recorded that it was "proud of what had been collected since 1885."[61]

Significantly, when requests for information went to division commanders, special reference was made to the reports required of all officers given leave for hunting—which had relevance to Canada. Furthermore in 1887 an MID confidential letter to the officers commanding several northern frontier posts instructed them to arrange technical reconnaissance patrols *into* Canada under officers carefully chosen for their tact and ability so that the military maps of certain areas in adjoining provinces could be kept up-to-date. The adjutant-generals of the National Guard were asked to provide similar information.[62]

The U.S. Army acquired much intelligence about Canada. Reports assembled by the Military Information Division later became part of the files of the Army War College's War Plans Division. The documents have unfortunately been destroyed, but the index to these files is in the National Archives. The card for "Canada" (which it must be noted is only one among many hundreds dealing with every manner of subject of importance to the army) has a number of significant items that show the amount of attention that the U.S. Army paid to the problem of a war with the United States's northern neighbour from 1885.

In that year a Mr. Colwell reported on Canada's strength, military resources, and lines of communication; and in January 1886 there was an anonymous essay on Canadian military resources with a plan for an invasion. Later in the same year Lt. Alexander D. Schenck of the 2nd Artillery wrote a paper on "The Military Geography of Canada"; and in October Capt. Daniel M. Taylor, an MID officer, reported on a trip along the Great Lakes and the St. Lawrence River, giving his opinion about the best way to defend the northern frontier and recommending a reconnaissance. On November 13, 1886, Capt. William C. Manning of the 23rd Infantry furnished a report on points in the vicinity of the St. Mary's River and Sault Ste. Marie. In 1887 Lt. George P. Scriven of the Signal Corps, who was attached to the Military Information Division, reported on the fortifications of Kingston and Toronto, and Lt. Andrew S. Rowan of the 15th Infantry, also of the division, wrote a report on the performance of the Canadian militia in the Northwest campaign. A year earlier the Military Information Division had obtained information from a Robert O'Byrne on the strength of the Canadian militia, from Lt. Sidney E. Stuart of the Ordnance on Canadian military resources and on his proposal for a plan of invasion, and from Brig.-Gen. Thomas Wilson, commissary of subsistence, on Canadian railroads and commerce. In 1889 a Dr. Lewis Balch supplied two reports, two sketch maps, and three hand sketches about a "proposed raid" down the Richelieu river from Plattsburg to Montreal, with a map of that city, and Brig.-Gen. John Gibbon, commanding the Department of Columbia, provided information about Puget Sound with a sketch of its defences.[63]

Then, in 1889, three years after the British reconnaissance, Lieutenant Rowan of the American army was ordered to report on the Canadian Pacific Railway and on the roads between it and the American Great Northern. In a forty-eight page report filed on March 1 of the following year Rowan listed the Canadian railway's most vulnerable points and indicated various possible lines of operation for attacking it between Lake of the Woods and Calgary with armies using parallel routes, or using one route for an invasion and another for withdrawal, "for the purpose of disabling or destroying portions of the enemy's territory and property." Rowan also provided information about stream crossings and bridge designs.[64]

Rowan's report on the CPR was only one of a number of MID intelligence papers filed in 1890 about Canada. Rowan himself also reported on the defences of Victoria and of Halifax and furnished descriptions of Nanaimo, the New Westminster district, Vancouver, and the Canadian waterways. There were also anonymous intelligence reports on the whole of the Canadian frontier, section by section, lists of British vessels capable of entering the Great Lakes, a naval intelligence report on Halifax, a report by a Captain Mills (possibly Samuel M. Mills of the 5th Artillery) on its fortifications, and an anonymous assessment of the financial value of Great Lakes cities, probably in connection with estimates for ransom in lieu of bombardment. Finally there was a paper described as "General considerations in regard to an advance into the Dominion."[65]

An article by Lieutenant Schenck entitled "Our Northern Frontier, in time of peace prepare for war," which was published in a military periodical in 1890, was also filed by the Military Information Division. As most of the intelligence reports in the files have been destroyed, published articles like Schenck's remain the chief source of information about military thought on many of these matters. Schenck repeated the traditional view that whoever controlled the Great Lakes possessed a predominant early advantage. He noted that the English had had the foresight to build canals that could be used for military purposes; that the American forts Ontario, Niagara, Porter, and Wayne, which had all been commenced between 1839 and 1843, had never been completed; and that, though the Fortifications Board had recently recommended rearming them, nothing had been done. Schenck warned, "We are living in a fool's paradise." He declared that it was impossible for the British to defend Canada's long border; but he believed that the United States "dare not" repudiate the Rush-Bagot agreement because that would mean a war for which preparation had not been made.

Schenck then outlined his view of an American strategy for war with Canada. A retaining force should hold Maine while an army secured or destroyed the St. Lawrence canals near Morrisburg and seized the Niagara River and the Welland Canal "which is entirely out of reach of guns from our shore." Schenck said that the Canadian railway system could not be more favourably situated for the defence of the Welland, and that the English would try to seize Detroit. In the West there were no military objectives for the United States Army except the CPR. On the Pacific Coast Victoria and Esquimalt must be captured. Finally Schenck concluded that it was easy to underestimate Canada's military strength backed by England, and to exaggerate that of the United States. The nature of the frontier, and winter conditions, made the conquest of Canada no easy task, especially as American military resources were undeveloped. Until they were developed, he lamented, "this country is bound hand and foot and under heavy bonds to keep the peace of nations even with a neighbour apparently so insignificant as the Dominion of Canada."[66]

The filing of Schenck's article by the Military Information Division is a link between secret planning and public discussion. It also demonstrates two distinct but related developments. On the one hand there was increasing tension between the United States and Britain, particularly about Canadian questions, with a concurrent American feeling of military impotence; and on the other the slow revival of American military strength on land and sea. It must be noticed however, that the first appeals for American military reform in the early 1880s, had preceded President Cleveland's precipitation of a minor crisis about American fishing in Canadian waters in 1885. Therefore, they were only partly caused by fear of an Anglo-American war over Canada.

American military and naval development in the 1880s had been produced by more general circumstances than the Canadian-American fishing dispute. In part an attempt to resolve the technological controversies that had hitherto served as excuses for the failure to rearm, reform of the army and navy was primarily motivated by growing evidence that, in an increasingly dangerous world where imperial powers were arming feverishly, the United States was being left behind by many other countries and was far weaker than its wealth warranted. Nevertheless, as Britain and Canada were obviously the two countries which, whatever their present intentions might seem to be, were in the best position to harm the United States, American military reform took a course which kept them in the foreground as the most dangerous, though not the most likely, enemies.

Articles on strategy were often written as part of training. Competitions for service officers were organized by the Military Service Institution and similar groups to encourage young officers to theorize on military problems. Speculation about a war with Canada furthered this objective because on subjects like "Our Northern Frontier" and "The Military Geography of Canada" the student could use personal knowledge and observation. One article that discussed American military relations with Canada was originally written as a thesis at the United States Infantry and Cavalry School by an officer of the 24th infantry.[67] A lecture on war with Canada was given annually at the school by Wagner, now a captain and later a distinguished member of the Planning Division of the Army War College. Wagner's theme was the responsibility of the military in the event of war. He said this was always an interesting subject but was also important "when the study is applied to countries whose interests are closely bound to our own, whose foreign policy may clash with that of the United States and whose territories may be the theater of operations of our armies. . . . Applied thus to the Dominion of Canada, the subject becomes one of great moment to every American officer."[68]

Wagner referred several times to Colonel Strange's "able paper" on the "Military Aspect of Canada," criticized some of its conclusions, and showed how circumstances had changed since it had appeared. He said there was no military objective in British Columbia, and Alaska was not, as Strange believed, a useful American base of operations. He noted that when Strange wrote his article there had been no worthwhile military objective in the Midwest. Now there was the CPR which "all the efforts of the British Empire probably could not save from the destructive forays of cowboys from Montana and North Dakota." Like Strange, Wagner saw the East as the crucial theatre. He said that geography dictated a defensive stance on the coasts and an invasion of Canada to cut Canada off from Great Britain. Wagner thought that Montgomery's invasion route via Montreal was the only possible one and that Strange was wrong in ruling out a winter campaign. As the United States lacked naval superiority, a winter campaign when Quebec was isolated by ice was the only hope. In the past strategic railways had always made it possible for Canada to act on interior lines. The Grand Trunk was therefore a most important objective. Britain could reinforce the Great Lakes by stationing gunboats on the St. Lawrence and this advantage had not been offset by enlarging the Erie Canal because American canal builders had sought commercial, rather than strategic, advantage and were opposed by railroad promoters.

Wagner went on to say that, after Montreal had been reduced, Quebec would be the next objective. The St. Lawrence River must be controlled so that the army would not be split in two parts. Heavy guns would be necessary to reduce Quebec, but American engineering technology could manufacture them and get them across the river. Wagner concluded that Canada could be conquered if the United States had a navy, but without one it would be difficult. "England could not hold Canada, and we could not conquer it." This last statement Wagner quickly qualified by saying that "complete conquest would be impossible without naval support," thus suggesting that a partial occupation might be undertaken.[69]

Study of the invasion of Canada in the American army was not a matter of indoctrination or preparation for war. The problem that a war with Britain presented would have been extremely difficult for the United States Army of that day to resolve. For the students of war it represented an intellectual challenge. Diplomatic historians have been misled by the fact that in a later period American army officers were prone to boast that Canada was a hostage for British good behaviour.[70] If this was so afterwards (which is not necessarily true) it certainly did not describe the situation throughout most of the nineteenth century, before the United States was adequately armed and when Americans might have been unwilling to endure the inevitable onslaught of the Royal Navy in a long war. Fascination with the complexity of war with Britain is shown by the large amount of attention given to this difficult problem in exercises and many published articles. A summary of their conclusions points to a consensus that an American victory could not be assured.

Study of war with Canada, even if only an academic exercise, must have conditioned the thinking of many members of the American forces and have made them aware that if war came as a result of the bankruptcy of diplomacy or the ambition of politicians it would create a situation that the army could not easily solve. In the long run, when American resources would become fully organized for war, the United States could certainly triumph; but the early course of war, which might be decisive, would depend on many unknown factors, including the relative degree of preparation on each side. Military preparations were essential to insure against all possible contingencies. But in 1895 the American forces were not ready to face a war with Britain. Lt. William R. Hamilton of the 5th Artillery declared that it was "utterly impossible for the United States to undertake a war of invasion against any country worthy of our attention with the means at hand."[71]

An American naval revolution intended to remedy that situation had begun at about the same time as the reform of professional development in the army, but with rather more momentum. In view of the Royal Navy's supremacy the possibility of a war with Britain, while not an immediate expectation, was obviously the most important question that naval planners had to take into consideration. The keels of the first American warships to be built since the Civil War (except for some inferior vessels launched in 1873) had been laid down in 1883, but although built of steel these were still experimental vessels that combined sail and steam.[72] The naval building program did not really get under way until 1889 during the presidency of Benjamin Harrison. His imperially-minded secretary of the navy, Gen. Benjamin Tracy, sometimes called "the father of the American navy," seemed for a time likely to pave the way for a more military approach to the settlement of Canadian-American differences. When Harrison was defeated in 1892, the *St. John Telegraph* said that it was just as well that he was "retired to private life," for if he had been re-elected there might have been war.[73] It was to be some time before the U.S. Navy constituted a serious challenge to British sea power.

However, the long-debated problem of coastal fortifications to protect American ports, needed in the event of a confrontation with Britain, had been moved nearer solution in 1885 when Congress had appointed the Board on Fortifications. This was presided over by the secretary of war, William C. Endicott. In its report the Endicott Board claimed that the greatest external danger to the United States came from exposure to a naval attack on ports and trade. It took note of the decline of American forts since their preeminence in 1860 and declared that they were now unable to cope with modern ironclads in order to prevent enemy vessels from entering American ports. The presidential message releasing the board's report showed what was in the minds of the administration. "Our nearest neighbour [Britain in

Canada], though reasoning from the past she should have no occasion to fear a naval attack from us, has nevertheless constructed armored forts at Halifax and Bermuda both as refuges for her fleets and as outposts for offensive operations."[74] Listing an order or priority among twenty forts to be brought up do date, the report placed New York first, San Francisco second, Boston third, and the Great Lakes ports fourth.

With regard to the Great Lakes ports, which could be as useful as the coastal ports in the event of a war with Britain, the board noted the "peculiar" circumstances resulting from the Rush-Bagot agreement of 1817, but indicated that since that time great cities had grown up and much property was now exposed to destruction. Canadian canals would permit the passage of many British gunboats now in commission to pass to the lakes where they could (in the words of a House committee report of 1862) "shell every town from Ogdensburg to Chicago." On Lake Ontario, Canadian commerce was superior, but it was inferior on the Upper Lakes. The board therefore noted a proposal that light vessels should be kept on the New York Finger Lakes ready to be sent by canal to Lake Ontario when needed. It was also noted that Sackets Harbor and Oswego could probably hold out long enough for the United States to develop resources to bring a force to their relief. West of the Welland Canal, British rail communications and naval supremacy would facilitate the concentration of a force that could easily overpower the "hastily formed, undisciplined, and poorly equipped force" which was all the United States could produce. However, preponderance of population meant that the United States, pursuing an "offensive defence" strategy, would soon gain control of the central portion of the province of Ontario between Lakes Erie and Huron.

The board therefore recommended that attention should be given to the state of the northern forts. The one at Rouse's Point would suffice to control entry from Lake Champlain if 9-inch rifles were installed, but also one or more forts should be built on the St. Lawrence River to command the approaches to the lakes from the sea.[75]

Although naval building had begun in the 1880s, Congress continued, despite the Endicott Report in 1885, to be niggardly with appropriations for fortification. It was not until 1890 that the secretary for war was able to report that the board's recommendations for the Atlantic coast were beginning to be put into effect. But by that time there had been a radical change in military thinking. Opposition had developed within the army to the fortification of the Canadian border. Gen. Oliver O. Howard, who commanded the Department of the East, said in 1893 that "it would be absurd to fortify where war is least likely to occur."[76] Earlier the secretary, Redfield Proctor, had suggested a radical departure from the Endicott Board's recommendations for the frontier with Canada. Noting that there was a very real danger of a bombardment of sea-coast harbours, and that to prevent it he hoped to get money for fortification over the next ten years, he admitted that the Great Lakes cities were in an even more defenceless condition. Furthermore, because of the Rush-Bagot agreement, ships could not be built to protect them. But he maintained that land fortifications were not the answer. Instead, he suggested, land forces, properly disposed, could ward off any danger.

Lt.-Gen. John M. Schofield, the commanding general of the United States Army, had noted that, as the Indian wars were ending, the army was now free to look after the other military needs of the country. He therefore proposed to establish garrisons at suitable points as nuclei for the concentration of regular and volunteer forces.[77] The American northern forts thus continued to be barracks rather than defended strongholds. Many troops were moved into them and they became very crowded. At Fort Wayne there was "not room to move in the quarters" and soldiers often wished for the accommodation that had been provided at San Antonio and other posts.[78] But at Niagara liberal appropriations after 1887 had made improvements possible by 1890.[79] Madison Barracks at Sackets Harbor, where there were already six companies, was to be another link in the chain of "important military stations" on the northern frontier.[80] Fort Sheridan near Chicago also grew rapidly and was reported to be in first-class condition.[81] Expansion was so noticeable that in 1892 it was reported in the London *Army and Navy Gazette* that, within the next three months, the United States military force along the Canadian border would be trebled.[82]

This report from Britain was based on statements made by the secretary of war when denying a rumour that the United States contemplated renouncing the Rush-Bagot agreement. Proctor had also referred to the probable direction of hostilities, "which he was careful to add there were no signs of and which he trusts may never come." In his view the vital point was the St. Lawrence canal system which would invite the first attack. One on the south shore of the river could be reached with ease and the others could be destroyed by gunfire. On the other hand Proctor thought the Welland Canal "naturally impregnable."[83] In the following year, when Major-General Howard said it would be absurd to fortify the northern border, new construction at Plattsburg provided room for eight infantry companies and, although there was opposition in Congress to spending money in "an age of peace" because "the Canadians are our friends," a new barracks, Fort Ethan Allen, was built fifteen miles from Burlington, Vermont. Described as one of the "best cavalry posts in the United States," it filled a gap in the chain of barracks across the north and was on the traditional invasion route which was now served by a railway.[84]

This major redeployment of the United States Army in the early 1890s, a result of the disappearance of the Indian frontier, was not initiated by hostility to Canada or by an expectation of war. Now that it was not required to control the Indians, the United States Army could be concentrated for training in larger units. It was natural to relocate the troops along the national frontier with Canada. Furthermore, the new locations had other uses besides the defence of the border. This was a time of considerable labour unrest and the troops were now conveniently located close to the heavily populated eastern and midwestern cities. The garrison of Fort Sheridan, for instance, played an important role during the Pullman strike of 1894 in Chicago.[85]

But by 1890, when the Military Information Division had compiled much information about the problem of war in North America, relations with Britain had begun to deteriorate again over a new North American issue. As early as 1888 British Columbia sealers had found it necessary to talk of arming their ships to prevent seizure by American cruisers in the Bering Sea.[86] To protect the fur-bearing seals which bred on the Pribiloff Islands, the Americans claimed that jurisdiction over a 100-mile off-shore limit had been obtained from Russia in 1868.[87] United States revenue cutters arrested many Canadian ships. In 1891, when American and British naval vessels were ordered to the sealing grounds, there seemed to be a possibility of a serious clash.[88] The *New York Sun* boasted that the United States Navy had twice as many sailors in the Pacific as the British and had two vessels faster and more powerful than any Royal Navy vessel there except the *Warspite*.[89] the British ambassador, C. A. Spring-Rice, reported to his government that the United States administration seemed to be attempting to manoeuvre Britain into an awkward position over the seal question by suggesting that Canadian and British sealers were conniving at the destruction of a valuable industry. He suggested that this was because the government wanted an election issue. The fact was, he said, that "the seal interest is quite as much a London, as an American interest and most of the smugglers are really Americans and not Canadians."[90] Britain thus rejected the American claim to have inherited control over the high seas from Russia; and when the British proposed to back Canadian rights with the Royal Navy's Pacific squadron, Canadian sealers were encouraged. Lord Stanley, the governor general, reported that when the activities of the United States cruisers were stopped, this silenced annexationists who had declared that Britain would never provide protection for Canadian interests.[91]

The sealing problem proved to be capable of solution because American opinion was divided about an issue that clearly had political implications, and because many thought "it would indeed be disgraceful to the civilization of this century that two of its greatest and most enlightened nations should be unable to adopt a peaceful mode of settling such disputed points as have arisen in connection with this matter."[92] Cordial relations between British and American sailors on sealing patrol were demonstrated by their cooperation in the Bering Sea the next summer when a Russian captain, allegedly acting on orders (but later committed to a lunatic asylum by his government) arrested five British sealers and one American. The commander of the U.S. Naval Force wrote a most friendly letter to thank Capt. H. A. C. Parr, RN, for information about Russian activities.[93] Negotiations for a settlement by British, American, and Canadian delegates ensued.[94]

Britain's strong stand on behalf of Canada-based sealers had seemed for a time to threaten a war that would have involved Canada, but it was only one among several influences upon the development of Canadian-American relations. American policy had been stiffened by an awareness of growing military strength, by a new interest in extraterritorial dependencies, and by the growth of protectionism. The McKinley tariff of 1890 was followed by the rejection of Canadian overtures for reciprocity. This was a source of great irritation in Canada, all the more because it was believed that rejection of reciprocity was in part motivated by the belief that such action might make Canada less prosperous and therefore more likely to sue for annexation.[95]

Among several other issues that troubled Canadian-American relations at this time, one that directly concerned the defence question was an American proposal to build two more revenue cutters on the Great Lakes, vessels that could also serve as warships.[96] The initiative stemmed directly from the naval building program. On April 9, 1892, Senator McMillan of Michigan introduced a resolution to ask the State Department whether the Rush-Bagot agreement was still in force.[97] His motive was to help Great Lakes' shipbuilders obtain a share of lucrative naval contracts. The secretary of state, James G. Blaine, argued that the agreement had not been intended to prevent shipbuilding. He proposed a codicil that would state that ships could be constructed in Great Lakes yards provided they were sent to the ocean before being armed.

In Washington Ambassador Sir Julian Pauncefote was suspicious.

As the canals would permit the passage of only very small vessels, he thought that the Americans intended to build ships for service on the lakes. The United States would gain an initial advantage at the outset of a war if there were ships in Great Lakes ports awaiting transfer to the sea to be armed. To investigate this problem the British Admiralty proposed sending an officer to survey the situation surreptitiously before it gave its opinion. The Colonial Office warned against this step. It said that Canadian government offices were "too leaky" to keep such a reconnaissance secret.[98]

Despite the warning, the Admiralty requested a report from Capt. Reginald Custance, formerly assistant director of naval intelligence, and now attached to the embassy in Washington as naval attaché. Custance recommended that the Dominion government should be given advice about measures necessary for the defence of Canada. His report was forwarded by the Admiralty to the War Office which replied that it also had an officer looking at the situation in the United States. This was probably Maj. C. Barter whose report will be mentioned later. Custance's report also went to the Colonial Office where an official commented that it seemed as if the Admiralty had only just discovered that the defence of Canada might involve a certain amount of imperial assistance. But the Colonial Office agreed that Canada had not lived up to a reciprocal obligation incurred when Cardwell withdrew the garrisons and Britain promised support in time of war. That obligation had been intended to relieve the British Treasury of expenses for defence in time of peace.[99]

Maj.-Gen. Herbert, the Canadian militia's GOC, preferred to see the Rush-Bagot agreement revoked rather than have it amended in the way the American secretary of state had suggested. Herbert recommended preparations to secure the necessary preliminary initiative on the lakes to offset the advantage which the Americans would eventually gain because of their greater resources. But the Canadian government was averse to renunciation of the Rush-Bagot agreement because that would further disturb the currently unsettled conditions for trade. It pointed out that the United States already had three revenue vessels on the lakes with treble the armament and more than treble the tonnage permitted by Rush-Bagot. Canada had none, although one was being built. It further noted that revenue cruisers were capable of being fitted out as warships in emergency. Yet it was not disposed to enter into a dispute about revenue ships. At the same time it was opposed to an alteration of the agreement to permit naval building because that could give the United States an initial advantage in the event of war.[100]

Although the governments of all three countries were concerned to ensure that discussion of North American disputes remained on the diplomatic level, the inflammation of public opinion, and the anxiety of professional service officers, caused some significant political, military, and naval developments. In 1891 Representative Butterworth, an old advocate of annexation, introduced a resolution in Congress to authorize negotiations for the union of Canada and the United States.[101] In December 1894 a similar resolution, probably drafted by Goldwin Smith, was introduced in the Senate by Senator Jacob Gallinger of New Hampshire.[102]

In the intervening period Maj.-Gen. Chapman, director of military intelligence at the War Office, had sent Maj. (later Lt.-Gen. Sir) Charles T. Leger Barter, of the King's Own Yorkshire Light Infantry, deputy assistant adjutant-general in the branch, to examine the military and naval aspects of the Canadian-American border. Barter wrote a 124-page report that included an assessment of American military and naval strength. He said that the naval revival in the United States had not yet been matched by one in the army which was not organized for war. He was also very critical of the military value of the American "militia." But he noted that geographic isolation would give the United States time to prepare if a situation showed signs of becoming critical.[103]

Similar investigations were being made in the United States with similar results. Capt. Daniel Morgan Taylor, an ordnance officer detached to special duty in the adjutant-general's office and temporarily attached to the office of the secretary of war in 1886, became the recorder for the Board of Ordnance and Fortifications in December 1889. He was in charge of the Military Information Division from 1890 to May 1892 and also with matters concerning the militia. During that time Taylor made a personal reconnaissance of the border. He started at St. Paul, Minnesota, and finished at Cornwall, Ontario. As a result he warned that British, Indian, and Australian troops could be quickly sent to Winnipeg by way of the Canadian Pacific Railway and could seize "our grain and flouring mills" by attacking Duluth. Taylor recommended hunting and fishing trips by officers to work out the best way of cutting the CPR in the West, that the adjutant-generals of militia from Ohio, Indiana, Pennsylvania, and New York should be invited to establish concentration points for the invasion of Canada, and that the Intelligence Branch should develop plans for attack on the Rapide Plat and Galops canals.[104]

On April 15, 1892, the adjutant-general of the United States Army had asked the generals commanding territorial departments of the army to recommend "the best plan to be adopted by the U.S. Military Authorities in case of war with Great Britain to protect our northern frontier." Maj.-Gen. Nelson Miles of the Department of the Missouri evidently did not consider the problem very urgent. He did not reply until February 27, 1893, "because of pressure of other business." He began by saying that a combination of Britain and Canada should not be underestimated and that Canadians would probably support it. Noting the vulnerability of the American coastal cities, he pointed to the strength of the Canadian position, protected by four deep lakes and the rapid St. Lawrence and with lateral communications permitting quick transference of defensive forces. Miles said that what was most likely to succeed was a winter offensive aimed at capturing Montreal and Ottawa. The invading force should then move on Quebec or, alternatively, mine the Lower St. Lawrence. If the offensive was launched in the spring it should cross the St. Lawrence in the same way, seize the canals, and penetrate to the heart of the Dominion. He presented a chart to show possible river crossing points which should be examined in advance by experts. Miles said that it was of great importance that an invasion should be launched quickly before the Canadian militia could be organized. Secondary attacks should be made simultaneously, from northern Maine to cut the Intercolonial Railway, in Manitoba to cut the Canadian Pacific, and in the West to seize its terminus at Vancouver.

Miles believed that a small force could subjugate Canada in one to two hundred days, but that a larger one could achieve the same end in ten days, which was to be preferred. To undertake the larger effort, the army should be expanded by recruiting intelligent volunteers in order to convert companies into regiments, battalions into brigades, and brigades into divisions. In peacetime the United States should be careful to match Canadian fortification of the border and all Canadian canal building that had military significance.[105]

Maj.-Gen. Oliver O. Howard, a Civil War hero and a great biblical scholar known as "the Havelock of the Army" who was the general in command of the Eastern Division had also filed a 13-page plan of campaign ("Project by United States against Canada") with the Military Information Divison.[106] Since Howard's plan, dated August 16, 1892, was drawn up by the responsible commander in the area most concerned, it must, like that of Miles, be regarded as something more than the contingency plans prepared by members of the Military Information Division or by young officers in training. These two plans may be compared in some respects with Admiral Mahan's contingency plan drawn up for the Naval Secret Strategy Board in 1890. All three are evidence that American professional officers at the highest levels, while not expecting war with Canada, were familiarizing themselves with the nature of the problem. They were the products of general military and naval development, of the redeployment of the army on the one hand, and of the expansion of the navy on the other.

Barter's reconnaissance had shown that the War Office was still of the opinion that it might be faced with war in North America. Significantly, after the death in 1891 of Prime Minister John A. Macdonald who had kept the brakes on military development, a vigorous general officer commanding in Canada, Gen. Ivor Herbert, by creating the first regiment of regular infantry,[107] was able to start the Canadian militia on the first stage of a long slow process of reorganization leading to operational readiness. On January 11, 1894, the governor general reported that the Canadian cabinet had agreed to order 8,000 Martini-Metford rifles and 500,000 rounds of ammunition.[108] This rifle had been selected by Herbert because it was more robust for militia use than the new magazine weapons, but it had been declared obsolescent by the British army and when issued to the Canadian militia the ammunition was found defective. It is not surprising that, after Canada took delivery of 1,000 rifles, the order was cancelled in May 1895 "for reasons of economy."[109]

Some progress had been made in Canada towards military security by the creation of the infantry regiment. But there was still no professional cadre of officers to make a study of military problems, as there was in the United States; and the Canadian militia's close tie with the British army meant that Imperial Defence dominated Canadian defence thinking. When the colonial secretary sent to Ottawa details of regulations recently introduced in the United Kingdom and Canda to forbid sketching and photographing military installations, Canada claimed that this was effectively covered by adoption of the British Official Secrets Act and that no further action was needed.[110] Canadian politicians did not take the danger from the United States seriously.

The motivation behind the hesitant military development in Canada that came in the early 1890s was mixed. General Herbert's immediate interest was in securing Canadian militia for the Halifax base and Canadian money for a garrison at Esquimalt. But his basic concern was the defence of the Empire as a whole. His militia reforms were thus intended to serve a dual purpose: to eliminate a weak link in the Imperial Defence system by strengthening Canada vis-à-vis the United States. On their part Canadian politicians were clearly still reluctant to accept increased financial responsibility for defence even though, since 1885, North American issues had cropped up to supplement previous arguments for a greater Canadian role in Imperial Defence, and even though Canadian interests were now more clearly involved than at any time since the Civil War and the Treaty of Washington. North American clashes with the United States had had less effect than British requests for aid for Imperial Defence, and that was minimal. Canadian politicians were not moved by them because they hoped for peaceful solutions. Resort to force would bring the horrors of an American invasion.

On the other hand, although American politicians had been reluctant to rearm, American soldiers and sailors responding to the obviously growing needs of American worldwide interests and alarmed by the possible implications of political errors, had begun to work towards rearmament. Although not directed primarily against Canada, this development inevitably focused attention upon the problems of a northern war even though one was neither expected nor wanted there, because that war with Britain was the most difficult the Americans could face, and because no other power then seemed more likely to come into conflict with the United States. Hence it is not surprising that, some months before the Venezuela crisis burst upon unsuspecting Canadians, the British Foreign Office learned from its ambassador, Lord Gough, that the *New York Sun* had reported that three American officers in succession had examined the strategic position of Canada and that precautions were being taken to prevent foreign officers from gathering military information in the United States. Gough believed that the first report was unimportant, but he said that the second was based on fact.[111] The United States was beginning to be concerned about its military secrets, a sure sign that it was beginning to be aware of the possibility that peace might not be eternal.

5

Venezuela and After
(1895–1900)

The long-smouldering dispute about the location
of Venezuela's border with British Guiana,
where British subjects had effectively occupied
and developed territory in areas claimed by both
countries, would have had little significance had
it not been for Secretary of State Richard Olney's conviction that Britain was bullying a small
American nation in contravention of the intent of
the Monroe doctrine. The prime minister, Lord
Salisbury, averse to surrendering interests of colonial planters in face of unwarranted American
interference, coolly took his time about Olney's
note of July 20, 1895, which contained the charge
that Britain was flouting the Monroe Doctrine.
News that Salisbury would reject his offer to ar-
bitrate angered the president. Beneath a veneer
of idealism Cleveland was, Joseph Chamberlain
believed, a "coarse-grained man [with] a good
deal of the bully" in his make-up.[1] On December
17 Cleveland sent his notorious message to Congress, in which he announced his intention to ar-
bitrate the question himself and to back his decision by force if necessary. His pronouncement
swept Congress off its feet and sent a jingoistic
tidal wave across the United States that seemed
to forebode war with Britain.

In Britain military opinion expressed in service periodicals looked on an Anglo-American war

over Venezuela as "preposterous" but agreed that if one did come it would be fought in Canada. The Dominion's strategic weaknesses were acknowledged but it was assumed that naval domination of the oceans and the availability of trained regular troops (perhaps including East Indians) who could be rushed to Canada would give Britain the advantage. These views were reprinted in professional journals in the United States without comment and were probably accepted there as a true appraisal of the situation at the outset of a war.[2]

For Canada the Venezuela problem was not a distant imperial question like those of 1878 and 1885. Even though the dispute was almost as remote from Canadian interests as the international incidents of those years, it raised the spectre of invasion. Goldwin Smith's periodical, *The Week*, reprinted a *Sunday Graphic* article warning that the Americans would combine with European countries to attack Canada. The writer of this article urged that the British Army should recruit a regiment in Canada to defend it against the United States.[3]

Gen. W. J. Gascoigne, GOC of the Canadian militia, was very pessimistic. In his mind everything depended on whether Canada would take measures for its own defence or would leave them to England. He reported to the adjutant-general in London that he had found politics and waste everywhere. "It is almost like dealing with children." The Canadian forts were in decay and there was no proper supervision of arms.[4]

Yet the people of Canada were not greatly disturbed. Many of them believed that they understood American political behaviour better than did the British. They dismissed Cleveland's message as meant for domestic consumption: there was an election in the offing.[5] But some militia officers feared that their countrymen were over-sanguine. Editorials in the next issue of the *Canadian Military Gazette*, and letters to the editor, pointed to the widespread, hysterical support with which the American public had greeted Cleveland's menacing gesture. Some Canadian military correspondents seized this opportunity to urge militia reform, the organization of a reserve militia, or contributions to Imperial Defence; but, notwithstanding their professed belief in the urgent need for military development, they expressed confidence that an American attack on Canada, the only form that operations against Britain could take, could easily be made unproductive. "Canadian resistance would be a hard nut for the invader to crack if the government would but carry out some sensible system of national defence." "The royal navy and the regular army would easily attend to the rest. . . . The great American spread eagle is quite a bird on his own dung-hill, but he will find himself pretty light poultry if he once causes the British lion to fight."[6] Expectation of British support was evidently the chief prop for Canadian confidence.

Indeed there appears to have been significantly little bravado about what the militia could do. C. F. Hamilton, the historian of the militia who knew it first-hand, noted later that his fellow officers had maintained a "prudent silence" at the time of the crisis. He claimed that this showed that they were "not militaristic."[7] It is more likely that they were prudent because they knew that the militia was not ready to fight. Canada's safety depended entirely on British support.

The crisis caused the Canadian government to show a belated concern about defence. The minister of militia authorized the purchase of 40,000 Lee-Enfield magazine rifles in England, a more effective weapon than the one that had been rejected in the previous year. He also ordered fifteen maxim guns and made arrangements for the progressive rearmament of the militia field artillery with a modern 12-pounder breech-loader, the gun used by the British horse artillery.[8] But these small steps would take some time to have any effect and were little more than tokens.

Meanwhile Gascoigne had begun to prepare to resist a possible American invasion. During the previous summer Capt. Arthur Lee, a brilliant young Royal Artillery officer then teaching at the Royal Military College, had begun to survey and map the border country with the aid of cadets.[9] Disturbed by Cleveland's bluster, the GOC instructed Lee to draw up a scheme for mobilization. Gascoigne also succeeded in getting the government to approve a reserve of officers to provide replacements in the event of war.[10] Working with Lee, Col. E. P. Leach, the Commanding Royal Engineer from Halifax, outlined plans for earthworks to protect Montreal which both officers saw as the key to Canadian defence. They were encouraged when they found some of the old Richelieu River forts "still in good condition" and therefore, in their opinion, of use as forward defences for the city.[11]

A few years later it was reported that if the Americans had invaded Canada at this time, the militia would have fought a holding action at Niagara, would have seized Ogdensburg, and would have attempted to capture Plattsburg.[12] That this may have been what Gascoigne intended is suggested by related proposals for securing control of Lake Ontario. In March the Toronto branch of the Navy League recommended that torpedo-boats should be brought by rail from Halifax to the St. Lawrence;[13] and Lee consulted Sir William Van Horne, president of the CPR, about the feasibility of this plan.[14] It would have been a means of drawing British power back to the vulnerable point in Canada's defensive strategy, the lower Great Lakes.

Joseph Chamberlain believed that Cleveland was not "just electioneering." He thought that many Americans who suspected Britain of "an assumption of superiority," and also "the Irish party," would not "look on war with Britain with horror."[15] H. O. Arnold-Forster, MP, the secretary of the Imperial Federation League, was convinced that the United States was bent on war. He recommended that if it broke out Queen Victoria should make an appeal to the people, with special versions addressed to each of the various self-governing colonies. Canadians should be reminded of the historic cooperation of their two founding peoples against the Americans. Arnold-Forster suggested that they should be told as soon as possible that cutting off American trade with Britain would benefit them. He wrote confidentially to Chamberlain, "If Canada leaves us in the lurch, the game is up as far as our American possessions are concerned"; but he added, "the moment Canadian blood is shed in defence of Canadian soil the whole situation will be changed. Not even in the United States can permanently destroy the liberties of over 400,000 if they are determined to protect them and if we are determined to assist them." Arnold-Forster argued that stopping American imports would permit the Royal Navy to concentrate on protection of the trade routes to the St. Lawrence and would force the United States into the open sea "which is exactly what we ought to desire."[16]

The British cabinet was not united on such a strong military stand. Chamberlain contended that the Monroe doctrine did not warrant American arbitration, but he suggested that Britain should temporize by expressing agreement with Monroe's intentions.[17] Sir William Harcourt, who was leader of the opposition in the House of Commons, wanted assurance that the government would move in a pacific direction. Chamberlain told Salisbury, "Nothing would induce him [Harcourt] to be a party to a war with the United States." Harcourt had declared that the Schomberg line which Britain claimed to be the Guiana–Venezuela border could not be defended and that the boundary question should be submitted to arbitration.[18]

Both Salisbury and Chamberlain, the leading figures in the government, were in fact not disposed to let the quarrel get out of hand. However, while the diplomats were arranging a compromise solution (one in which Britain submitted to accept international arbitration that eventually decided substantially in her favour), the military implications of failure in diplomatic negotiations were being examined by British military and naval officers. On January 16, 1896, the adjutant-general called a meeting of senior army officers which approved a report by Maj. Hubert Foster, RE, who had reconnoitred in the United

States. Foster had apparently said that an American attack would be aimed at Montreal which must therefore be the main concern of the defence. The meeting concluded that Kingston, and possibly Hamilton as well, should be defended, that the defence of Canada was partly a naval problem, and that therefore the Admiralty should be consulted.[19] Thus far British military leaders appeared to support Gascoigne's idea of a forward defence strategy covering the lower lakes.

Col. Percy Lake, DQMG of the Canadian militia, brought Gascoigne's plans before the Colonial Defence Committee on March 27. The committee complained that the Dominion had not yet prepared and filed the defence plan requested of it eight years before, and that an examination of the 1895 Militia Report showed that in the event of war Canada would suffer great losses through lack of planning.[20] It went on to say that when a possible enemy had great resources that would become more and more available as the war progressed, the effect of victories at the outbreak of hostilities could scarcely be exaggerated. They could cause a war to be of short duration. If Canada's defenders were unable to gain strategic positions at the outset and the campaigns were prolonged, the resources not only of Canada, but also of the Empire, would be strained. The implication was that detailed advanced planning was absolutely essential to ensure early succes.[21] Lake contributed a paper of his own on "Canadian Naval Action in Defence of the Great Lakes," stressing the need for help from the Royal Navy.[22]

Gascoigne's proposals for defending Canada did not come before the Joint Military and Naval Committee until April 23. This committee, a professional body of senior officers of both services presided over by the parliamentary undersecretary of state for war, St. John Brodrick, approved the central features of the GOC's plan, the defence of Montreal, but warned him that his forces needed to be more concentrated for the purpose and that distant diversionary raids, like one contemplated on the Sault Ste. Marie canal, should be avoided. It also agreed that in the event of war the Admiralty should be asked to send ships that could pass through the St. Lawrence canals to Lakes Ontario and Erie. An officer should be sent over, apparently immediately, to select vessels suitable for service as auxiliaries.

The Joint Committee had probably had access to Foster's report which may have outlined a plan for an invasion of the United States.[23] At any rate the committee asserted that the best way to ensure the safety of Canada would be, if conditions in Europe permitted, "by landing a British force on American territory and making a vigorous offensive movement"; but it was of the opinion that "in any case such military assistance should be afforded to Canada as would secure the safety of Montreal."[24] Foster was then sent back to find out more about the American land forces.[25] Noticeably the committee had said nothing about Gascoigne's intention of defending the Niagara Peninsula or the Upper St. Lawrence, or even about sending troops to Montreal before war started.

Sir John Ardagh, director of military intelligence at the War Office, had warned almost before the Venezuela crisis was over that in a long war the superiority of American numbers would mean the conquest of Canada. He concluded that a land war on the American continent "would be perhaps the most hazardous military enterprise that we could possible be driven to engage in."[26] A year later, referring to the role of the militia in Canadian defence, Ardagh said, "The numerical superiority of the Canadians [in arms] can only last for a short time after the outbreak of war, and it is very essential that Montreal should be secure as its loss would probably decide the fate of Canada."[27] But the War Office and Admiralty had agreed that the small vessels that Lee had wanted brought by rail could not gain command of the lakes. Naval supremacy there would only be possible when the St. Lawrence canals were deepened.[28]

Despite, or perhaps because of, these views there was no disposition in Britain to give advance commitments in peacetime to seize control of the Great Lakes or even to help to defend Montreal. After a realistic look at the strategic problems of defending Canada, professional opinion in Britain had turned against deep involvement, especially when Canadians were doing little in the way of preliminary preparation themselves. One reason for British equanimity may have been a growing confidence that the United States had no aggressive intentions. The strident tone of a part of the American press in response to Cleveland's aggressive message, a cause of foreboding and of advance planning, was not universal. The *Canadian Military Gazette* reported in January that some U.S. Army officers explained "for the edification of the great unwashed how Canada could be licked in short order"; but it pointed out that "the bottom was literally dropping out of Wall Street . . . while loud-mouthed apostles of unreasoning spread-eaglism were threatening the conquest of Canada." It claimed that while Canada was united from end to end, there was a "large and influential element in the United States as anxious for peace as any of us on this side of the line."[29]

Indeed, during the crisis, cross-border social contacts between Canadian and American officers continued as usual. In February Colonel Bartlett of Madison Barracks, Sackets Harbor, gave a farewell reception for a hundred guests among whom "were delightful officers from the barracks at Kingston."[30] About the same time the *Army and Navy Journal* reported that a newspaper, the *New York Evening Sun*, had carried a "very discouraging picture" of Canadian military capability. It had said that there was little to show for the thirty million spent on the militia since Confederation, that its eighty-three muzzle-loading rifled guns were "as obsolete as a Queen Anne flintlock," and that in Canada money had been spent on "indulgence in boodle—quite an orgy" for public works that never had any prospect of being productive. The Dominion could muster 150,000 men for self-defence, but taxes could not be raised to train them.[31] This was a curious tone for an American military journal to use about a potential enemy. The notable lack of belligerency contrasts strongly with the militancy of a part of the American civilian press. But Foreign Office reports noted that there was no unusual activity in American naval yards.[32]

The United States War Department was also apparently very little disturbed by the Venezuela crisis. During the months of tension, Brig.-Gen. Thomas M. Vincent, who had been appointed to command the Military Information Division in October 1895, calmly reported matters that were clearly not urgent: contemplated reforms of the Canadian militia, its new valise equipment, and the budget estimates of the Militia Department; and he collected missing annual militia reports by courtesy of that department. In July, when the crisis was over, Vincent visited New Brunswick and Nova Scotia.[33] Some months later he sent the secretary of war an eleven-page plan for the protection of the northern frontier in a war with Britain.[34] But this was routine contingency planning undertaken as if the situation had not recently been critical.

In other respects Canadian-American relations with a defence or military connotation also proceeded as if there was no cloud in the sky. At the height of the crisis Canada and the United States were negotiating about the deepening of the St. Lawrence canals to fifteen feet for commercial purposes.[35] Strategic implications did not impede discussions that would give Britain an advantage in putting a fleet of small warships on Lake Ontario. A year later the chief of the Engineers of the United States Army told Congress that the deepening of the Erie and Oswego canals to eight feet, which was now being done, would permit ordinary torpedo boats, but not torpedo-boat destroyers or gun-boats, to pass to the lakes.[36] Although this was less than the prospective depth of canals planned by Canada, the potential disparity produced no really significant military reaction.

Nevertheless Cleveland's message had in fact initiated concern and activity in certain professional service quarters in the United States. Two articles that had appeared soon after the menacing presidential message, but had been written earlier, had proclaimed that "energetic efforts [had been made] since 1884" to build an American navy, and also that "wonderful strides [had been made] in the production of war material."[37] However, when war seemed imminent one of these authors revealed that a year earlier, when the United States Naval War College had studied war with Britain, a naval expert had told the students that it was still a moot question whether land batteries could impede the advance of a hostile fleet. He said that in any case American coastal fortifications were out-of-date. The author of the article concluded from this that the American fleet was too weak to repel a British invading force; and he added that if the navy were defeated the U.S. Army was too small and scattered to prevent the British from landing on the coast. One reason for professional American caution was the knowledge that war with Britain would not be easy and that victories could not be guaranteed.[38]

In a personal letter to Rear Adm. L. A. Kimberley, USN (Ret'd), Capt. H. C. Taylor, president of the United States Naval War College, had posed the problem of the defence of the country against a British attack. Kimberley replied that five armies totalling 600,000 men should be put in the field, two to defend the Atlantic and Gulf coasts and the others to invade Canada, one through New Brunswick and Nova Scotia to seize Halifax, a second via Niagara to capture Toronto, Montreal, and Quebec, and a third "the army of the North West" [sic] to cross at Detroit and hold all the country west of Niagara to Winnipeg. In addition a force should be raised on the Pacific coast to invade British Columbia and all American ships on the Great Lakes and Puget Sound should be armed as gunboats to cooperate with the invading armies. In a later letter Kimberley added that he would also attack up Lake Champlain and that his objective in the West would be Vancouver Island. "The conquest of Canada as a defence to our own country would be the solution of the Problem as I understand it and would settle for ever the question of future attacks in force."[39] Taylor had anticipated the Venezuela crisis by several months.

American professional service attention had long turned to Canada to find a way to victory should war come. For ten years the army's Military Information Division had been studying the problem of war on the northern border; but when war seemed imminent the question was regarded as primarily one of naval concern because it could be decided by early control of the Great Lakes. Therefore, although no special

American measures were taken on the Atlantic coast or to deploy the army on the border during the emergency, some preliminary plans were made very secretly for a war in the North. The secretary of the navy, Hilary Abner Herbert, ordered Com. Charles Vernon Gridley, a lighthouse inspector at Buffalo, N.Y., to seek out 130 ships which, armed with guns and torpedoes, could seize control of Lakes Erie, Ontario, and Champlain, and the Upper St. Lawrence River.[40] Herbert wanted to be able, in the event of a breach of the peace, to take Canada by surprise.

Brought up in Michigan, Gridley had commanded the American warship *Michigan* on the Great Lakes from 1870 to 1872. Now on his second tour in the Lighthouse Service, he knew the lakes well. His technical expertise is suggested by his introduction of a gas buoy.[41] But Gridley was no mere lighthouse man. That he was one of the most respected of American operational officers is shown by his appointment, two years later, to command Dewey's flagship in the Pacific. At Manila Bay, he was to receive Dewey's famous order, "You may fire when you are ready, Gridley," which conferred upon him the responsibility and honour of beginning the action.[42] In January 1896 Secretary Herbert instructed Gridley to make sketches of ships suitable for armed operations on the lakes, to investigate the need for more branch hydrographic officers there, and to suggest places where they could be stationed away from local influences.[43] In other words Gridley was to plan an improvised fleet, an improvised intelligence service, and an operational communications system for war with Canada on the Great Lakes.

Capt. Henry C. Taylor, president of the Naval War College, which was at that time the navy's only operational planning agency, supervised Gridley's work. It was probably Taylor, one of the leading advocates of contingency planning and preparedness in the United States, who had inspired Herbert to order secret warlike preparations. Taylor was an older brother of the Capt. Daniel Taylor who had recommended planning for war with Canada some years earlier. It is tempting to assume that the Taylor brothers had much to do with developing American professional concern about war with Canada. In 1900 Daniel was ordered to the U.S. Naval War College to lecture on "Military Questions of the Great Lakes."[44]

Gridley was given the information that he would need to carry out operations on the Great Lakes.[45] After receiving detailed instructions from Taylor about what further information would be needed to plan the campaign, Gridley went to Oswego and Ogdensburg. In January he found that all the American vessels on Lake Ontario were built of wood and so were unsuitable for naval use. Ogdensburg did not have facilities for building the torpedo boats, which Herbert counted upon to make up for American weakness. Gridley therefore recommended that four torpedo boats being built elsewhere for service in Maine and Texas should be shipped to Lake Ontario by rail.

Before returning to Buffalo by way of Kingston and Toronto, Gridley recommended that when war came the canals below Ogdensburg should be seized and the Grand Trunk Railway cut.[46] In Canada Gridley learned that a thousand rifles had been received from England (probably old news about the Martini-Metfords received in 1895 and then rejected) and that Canadian Yacht Club members were organizing a naval brigade to attack American forts on Lake Ontario and to destroy the Welland Canal. But Gridley had noticed no signs of war material being shipped on the Grand Trunk; and in Kingston he saw that the guns of Fort Henry were neglected and covered with snow.[47] In Toronto Gridley recruited a spy, Albert A. Crandall, an Annapolis graduate who had resigned his naval commission in 1875 and who now worked for an insurance company in Canada. Crandall claimed that he could provide valuable information about Canadian ships from his company's books.[48] In February Gridley earmarked vessels in Buffalo for one of the proposed auxiliary squadrons and also made plans for forming a naval brigade to man them.[49]

A few weeks later Taylor, who had been summoned back to Washington, advised Gridley that the war scare had subsided and that there would be no further naval preparations until it revived again, which he thought might be in April;[50] but Gridley nevertheless went to Lake Champlain to complete his survey. There he was unable to get close enough to examine ships because they were ice-bound.[51] Meanwhile he had furnished Taylor with a list of "look-out stations" and with a means of communicating with them;[52] and he reported that Crandall had informed him that the three Canadian revenue cutters were not on Lakes Erie or Ontario (which he had already observed himself) but were probably down in the St. Lawrence or up on Georgian Bay.[53] Taylor then wanted to know whether a considerable force could be sent into Canada across the Niagara River. Gridley replied that some such action would be necessary in order to seize the Welland Canal before it was destroyed.[54] In July Taylor personally reconnoitered crossing points from Detroit to Massena, N.Y.[55] But Herbert's interest in planning war on the lakes had now waned because international tension had been reduced.

Herbert had warned Gridley from the first that he must work in strict secrecy. "The political situation might be seriously disturbed

should these preliminary preparations become public." There was to
be no sketching or investigating that could not be done without risking
discovery.[56] This precaution was obviously dictated in part by the need
to surprise the Canadians; but it was also made necessary because
any suggestion of a breach of the Rush-Bagot agreement would have
aroused discussion and opposition in the United States. It is possible
that even Cleveland did not know that his secretary of the navy had
initiated a plan for war with Canada. What is significant is that, in the
United States as in Canada and Britain, when war seemed possible,
professional opinion had at once fastened on the Great Lakes as the
vital point and had sought a way around the restrictions on military
preparations there. Furthermore, henceforward the problem of war
with Britain continued to be studied at the Naval War College. The
superintendent referred in his opening lecture in 1899 to that subject[57]
and, as has been said above, Captain Taylor's brother was invited to
lecture on the northern defences in 1900.

American planning for war at the time of the Venezuela crisis had
thus gone much further than that of Britain and Canada; and it aimed
at anticipatory action, or a preemptive strike, to forestall a long war
that the United States would win in the end only if the American public
remained steadfast. Secrecy had been necessary because, although a
British attack might have consolidated American opinion in defence of
the country, the knowledge that American officers had planned the
first blow might possibly have been divisive in the United States and
might have destroyed the essential patriotic unity required for pros-
ecuting the war.

On the other side of the Atlantic the important effect of the Venezuela crisis was to draw attention to Canada's vulnerability as a weak
spot in the Empire's defences. In October 1896 Chamberlain forwarded to Lord Aberdeen, the governor general, a complaint that
Canada was the only part of Her Majesty's dominions that had not yet
prepared a defence plan to be kept up-to-date by regular revision. He
warned about the danger of hasty mobilization. He hoped that the
long-awaited Canadian defence committee would soon be organized.[58]
Two months later, the Defence Committee of the British cabinet, a
political body that was somewhat resented by the service departments, required its chairman, the duke of Devonshire, to announce
publicly what Britain would do to defend colonies and what they were
expected to do themselves. The duke explained that the Admiralty
would protect colonies against organized invasion from the sea but
could not prevent small predatory raids. Except at selected imperial
bases, the provision of fixed defences and other measures was a local

responsibility.[59] The inspector-general of fortifications, Sir Richard Grant, then obtained a report on the defence of Montreal. Lt.-Col. George Barker, RE, an assistant in his department, declared that Leach's plan to delay an invading force by occupying Fort Lennox on the Île-aux-Noix was "illusory" because modern howitzers would make it untenable. He urged reliance on field forces, the clearing of ground, and the preparation of lines of communication. Despite this advice, Sir John Ardagh, director of military intelligence, instructed the GOC to ask Leach to prepare plans for fixed defences.[60]

Defence works were favoured in Britain because they could give untrained troops more confidence. Canadian militia officers were, however, well aware that European opinion was divided on the value of fortifications. They argued that money would be better spent on the militia to fit it to be a field force. One said that the Canadian Pacific Railway, built in part with the loan that was to have gone to fortify Montreal, was worth more for the defence of Canada than were fortifications.[61] But British officers in Canada had reported to Ardagh that politics riddled the militia and that it would be weak in the field. However, to have complained openly about the Canadian militia would have betrayed Ardagh's confidants and would have destroyed their efforts to bring reform about. He therefore decided against an official approach on that subject. Instead he asked Chamberlain to speak to Laurier at the Colonial Conference about the state of the militia.[62]

Wilfrid Laurier, who had become prime minister in 1896, always disclaimed any military expertise. He was now bombarded with contradictory opinions about this difficult question of peacetime planning for defence against the United States. A retired army captain, Thomas Maxwell, warned him that "our so-called cousins, I call them our hereditary enemies," had built large posts on Lake Champlain, a new cavalry post at Fort Ethan Allen, and a formidable fort at Rouse's Point within ten miles of the Canadian frontier. Maxwell said that Canada was undefended. He deplored the neglect of the militia which he described as "criminal folly" and "treason."[63] On the other hand, another correspondent drew Laurier's attention to the "scattered, anomalous, and comparatively defenceless position" of British and Canadian possessions in the Gulf of St. Lawrence and urged that Canada should take over Labrador by uniting with Newfoundland. He declared, "We have little to fear from our cousins south of us, blood is thicker than water, and relatives who are neighbours cannot afford to quarrel."[64] Others argued that American intentions were ambiguous. It was reported that the New York Republican Club's Committee on National Affairs had claimed that Canada was bankrupt yet at the same time it had shown a desire to take it over.[65] In London Laurier told Chamberlain that the Americans were a "peculiar people" whom he found irritating in their conduct of international relations. But he added that they had so many valuable qualities in common with the British and Canadians that he thought there must be some way of getting a better understanding with them. As Canada was the chief source of friction, he thought a Canadian attaché should be attached to the British embassy.[66] Although nothing came of the suggestion, it was evident that diplomacy rather than preparation for war was Laurier's answer to the alleged American danger.

But military considerations could not yet be so easily ignored. Although the extent of planning on both sides for war on the Great Lakes was not known to the public, anyone who thought at all about the course of a possible war between Canada and the United States was aware of the advantage that an early control of the lakes would give to the side that seized it. In the years immediately after the Venezuela affair, progress towards canal development for commercial purposes had led military personnel to speculate on its strategic implications. Canada was building a fourteen-foot deep canal up the St. Lawrence and to Lake Erie. But the bigger warships that could be sent that way would be safe only if Canada held both banks of the river. Consequently a proposal for a twenty-foot canal from Montreal by the Ottawa to Georgian Bay was attractive to British strategists. It was believed that this would make possible an offensive campaign in the West that would compel the Americans to divert forces from an attack on Montreal in order to protect Illinois. Nevertheless, although this Georgian Bay canal was declared to be commercially feasible, it failed to arouse interest because it would probably not be able to compete commercially with the St. Lawrence route.

On their side, American officers, having looked into the possibility of a ship-canal from the Hudson River to Ontario and Erie, had decided that it would bring the United States no military advantage. They believed that ocean ships were not suitable for passage through the canals and locks, and they declared that the deepening of the enlarged Erie canal to nine feet was all that was needed because the United States had 89 per cent of the shipping on the lakes and had superior facilities for building there. They said that the United States would hold the upper hand as long as Britain could not get reinforcements to the lakes. Thus American officers and the British Colonial Defence Committee were in agreement that a satisfactory policy for preparing to get military control of the lakes was to stimulate commercial shipping.[67]

An American request for permission to send officers of the Corps of Engineers to make surveys on Canadian soil in connection with the proposed ship canal from the Hudson to the St. Lawrence had stirred up British concern about security. The Canadian government had seen no reason to object, but the Admiralty was suspicious that the American intention was to obtain valuable strategic information about "a major invasion route." The War Office had fewer doubts; and Lord Salisbury overruled the Admiralty on the grounds that as the area was wide open the Americans could get any information they wanted about it in other ways. [68]

A yet more sensitive question was the presence of armed vessels on the Great Lakes in apparent contravention of the Rush-Bagot agreement. In October 1896 the Colonial Defence Committee had decided not to object to American construction of revenue cutters on the lakes because it knew that Canada wanted similar vessels. It advised that the only restriction on the Canadian ships should be that they should not exceed in size those built by the United States. [69] A year later the secretary of the Royal Military College Club reported that the United States was arming the steamer *Yantic* for the use of the Michigan Militia. [70] The *Yantic* was 900 tons, much larger than any other armed ship on the Great Lakes but was described as an old wooden vessel "of little military value." Putting her through the St. Lawrence locks left her "ruined for naval purposes"; but the U.S. Navy Department had seized the opportunity to send an officer to watch her progress and, incidentally, to reconnoitre the frontier. This officer, Lt. J. B. Murdoch, reported that "the true focus for aggressive action is not at the Welland but against the St. Lawrence canals." [71]

When the American revenue ships were wanted for service in the war with Spain, on the very day on which a request was made, Canada gave permission for them to pass through the canals to the sea. [72] The Canadian ministers were reluctant to "give rise to ill-feeling in the United States" and were willing to accept American assurances that the ships would proceed straight to an Atlantic port without being involved in hostilities. [73] This operation would probably have been completed before the British had time to comment had it not been that late winter ice delayed the passage, and also that one vessel proved to be too long to go through the locks and had to be cut in half at Ogdensburg and sent through in hermetically sealed halves. [74]

When informed about the American request, the Colonial Defence Committee, reviewing the situation, noted that the United States had vessels on the lakes larger than Canada's, and that they also had the old warship *Michigan* of 685 tons; but that they had refrained from building the additional vessels planned in 1892.[75] Nevertheless the War Office registered its concern that "the facts [now] brought to notice very naturally affect the defence of the Dominion of Canada in the event of a war with the United States."[76] What made this seem more serious was that there were reports that the United States had ordered replacements for the revenue cutters they had sent to the ocean. It was feared that this was a step towards abrogation of the Rush-Bagot agreement. Another complication was that the Spanish consul in Montreal had complained that Canada had committed a breach of neutrality.[77] But the Colonial Defence Committee concluded that the United States was merely trying to see how far it could go without provoking a British protest. It suggested that "in the interests of peace and in the military interests of Canada in the event of war," the Americans should be urged to adhere to the Rush-Bagot agreement "as closely as possible."[78] At the same time Chamberlain did not want neutrality laws to be enforced "in an unfriendly fashion" against the United States which was now at war with Spain.[79]

In the years immediately after the Venezuela crisis, there was further discussion concerning the provision of guns for the defence of Montreal, "to strengthen that city against capture by a coup-de-main." Again the British and the Canadians had different points of view about the need for the defences against the United States. The Colonial Office had asked whether £20,000 would be enough for guns for Montreal, Kingston, and Quebec. The Colonial Defence Committee recommended that a sum as small as that should all be expended on Montreal. It added that Canada ought to purchase twelve 40-pounder rifled breech-loaders and eight five-inch howitzers. These the War Office agreed to supply.[80]

Col. Percy Lake, quartermaster-general of the Canadian militia, disagreed with the proposal to place guns only at Montreal, especially if the Royal Navy intended to send forces to the Great Lakes. However, when the Colonial Office tried to hasten the transfer of the guns to Canada, it was revealed that Canada had not yet made a formal request to the War Office for them. The Colonial Defence Committee then proposed that six nine-inch rifled muzzle-loaders no longer needed at Halifax should be given to Canada without charge, a departure from the general principle of making self-governing colonies bear the cost of their defence. Four of these guns were for Montreal and two for Kingston.[81] Apart from the rearming of the First Battalion of Canadian Artillery and the 63rd and 66th Active Militia (who were to be employed with imperial troops on mobilization) with new Lee-Enfield rifles bought by Lake in England,[82] the acquisition of these six obsolete guns from Halifax was about all that the Canadian government did to strengthen its defences after the Venezuela excitement had died down.

Meanwhile the imperial naval base at Halifax was being rearmed, but here British policy was in process of revision and London was encountering difficulty in obtaining Canadian cooperation. Although American naval strength was increasing, the three new American battleships would have to be sent to Halifax for dry-docking because the United States had no facilities large enough for them on the Atlantic coast. This "humiliating" circumstance meant that in a war the U.S. Navy would be without the means to repair them.[83] Nevertheless, growing American naval power appeared to threaten that in the event of war the Royal Navy would lose local supremacy in the Western Atlantic. Hence British policy called for a distinction between defending Halifax against a "sudden raid" as against a "serious land attack," and ruled that the latter was most unlikely. To provide against the former, an increase in the covering field force was needed.[84] Here there were problems in getting the Canadian militia, part-time soldiers who made up much of its strength, to turn out for training. Furthermore the Canadian Militia Department was reluctant to agree to commit another battery of Canadian field artillery to the GOC of the Halifax fortress because one battery constituted one-eighteenth of the artillery strength of the whole Canadian militia which was now only one-third as large as the organized American regular army.[85]

On the other coast, the growth of Russian and American naval strength in the Pacific had made more urgent a settlement of the vexed question of arrangements for the defence of the Esquimalt naval base.[86] The Colonial Defence Committee said that Canada could not bear the whole cost; but the decision about how the cost should be shared depended on the amount required and whether defence was to be provided merely against one or two cruisers or to enable the naval base to resist a "determined American attack." The local militia was deficient in strength; the Canadian Permanent Force to reinforce Esquimalt was four thousand miles away in Quebec city; and the Canadian Pacific Railway would inevitably be cut in wartime.[87] In 1898, when Britain decided that Esquimalt need be defended only against raiding cruisers, the way was cleared for a settlement of the dispute with Canada about responsibility and cost-sharing.[88]

Developments regarding Esquimalt had not gone unnoticed in the United States. Lieutenant Rowan, the army's most experienced intelligence officer, had been sent to spy out the situation on the spot in 1897. As security measures prevented "unauthorized persons" from viewing the interior of the works, he looked them over surreptitiously from "coigns of advantage," rowed around them in a boat, and questioned the boatman and his hotel-keeper. He drafted and sent a preliminary report to avoid carrying incriminating notes. Rowan reported that the construction at Esquimalt was designed to protect the naval base rather than the nearby city of Victoria and that there were no plans to fortify Vancouver which, as the terminus of the CPR, was much more important. Three forts were being built at Esquimalt, well-sited to cover the harbour, and "splendidly constructed." Rowan could not learn the calibre of the guns that were being installed, but he knew that they were few in number. He was told that there were mines in store. However, Rowan said, as the planning had been done some years ago, Esquimalt's defences were already obsolescent. He believed that they would not prove formidable.[89] Three years later, in 1900, a navy intelligence officer confirmed Rowan's general conclusions and added the missing details concerning the ordnance. But he warned that Esquimalt was well planned strategically to be a base for naval operations against the American Pacific coast.[90]

In the intervening period the question of the future of the Rush-Bagot agreement had emerged as an important obstacle in the discussions of the Anglo-American High Commission which sat from August 23, 1898, to February 20, 1899, in an attempt to eliminate friction between Britain and the United States. This joint approach to the problems involved in a rapprochement had been made possible by the coincidence of Joseph Chamberlain's pro-American sympathies and the Anglophilism of the secretary of state, John Hay. Leading British statesmen had become increasingly aware of the potential hostility of European powers and of the danger of isolation. They sought to obtain American support to preserve the "Open Door" in China in order to protect British trading interests there, and at the same time to reduce the possibility that the United States might take advantage in North America or the Far East of British involvement elsewhere.

Hopes for success were greatly increased by a dramatic surge of popular feeling in the United States in 1898. Early in January of that year it had seemed unlikely that, with Gen. John W. Foster, the American negotiator, "a tricky lawyer playing into the hands of the Alaska Commercial company," it would be possible to get a settlement of the difficult dispute about pelagic sealing.[91] But by May Chamberlain's policy of benevolent neutrality in the war with Spain had produced what Ambassador Sir Julian Pauncefote called "the most astonishing . . . sudden transition . . . from Anglophobia to the most extraordinary affection for England." Pauncefote told Salisbury that they must seize the opportunity to "straighten out . . . our Canadian difficulties."[92] Chamberlain called this change in American opinion "an explosion" and foresaw "far-reaching and beneficent consequences . . . from a candid understanding between the two great branches of the Anglo-Saxon world."[93]

The issues that had to be resolved between Britain and the United States primarily involved Canada. Besides the Rush-Bagot question, they were pelagic sealing, the old Atlantic fisheries dispute, the location of the Alaskan boundary, and Canadian hopes for reciprocity. Under the chairmanship of a distinguished British lawyer, Lord Herschell, the other "British" delegates were all Canadians who were determined not to surrender their country's interests, especially as public opinion in Canada was strongly against concessions without adequate recompense.

Gen. E. T. H. Hutton, newly appointed GOC of the Canadian militia, had written to warn the earl of Minto before the latter came to take up his appointment as governor general, that no one in Canada believed in the *entente cordiale* with the United States. "It is pronounced bunkum."[94] After his arrival in Canada, Minto had advised the Prince of Wales that the negotiations in Washington were coming to an end without reaching fruitful compromises and that "the Canadian public is not inclined to profess rapturous affection for their cousins over the border." He said that Canadians did not understand British admiration for everything American. The Canadian delegates had found the Americans to be "hard bargainers." Minto pointed out that Canadians were in a much better position to know the United States than people at home. He commented that, while leading men in both countries saw the advantages of friendly understanding, "the general public of Canada . . . considers the proof of the pudding is in the eating."[95] Minto also informed Chamberlain that "the value of the goodwill of the United States had probably not made itself felt here beyond the leading men of the country";[96] but he told his brother that a rapprochement with the disliked and distrusted Yankees went "against the grain" with Canada's leaders as well as with the Canadian people.[97]

It is certain that some Canadians were still suspicious of American intentions. When the Anglo-American commissioners were about to meet, Colonel Denison told Laurier that to permit the Americans to use the canals to send warships to the sea was "madness." They would build the dockyards and arsenals on the Great Lakes and, when they wanted to commence hostilities, they would send warships down the canals timed to be at Montreal, "our most strategic point," at the outbreak of war.[98] American ships sent to the lakes to train a naval militia caused Denison further alarm.[99] But the Canadian government refused to establish the Canadian Naval Militia recommended by him, by General Hutton, and by Commander Spain, the commodore of the Canadian Fisheries Protective Fleet.[100] Thus while opposing concessions to facilitate an entente with the United States, Canada simultaneously rejected measures to strengthen her defences.

Hoping to capitalize on what they saw as Canadian fear and dislike of Americans, British officers concerned with the defence of Canada pushed for military reform. For over a decade Canadian Conservative governments had resisted or ignored appeals for the establishment of a defence committee, but Laurier had apparently agreed informally at the 1897 Colonial Conference to set one up. When he was slow to do so, Gen. Sir A. Montgomery-Moore, the GOC at Halifax, urged the need for action in November 1897 and again in January 1898. Moore pointed out that all nations were arming, "the Americans quite as much as others." He expressed the hope that concern for American susceptibilities would not prevent Canada from considering the question. European countries, he said, had schemes to protect themselves against their friends as well as against their enemies. He warned that the St. Lawrence frontier was wide open to either raids or an invasion in force. He said that the Canadian militia was not organized for war but was merely a mass of "men with muskets."[101] The Colonial Office also pushed for the creation of a committee to look into the defence of Canada.[102] In February the Canadian Privy Council gave its approval of a committee but asked that, as a vote in the House of Commons to provide funds might attract the attention of the United States, and as talk of mobilization plans might stir American jingoism, Britain should undertake to pay the members. Canada would provide travel expenses.[103]

Gascoigne had been selected chairman of this committee for Canadian defence but he resigned his post as GOC soon afterwards. His place on the committee was given as a special assignment to Maj.-Gen. Edward P. Leach, VC, the planner of Montreal's defences. Apart from two Canadian ministers whose presence was disliked by the Admiralty, all the members of the committee were British officers.[104]

The Leach Commission, as it was popularly called in Canada, assembled in August 1898, the same month as the Anglo-American High Commission in Washington. Great secrecy was to be observed. General Hutton suggested that to avoid an appearance of interference in Canadian affairs, the Leach committee should be called, "The Commission upon the Inter-Ocean Communications of Canada for Imperial Purposes and their Defence."[105] It was to be given out to the public that the Leach Commission was investigating the relations between colonial and imperial forces in carrying out agreements for "colonial military federation" made at the recent Colonial Conference.[106] This relationship was indeed the first point in the committee's terms of reference; but the committee was also instructed to examine local defences, to submit a detailed scheme for the defence of the Dominion, to report on the militia's organization for mobilization, and to suggest what more complete scheme of defence could be established, presumably with a permanent committee to keep it up-to-date.[107]

The Canadian Defence Committee of 1898 was in fact a one-shot investigation to explore the question of the defence of Canada against the United States. The first of a series of memoranda submitted to it suggests that this was what was really intended. Edward Francis Chapman, formerly director of military intelligence (1894–96), said that it was "practically acknowledged" that in the event of war the United States would attempt to annex Canada. He requested that the defence of certain Canadian cities should be emphasized by the War Office in order to strengthen the hands of the GOC in recommending to Ottawa what was needed to organize his command for war.[108] Chapman meant war with the United States.

From the first the Canadian Defence Committee acted as if it assumed that Canada's greatest danger was from the proximity of the United States. The Americans had now had experience of actual war in Cuba and the committee made an estimate of the rate at which an American force could be built up for the invasion of Canada. It noted that an estimate three years earlier had said that within a week there would be 3,000 American regulars and 2,000 militia available for raids. A month later the Americans could have 10,000 regulars and 20,000 militia in the field. After two months that militia force would have doubled. This could now be bettered.

The committee accepted the traditional assumption that an American attack would be thrown against Montreal. It declared that the American forts and barracks built on the direct Champlain–Richelieu route confirmed that this was the case. It assumed that the proper Canadian strategy should be an offensive-defensive and it discussed the problem of mobilization and deployment for that purpose. A most serious difficulty was that Canada had no officers trained to command and staff higher formations. These would have to be borrowed from Britain and might not arrive in time. But there would be jealousy if they took over from Canadian militia officers. Also, most seriously, the complete lack of a transport and supply system made effective mobilization impossible. Without these auxiliary services, and without reorganization and staffing for operational purposes, the militia was unfit to take the field either offensively or defensively. "Effective action by Canada in the early stages of a war [was] a matter of considerable doubt."[109]

The committee's report was kept secret by the Canadian government. Nevertheless its activity was widely known and some of its proposals were vigorously discussed behind the scenes. The governor general, concerned lest his ministers seek any excuse to avoid taking effective action, told Leach that he thought the Canadian public would not accept defence plans that did not cover Winnipeg.[110] Leach's reply was hardly reassuring. Winnipeg would be another "Mafeking" defended by local forces.[111] General Hutton criticized the committee's emplacement of guns for the defence of the St. Lawrence River and asked where the guns to defend Quebec were to come from.[112]

Hutton had worked in secret collusion with Leach in the preparation of the report. Fearing that it would be permanently shelved, he included in his own *Annual Report*, published in the Sessional Papers, a section on "Principles Governing the Defence of Canada," which stated the Leach report's general conclusions.[113] He believed that his opinions would carry more weight if it were made to appear that he had arrived quite independently at the same conclusions as the committee's. He therefore alleged that he had not seen the Leach report before he wrote his own,[114] a misstatement that Leach asked him to correct.[115] Chamberlain also feared that the Leach report would be suppressed. For a time he considered requesting the governor general "in a public despatch" to ask the Canadian ministers to publish it;[116] but he abandoned this impolitic attempt to force their hands.

Neither Hutton nor Chamberlain was apparently concerned that the publication of Canada's weaknesses might precipitate an American attack or strengthen the American diplomatic position at the bargaining table. Undoubtedly this was because they were motivated more by a desire to strengthen a weak part of the Empire than to protect Canada. The Leach Commission was one means of achieving this objective. With his customary tactlessness Hutton complained that the commission had not dealt with the question of Canada's contribution to the defence of the Empire.[117] He thus revealed what was undoubtedly his principal objective, which was also that of most of the British military establishment.

British efforts to persuade Canada to arm against the United States, pursued through the agency of the Leach Commission, had paradoxically coincided with the British attempt to reach an understanding with the United States on outstanding questions through the agency of the Anglo-American Commission. This was the first faltering step towards the diplomatic entente that was to be achieved by 1903 and was to lead to alliance in 1917. Already in 1898 there was ample evidence that in the two years that had passed since the Venezuela crisis the American mood, influenced by gratitude for the sympathy that Britain alone of all European powers had shown during the war with Spain, had switched from bellicosity to a desire for friendship.

Much of this evidence related to Canada. When Fenians and pro-Boer sympathizers tried to stir up trouble in the West, and when there were "outrages" at the Welland Canal and in Kingston where suspects were gaoled,[118] General Hutton, although he knew that the McKinley government would not tolerate such activities from American soil, had organized "flying columns" of militia cavalry to deal with them.[119] But the *New York Tribune* had asserted that incidents of this kind could now be safely left to the care of the American authorities, since there was no doubt that the attitude of the American government and of "thinking Americans," if not of a few extremists and the "ill-informed rabble," was pacifically inclined towards Canada.[120] The Spanish war had absorbed American imperialist urges and had diverted attention from the north. Northern garrisons had been stripped of troops for the war in Cuba.[121] Intelligence reconnaissance on the frontier (and into Canada) had declined.[122] When Hutton's Militia Report revealed Canada's weakness, this caused a mild sensation in the United States;[123] but it provoked no desire to take advantage of the situation. When a member of the House of Representatives noted that fortifications were being built at Esquimalt, he added that there was no need to fortify the American border.[124] The guns were not pointed to the United States.

With the American danger thus declining, the Leach Commission's emphasis upon it seems to have been deliberately calculated to play upon ancient Canadian fears. Canadians could be swayed because long memories of past American threats and invasions quickly aroused chauvinist reactions. At about this time the proposed lease of an historic Canadian fort, Fort Erie, by an American golf club was thought so sacrilegious that the proposal was referred to Prime Minister Laurier.[125] But Minto and Arthur Lee were received in friendly fashion by the army in the United States and were impressed by the quality of the troops they saw; and Lee noted that the toast "The Army and Navy" given at a great Anglo-American banquet in New York gave no indication which country's forces were meant.[126] When the 14th Battalion of the Canadian militia went with government approval to take part in Fourth-of-July celebrations in New York, the *Cana-*

dian Military Gazette found this "incomprehensible" and suggested sarcastically that next year the New York National Guard should be invited to fight the battle of Queenston Heights over again.[127] On the other hand, Lee believed that the more American and Canadian soldiers saw of each other, the better would be the prospect of peace.[128] However, many Canadians saw this as no reason for giving in to the United States on every issue. They regarded British willingness to make concessions as a threat to ancient imperial ties.

Canadian attitudes towards problems of defence against the United States were thus still confused and complex. Sir Louis Davies, the minister of fisheries, had served simultaneously on the Anglo-American Commission to reach a rapprochement with the United States and on the Leach Commission to plan for defence against an American attack. Minto noted that, despite their supposed American antipathies, Canadians "took full part in the Empire's manifestations of affection for the Great Republic."[129] The *Times* of London's correspondent noted that in 1900 it was possible for an American to visit Canada and never find a trace of ill-feeling or of contentious feeling;[130] but British officers had been able to exploit Canadian fear of the United States in order to develop Canadian military strength for imperial purposes.

The Venezuela crisis had in fact impressed British and American military opinion with the fact that the outcome of a war in North America would be very uncertain. On both sides advance planning and preparation, especially on the Great Lakes, had been seen by soldiers as a possible solution. But when no political and popular support for this was forthcoming, the prospect of war in North America became less attractive.

Meanwhile international tensions and complications elsewhere had diverted attention and had absorbed military energies. In 1899 the war in South Africa had much the same effect on Britain as the Spanish-American War had had on the United States. It demonstrated the need for military reform and development but at the same time it downgraded interest in, and the need for, preparation for the less likely, but more dangerous and difficult, North American hostilities. Hutton believed that a war in South Africa would serve Chamberlain's purposes of "unifying and consolidating the Empire more than any scheme of federation for co-operative movement that could be devised."[131] The emphasis on the American menace had become less necessary.

Canadians were slower than Britons and Americans to appreciate these trends because Canada was less affected by imperial rivalries outside the continent. Canadians continued to expect British support for their interests against American pressures and did not relate this support to changes in the strategic situation. The experience of the Venezuela crisis had not taught them that resistance to American demands depended on military strength. By a fortunate coincidence the Americans had also become less inclined to assert military pressure in the north. Hitherto Britain had provided in the background an umbrella which Canadians had taken for granted would shelter them in dire emergency. They had become accustomed to thinking of Canadian national development in its relation to the United States in economic and political, rather than military, terms.[132] When the umbrella was removed they must continue to bargain without a basis of military strength—the disparity with the United States was too great to be overcome. On the other hand, if Britain were no longer a potential enemy, the United States would have less reason to develop military force for use against Canada. Whether in the long run Canada would suffer was not clear then, and might never be.

6

Canada's dilemma
(1900–1907)

The surge of American good will for Britain that
was said to have been stimulated by gratitude
for benevolent neutrality in the war with Spain
did not last very long. In the last decade of the
century most signs pointed in the opposite direction, to a possible Anglo-American confrontation
caused by American ambitions that echoed the
growing imperialism of Europe. But some of
Britain's leaders had begun to realize that they
could not maintain unlimited global responsibilities indefinitely. The Venezuela crisis of
1895–96 may have indicated an area where re-
traction was possible with least injury to Britain's widespread strategic and commercial interests. Withdrawal from the Americas in face
of United States expansion in the Caribbean and
the Pacific could be made less unpalatable to
British voters by reference to kinship, and even
to a suggestion of an Anglo-American mission
"to save civilization." Hence, although their
American "cousins" signally failed to coordinate
policies in the Far East to preserve the "Open
Door" in China, the British persisted in diplomatic efforts to hold off a revival of traditional
American hostility. The price that had to be paid
was surrender to pressure for what had become
an urgent American need, agreement to an isthmian canal under American control. What Brit-

ain desired in exchange were concessions for Canada in the Alaskan border dispute.[1] All this had implications for Canadian-American military relations.

The Alaskan boundary question, now the most contentious issue between the two countries, stemmed from non-military concerns. Until gold was found in the Yukon in 1897, failure to agree on the location of the border between the Panhandle and British Columbia had been of little moment. Thereafter the dispute became inflammable. Where the boundary was eventually established might not only decide who possessed future gold discoveries, it could also affect access to the goldfields. As the dispute jeopardized law and order, and therefore threatened Canadian sovereignty, it involved defence measures.

Because it would decide access, the location of the border seemed the most vital matter for both sides. Fjords like the Lynn Canal cut deep into the mountains; ports lay far inland. As the coast had long been settled by American whalers and fishermen, the United States claimed all the existing ports by right of occupation. But the winter routes from the ports to all points on the Yukon river in Alaska lay through Canadian territory "with all that that implies." In 1898 and 1899 American officers were sent to open up an all-American sled trail.[2]

The location of the international boundary set down by the Anglo-Russian Treaty of 1825 was "the height of land"; but this was quite impossible to determine in such rugged terrain. Canadians hoped that a favorable interpretation, with the boundary following the general lines of the shore at a set distance, would give them the head of one or more of the fjords and an all-Canadian means of entry. This would enable them to overcome restrictive American coastal shipping regulations that impeded transportation through the ports. Although there was little talk about strategic implications, the military aspects of the access problem were implicit.

Unfortunately for Canadian aspirations, and largely because Britain's deteriorating international situation at the outset of the Boer War had made her somewhat dependent upon the United States, the mother country had now become less willing to support the Canadian case and had begun to press Canada to yield. Anglo-American negotiations for the settlement of the isthmian canal question, resumed early in 1900, led to the Hay-Pauncefote Treaty without obtaining the desired concessions for Canada.[3] The treaty provided for settlement by a Joint Commission.

The law and order issue in the gold fields had had military repercussions a little earlier. In 1898 Canada had had to send the Yukon Field

Force of volunteers from its miniscule militia to aid the civil authorities in keeping order. This operation, being very small, had been little more than a symbolic demonstration of Canada's military capability, though it incidentally backed Canadian territorial claims. Complaints persisted of disorder, or of possible preemptive action by Americans in Alaska to anticipate or thwart a settlement by diplomacy. In the Klondike Irish-Americans, Germans, and Russians were alleged to be at the bottom of trouble which was variously described as "almost a reign of terror" and a "conspiracy." Lord Minto told the foreign secretary, Lord Lansdowne, in June 1902, that hotheads anxious to capitalize politically on the undefined frontier might precipitate dangerous turbulence in an area where the population was "rough and mixed." [4]

American officers had dismissed such reports as a "Canadian fancy" that no one took seriously because they were disseminated for ulterior motives; [5] but Pauncefote, the British ambassador, notified Secretary of State Hay that the superintendent of police at Dawson had investigated and had discovered that "a conspiracy of the sort did in fact exist . . . [but] probably [one] conceived by the keepers of amusement halls and gambling houses solely for the purpose of making money." Although he admitted that "nobody of any standing or importance was associated" in it, the ambassador cautioned that there might be trouble when the ice broke up. [6] The United States therefore quietly moved a few more troops to southern Alaska "so as to be able promptly to prevent any disturbance along the disputed boundary line"; and a "discreet" American officer was sent to reconnoitre the border to find whether there were signs of either Canadian agression or improper action by Americans. This officer, Capt. W. P. Richardson, reported that he could find no signs of either. He declared that what Americans in the gold fields really resented was an "overzealous" Canadian customs officer. [7] Both governments cooperated in the movement of each other's police or troops for the preservation of order. Clearly both were anxious to avoid violence.

However, a permanent settlement of the border dispute had still to be worked out by diplomacy and arbitration. Canada, perhaps suspecting that an international commission with equal representation might decide against its case, was adamantly opposed to arbitration by a body so constituted. The situation had reached an impasse of the kind that often can be resolved only by resort to war. But as Britain was now courting the United States, there seemed to be less danger of that, even though the Alaskan boundary and other problems still profoundly disturbed Canadian-American relations.

Nevertheless in these first years of the new century the British War

Office vigorously stepped up its interest in Canadian defence. This was not so much because the military were lagging behind the politicians in thinking realistically about the improbability of an Anglo-American conflict, or because they looked to war for the settlement of outstanding differences. It was merely because Britain now had better facilities for contingency war planning. Furthermore, British intelligence had learned what the United States had intended to do during the 1896 Venezuela crisis if war seemed likely. Capt. Cecil B. Levita of the Royal Artillery had talked with Senator Redfield Proctor, the former American secretary of state for war whom he described as "a fairly shrewd old gentleman." Not knowing that Levita was a British officer, Proctor had spoken of American determination "this time to wipe Europe off the face of the continent," and he had leaked details of plans made during the crisis. He said that the United States would have seized the canals and that this might have been done simultaneously with a declaration of war. Three American columns would then have cut rail communications, one operating from Maine, a second against Medicine Hat, and the third, the main thrust, by way of the Great Lakes and canals in the centre. These attacks, made by regulars, would have been designed to offset the landing of British troops in Halifax and Esquimalt until such time as mobilization gave the United States the advantage of numbers. Levita thought this information accurate; and Col. Percy Lake, the British quartermaster-general of the Canadian militia, advised him to send it to Maj. Edward A. Altham, DAAG in the Military Intelligence Division in London.[8]

With information of this nature about recent American planning for war, British military authorities would have been negligent in their duty if they had not investigated the defence situation in North America. In 1901 a staff officer in intelligence at the War Office, Capt. W. R. R. Robertson (the future field-marshal and CIGS during the First World War), prepared a long appraisal of the problem of defending Canada. He outlined strategic planning since 1846 and analysed developments that had occurred since the Leach Commission reported in 1898. Robertson recalled that Leach had indicated the need for an offensive strategy; but he noted that the improvements in the Canadian militia necessary for such a strategy had not yet been made. He pointed out that the tactical information required for operating across the American border was still lacking: Canada's intelligence officers were only part-time militia officers unequal to the task. Robertson then gave details from Col. Hubert Foster's reports of 1895 and 1897. He said that Foster had proposed a two-corps invasion of the United States Atlantic coast. Nothing that Foster's plans had been submitted to the Admiralty, Robertson said that no response had been received until the present year. Naval Intelligence had replied that since Foster wrote events (they meant the growth of the American Navy) had "completely altered the conditions and every day which passes tends to accentuate this change." The Admiralty declared that comment on Foster's proposals was now pointless.

Col. Herbert A. Lawrence, a DAAG, who sent Robertson's report on to the director of military intelligence, agreed with Robertson that it would not be possible to launch an offensive from Canada at the outset of a war. Planning for one depended on promise of naval support. He believed that although a British occupation of a part of the United States would not necessarily upset other parts of that country, it would have less effect than dislocation of American overseas trade by the Royal Navy. Returning to the prospects for an offensive, Lawrence said that an imperial army sent to Canada to be in action within two months of the outbreak of war would need the cooperation of the Canadian militia. Its best invasion route would be by the Lake Champlain route to the manufacturing towns of Springfield, New Haven, and Hartford. The progress of American mobilization would then determine whether other offensive operations were also possible, e.g. against Buffalo, Detroit, and Cleveland. However, like Robertson before him, Lawrence repeated Ardagh's dictum of 1897 that a war on the American continent was the most hazardous enterprise in which the Empire could be driven to engage.[9]

The War Office then took new steps to bring its intelligence information from Canada up-to-date. Lt.-Col. Charles V. Townshend of the Royal Fusiliers reconnoitred the border. He reported that Canada would have to adopt a defensive posture; but he believed that, as in 1812–14, it could be an "active defence." He assumed that the Americans would invade as they had done in 1775 and in the War of 1812. Canada's great extent would then provide opportunities for the non-Active Militia, whom Townshend described as "patriots armed with rifles." He was apparently proposing guerrilla warfare. But Townshend threw little light on the way in which the position had changed since 1898, except to suggest the need for minor tactical revisions in the disposition of defence forces in front of Montreal. He did indicate one thing, however, that could be an impediment: Canadians might be too interested in commerce to fight to defend their country. Furthermore he had found that as a result of the South African War they distrusted British officers. French-Canadians were inclined to be over-confident, saying, "We beat the Americans before and we can do it again," and were therefore unwilling to prepare.[10] Townshend thus called attention to what was to be a growing problem in planning for defence. The traditional concept that defence preparation was needed against the United States had ever-decreasing credibility in Canada. War Office planning for the defence of Canada rested on unreliable foundations.

Capt. J. Aylmer Haldane, who brought the War Office's plans for the defence of Canada up-to-date in March 1902 and, as a lieutenant-colonel, revised them again in January 1903, developed this reasoning further. In a paper headed "Military policy in a war with the United States" he began by taking the line that early boldness on land could lead to disaster, but that naval supremacy could permit the dispatch of three army corps to Canada. While noting a widely held belief that the weakness of republics lay in their constitutions and that democracy is proverbially unstable, and admitting that no democratic government could carry on for long a war that "entailed sacrifices on every member of the community" unless it had popular support, he nevertheless argued that the loss of any part of the United States would be intolerable to Americans. The capture of towns would not shatter morale in the United States. Instead it would arouse American ire and spirit. On the other hand the loss of Canada to the British Empire, "though a heavy blow would not mean national ruin or disgrace."

Haldane's suggestive opinions, perhaps inspired by Townshend's report, were supported by Capt. Arthur Lee and Col. G. C. Kitson, successive military attachés in the United States who had both served at the Royal Military College of Canada and who both knew the Dominion well. They believed that, once aroused, the Americans "would never stop." Haldane said that war in North America would probably mean the loss of Canada. He therefore recommended that the thrust of the attack in any conflict should be a naval assault on American trade.[11] British army authorities were thus coming to accept the impossibility of saving Canada in a war with the United States.

Certain aspects of the changing global strategic situation, and British adjustment to it, also affected the problem of defending Canada. Redeployment of the British imperial forces overseas was greatly facilitated by the formal setting up of the Committee of Imperial Defence in 1904, completing a reorganization of the cabinet's defence committee begun in 1902. Although it lacked executive authority to compel service obedience, the CID provided the first really effective forum for professional discussion of Britain's worldwide strategy, a permanent secretariat to initiate investigation, and direct access to the seat of power, the cabinet.[12]

In the first years of its existence the new committee took up, among many other problems, the effect of the growth of American naval capability on the retention of imperial naval bases in North America, maintained in the belief that they were essential for the exercise of sea power. The War Office had recently spent large sums on the improvement of Halifax's defences. An overland attack was considered unlikely or impossible and the theory was that Halifax should be defensible against sea-borne raids. For this it would need the cooperation of the Canadian militia. However, it was now known that American planning in 1896 had ignored Halifax. Furthermore, when asked in 1903 for an opinion, the Admiralty had admitted that in a war with the United States the fleet would have to be withdrawn from the Western Atlantic if European powers were unfriendly. It seemed that Halifax was "of minor importance."

This cast an entirely new light on the problem of defending the base. Despite Admiralty protests, the War Office had always acted on the assumption that the presence of fleets would deter or frustrate attacks on naval bases. If there were to be no fleet there, Halifax would be less secure as well as less necessary. The base would be needed, and could be used, in a war with a European power, but only if the United States were neutral or friendly. As it was asserted that the port was now of greater value to Canada than to the Empire as a whole, the CID, on December 11, 1903, when Frederick Borden, the Canadian minister of militia happened to be present, proposed the withdrawal of the British garrison. Eventually this step was completed even though the Canadian militia was not yet ready to defend the base unaided.[13]

The CID had assumed that Canada would continue to maintain Halifax in a state fit to withstand a fleet including battleships and also, for a considerable time, an enemy who had landed in the vicinity.[14] But, unless the Royal Navy lost control of European waters, only the United States could launch such an attack. In the years that followed, Canada's garrison did not have the strength to meet that test. The new military facilities that had been built by the imperial garrison between 1901 and 1906 were not developed after the British left. The outer forts were used only for summer militia training, and the dockyard had become "a place of rust and ghosts."[15] Perhaps Borden's interest in taking over the base had been its potential for patronage. The step had enormous incidental consequences for Canada's Permanent Force. But Canada's neglect of the base, although it had several causes, is clear evidence that the prospect of a war with the United States was not a sufficient incentive to get Canadians to build up Halifax's defensive capability.

Esquimalt, on the Pacific coast, was dealt with at the same time. In

1902 Colonel Lawrence, the DAQMG, had listed the overwhelming land forces that the United States would be able to send against the Pacific base; and the Admiralty stated it could see no reason to revise the Carnarvon Commission's conclusion in 1882 that the base could not be defended against the United States. Esquimalt had been established as an imperial naval base because of Russian naval ambitions in the Pacific. After the Anglo-Japanese Treaty of 1902 it was less needed. The defeat of the Russian fleet in 1904 confirmed this. As there was no longer any reason for maintaining a base in the North Pacific, the navy wanted to spend no more funds on it.[16]

As a result of these opinions and developments, the arrangement between Britain and Canada for the loan of British garrison troops at Canada's expense was terminated. A continuing Canadian concern about a "Yellow Peril," as much as the deep-seated, but unfounded, Canadian belief, never contradicted by Britain, that Esquimalt was a defence against American attacks, caused Canada to take the base over and maintain it after the British left.[17] Esquimalt was, however, very much weaker than Halifax. Canada's decision to take it on while at the same time failing to maintain the Atlantic fortress at full strength shows something of the dichotomy of Canadian thinking about defence in general and the American threat in particular.

Despite the great global strategic revolution of which these changes were a part, which obviously affected the defence of Canada as a whole, the War Office was slow to abandon responsibility for the defence of the Dominion against any foreign assault, including one by the United States.[18] But with responsible government Britain had no effective means of ensuring that Canada would fulfil its end of the bargain of 1865, the maintenance of an effective militia. The only means by which this might have been secured was through the agency of the British general officer commanding the Canadian militia. But the GOC was responsible to the minister of militia and to the Canadian cabinet, which, in the eyes of the War Office, was inclined to shirk its responsibilities. Colonial Office officials pointed out that the GOC could only achieve results if he had the support of the Canadian people and if they were convinced of the need. Vigorous GOCs like Major-Generals Herbert and Hutton had therefore been tempted to appeal directly to the Canadian people, thus contravening their own constitutional subordination to the Canadian government. Most British GOCs of the Canadian militia had come into conflict with their political masters over this issue, and Major-General Hutton had been forced out.[19] History repeated itself when one of his successors, Lord Dundonald, who had been a popular commander of colonial forces in South Africa, attempted to expose the Canadian government's failure to carry out reforms recommended by the Leach Commission. Sir Frederick Borden's determination to make it possible for a Canadian to succeed Dundonald was not entirely due to the behaviour that had culminated in Dundonald's dismissal, but that was a contributing cause.

Dundonald, like many British officers, was still preaching that defence against the United States was the primary reason for a Canadian militia.[20] But the new Militia Council ruled in 1905 that the first duty of the militia was "support of the civil power." Defence against a foreign power was placed second.[21] Sir John Anderson, undersecretary in the Colonial Office, discussing the Dundonald incident and the Militia Bill, talked of the "extinction" of Canada in the event of a war with the United States, and incidentally revealed what had become Britain's real interest in regard to a Canadian militia. If war with the United States were left out of consideration, Canada was invulnerable. Therefore, said Anderson, "We need not trouble ourselves about their internal defence [that is to say, within North America] except in so far as we may legitimately look to them for material assistance in a European War."[22] The wording of the 1904 Militia Act had in fact quietly made possible overseas use of the militia by changing words which had been assumed to imply use in hot pursuit into the United States "within or without Canada . . . by reason of war, invasion, or insurrection" into the more general phrase "beyond Canada, for the defence thereof."[23] On the other hand, Minto asked Sir George Clarke, secretary of the Committee of Imperial Defence, to avoid any reference to the employment of Canadian troops outside Canada, apart from individual officers, "because it at once puts up the backs of the people in high places."[24] British officials thus tacitly admitted that the chief purpose of the Canadian militia was to help to defend the Empire elsewhere. But this was not yet politically acceptable in Canada.

However, some British officers continued to assert that, because of their obligation to defend Canada against the United States, they not only had a moral right to know the militia's condition, but also to investigate the problems of fighting a war in North America. In 1903 the British General Staff had directed Lt.-Col. G. M. Kirkpatrick, an engineer officer who was DAQMG of the British garrison at Halifax, to survey the situation. Kirkpatrick was a Canadian by birth and a graduate of the Royal Military College of Canada who had made his career in the British Army. In 1904 he produced a report on the defence of Canada that ran to 109 printed pages.

Starting from the premise that the growth of the American army and navy had completely altered the strategic situation since the

Leach report of 1898, Kirkpatrick examined tactical problems on the border, section by section. As in most previous defence studies the stress was on the need for naval control of the Great Lakes and the St. Lawrence. He noted that new canals north of the river had improved Canada's position but that the building of the international bridge at Cornwall in 1898 had provided the United States with the opportunity of seizing a bridgehead across the river. Kirkpatrick said that the completion of the Great Northern Railway in 1901 had given direct contact from Quebec to the West and this could be maintained even if Montreal were lost; but west of the lakes the CPR was vulnerable. Canadian prairie farmers, unable to export, might be prepared to make terms with the enemy. Kirkpatrick also argued that the American railway system was capable of handling the movement of troops for mobilization but that the Canadian railway system would be strained. Referring to an opinion expressed by the "Director" of the American War College in annual lectures, that a winter campaign would be America's best opportunity, Kirkpatrick argued that only small raids, and not a major invasion, were possible at that time of the year. Finally, stressing the need for a professional Canadian intelligence system, he contended that American immigration into Canada was dangerous to Canadian security and that Americans employed on the railways should therefore be compelled to take an oath of allegiance or be replaced by Canadians. "The fewer Americans employed in peace time the better."[25]

At the War Office, Lt.-Col. Charles E. Callwell, DAQMG in the Mobilization Branch, who was later to become well known for his writings on strategy, had also prepared a revised study of the defence of Canada; but he had held it back until Kirkpatrick's report was received. When he submitted his paper to Maj.-Gen. J. M. Grierson, director of military intelligence, in October 1904, Callwell stated that Kirkpatrick had not considered the broad strategic principles involved. Callwell asserted that in a "fight to a finish . . . we should lose Canada" because the Canadians were incapable of defending themselves for more than a few weeks. Any military force that could be sent from the United Kingdom might defend important points for a time but would eventually be overborne by weight of numbers. So even if the Royal Navy retained command of the sea, Canada could be lost. Callwell then went on to discuss the likely course of operations in the event that war came. He stressed that Britain should avoid arousing the American people so as to make them believe that their honour was involved. Strategy should concentrate on the attack on American

trade. He thought that operations in the Maritime provinces were unlikely but that the prairie provinces and British Columbia were indefensible. However, if the main points in "Canada proper," Toronto,
Montreal, and Quebec, could be held, a balance might be struck, but
this would depend on quick naval action to seize the lakes. Callwell
volunteered his opinion that the threat of bombardment of lake cities
might perhaps bring the United States to make terms.[26]

Despite Callwell's desperate clutch at the old determination to seize
the initiative against the United States, it is clear that by 1904 the
British military establishment had come to accept that in the event of
war with the United States operations in Canada would be defensive,
and that even in those circumstances Canadian participation might be
doubtful. There were, however, some Canadians who differed from
this appraisal. Col. Sam Hughes, the future Conservative minister of
militia, had been given a special post as railway intelligence officer, in
order to maintain his connection with the militia and at the same time
keep him under control. He was described by Dundonald as "eccentric
and extravagant" but a "good officer."[27] Hughes prepared a paper on
the defence of Canada which proposed a major invasion of the United
States thrusting from Sackets Harbor to Portland, Me. He sent his
paper to Leopold Amery, a journalist and future British cabinet minister and it came to the knowledge of Lt.-Gen. Neville Lyttelton, chief of
the Imperial General Staff, who declared it quite impractical.[28]

More impressive was a British opinion, that of Lt.-Col. Hubert Foster, who argued that the big danger was an American surprise attack.
Foster said that an invasion would be aimed at Montreal, the historic
objective, and that by the end of the year the United States would
have 400,000 men in the field and would greatly outnumber her opponents. He argued that Canadians must depend on themselves for defence, but he declared that "a vigorous resistance in the first year
would disappoint the invader and possibly tire him out." Foster admitted that the morale of the American soldier was high, and that the
training of the West Pointer was excellent, but he rated Canadians as
"hardier" than Americans. He suggested that there was a useful lesson in the Civil War: "In fierceness of patriotism and determination to
succeed in a desperately overmatched struggle, Canada should at least
equal the South and, with the assistance that the mother country is
pledged to give her, there is no reason why she should not successfully
resist the invasion." Discussing the various theatres of war along the
border, he was optimistic that an attack could be contained. Yet it is
noticeable that Foster, like other British officers, now talked only of

defensive operations in Canada.[29] He no longer recommended the invasions launched from the sea and from Ontario that seem to have been the main thrust of his lost reports of 1895 and 1897.

At the end of 1904 the British Imperial General Staff was of the opinion that a successful invasion of Canada would be an imperial disaster of the first magnitude and that defence of the country was a far more difficult problem than the protection of India. This warning was contained in a memorandum for the CID in which it was also noted that "war in North America is less likely than war in Central Asia." The memorandum asserted, "There can be no offensive campaign by Canadian forces" and, at least during the early months of the war, "it would be fought on Canadian soil." The War Office had long thought that the key to holding Lake Ontario, which was vital, was naval action, but "unless we get the start of them with fighting ships actually ready and in commission . . . our opponents must beat us at that game." The British General Staff therefore decided to ask the CID for a ruling on the action the navy should take.[30]

Three months later Maj. Hugh B. Williams, RE, of the intelligence staff, reported on the military resources of the United States. Commenting on this report, Colonel Robertson said that it was known that American commanders along the border had been ordered to study the terrain and to report to the chief of staff on plans for mobilization and concentration for an invasion of Canada. He said that "recently" a member of the U.S. General Staff had lectured at the War College on "the Military Geography of Canada." "Moreover we have good evidence that special reconnaissances have been made across the Canadian frontier." He went on, "It is not pretended that these proceedings indicate any aggressive design, but they do nevertheless show that war with Great Britain is considered by the [American] authorities to be sufficiently probable to merit preparations for it."[31] War Office concern to learn what the navy would do was thus being justified by fear of an American attack.

With the renewal of the War Office's long-standing advocacy of precautionary action to secure the Great Lakes, the Admiralty's position was at last made quite clear. True to his reputation for plain speaking, Admiral Sir John Fisher, first sea lord, asserted that the Royal Navy could not defend the lakes or do more than prevent a major enemy invasion fleet from entering the Gulf of St. Lawrence. He added that to station submarines or other small craft at Halifax in excess of local defence requirements, which had been proposed, would arouse the suspicions of the United States. However, the CID held that Canada must still be reassured that Britain would not withdraw its pledge of support for defence. It said that to fail to do this would be tantamount to dismissing Canada from the Empire. Therefore the Imperial General Staff decided to look for other means of obtaining the necessary naval support on the Great Lakes, and it talked of asking Canada to assume the responsibility.

The Admiralty urged instead that Canada should contribute to the Royal Navy; but the Imperial General Staff now made a surprising statement that contradicted the view generally held about Canadian backwardness in defence. It said that Canada contributed more to its own defence relatively than did any other colony and Canadians should therefore not be asked to subsidize the navy. Indeed, the Dominion should be discouraged from doing so and should be invited to devote all its defence funds to the improvement of its military organization and to the development of its preparations for war on land.

The weakness in this proposal, which must really have been directed towards obtaining Canadian help in a major war, was that at the same time the General Staff was still implying that defence was needed against the United States, and in Canada this was no longer very persuasive. The chancellor of the exchequer, Austen Chamberlain, raised another objection. Although he looked forward to the time when colonies would have their own naval forces, he disliked the General Staff's suggestions because they seemed to imply that colonies should be urged to look only to their own defence.[32] Nevertheless, at the end of 1905 the CID's decisions, including the promise of British succour, were conveyed to Canada along with recommendations that Canada should organize a naval militia and should also make plans to destroy the Welland Canal in the event of war.[33]

Having failed to get a promise of naval support, either on the Great Lakes or even for the defence of Halifax, Lt.-Gen. Sir Neville C. Lyttelton, CIGS, may have recalled Balfour's reminder at a CID meeting that Canada had a right to the support of the whole resources of the Empire. No doubt Lyttelton was also of the opinion that a guarantee of defence could help to get reciprocal aid from Canada. In January 1906 he repeated the suspicion that American military preparations had been made with a view to a possible conflict with Britain. A month later Lt.-Col. Callwell reiterated that the problem of defending Canada was one the General Staff must keep in mind "unless a conflict between the United States and the British Empire be looked upon as an impossible contingency."[34]

The extent to which British intelligence officers and the Imperial General Staff continued to investigate the problem of defending Canada against the United States at a time when détente was in the air may now seem remarkable. But such planning must not be written off as "the lunatic fringe of official documents" or as "airy nonsense."[35] These reports, which took the form of appraisals of the situation rather than of specific mobilization or operational plans, were not simply a part of training nor were they mere "doodling" or "five-finger exercises." Representing only a small portion of the work of some of the best minds in the British army, they were sensible assessments of contingency military measures that might be called for if the unexpected happened. While the navy could never forgive Canada for refusing to contribute to the fleet, British soldiers felt unable to write the Dominion off so easily because they were aware of Canada's potential as a source of manpower.

The Imperial General Staff had returned to the old frustrating task of attempting to persuade Canadians to fill in the gaps in their own defences. But in so doing it may have helped to foster, if only in official circles in Britain, a realization that, if the navy could not take effective action against the United States by launching an invasion from the Atlantic or by destroying American sea-borne trade and coastal cities, Canada could not be defended by the British army. In that case the Dominion might prefer to think in terms of securing an accommodation with the United States by non-military means. It might therefore fail to develop the land forces that could help Britain in a major war elsewhere. Accordingly, after the Admiralty have given it up, the War Office persisted in talking of the defence of Canada. The soldiers thus helped to stress the folly of a war in North America. But they also had a realistic understanding that Canada's defence preparations had other possibilities than for war with the United States.

The War Office's concern about protecting Canada was not a view held by the military alone. The Foreign Office also still took the question of Canadian defence seriously. In 1905 and 1906 it printed for private circulation a *Military Report on the Northern Frontier of the United States*. This had been prepared by the Imperial General Staff, so that publication by the Foreign Office was an endorsement of the military view. It was comprised of four regional reports of a very comprehensive nature. They included information about the available armed forces, about terrain, about means of communication, and even such minor tactical details as was conveyed by photographs of bridges. Part II, which dealt with the Great Lakes, noted that "few Englishmen who have not visited Canada and the United States can estimate the vast commercial development which has taken place—but this development furnishes the strength and the weakness of the northern states." Industrial development in an area where military concerns had not been important had led to the growth of great American cities which, in time of war, would make heavy demands on the government for their defence.[36]

In his annual report on the United States in 1906, Sir H. M. Durand, the British ambassador, assessed the qualities of American political and military leaders and their disposition towards Britain. He was of the opinion that some issues like the fisheries question might still make the United States as aggressive and uncompromising as it had always been. He noted significantly that American coast defences were elaborate but that there were not enough men to man them.[37] Durand had made conscious efforts to improve Anglo-American relations but, partly because President Theodore Roosevelt had not wanted him to be appointed, and partly because the ambassador was rigid in advocating British and Canadian interests, he was not too successful. His report is, however, a useful reminder that some British diplomats, like some British soldiers, were not yet completely confident that war was out of the question.

In January 1908 an anonymous Foreign Office paper on Anglo-American relations asserted that there was evidence that the United States government wanted to come to a definite settlement and that the outlook for Anglo-American amity was more favourable than it had been since the Declaration of Independence. But the paper then went on to list issues that were still outstanding in 1907. It stated that the outlook along the frontier, the greatest source of friction, was more favourable than at any time since the War of Independence. This paper concluded that every effort should be made to convey to Americans the idea that a war between the two nations would be "little less than fratricidal" and that together the British and American navies could maintain exclusive possession of the oceans. The Foreign Office's approach to the situation in North America, while taking into account the possibility of war, was thus directed towards advocating the need for an Anglo-American entente.[38]

British intelligence reports that the Americans were still investigating the problems of fighting a war with Britain in North America were quite correct. Gen. Nelson A. Miles, commanding general of the United States Army, made public references to the indefensibility of Canada that were a reminder that Anglo-American friendship was far from secure.[39] The reform of the American military and naval services after the Spanish-American War had led to an improved capacity for war planning somewhat similar to that which had developed in Britain. Elihu Root's reorganization of the army and of its educational system, begun in 1901, had produced, among other things, the Army War College.[40] This institution continued to show the interest in Canada that had been developed earlier by the Military Information Division to whose files and reports it had access. On March 24, 1903, it added to its collection of information about Canada an invasion plan made by Brig.-Gen. Leonard Wood,[41] a former governor of Cuba and future chief of staff of the U.S. Army, who had just returned from visiting European military headquarters. On June 13 the War College also collected surveyor-general's maps of Canada from the Military Information Division.[42] In November the new Third Division of the General Staff reported that it had been considering the strategical problems of Canada;[43] on February 4, 1904, the college filed information for use in the preparation of a plan for the invasion of Canada;[44] and in April the Military Information Division received a new batch of publications and maps from the consul-general in Ottawa.[45] Only one month after the first War College course began in 1904, it took up the disposition of Canadian troops from Lake Nipissing to the Pacific Ocean, and also operations on the Canadian frontier from Sault Ste. Marie to the Rockies, "with provisions for guarding Detroit and Sault. Ste. Marie."[46]

There have been differing interpretations of the precise purpose of this American War College planning. Masland and Radway state that after the passage of the Army Reorganization Act of 1903 and the creation of the General Staff, the college became primarily an educational institution; but they add that, in association with the General Staff, it continued to engage in planning activities up to the First World War.[47] This assessment tends to under-rate the role of the college. When it opened in 1903 the Army War College had no students. Its president, Gen. Tasker Bliss, who had served as the army member of the Naval War College's Directing Staff in 1885–88 and had also paid recent official visits to European staff colleges, was well acquainted with current practice in war gaming and war planning. He and Secretary of State Elihu Root both thought of the college in the sense of the old meaning of *collegium*, a group of men working together with the object of doing something rather than merely of learning to do it.[48]

Because the development of a General Staff was feared by politicians, the War College was the army's only planning agency in 1903. Even after courses for students began in 1904, the college continued to work in close cooperation with the Third Division of the General Staff, created in that year, which soon became primarily involved in mobilization planning built upon the strategic analyses made by the War College as well as in the division.[49] The fact that the War College was deeply involved in the planning function was to be confirmed in 1911 when the Third Division of the General Staff was renamed "The War College Division." [50]

The United States now had more effective machinery for studying and planning war. There was even an attempt to coordinate planning by the army and navy. In the last years of the nineteenth century the U.S. Navy had been ahead in war planning activity, but had then merely collected charts and data on areas of strategic importance. In 1904, after the creation of the General Staff, its chief, Lt.-Gen. A. R. Chafee, suggested that the new Joint Board of the Army and Navy should work with the two services to prepare plans for war with specific countries, each country to be assigned a distinctive color by which the plan would be known. This did not lead, as is sometimes believed, to the production of a complete set of "color plans" for every conceivable or inconceivable occasion. The strategic analyses made by the Joint Board, the General Staff, and the War Colleges varied in their nature in accordance with the degree of expectation and of difficulty of a war with the country concerned. [51] The Army War College's interest in Canada, even though it produced something less than a complete set of operational plans, was something more than an academic exercise.

How far did this American war planning affect national policy? Richard Challener, examining this question, pointed to difficulty in giving an answer because of the episodic nature of the involvement of the American military in policy making, because of the paucity of materials, and because of the belated development of institutions for the coordination of military thought and political decisions. However, Challener concluded that by 1900 Anglo-American rapprochement had reached the stage where Britain had virtually ceased to be an enemy. He noted that Anglophilia was especially rampant among American service officers. War with Britain was regarded officially at the Army War College as the "least possible of all conflicts." But he noted as well that American officers were quick to point out that Canada was a hostage for British good behaviour and could be compensation for losses suffered at British hands elsewhere. Planning for an invasion of Canada, therefore, although not the chief preoccupation of the American General Staff and the Army War College, made good sense. But Challener also showed that professional soldiers and sailors were deliberately "kept down" by American politicians, and that the professional input into policy making was small. [52]

Military input into political decision-making usually produces greater preparations for defence. But it does not necessarily do so. It can also caution against unwise involvement in situations that might lead to defeat. The CID had established a more effective relationship between Britain's military and political leaders and thereby weakened belief in the need to prepare for war against the United States. In Canada the case was different but the results were similar. The 1904 Militia Act, by opening the command of the militia to Canadians, had further reduced the dwindling influence of professional British officers on Canadian political decisions. At the same time it had served to entrench the minister of militia's control of defence policy and also that of the cabinet. British military advice, tendered through the Imperial Conferences, the Committee of Imperial Defence, the Colonial Office, and the Imperial General Staff and its representatives in Canada, was henceforward suspected to be directed towards British rather than Canadian interests. The natural inclinations of Canadian politicians to avoid expenditure on expensive military development was therefore not merely unchecked but was in fact enhanced.

Politicians are responsive to public opinion. On matters like the need for defence preparations there are always several conflicting points of view. There is no monolithic public opinion, just many separate opinions. Modern computing techniques can be used to assess the strength of various attitudes and hence their influence on policy. But without the statistics on which such computations can be based it is necessary to attempt to evaluate popular influence by other means.

In North America defence questions and military matters found little place in legislative debates, in public speeches, and in newspapers and periodicals. Lack of evidence in the form of discussion of military problems in the press and on public platforms is in itself suggestive of public unconcern about military affairs. In Canada debates in the House of Commons on militia matters had rarely touched upon the basic question of the purpose for which a militia was needed. Arguments in favour of a contribution to Imperial Defence, or based upon a suspected American threat, had in the past been advanced to justify expenditure on a citizen force which militia colonels wanted for reasons that were not necessarily very closely connected with the security of the country. However, in Canada, perhaps even more than in the United States, in view of the lack of military input in decision making, defence policy was likely to be proportionately more affected by popular sentiment. As some British intelligence officers had noted, many Canadians had taken little interest in defence questions, especially in defence against the United States. The rapid defence expansion which came after 1904, unmatched until the 1950s, may therefore be assumed to have been due to realism in Canada about the overseas situation, a disposition that had never existed while the supposed enemy was the United States.

The discussions about war in North America which have been outlined thus far in this chapter were restricted to confidential memoranda. Canadians and Americans were completely unaware of the extent of professional military contingency war planning. Occasionally references to the reconnaissances appeared in the Canadian press, but usually without comment. Lack of comment may indicate a public refusal to take the obsessions of soldiers seriously. On one occasion it was suggested that public knowledge of military activity could be dangerous or disadvantageous. Lord Dundonald, reporting to Minto about alleged American spying on the St. Lawrence, complained that Colonel Townshend's reconnaissance in 1902 had "done harm" because his mission was "trumpeted about." The GOC said that it would be known in the United States, Townshend having crossed the border several times. Dundonald said that he had had his "own man" doing "good work" over there several times without attracting attention.[53] However, as there is no other evidence of public reaction to Townshend's work, the GOC may have merely been motivated by dislike for War Office interference in his command. The public on both sides of the line seems to have been undisturbed.

On the other hand, Americans and Canadians were well aware of the current reform and expansion of their military forces. The doubling of the Canadian militia to enable it to take over the garrison at Halifax was enacted in Parliament. When the American army retained its wartime strength after the war with Spain, the increases were approved by Congress. Congress was also informed of the work on Atlantic and Pacific sea-coast fortifications, of the trend towards larger army posts away from urban centres, and of the increase of troop concentrations in the Northwest. This last development was justified in 1902 with the aid of a letter and a report written in 1894 by Brig.-Gen. E. S. Otis who then commanded the Department of the Columbia. It was also supported by two letters from the Seattle Chamber of Commerce, one of them undated. The chamber reasoned as follows:

> There is every reason why a strong infantry force should be stationed on Puget Sound for both international and domestic reasons. The proximity of the Canadian boundary, only a few hours distant by either rail or water, renders this a peculiarly suitable place to station a large enough force to at least hold in even balance that maintained in British Columbia. It has been the policy of the Government to cover the Canadian border with a chain of military posts, of which Fort Lawton is the one farthest west, and being the terminus it should be one of the strongest,

especially as at no point on the line this side of Detroit has Canada such a concentrated population and available military strength as about Victoria and Vancouver, B.C.

This rationale for American military deployment, based on an exaggeration of the strength of forces in Canada, was accompanied by stress on the need to preserve law and order and on the need for a Western depot for possible expeditionary forces for either Alaska or the Far East.[54] Reports to Congress in favour of western defence measures made no reference to what must have been an even more important motive, the desire to take precautions lest Canada's military weakness enable some other power to use British Columbia as a base for attacking the United States.

There appears to have been no contemporary criticism of these questionable justifications for military development in 1902 which cited outdated arguments based on inaccurate reports of British strength in Western Canada. One can only assume that this was because the American people were now more ready to accept an expansion of their armed forces to suit the nation's new world status. References to Canada, like other explanations, were rationalizations repeating old concepts. Not that military budgets were passed unanimously, for opposition on grounds of the need for economy continued in the United States as in Canada. But as it was accepted that there was less fear of war in North America, from that point of view the public in both countries was paradoxically less afraid of an inevitable, though it was hoped small, military expansion to match in some way the growth of military strength throughout the world. Diminution of the fear of war between Canada and the United States had not meant abandoning military development. It had made it more possible.

The possibility of war in North America had in fact lost much of its force as a pretext for military preparation. Albert K. Weinberg, in his study of Manifest Destiny, showed that at the turn of the century American interest in Canada, which he called "a first love," "rose from a flicker to a high flame," but that it was aimed at absorption by nonviolent means. Many Americans regarded reciprocity with Canada in trade as a potential source of profit, and some believed that political union would follow. Weinberg considered this to be a new trend in American opinion caused by disillusionment with overseas imperialism and by belief in the political affinity of the two North American countries. He quoted Champ Clark, the Democratic house leader, Canadian-born Dr. Jacob Schurman of Cornell, Andrew Carnegie, John R. Dos Passos, and numerous others, to show the strength of the belief in Anglo-Saxonism and in the peaceful achievement of continental union.[55]

As has been shown in an earlier chapter, the American belief that Canada need not be conquered because eventually it would attach itself voluntarily to the United States was not new. This concept had a long history. What was different after 1900 was that disillusionment with the brief American flirtation with imperialist conquest of overseas alien peoples had revived the old dream of expansion to the north. There were fewer voices than in the past calling for military action to speed political union, yet occasional references were still made to the possible use of force.[56] Theodore Roosevelt, who was said to be holding back a demand for a settlement of the Alaskan problem while Britain was involved in South Africa, was quoted by Senator Henry Cabot Lodge as having told him and another "very conservative senator" that, in case of a "row" in the disputed territory, he would at once order American troops to occupy it and hoist the American flag. Lodge informed Colonel Kitson that that "very conservative senator" had replied, "If you will say so from the steps of the White House, Mr. President, you will have the next nomination for President by acclamation." Kitson warned Minto that a "row" could easily be staged.[57]

It has never been clear whether Roosevelt was bluffing when he hinted that he might take the big stick to Canada. No doubt some ethnic groups in the United States would have supported him in a militant policy. But in general American opinion was now less likely to countenance war than had previously been the case. The Toronto journal, *Saturday Night*, noting the revival of American discussion of annexation, said, "Force is rarely thought of as a means of obtaining our consent." Talk in the United States was said to assume that American capitalists, and American immigrants to Canada, "will give body to annexation sentiment when the time is ripe to coax us woolly natives into the fold of Uncle Sam." The article added, "the matter really does not need discussion, as it is not causing the slightest alarm."[58]

One reason for the decline of Canadian fear of war was that the American menace seemed to have become that more subtle danger, peaceful absorption. In this regard, a Canadian writing anonymously in the *Saturday Review* of London thought American immigration into Canada dangerous and pernicious;[59] and J. A. Macdonnell, a Glengarry correspondent writing in the *Montreal Gazette*, agreed.[60] Other Canadian papers took a somewhat different, but equally pacific, line. One said that French-Canadian immigration had infiltrated into the United States large numbers of Canadians who by and large wanted to return to Quebec to spend their money, Americanization had broken down. It added that the influx of Americans in Canada could be offset by immigration from the United Kingdom.[61] The imperialist *Montreal Star* alleged that a French-Canadian journal, *La Verité* (the platform of Jules Tardivel, most extreme of Quebec nationalists and well-known for anti-Americanism) had plumped for union with the United States because "annexation means peace" while imperalism could drag Canada into war. The *Star* countered that Canada would probably be formed into one American state and one territory and, although French influence in that state would counter-balance the English influence, French influence in Washington would be swamped and would amount to nothing.[62] Henri Bourassa, advocate of French-Canadian interests within the federal structure, argued that Canada had always maintained a sufficient force to preserve order and prevent aggression. English-speaking critics denied this.[63]

The governor general, Lord Minto, who carefully collected these expressions of contemporary Canadian opinion, reassured a Canadian MP in 1902 that American capital and immigration could be beneficial. He suggested that the influx of capital and people might not serve to Americanize sympathies in Canada. "Possibly the business men, and the immigrants from over the frontier, may succumb to Canadian influences, happier legislation, and freedom from the great difficulties that the United States will have to face." But he added that it was impossible to say what would happen.[64] However, in writing privately to his brother he was less sanguine. Developing the theme that Canada had met "nothing but sharp practice" from the United States, he said that he had many American friends but he believed the best of them would say that "[American] friendship is absolutely unreliable." There were influences at work across the border that were "full of danger as regards our continued possession of Canada."[65]

It was part of Minto's duty to report to the Colonial Office on Canadian attitudes. When not bemused by his own imperialist aspirations, the governor general was frankly puzzled by the complexity of the strands of opinion in Canada revealed in these disturbing assessments of American intentions and influence. But when he could shake himself free from his fear of the American challenge to Britain's imperial position, Minto apparently anticipated a peaceful future for North America and the absorption of American and other immigrants into an autonomous Canada.

The Canadian government had to attempt to ensure that Canadian interests were effectively represented in negotiations with the United States about all outstanding issues, including Alaska; and it now had to do this in conditions that were new because there could no longer be a comfortable reliance on British military support to facilitate dealing from strength. For, just as the British had begun to realize that Canadians might shy away from war with the United States in imperial disputes, so Canadians now knew that Britain could not fight the United States for Canadian interests. New techniques had to be worked out.

Canada's formal relations with the United States were still conducted through the Foreign Office and the British ambassador in Washington, but communications to the latter sometimes went direct from the Canadian government through the governor general. Long before formal and permanent Canadian representation in Washington was possible, Laurier carried on some discussions with American leaders through an intermediary. Edward Farrer, his agent, was a retired journalist. In 1891 Farrer had composed an article on political union and had planned to publish it in the United States in the name of a friend. A stolen copy had been used effectively by Sir John Macdonald against the Liberals. Farrer, who thus had Liberal connections and American sympathies, was on close terms with Senator Lodge and may have known Secretary of State Hay personally. The British were opposed to Farrer's activity in Washington, on the ground that he might make statements to the Americans that differed from the position taken by their ambassador. They claimed that he was causing delay in the settlement of the Alaskan dispute.[66] Lord Lansdowne labelled Farrer "an able but dangerous person, not fit to be in a confidential position in Laurier's office." What the British obviously feared was that Farrer might jeopardize Britain's imperial interests.

Farrer was supposed to have abandoned his extreme views on political union, but in 1903 he published another article entitled "Canada and the New Imperialism" in which he advanced views held by Goldwin Smith, the high priest of Canadian continentalism.[67] Laurier was, of course, not sympathetic to the idea of political union with the United States, but he must have found Farrer, who leaned in that direction, useful in gaining access to American leaders. Farrer was indeed able to report back to Laurier that the Americans had liked the stand the prime minister took against Imperial Defence at the Colonial Conference of 1902; but he does not seem to have achieved much towards Laurier's ultimate objective, a modification of the American position on the Alaskan issue.[68]

Laurier's use of Farrer shows that the balance in the North Atlantic triangle was rapidly changing. In 1902 the *Toronto Globe* recalled that Richard Cobden had once said to a friend that the only serious danger between the United States and Canada arose from the connection of

Canada with England. The *Globe* editor said that that had indeed been the position during the American Civil War. But he noted that conditions had changed since Cobden's day. "The only serious danger of a quarrel between the United States and England now arises from England's tie to Canada."[69] He could have added that as the shattering impact of a war would fall on Canada any Canadian government would want to avoid it. Britain could now do little to help, Canada must now more than ever before look for policies in time of peace that would maintain her interests without resorting to force.

However, in addition to the Alaskan boundary question, a number of issues that in another place or age might have been a cause of war, continued to cloud Canadian-American relations. Anglo-American harmony was being nourished by references to common interests and ideologies, and many Americans, including some who had championed Irish nationalism, sympathized with Britain over the illness that had delayed the coronation of Edward VII.[70] Canadian-American relations, however, were deteriorating, according to the *Springfield Republican*. As reported by the *Globe*, the American newspaper had said that Canadians were friendly to Americans as individuals but regarded their nation "as a huge political and social organism whose first law is supreme selfishness and from whom Canada can hope for no kindly consideration whatever."[71] Canadian antipathy toward the United States had recently been inflamed by tariff issues.[72] It was alleged that as a result (so Minto told the Prince of Wales) the ordinary Canadian "hates a Yankee as he does the devil!"[73] This was the atmosphere in Canada when the Alaskan question was nearing its climax. Canadians were very disturbed. They would have been more disturbed had they known that Roosevelt had warned Kitson, the British attaché, that "he feared he would have to get nasty about it."[74]

But Laurier had probably long realized that he would eventually have to accept arbitration by a panel with parity of American and British representation, and at the Colonial Conference in 1902 he may have agreed to do so.[75] If so, he was slow to tell his colleagues because the Canadian public was bitterly opposed to arbitration on those terms. Minto reported in October that there was a point beyond which public opinion would not let Laurier go.[76]

Despite promises that the Alaskan Boundary Commission would be judicial in nature, Roosevelt made appointments to it that were frankly partisan. Lord Alverstone, the British lord chief justice and leader of the British-Canadian delegation, accepted American arguments and ruled against his Canadian colleagues. Subsequently Minto complained that the Canadian commissioners had rushed to publicize what they claimed was a political, rather than a judicial, decision that had sold Canada's rights in return for American friendship for Britain. Although international legal specialists have tended to agree that in law the Americans had the better case, Canadians believed that they had been defrauded. There was a revival of the debate about the merits of reciprocity, annexation, and independence which had seemed dormant for some time. Yet Minto was still convinced that the Canadian people were infinitely more devoted to the mother country than was their government. "They lose their tempers over Alaska, know their growing strength, and talk of setting up for themselves, but it is simply the hot-headedness of youth which I am sure could be controlled and directed."[77] Minto's imperial bias is evident in this opinion. What was closer to the truth, and more important, was that some Canadians, including Sir Wilfrid Laurier, had come to realize that, having lost British protection and backing, Canada must in future look after her own relations with the United States.[78]

Some also believed that the Alaskan settlement had potentially dangerous military implications. A. B. Aylesworth and Sir Louis Jetté, the Canadian members of the tribunal, bitter about their defeat, spread the word that Port Simpson, the proposed Pacific terminus of the northern Grand Trunk Railway from Alberta, would be commanded by guns which the Americans could mount on two of the islands granted them by the award, Kannaghunut and Sitklan. Lord Dundonald, the GOC, and Col. Hubert Foster, the military attaché in Washington, were instructed to look the situation over. Foster's trip was blocked by Minto, but Borden, the militia minister, eventually agreed to receive Dundonald's report. This confirmed what British naval and military intelligence had declared, that the islands were strategically unimportant.[79] Furthermore, the *Canadian Military Gazette*, which had thought the Canadian case for the Lynn Canal was weak, and which had rejoiced that the award had at least removed a dangerous source of international tension, asked why Washington would want to fortify the islands. It pointed out that they were dominated by Pearse and Wales Islands which were still in Canadian hands.[80] Nevertheless, Laurier, taking no chances despite the advice of the military, ordered that the terminus be removed to a less vulnerable location. It was eventually established at Prince Rupert.[81]

The Alaskan decision also caused Laurier much concern about American intentions in other directions. Press reports alleged that Senator Henry Cabot Lodge, a member of the Alaska Boundary Commission and one of the president's closest advisers on foreign policy, had revealed that the United States had proposed to acquire from

France the islands of St. Pierre and Miquelon in the Gulf of St. Lawrence. Laurier told Minto that he thought that Lodge had been misrepresented; and the governor general later found that the statement had in fact been attributed to "a crank named McGraw or McGrath." But he informed the Colonial Office that Laurier was in fact really worried, not merely about American intentions in those islands, but also about American plans for expansion in Hudson Bay, in the Arctic, and in Newfoundland. The prime minister feared that there was an "evident American wish to acquire further territory in the North American continent." He believed that they could set up and occupy posts in the Arctic for some years without anyone knowing it and that they could then claim possession by right of settlement. He had therefore sent expeditions north and had arranged to levy customs duties on American traders there.

Questioned by Minto, Laurier admitted that he thought the Americans might be planning to take Newfoundland, and that he therefore intended to reopen negotiations with Newfoundland about confederation with Canada.[82] Laurier confessed that he considered the grasping nature of American policy with regards to territorial acquisition to be dangerous, "not immediately so, but decidedly dangerous." Yet he did not fear that the policy of appeasement, through reciprocity, Canada's alternative to Chamberlain's imperial preference, would lead to continental union.[83] No doubt Laurier's pessimism about American expansion, if Minto reported him correctly, was inspired by the recent shattering decision about Alaska and by the nature of American claims there. These developments were sufficient to suggest to him that Canada might be faced with more American territorial demands in the near future.

Laurier was thus faced with a very difficult question. Now that Britain could no longer threaten the Americans or, in the last resort, come to defend Canada, how could the Canadian government cope with American pressures? An answer to that question would have been easier if a reliable assessment of American public opinion could have been made. But public opinion is always difficult to determine and was particularly so in this instance. By and large the American people, their political leaders, and the media, when not striking a pose, seemed more concerned with trade expansion and peaceful relations, and they appeared to pay little attention to military questions. But this might be misleading. Public opinion is notoriously fickle.

The reaction of the American military press, which could be assumed to be more knowledgeable about military matters and perhaps more inclined to strong measures, is informative. The American *Army and Navy Journal* was in many ways the equivalent of the *Canadian Military Gazette*. It catered both to part-time and to regular service personnel, the proportion of the latter being greater in the United States. The *Journal* was accustomed to express views on military policy. Its columns show that its American military correspondents were quite taken by surprise, apparently genuinely, by Canadian anguish and anger over the Alaskan award.

Eighteen days after the formal announcement of the commission's decision on October 20, 1903, when the Canadian House of Commons was debating appropriations, Col. Sam Hughes had stated that during the Venezuela crisis Washington had asked the governors of the border states how many men could be mobilized for the invasion of Canada. He declared that Canada was saved from the horrors of invasion only because fifty thousand Americans could not be put in the field in two weeks. The *Army and Navy Journal* ridiculed Hughes's excessive charges. It was able to point out that the United States would not have needed fifty thousand men to launch an attack on Canada and that Hughes's statement therefore "curiously illustrated the touchiness of our neighbours across the border on questions affecting their relations with the United States."[84]

Later the *Journal* commented on Canadian plans for the development of the militia in the new bill and also on Canadian complaints about American plans for a new naval training station on the Great Lakes. It declared that if Canadians ever wanted to establish naval training stations they would find the American government more kindly disposed.[85] The *Journal* remarked that some Canadians had an inferiority complex, that they pretended that Americans were the worst enemies, and that they were continually suspecting "republican" designs on their territory. It noted the allegation of the *Toronto Evening Telegram* that Americans had magnified their own military feats by claiming that other people's victories, for instance those of the Japanese against Russia, were the work of "American lieutenants who were directing Tojo's fleet while on holidays." the *Journal* believed that all "broad-minded Americans would regret such exhibitions of childish petulance on the part of their Canadian neighbors" and went on, "Canada is doing well in a material way, there is no reason for their discontent."

The *Journal* also showed that on the other side of the border some Canadians had taken up a position very similar to its own.[86] The *Toronto Globe* had complained about the tendency of some Canadian "carpet knights" to brag when visiting New York during the Military Tournament. "One bare-legged hero gravely informed his audience

. . . that in 25 years Canada would exceed the United States in population as it now does in area." As reported in the *Army and Navy Journal*, the *Globe* said that such behaviour might one day lead to consequences that no sane man, even if he is a "veteran" and a "hero," can fail to see might be unpleasant.[87]

The *Journal* was also amused by the *Ottawa Citizen*'s fear that American warships on the Great Lakes could only be designed for the invasion of Canada. "It indicates an unneighbourly disposition to take offence where no offence is intended and this causes needless friction in our relations." By contrast the *Journal* asserted that the United States approved of military improvements in Canada.[88] At a later date the *Journal* reiterated that the Canadian Militia Act's reforms would be met with sympathy and approval in the United States.[89] The American military establishment thus implied, probably sincerely, that it could see no reason for the Canadian suspicion that the United States' new strength would be turned against Canada.

But the Canadian government did not react in the way the American military journalists apparently feared it might. Although most Canadians believed, with some anger, that they had been defrauded by the International Tribunal, their government, while apprehensive about future American territorial ambitions, turned not to force, which could have been counterproductive, but to the idea of managing its own foreign relations by peaceful means, a procedure that Minto had once declared was impossible as long as the Dominion depended ultimately upon the strength of Great Britain.[90] This new policy Laurier implemented by means of the International Waterways Commission of 1905, by the creation of the Department of External Affairs in 1909, and by the International Joint Commission set up by Canada and the United States in that same year.

The Laurier government's reaction may have been partly inspired by the traditional pro-American sentiment in the Liberal party (which the *Globe* had long expressed), and also by its incipient pacifism. But in fact no other course could have been followed realistically in face of the superior American military potential. Sections of Canadian opinion had for some time been moving to the realization that military strength was no longer available to defend their interests in their relations with the United States.

In 1902 Henry J. Morgan, one of the founders of the Canada First movement, had written to ask whether Laurier had seen the statement by the governor general, Lord Lansdowne, who had said that he hoped Canada would never be a military nation like the European powers because that would be a curse.[91] There was indeed no enthusiasm, even among the militia, for competition in arms with the United States. Surveying Canadian newspapers before the Alaskan award, the *Canadian Military Gazette* noted that the *Vancouver Province* had asked, "How are the people of Canada, with a population of six millions, to provide any adequate defence for a frontier of 4,000 miles? It would be utterly impossible even for a populous and rich country like the United States to safeguard a boundary of such dimensions." The *Province* had concluded, somewhat vaguely, that in Canada the best defence consisted in the loyal devotion of her children.[92]

After the British election of 1906 the *Montreal Daily Herald* gave full coverage to a speech by Sydney Fisher, minister of agriculture in Laurier's cabinet, who had argued that militarism does not make nations great. In the same place it referred to Leopold Amery's assertion that Canada's greatest contribution to Imperial Defence would be to build up its own population. The *Herald* went on, "In Canada, for the Empire's sake as well as our own, let us build up our population; spend our substance on such administrative works as will draw settlers; and conduce to their prosperity as Canadian citizens, and therefore as good citizens of the Empire."[93]

The year after the Alaska award had fuelled Canadian anger at being let down by Britain in face of American pressures and threats, the editor of the *Canadian Annual Review* reported that during the past twelve months there had been a marked growth in friendly relations with the United States. He stated that there was now an utter absence of the old-line discussion of the annexation idea.[94] He also quoted Charles W. Fairbanks, vice-president of the United States, who, noting that there were neither fortifications or warships along the Canadian-American border, had declared that they were not needed. It apparently did not seem ominous to the editor that Fairbanks went on to say that American policy was the spread of commercial control and that conquest would be achieved by men of trade not men of war. This, said the American sententiously, was "an inevitable law of commercial gravity."[95]

It was becoming understood in some quarters in Canada that what Cartier had preached when he introduced the first Militia Bill in 1868, that every state needs military strength at its own disposal, did not have relevance only to the possible attack of a particular enemy. Imperial Defence theorists had always taught that Canadian military strength was a contribution to the general strength and well-being of the Empire. Admiral Sir Archibald Lucius Douglas, the Canadian-born commander-in-chief of the Royal Navy's West Indian and North

American stations, criticized certain members of the Committee of Imperial Defence for being superficial in their attitude to Canada's failure to contribute to the Royal Navy. Departing from the customary naval position, he told Minto, "the fact that we could not possibly defend Halifax and Esquimalt against the United States does not seem sufficient reason for dropping suddenly the military education of a young colony or for relinquishing Imperial power or influence when it can still be useful to them and creditable to ourselves." Douglas may have been better able to see Canada's point of view because of his Canadian background.[96]

Similar views were being expressed in Canada. Commenting on proposals made by Raymond Préfontaine, minister of marine, for the creation of a Canadian naval militia, the *Toronto World*, although it claimed somewhat questionably that "rational Canadians know that Canada is no freer from invasion than any other country in the world," then went on to say with greater power of conviction, "Every other nation of consequence has an army and navy. For Canadians to assert the doctrine that we have no need of land and naval forces is to practically declare that every other nation in the world is a fool and that we alone are wise. The conception is absurd on the face of it, and has been put forward as an excuse for failure to perform an obvious national duty."[97] The *World* apparently did not take Canada's assumption of a larger voice in Canadian-American affairs, with less reliance on the backing of its position by British or Canadian armed strength, to mean that Canada could be free of the responsibility of bearing arms. However, the means by which Canada could build up military and naval strength to protect its interests in a world where the danger of war was increasing had to be disentangled from the lingering traditional belief that Canadian military preparations were needed only to meet a possible American invasion.

Meanwhile in the United States an important influence was at work to reinforce the growing conviction that preparation for a war in North America was unnecessary. From early in the nineteenth century pacifist movements had flourished in the Republic. One of the most influential of these was promoted by two brothers, Albert K. and David Smiley, Quakers who from around the time of the Venezuela crisis in 1895, had organized annual conferences with an invited membership at their vacation resort at Lake Mohonk, New York.[98] The Smileys' objective was the promotion of arbitration instead of force in international relations and they were thinking particularly of the current situation in Europe. Although the International High Commission of 1898 was noted as an example of peaceful settlement, no Canadians attended until 1905. In that year John Murray Clark, KC, a member of the Toronto bar, was one of the speakers. Clark said that the Rush-Bagot agreement accounted for naval limitation on the Canadian-American boundary but "as regards the land boundary, the matter is governed by the good sense and justice of two great peoples."[99] In the following year Boards of Trade and Manufacturers' Associations in Canada as far west as Winnipeg were represented at Lake Mohonk.[100] Shortly afterwards a Canadian Peace Organization was founded with Sir William Mulock as its president.[101] In 1908 Clark Olds of the Erie Chamber of Commerce spoke at Mohonk about "The Lessons of the Great Lakes."[102] A year later John Murray Clark drew attention to Mulock and a "brilliant young protégé of President Eliot of Harvard," William Lyon Mackenzie King, who were using conciliation effectively in labor disputes.[103] In 1909, the year when the International Joint Commission was established, the Lake Mohonk Conference in effect discovered the Canadian-American practice of peaceful settlement of disputes as the best example of its tenets.[104] The conferees then proceeded to plan for celebration of the centenary of the Treaty of Ghent in 1914. They made contact with many interested organizations in both the United States and Canada in order to provide appropriate forms of commemoration.[105]

Meanwhile Mackenzie King, Henri Bourassa, and Hon. W. R. Riddell, the Ontario legal historian, all spoke at various times at Lake Mohonk about Canada's experience and views on domestic and international arbitration.[106] Although the Lake Mohonk conferences were relatively small affairs, the idea that war between Canada and the United States was now unthinkable was carried far and wide in both countries by the promotion of plans for the celebration of "a century of peace."[107]

7

Lingering Confrontation
(1908–1917)

By 1908 a watershed had been passed in Anglo-American relations and in trends in official attitudes towards the problem of the defence of Canada. The War Office's long-sustained effort to find a way to guarantee the security of Canada against an American attack had finally succumbed to the Admiralty's evasion of that difficult problem. It was now accepted that a British guarantee was not possible. This admission had been in part responsible for bringing about a new analysis of British foreign policy in which the United States was cast in the role of potential friend rather than potential enemy.[1]

In Canada, in the early twentieth century, as a Canadian military historian has said, "the possibility of conflict with the United States was receding more and more into the limbo of forgotten things."[2] Nevertheless, despite this diplomatic entente, or the approximation thereto, and despite declining fear of invasion, some aspects of the problem of defending Canada against the United States were examined in the years immediately preceding the First World War.

In Britain some members of the Imperial General Staff, although admitting that relations with the United States were now good, worried about the security of Halifax in Canadian hands because they still looked upon it as the port through which reinforcements would have to pass to help to defend Canada in the event of a war with the United States. Because Naval Intelligence had said that it might be six months before naval reinforcements could go to Canada, Maj. A. H. Grant of the Directorate of Works, when commenting on the Halifax Defence Scheme in 1908, said that it might be a year before British troops could get there. As a result, at the outset of a war the United States might attempt to seize the port. He considered that it was imprudent to limit planning to defence against a possible attack by 15,000 men, or to build hopes on the "fears of the ignorant [in the United States] for the safety of Boston and Portland." Grant believed that, because of the growth of the U.S. Navy, the American populace was losing its fear of bombardment.[3]

In response to these representations, the CID's review of the Halifax Defence Scheme in that year repeated that an overland attack was unlikely, and it supplied detailed reasons. It also asserted that Halifax would probably be only a secondary objective in the early days of the war. But it agreed that if the Royal Navy gained control of the Western Atlantic the United States would then want to sever communications between Britain and Canada through the port, and in those circumstances a land attack would be possible. However, the review shelved further discussion of that question by saying that that problem would have to be considered in connection with the defence of Canada generally, a problem that it did not take up.[4]

A year later the CID declared that if Bermuda fell in a war with the United States, Halifax would be the only British base in those waters and the only terminus for landing reinforcements when the St. Lawrence was icebound. But it again said that the port would probably only be a secondary objective in the early stages of a war. It added that the United States might want to eliminate the port as a base for the Royal Navy, either before the fleet could reach it, or during possible temporary absences; and it was also possible that the U.S. Navy would resort to torpedo raids. But it said that these efforts would be hazardous at a distance of three hundred miles from American bases.[5] In 1910, as a result of these considerations, the CID's Halifax Defence Scheme included a long discussion of the effectiveness of a naval bombardment of a naval base; but it repeated the previous conclusion that the base in Canada would not be so attacked.[6]

Although the Royal Navy had retained the right to use the repair facilities in Halifax, and although it had been said at the outset of negotiations for the handover that the Admiralty should be able to "resume possession at any time when naval interests require it,"

British orders in council in 1910 concerning the final transfer said nothing about resumption by Britain in the event of war.[7] Nevertheless, even after that date the British Committee of Imperial Defence maintained its Halifax Defence Scheme which was still chiefly concerned with the possibility that the port might have to be defended against the United States. In 1912 a possible American attack was again discussed and it was once again urged that Canada's assumption of responsibility for defence of the base had increased the need for the British to take precautions because it was the port where reinforcements for Canada would disembark; and the CID admitted that the United States might attempt to capture Halifax because of its strategic importance "to us," which appears to mean to Britain rather than to Canada.[8]

The problem came up yet again in 1913 when the Imperial General Staff indicated that it considered Canadian defence measures inadequate because the militia could not reinforce the garrison in Halifax soon enough to be of assistance in the event of an American attack. Maj. S. H. Wilson, secretary of the Overseas Defence Committee (formerly the Colonial Defence Committee), a future permanent undersecretary in the Colonial Office, asked whether, in view of the remoteness of the contingency, Canada should still be urged to prepare for an American attack; but he confessed that he was not one of those who believed that the possibility could be entirely ignored. "In my mind it is conceivable that we might be forced to go to war with the United States, however inconvenient it might be for us to do so, and however hopeless it might be to expect a successful issue to a campaign." Wilson warned that to tell Canada now that a war with the United States should not be taken into consideration would raise questions about past advice and would slow the present defence build-up.[9]

British military planning up to the outbreak of war in 1914, even though pressed by far weightier matters arising from the growing German menace, had thus continued to be concerned with the defence of Halifax against an unlikely American attack. The planners appeared to have been less worried about the defence of Halifax in a European war, perhaps because they thought that Canada could take care of that; and it is a strange reflection on the perspicacity of men who tried to examine every possibility, however unlikely, that the members of the CID apparently did not anticipate the use to which Halifax was put in 1914, as a port of embarkation of Canadian troops and supplies to reinforce Britain in Europe.

On the Pacific coast, the fact that an American attack was unlikely did, however, restrict planning. Esquimalt was no longer classed as a defended base.[10] Even though the dockyard remained in British hands until 1910, the CID gave it little individual attention after the withdrawal of British troops from its garrison. But the establishment of the Pacific terminal for the new northern transcontinental railway at Prince Rupert caused the Canadian government to ask about areas that should be reserved for military purposes. In reply the Colonial Defence Committee of the CID stated that, "In view of the remoteness of the contingency of a war with the United States, the scale of attack that could be brought to bear by that power has not been taken into consideration."[11] When the CID began to discuss the scale of attack that could be expected in the Pacific, Sir Edward Grey, the foreign secretary, intervened to say that there should be no reference to the Anglo-Japanese Treaty or to its possible termination, and that discussion should be limited to the possible scale of attack on Prince Rupert.[12] Esquimalt, closer to the American border, was not considered at all, even in connection with attack by any other power than the United States.

Despite the improvement of Anglo-American relations, British planning in these years was also concerned about some aspects of the defence of Canada as a whole. In response to questions put to the CID by the British General Staff in 1905, the Admiralty had refused to consider operating on the Great Lakes. The 75th meeting on July 13 had then decided against making advance commitments to operate within Canada against the United States. Nevertheless, the Imperial General Staff brought the matter up again on January 17, 1908. Maj. A. Grant Duff, DQMG, suggested that, as British relations with the United States might deteriorate in the future over the Anglo-Japanese alliance, St. Pierre and Miquelon, or Panama, and in view of the continuing imperial obligation to defend Canada, Britain had a right to demand that the Dominion take steps to ensure her own defence. Duff and General Staff Col. E. Callwell both thought that those steps should include preparations for an offensive. "We should punish the United States to the uttermost before she has time to turn on us, which she may not in the end decide to do."[13]

The CID, however, noted that "no request had been received from Canada since 1904 for an expression of opinion on this subject." Hence, because of the decision taken in 1905, Lord Morley, secretary of state for India, objected to the question being raised. The CID thereupon rejected a proposal to discuss action to be taken in the interior of North America in the event of a war with the United States, on the grounds that, apart from the remoteness of the contingency, it was impossible to defend the long frontier. It added that this matter should also not be discussed because Sir Wilfrid Laurier was "opposed to taking any special measures for defence against the United States." The committee was, however, in agreement that it might have to consider the implications of the termination of the Rush-Bagot agreement because that was a question on which Canada might request an opinion.[14]

Laurier, sensitive about naval matters in view of the current debate about the policy of creating a Canadian navy as opposed to contributing to the Royal Navy, did not raise the question of warships on the Great Lakes until 1911, when Robert Borden, leader of the opposition, drew his attention publicly to reports that the United States was planning naval manoeuvres, including a "sort of bombardment" of Chicago where a fortified naval training school was said to be in process of construction at Lake Bluff for the training and drilling of naval militia. Laurier did not make a formal submission to the CID for advice; instead he directed personal enquiries to Lord Bryce, the British ambassador in Washington. He complained to Bryce that the proposed naval armaments were a contravention of the spirit of the 1817 convention. Bryce advised the foreign secretary, Sir Edward Grey, that Laurier considered the question important because it would arouse sentiments hostile to the United States, adversely affect trade negotiations then in progress, and tend to confirm the fears of annexation held by persons indisposed to more friendly relations.

After making enquiries, Bryce reported that the U.S. secretary of the navy, George Von L. Meyer, had assured him that the reports were spread by individuals trying to organize a land boom in North Chicago and were false; and he had also given Bryce details of American ships and naval training establishments on the lakes which he said were virtually unarmed. Laurier was not satisfied with this answer. He said that the naval authorities in Washington seemed to wash their hands of what was happening on Lake Michigan, and he feared that the Canadian public, if it became alarmed, would demand the raising of its own naval militia on the lakes. As a result, the American navy secretary agreed to cancel the assembly of what he said was "the usual yearly naval review on the Lakes"; and President Taft told Bryce personally that he hoped nothing would be done to perturb Canadians or to give newspapers opportunities to make mischief. Laurier now declared himself content; and Bryce concluded his report to Grey by hoping that such reviews would not be held in future even though they were valuable to the United States for recruiting purposes because, "absurd as it may appear," they caused apprehension in Canada since

they occurred at a time when the summer resorts on the shores of the
Great Lakes were crowded and there was little else to occupy public
attention.[15]

The Rush-Bagot question was raised yet again in 1912 in an exchange of letters between the private secretaries of the governor general and the colonial secretary. Laurier had apparently felt that the
position which he had taken on reciprocity in trade with the United
States had given him a special pull in Washington. He had believed
that a revision of the agreement for arms limitation to bring it up to
date with modern needs and developments might now be possible. The
British colonial secretary, Lewis Harcourt, had been prepared to follow this up: replacement of a treaty that had been repeatedly broken
as it suited both sides in the course of the past ninety-four years
seemed on the surface to be a sensible move; and it might make naval
training schemes and shipbuilding possible under conditions that
neither country would consider dangerous.

However, any talk of the building up of American naval strength in
what one British official called "the bowels of Canada" invariably provided ammunition for local politicians to use against the government.
Furthermore, the British found that Canadians were "strangely
touchy" about American maritime force on the lakes although they
would not take measures to protect their ocean ports from similar dangers. When Robert Borden's government rejected reciprocity in 1912,
the possibility of a revision of the Rush-Bagot agreement receded. The
secretary of the duke of Connaught, the governor general, consulted
Sydney Fisher, former Liberal minister of agriculture, about the matter. Fisher advised that it was best to leave things as they were. With
all its faults, the historic convention still had some value as a brake on
American ship-building and any attempt to revise it seemed likely to
do more harm than good to Canadian interests.[16]

It must be stressed that, with increasing clouds of war in Europe,
these discussions arising out of the CID's vestigial interest in defending Canada were a very small part of its activities. Amidst many other
problems resulting from increasing tension in Europe, British contingency planning had continued to consider the defence of the old imperial naval base at Halifax against the United States, but had been
diverted from considering the defence of Canada as a whole because
the Canadian government was anxious not to disturb relations with the
Americans. The possibility of a revision of the Rush-Bagot agreement
had been brought up chiefly because it was thought that happier relations with the United States might now make a more practical agreement possible. However that possibility had been thwarted by the fact

that there was still enough left of the traditional Canadian fear of the United States to make the issue one that Canadian politicians could exploit. Furthermore, the agreement had become a popular symbol of unusual harmony between two independent neighbours and it was thought better to avoid tinkering with it, despite its imperfections, lest discussion of the matter lead to its termination.

Less inhibited by the Anglo-American rapprochement, American military authorities had continued to consider the problem of fighting a war against Canada. In 1906 Capt. Samuel Curtis Vestal lectured at the Staff College at Leavenworth. Inspired no doubt by recent proposals for the reform of the Canadian Militia, he said that this force had hitherto been regarded with contempt by the United States Army because of its small numbers and lack of training; but he warned that it had certain advantages that had been overlooked. It was federally controlled, and there was no prejudice in Canada against a militia force as there was in the United States.[17]

Three years later the commanding officer at Fort Wayne forwarded to the adjutant-general of the Department of the Lakes an essay written in a postgraduate course in accordance with instructions from that headquarters. The subject was the defence of the northern border of the United States. The author, Lt. Frederick E. Wilson of the 27th Infantry, said that any country or countries attempting to launch an invasion there must be in alliance with, or have conquered, Canada. He found there were nine possible invasion routes, but he eliminated all but three from consideration. The most important was in the Great Lakes-Hudson area, but Wilson said that the British might also invade New England in order to cut off New York and they might attack the Pacific coast. He declared that the present military resources of the United States were inadequate to prevent invasion, therefore the American plan would have to be to draw the invader deep into the country in order to lengthen his lines of communication while volunteers were recruited and trained to cut him off from his bases. Despite this very gloomy prospect, Wilson claimed that eventual victory was sure.[18]

These two incidental discussions of the military situation vis-à-vis Canada were merely a part of the process of educating American soldiers to think about strategic problems in general, and they may be assumed to have had little bearing on the development of military policy or on Canadian-American relations. But this was not necessarily the case with the work of the Army War College which, in collaboration with the Third Division of the General Staff, was responsible for all army planning until the General Staff was reorganized in 1911–12.[19]

The War College combined training with contingency planning. Having been taught how to make estimates of military situations, students on courses made strategic plans that were to be "put in shape for future use . . . [after they had been] fully revised by the officers of the permanent personnel." This program got into full swing in 1908. Thenceforward three strategic problems were to be studied: a war in the Pacific, war with a country south of the Rio Grande or on the Caribbean, and a war on the northeast frontier and the Atlantic coast. In 1909–10 this order of priority, if such it was, was changed. Plan Red and Blue, that is war with Britain and Canada, was raised to second priority after war with Japan. But during that year the officers who had been assigned to it were transferred to the study of Plan Orange (Japan). Completion of plan Red was left to a subsequent course.[20]

Geographical information had, however, already been compiled and presented to the course by Maj. William Carey Browne of the 3rd Cavalry and Capt. Alexander Lucien Dade of the 13th Cavalry who stressed the strategic importance of the St. Lawrence canals where the locks were vulnerable. These officers said that the United States must act promptly in that area if war with Britain became imminent. Brown and Dade added that the completion of a proposed Georgian Bay canal would menace American cities on the Great Lakes.[21] In addition Maj. David Jewitt Baker, Jr., of the 11th Infantry prepared a paper on "The Invasion of Canada and the defence of our Atlantic coast" which discussed the relations of these operations to the strategy of a war with Great Britain. Baker suggested that previous planning had proposed frittering away the few resources available for the defence problem. He believed that in view of American inferiority in the early days of a war, both at sea, and in trained, equipped, and organized land forces, the United States should concentrate on an attack on Montreal, the commercial capital of Canada, and Quebec, the military capital.[22]

A third detailed study was made in that same year, 1909–10. Capt. Richard McMaster of the 1st Field Artillery noted that Laurier had said that the supremacy of the St. Lawrence as an export route must be maintained. McMaster warned that competition for trade "is known to be a prolific cause of war" and went on to discuss details of likely operations in a war arising from this difference with Canada. He recognized that Canadian canals could bring to the lakes bigger vessels than could pass through the Erie Canal but pointed out that the United States could control the St. Lawrence route by building a fort on the New York bank of the river. He expected that as a result of this Canada would construct the Georgian Bay canal which would be inaccessible to the U.S. and would necessitate new American forts at Detroit, Sault Ste. Marie, and Mackinac. McMaster believed that British landings on the American coast were also possible, but that they would be risky for the attackers; that the new northern transcontinental railway, when completed, would give Canada safe communication from east to west; and that the British would probably attempt to seize Buffalo and Pittsburgh to cut off New England and New York from the West. Eastern financial interests might then demand peace, but history showed that they would not be heeded.

McMaster recommended that the size of the army be increased, that it be organized on a divisional basis, that a reserve be established, that the militia be improved, that new forts be built at Albany and on the Great Lakes and the St. Lawrence, and that the Rush-Bagot agreement be revoked. Endorsed "an excellent paper," this strategic study was filed by the new War College Division of the General Staff, along with Brown's paper on the geography of Canada, as a basis for further planning.[23]

The War College's intention to develop operational plans for the north was not carried out in the following year (1910–11), when the major study was war in the south which had been restored to second priority.[24] Nevertheless, Maj. George Le Roy Irwin of the 3rd Field Artillery discussed the course's handling of Problem No. 61, "The Canadian Frontier, Central Section," which questioned the theory that a war in the north should be fought principally in the East. He said that if the enemy could be held in both the East and the West, Winnipeg would be vulnerable and the three thousand Americans newly settled on the Canadian prairies might aid an invader. Irwin remarked that Gen. Sir John French, who had inspected the Canadian militia, had described the West as cavalry country. Irwin was also probably borrowing from French when he said that the Canadian militia was no better drilled and disciplined than were the states' national guards. He concluded by saying that the whole class was in agreement that in the event of war with Britain Winnipeg should be attacked and the railroads destroyed. He added that all but one member of the course planned the attack by way of Pembina.[25] In 1911–12 the course included selected map problems connected with the invasion of Eastern Canada in a Blue-Red war. One of these problems was a Red plan for the defence of Toronto which concluded that Canadian troops would be concentrated at Hamilton.[26]

The operational plan for war in the north was at last considered in its entirety in 1912–1913, but Mexico was studied as well. The map problems numbered 47 to 54 dealt with the northern frontier. The basic premise was that diplomatic relations had been severed with Britain on August 8, and that war had been declared by the United States on August 20. The American strategy was to cross the St. Lawrence River at Cornwall. Maj. R. A. Brown, who had prepared the geographic study in 1910–11, supervised the work. He repeated much of what Colonel Irwin had said in the previous year but added that Kingston was the most strategic point and was "well fortified as far as fortifications go in Canada." The course prescribed an advance on Ottawa to destroy the Rideau Canal and hold the Ottawa-Cornwall line with auxiliary divisions while Montreal was attacked from the south. Simultaneously raids would destroy the Welland Canal, cross into Ontario from Detroit, and also seize Sault Ste. Marie, Fort William, and other places further west. By these means the plan was expected to neutralize Red superiority on Lake Ontario.[27]

In this same year Lt. Thomas B. Dugan presented a different opinion in a 97-page paper on the military geography of Ontario and Quebec which discussed an attack on those provinces. Dugan said that it was hardly likely that Britain would attempt to invade the United States but, if she did launch an attack on the east coast instead of from Canada, the American army must give up its plans for invading Canada and must concentrate to resist the invader from the sea. Therefore, said Dugan, at the outset of a war the United States should wait for a month to find out what British strategy would be. Meanwhile the Canadian militia could be neutralized by use of American volunteers who would be raised in greater numbers and would be as well trained, and probably better armed, than the Canadians for whom there were arms sufficient only for 200,000 men.

It is noteworthy that Dugan, although writing in connection with a possible American-Canadian War, was curiously disturbed by the failings of the supposedly hostile troops. He said that it was "regrettable to notice how many [Canadian] officers are absent without leave and that the grounding of squadrons, companies, and batteries in the elementary parts of their duties is far from perfect." He advocated better pay and longer training for the Canadian militia which, although more ready than the troops of any other dominion to go abroad, was still "not on a level with Canada's position in the modern world."[28] It seems almost as if Dugan were more concerned with the efficiency of Canada as a potential ally than as a potential enemy.

Yet in the same year Dugan took up the study of a means to invade Canada by crossing the St. Lawrence on a pontoon bridge. As no study of such a crossing had been made before, he recommended that officers should be sent to make exhaustive reconnaissances of the river at various seasons of the year. Meanwhile other members of the college prepared very detailed plans for an invasion of Canada from a base at Moira, N.Y., which identified units for the task and were by far the most sophisticated operational plans in this series. These plans were also filed away for possible future use.[29]

The course in 1913–14 was preceded by a lecture given by Maj. Benjamin A. Poore of the General Staff to a conference of officers "to explain such lines of action [in Red Plan] as are not to be studied by the Army War College class." Poore stated that the map problems in the course were based on "existing war plans" and that the first series assumed that the United States was in a state of war with Great Britain. He inserted parenthetically that "happily" the prospect of war was remote, but that there had been crises in the past. "Although war is not probable, yet it seems reasonable and prudent to provide in time of peace for any possible contingency." In the event of such a war, Britain would be the aggressor and the war would be principally in the East. While no opportunity for local action would be overlooked, the American strategy would be defensive; however the object of the U.S. forces would be to transfer the theatre of war from American to Canadian territory. Britain, having seized control of the North Atlantic, would perhaps strike within a month with 160,000 or more men at some point on the eastern seaboard, leaving the defence of Canada to the Canadians. The United States would attempt to divert the British attack by a prompt and rapid movement on Canada while concentrating all other available forces for the defence of the Atlantic coast. Poore said that the Great Lakes system was not impassable; and that when rail centres at Montreal and Ottawa in the East, and at Winnipeg in the West, were severed, the flow of Canadian grain would be disrupted and reinforcements and supplies from the Pacific dominions and India would be cut off. Several separate expeditions would be launched. Strong batteries would be set up on the St. Lawrence and the Richelieu.[30]

Dugan's papers were made available to the 1913–14 course and two further studies were then prepared. Lt.-Col. B. H. Fuller of the Marines repeated Brown's statement about the importance of Kingston and added details from a fresh report on the Canadian militia by Gen. Sir Ian Hamilton. Fuller said that if she were left without outside aid, Canada would be easy to conquer. Therefore Quebec City must be seized. He suggested that the operations contemplated against Montreal would require a large army but that an advance on Montreal as a preliminary to a major attack on Quebec could be carried out swiftly and without heavy artillery.[31] In another paper, Col. Abner

Pickering repeated Dugan's point that Britain would promptly invade the eastern seaboard. He said that the war should therefore be carried swiftly into Canada to relieve the American people of hardships. Quick action could also prevent reinforcement from Australia, New Zealand, and India, and perhaps even the naval attack on the coast. The aim of American operations in the West would be to sever communications with the East in order to cut off possible reinforcement from the Pacific while the U.S. Navy was occupied in the Atlantic. But Pickering believed that Britain would not be diverted to the West and that the only opposition there would come from Canadian troops.[32]

As war came nearer in Europe, and with its approach even less likelihood of Britain and Canada attacking the United States, American planning for war with Canada had become more detailed; and in the later years it was done by officers of higher rank. This work reached the top of the army's hierarchy in 1915, by which time Britain was deeply involved in Europe. On March 18, the chief of the War College Division, Brig.-Gen. M. M. Macomb, sent detailed plans for a war with Great Britain to the chief of staff of the United States Army. These showed troop disposals and concentration for an invasion of Canada.[33]

In June Macomb followed this up with a statement concerning the military problems of the United States "at home." He said that England had enough tonnage to transport 1,300,000 men in a succession of fleets, and that in alliance with Japan she absolutely dominated the seas. The troops of the two allies could land in British North American territory without much interference even by American submarines. By exploiting Canada's excellent railroad system, they could choose the most embarrassing place to strike. Macomb declared, "The practical military effect of that alliance has been to place a powerful army on our northern frontier." He knew that many people might think that Britain would not use the Japanese army in that way, and would not permit the Japanese to so use it; but he stated that, like any other nation, Britain would do whatever she thought her vital national interests demanded. In what was evidently a reference to the Anglo-Japanese Treaty, he said "England never violates a treaty," and he showed that the Japanese could seize Puget Sound, a part of the United States that was completely cut off from the rest of the nation by great natural obstacles. It is probable that Macomb's underlying purpose was to play upon American fears of Japan and dislike of the Anglo-Japanese alliance in order to build up the army's case for expansion.[34] Therefore it is not surprising that in presenting his case he neglected to take into consideration the likely Canadian reaction against a Japanese army on Dominion soil.

On May 21, 1916, a plan for an invasion of Canada by three American army corps was filed by the War College Division of the General Staff. It is very brief, only a seventeen-page outline and not a detailed operational plan. Accompanying the plan to invade Canada in the National Archives is a rough sketch map of Lakes Ontario and Erie and the St. Lawrence River (plate 5). This map indicates the lines of advance for American troops invading Canada and the timing of their operations. But for two years Britain had been too much distracted by war in Europe to harbour aggressive designs against the United States; and by 1916 the United States was close to involvement in the war with Germany. The last map and plan for a war with Canada prepared before American entry into the First World War is in fact filed incorrectly in the General Staff papers in a volume of papers discussing various military implications of a possible war with Germany.[35]

The 1916 plan was the culmination of nine years of War College and General Staff planning of war with Britain and Canada in the course of which the existence of various unknown factors and consequent uncertainties in strategy had caused many different suggestions to be put forward. American planners always assumed that the Canadians would resist, but there were differences of opinion about the ability of Britain to control the West Atlantic and to launch an invasion across the Atlantic. Lack of military preparedness in the United States and possible disunity with regard to the object and conduct of the war led to disagreement among military planners about the strategy of invading Canada even though it was now clearly a less difficult operation than it had been in the nineteenth century. If Canada were to resist, the invasion might be no walkover.

Since planners habitually ignored the realities of the political situation, the planning outlined above has an air of fantasy. In particular, it is noticeable that American planners were considering a kind of war that the British no longer contemplated, a war in the interior of North America, and that the United States had no plans to seize Halifax, about which the British were still worried.

American officers engaged in this work had acted consistently on purely professional considerations. Many were Anglophiles. They regarded a war with Britain and Canada as both undesirable and highly improbable. Yet military caution had made them regard such a war as not impossible. The fact that this was planning for an unlikely contingency, as well as for training purposes, may be justification enough

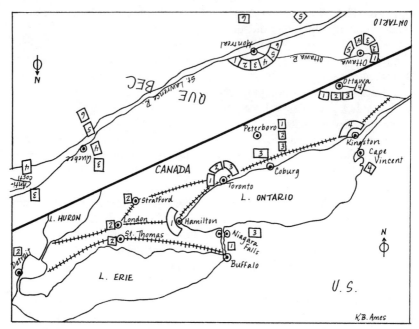

5. "Alleged Plan for the Invasion of Canada" (redrawn), War College Division, U.S. General Staff, 1916. The invading forces consist of I Army Corps, First and Second Divisions (1 and 2); II Army Corps, Third and Fourth Divisions (3 and 4); III Army Corps, Fifth and Sixth Divisions (5 and 6). Railroads are indicated

for the secrecy with which it was carried out. Secret planning did not disturb amicable international relations or domestic politics. Strategic planning in the United States was in fact done so secretly that the civil authorities were largely unaware of it. Unrealistic secret planning not related to political developments did not promote war with Britain.

On the other hand, when planning touched upon possible, rather than impossible, wars, the question was different. President Wilson is said to have threatened to dismiss all the members of the General Staff in 1916 if he found that a report that they were planning for war with Germany was true.[36] In a democracy it was paradoxically easier to plan war with a friend than with a potential enemy because the former course would involve fewer political liabilities; and planning of any kind could be useful for training and also for general military preparedness.

On both sides professional investigation of the possibility of war between the English-speaking countries in North America was insulated from policy by constitutional structures. Britain, it is true, now had the CID to coordinate military policy and professional advice; but the evolution of responsible government in Canada had transferred important elements in decision-making to the Dominion government, which had few if any facilities for the discussion of strategic problems. In the United States the War Colleges had developed more efficient organs for the study of strategy, but they were not harnessed to political decision-making as effectively as was the CID. However, in an age when technical complications were much less sophisticated than they are today, the tradition of civil supremacy over armed forces meant that policy was determined by politicians who were much influenced by public opinion, and there was little, in some cases much too little, input from military experts.

The general public learned almost nothing about military planning, but public opinion was more important than professional study in the establishment of long-term attitudes. In Canada and the United States it was of great importance in the development of a special pacific relationship. Public opinion and public policy must therefore now be examined.

On indicator that shows the direction in which an informed element of American opinion was moving on the question of the possibility of a conflict with Canada, and of the course of such a conflict, is the military periodical. The well-established *Army and Navy Journal*, produced for all Americans in full or part-time service, continued to watch Canadian military developments with a benevolent eye and perhaps even more closely than in the past. In discussing the effect of a Georgian

Bay canal, the *Journal* said that such a canal would be built primarily for commercial reasons but would be built primarily for commercial reasons but would have military implications which American authorities should keep in mind. But the discussion of Canadian-American relations in the *Journal* was usually concentrated on the commercial competition between the two countries, on the development of the Canadian militia, and on the possibility of a Canadian navy and of reciprocity in trade. It showed no evidence of rancour and made no suggestion that these things were a prelude to conflict or related to it.[37] In 1910 the *Journal* sympathetically reported Canadian resentment at a *New York Sun* article on infantry manoeuvres in New York state that was headed "Canadian Army crushed." It learned that the word "Canada" had not appeared in the operational orders for the manoeuvres, and that a newspaper correspondent had been trying to be "funny" and had "made a mess of it."[38]

The amicable attitude of unofficial American military opinion, shown in these references to Canada in the *Journal*, is further demonstrated by the fact that the new *Infantry Journal*, established in 1904, made no reference at all to Canada or to the northern frontier of the United States until 1914 when it carried an article that declared that, although the average American assumed that Canada would seek to join the United States, nothing was more unlikely. The author, a Michigan National Guard officer, said that Canada would always be friendly to the United States because of the large number of Americans who had settled on the Canadian prairies; and he praised the Canadian militia and Permanent Force for discipline and lack of snobbishness, and for giving value for the money spent on them by the Canadian government. He said that the men in the Permanent Force were "as hard as nails" and that there was no sky-larking after Last Post which, he explained, was the Canadian equivalent of Taps.[39]

Public policy in the United States reflected these amicable trends in American military opinion. Under Elihu Root, secretary of war (1899–1904), who understood the relation between power and responsibility, and Gen. Leonard Wood, army chief of staff (1910–14), the American army was transformed from its organization for a police role on the Indian frontier to that of a modern force of four regular and twelve National Guard divisions that could be expanded to match European continental armies;[40] but there was no sign that these reforms and reorganization were in any way related to the possibility of war with Canada. From 1902 to 1911 the United States spent $71 million on fortifications, mainly along the Atlantic and Pacific coasts;[41] but although Britain was still the most powerful potential rival on the Atlantic, references to that fact, frequent in the past, had now become rare or nonexistent. In 1912 the War Department recommended the abandonment of Fort Brady, Madison Barracks, Fort Niagara, Fort Ontario, Fort Wayne, Fort Ethan Allan, and Plattsburg Barracks. Location of the last-named on "a natural line of advance from Canada" was no longer considered to justify its maintenance in peacetime. Dispersion was stated to be fatal to economy. Modern armies must keep all arms together and lie readily available for movement elsewhere.[42] The organization of the American army was thus being adjusted for possible service overseas rather than for defence against the neighbour to the north.

Faced with many more urgent problems at home and abroad, American public opinion generally, like unofficial military thinking, did not envisage a possible need to take Canada by force. A few notorious demagogues like Champ Clark, speaker of the House of Representatives, still talked of annexation, but the movement for reciprocity in trade, which will be discussed later, was not an alternative to conquest as it had been in mid-nineteenth century. Annexation now invariably meant political union by agreement.[43]

On the other hand, Canadians appear to have been unaware of the extent to which American opinion had changed for the better. They had inherited antipathies that still persisted because the United States loomed ever larger in Canadian eyes. A century earlier, because of their innate conservatism, a majority of Canadians had intensely disliked American institutions.[44] Extension of the franchise had since mellowed Canadian acceptance of democracy; but this had come about without greatly weakening the conviction that the American system of government, which seemed to them to lack responsible nonpartisan leadership, was inferior.[45] The Canadian outlook on this question was highly subjective, a reflection of the fact that Canadians were becoming more aware of their own values and character.[46]

Nationalism in Canada reinforced, rather than diminished, certain aspects of the traditional attitude towards the United States that Canadians shared with the British. It helped to maintain the desire to resist an Americanization that now seemed more likely to come by infiltration rather than by invasion. The switch from fear of invasion to fear of infiltration did not, however, come about overnight or without anguish and dispute. Anglo-American understanding, coupled with Canada's desire to obtain a greater say in relations with the United States, in order to forestall a future diplomatic reverse like the Alaska award, had presented the Dominion with the need for a clearer definition of its external relations.

This reappraisal, as Minto had foreseen, took the form of a renewal of the old vigorous debate about the relative merits of reciprocity, annexation, and independence, each of which could have been an alternative to the loosening of the imperial tie. Carl Berger has established that, for Canadian imperialists, the imperial tie was a means of developing Canada's national potential and was therefore an aspect of Canadian nationalism.[47] But Canadian imperialists did not always see that Canadian and British interests might seriously diverge.

At the other political pole, Goldwin Smith, who had begun his career in North America by nurturing Canadian independence in the 1870s, had moved on to suggest the inevitability and desirability of continental union. Smith was reacting against proposals for Imperial Federation that were urged from 1885 on, despite obvious practical impediments such as the British Parliament's unwillingness to share power. According to his biographer, Smith had never really understood the spirit of nationalism, Canada's most pervasive characteristic in the half-century after Confederation, which he had encouraged. Although he was frequently labelled an "annexationist," Smith never talked of "annexation" which in fact he abhorred.[48] Yet he and others like him, at that extreme of the political spectrum which rejected the continuation and extension of the imperial connection, failed to see that the growth of a consciousness of "being Canadian" could offset the gravitational pull of the United States.

Bitter disputes that raged between the extremes of imperialism and continentalism have tended to obscure the fact that there was a pervasive growth of nationalism in Canada that affected not only imperialists but also many of those accused of continentalism. While there was great divergence of opinion in Canada about the advantages and disadvantages of closer British or American ties, there was considerable common ground on the question of unsought absorption.

Common elements in imperialist and nationalist thinking in Canada with regard to the United States can be seen in the views of two governors general at the beginning of the century who have been associated with those differing philosophies. Minto was, as has been seen, a vigorous imperialist. Before the Anglo-American rapprochement, imperialism had usually been considered as strongly anti-American. A. C. Gluek has said that Minto's anti-Americanism combined with that of Laurier to obstruct good relations with the United States.[49] Leaving aside for the moment the question of Laurier's anti-Americanism, it should be noted here that in Gluek's opinion the arrival of Minto's successor, Grey, "worked wondrous changes" in relations with the United States. Grey is usually considered to have identified himself much more than Minto with Canadian interests and aspirations, yet he could, on occasion show himself as suspicious of America as Minto had been. Contrasting the "amazing wealth" of Canada with the "alarming poverty" of the United States, Grey told W. T. Stead in 1909 that when the Americans had squandered their inheritance they would "seek to share ours." He followed up this prophecy by saying that Roosevelt had told a confidant that "celibacy and sterility were eating their poisonous way into the heart of the United States and that the effort of the Anglo-American stock to Americanise the annual flood of non-Anglo Saxon Vandals, Goths, and Huns was becoming Sisyphean."

Despite such critical views of American society, Grey believed that the Republic's relations with Britain and Canada were improving. He said that he regarded every American ship as a British reserve.[50] In his way he was as strong a believer as Minto in the imperial connection, and his views about the United States, like Minto's, probably reflect his British origin and official connection. But if he had a better understanding of the growth of Canadian consciousness of a distinctive identity, this serves to demonstrate that Canadian nationalism clearly harboured elements of anti-Americanism not unlike those formerly associated with imperialism. In the heat of debate in the first decade and a half of the twentieth century this aspect of the nationalist attitude was often forgotten.

British observers had frequently commented with surprise on the virulence of Canadian antipathy for all things "Yankee." Their surprise was occasioned by the fact that, while the British themselves could be expected to react adversely to Americans, English-speaking Canadians seemed to British visitors to have in some ways moved away from British characteristics and to have become more American and therefore less inclined to dislike the American people. But what was happening was that, in Canada as everywhere else, national characteristics were more easily identified and demonstrated by contrast with the qualities of other peoples. The identification of positive distinctive national characteristics comes later. Canadianism could more easily be defined by revealing its differences from things British and things American than by attempting to distil out pure Canadian qualities.

John S. Galbraith has said that "The catalyst of the power of the republic of the United States" forced the growth of nationalism in Canada.[51] The rise of nationalism strongly tinged with anti-Americanism might have been expected to lead to a more militant Canadian stand against the United States on points of difference. In the wake of the Anglo-American entente, desirous of shaping their own destiny in North America, and moved by dislike of some aspects of American life, Canadians had to make fundamental decisions about the nature of Canadian-American relations. But they were slow to take a positive stand.

However, Grey had come to Canada to work for the removal of outstanding questions that made for friction.[52] Since Canada's external political contacts were still made through his office, his influence was powerful, the more so because Laurier, despite his desire to get a grip on relations with the United States, and despite the nationalism arising from his French-Canadian background, was over-cautious lest new procedures or new approaches should arouse political opposition. Laurier could talk like an imperialist to one audience, suggest the need for administrative changes in relations with Britain to another, and end by declaring that present arrangements were satisfactory. In his American policy he avoided anything that appeared to call for constitutional change even when he was doing things that worked towards it. Consequently the fact that the crown's representative in Canada was sympathetic to closer American-Canadian ties was relatively more important than it would otherwise have been.

Had Laurier been willing to move that way, the creation of the Department of External Affairs in 1909 might have been a big step towards the independent foreign policy that some Canadians now wanted. Instead, the act that created the department and received royal assent on May 19 was designed only to adjust existing administrative procedures in order to give the secretary of state (in Canada a minister concerned with domestic matters) the means of coordinating the policies of government departments in contact with other countries. Although an order in council in September 1909 referred to a "secretary of state for external affairs," it was not until 1912, when new legislation conferred that office on the prime minister (by then Robert Borden) that the department was put in a position to exercise any influence on policy; and that influence arose chiefly from the fact that its head was paramount in the government. The department's impact continued for some time to be restricted by the fact that it had only a very small staff in Ottawa, and no diplomatic representatives overseas.[53] In 1914 it was still only "a filing bureau without responsibility for policy."[54]

Nevertheless, the rise of Anglo-American friendship had in fact given Canada greater potential for independent action, and Canadian-American relations soon began to take on a different appearance. An example of this was the machinery for the peaceful settlement of disputes, the International Joint Commission with authority to deal with boundary waters, established in 1909.[55] As in the case of the Department of External Affairs set up in the same year, the creation of this agency could be claimed to represent no drastic change in the constitutional position of Canada as a dependency of Great Britain. It was therefore in conformity with Laurier's cautiousness as well as with Grey's wish to improve the relations of a strong autonomous Canada with the United States.

Where Laurier was eventually less reluctant to act positively in Canadian-American relations was in the sphere of trade policy. He and his Liberal colleagues were conditioned by traditional Liberal principles to be theoretically disposed towards the promotion of national prosperity and harmonious international relations by the lowering of tariff barriers. For half a century Canadian governments had from time to time sought to increase trade with the United States, either by reciprocal tariff reductions or by the total elimination of duties and the establishment of a common tariff. But at the time of the Colonial Conference in Ottawa in 1897 Canada had granted imperial preferences to the United Kingdom to promote Empire trade. About the same time, after the enactment of the highly protectionist Dingley tariff in the United States, Laurier had vowed that there would be no more pilgrimages to Washington in search of trade agreements.

However, the Liberal victory in Britain in 1906 rejected Imperial Preference as a breach of universal free trade; and Canadian imperial preferences had aroused American concern. When the Republicans won the election of 1908 on a platform of tariff reform, what had ostensibly been a program for lowering tariffs emerged instead as the Payne-Aldrich Act that authorized "fair" tariff rates to offset the higher cost of production in the United States and also permitted discrimination against countries that did not give American goods equal treatment. President Taft was disposed to agree that Canada's imperial preferences did not constitute discrimination against the United States and he was even ready to accept Canada's trade agreement with France in 1910; but his squabbles with a hostile Congress led to American efforts to revise reciprocity with Canada.

Interest in the idea of reciprocity was widespread in Congress and throughout the United States, much more so than in the middle of the previous century when the first short-lived agreement had come into force. This was largely because Americans were now prepared to sublimate their expansionist urges by proposing union with a more congenial mate possessing characteristics similar to their own. But some groups in the United States offered the proposal for their own reasons;

and it has even been suggested that the alleged political implications of a trade agreement were contrived in the United States for the express purpose of frightening Canadians from accepting one.[56] American newspapers, afraid that too much stress on political union might thwart the reciprocity that would get them cheap newsprint, soft-pedalled references to possible political consequences of an economic agreement with Canada. However, those Americans who were opposed to tariff reductions for specific reasons made sure that this aspect of reciprocity was well publicized.

In Canada, Earl Grey had suspected as early as 1908 that there were underlying American designs. He wrote then, "It is evident that the Americans have at length realised that their endeavour to kick Canada into the United States is doomed to failure and that their only chance lies in the substitution of a policy of kicks by one of kisses." But he added, "It is fortunate that they did not find this out before. They have kicked a National Soul into Canada and I come across no evidence of any desire on the part of Canadians to play the American game by lowering the tariff against them."[57]

The ruling Liberal Party was deeply divided over the tariff issue because it would affect various parts of the country and various economic interests differently, and some adversely, and so would split the party and the country. Touring the West in 1910, one not unbiased observer, Col. G. T. Denison, had found what Grey had discovered elsewhere, that people there "were in no mood to listen to the advances of the United States."[58] Yet Laurier, when campaigning in the same region, discovered enough support there for reciprocity to convince him of the political value of adopting it as his government's policy.[59] In 1911, therefore, he reversed his earlier stand and introduced proposals for the reduction of tariffs against the United States on natural (but not manufactured) products.

By the time reciprocity was reintroduced into practical politics as a means of cementing Canadian-American peaceful relations Canadian national consciousness had become considerably advanced. G. E. Foster, a leading Conservative, had said in 1909, "We hate the idea of absorption as much as we do extinction, for we have red blood in our veins and feel the impulses of a great life throbbing within us. . . . You can never make us into states of the United States." Foster, an imperialist, went on, "British-Canadians we are, and as such we intend to remain."[60] Events were to show that this sentiment prevailed widely among many other Canadians who were not as enamoured as Foster with strengthening the British connection.

The Rouge tradition in French-Canada, with its American sympathy, was not entirely dead in the early 1900s and many French-Canadians had long believed that Canadian difficulties with the United States were invariably caused by the tie with Britain. But they were now sometimes even more suspicious of American intentions than were their English-speaking fellow-citizens. "In the United States we can have no faith. The amiable nation of pirates which stole Texas, Cuba, Porto-Rico, and the Philippines, cannot be depended on to act justly towards a weaker nation. But if you own that England will not go to war with the Americans for our sake,—and this seems more likely than ever,—how can you pretend that the national status would more fatally bring us under the American hegemony." So in 1909 wrote Olivar Asselin, founder of the Nationalist League, who had served in the U.S. Army during the Spanish-American War.[61] Henri Bourassa, editor of *Le Devoir* and a leading French-Canadian nationalist politician, similarly alleged that British expenditure on the defence of Canada was because of British wars, that Canada had never been a cause of trouble between Britain and other countries including the United States, and that Macdonald had had to fight for three months to prevent British diplomats from handing over the whole of Canada to the United States, hyperbole that served to demonstrate not only the strength of Bourassa's feeling against imperialism but also his aversion to continental union.[62]

As a French-Canadian Laurier may have inherited some suspicions of the United States to match his distrust of British intentions, but he was aware of the need to accommodate the views of many different elements in the Canadian electorate. Therefore, along with reciprocity, he introduced a proposal for a Canadian navy which could, if the Canadian government and people agreed, be sent to aid Britain in a naval war. The naval bill, belatedly carrying out a suggestion he had made to the first lord of the admiralty in 1902, was Laurier's answer to the growth of German navalism and to Canadian Conservative pressure for direct contributions to the Royal Navy. Although not related directly to the problem of relations with the United States, except in so far as a Canadian navy might be considered less of a challenge to the United States than a contribution to the Royal Navy would be, the naval bill and reciprocity were linked together to preserve Canadian autonomy in foreign policy as well as to establish closer economic ties with the United States, which, in the prime minister's view, would not be a step towards political union.

The public's reception of Laurier's twin measures was conditioned by contemporary discussion of the nature of imperial relations and of relations between Canada and the United States, topics that were

closely connected. Some British imperialists were still inclined to re-
mind Canadians of historical American hostility and aggression in
order to strengthen the case for participation in Imperial Defence.
Urging the need for a larger citizen army in Canada in 1905, Leopold
Amery had been willing to agree that there was less need for defensive
measures in America than in Europe. But he asked, "Has the expansion of the United States been entirely peaceful and unaggressive in
the past?" He declared that Mexico and Spain would not think so.[63] He
appeared to imply that if Canada did not play a part in Imperial Defence she must philosophically await absorption by the United States
because no resistance would be possible. Similarly, an anonymous correspondent of the *Canadian Military Gazette* said in 1909 that war had
already started in Europe even though blows had not yet been struck,
and he argued that Canada must make up her mind. "She must maintain her connection with the British Empire or be absorbed by the
United States." If Canada adopted the former choice then she must
shoulder responsibilities by developing a well-thought out scheme of
defence.[64]

However, by the time of the German naval scare in 1909, it had
begun to be widely accepted in Canada that the Americans would not
attempt the acquisition of Canada by force. A military confrontation
was no longer expected by either side. The *Canadian Military Gazette*
announced that in its opinion "President Taft is pacific," and it based
this belief on the fact that he appeared to be determined to cut the regular forces and to rely on a civilian militia as a "preventative of war."
This, it said, was an example that Canada, and perhaps even Europe,
might follow.[65]

The German crisis impelled some Canadians to call for a more vigorous Canadian military and naval effort. Lt.-Col. Hugh Clark, commanding officer of the 32nd (Bruce) Regiment of Militia, and editor of
the *Kincardine Review*, who was a Conservative MP and a future parliamentary undersecretary for external affairs, asked whether Canada
was "worth defending." Clark was thinking of the survival of the
British Empire and not of the defence of Canada against the United
States.[66]

On the other hand, a few Canadians still believed that the exposed
Canadian border presented a serious defence problem. Charles Hazlitt
Cahan, KC, leader of the Conservative opposition in Nova Scotia, discussed Canada's maritime situation on the Atlantic and the Pacific and
the need to protect the Dominion in the event of war "by such defences
as we can provide in our own territory." Although he acknowledged
that the greatest danger was a European War, he declared that the

4,000-mile border with the United States was also a source of danger. "I do not say that a conflict between Canada and the United States is probable, but no intelligent observer of political events can deny that it is quite possible; and that possibility is in my opinion increased by the evident determination of the Canadian people to maintain their independence of the United States." He said that the great expansion of the United States, and its need for resources, was an ever-increasing danger that implied the possibility, if not the probability, of conflict. He alleged that this possibility was being "seriously and intelligently contemplated" by the American military authorities. Cahan noted that American merchant ships on the Great Lakes were capable of being armed and that "the authorities who are responsible for the defence of Canada cannot long ignore the military and naval preparedness of our peaceful neighbours to the south and must in due course take adequate measures for the due protection of our internal waterways and great transcontinental lines of railway communication." Cahan recommended completion of the Georgian Bay Canal, "a work of supreme military and naval importance to Canada." Cahan concluded by asserting that Canada was morally bound to contribute to naval defence, and he advocated Imperial Federation.[67] Writing at the height of the dispute about Canada's naval bill, he was obviously stirred by that great dispute about a Canadian role in Imperial Defence, and his discussion of the details of defence against the United States may have been an attempt to use any conceivable argument, however wild, to tip the scales in favour of military preparations for other purposes than to fight the United States.

Even so, imperialists like Cahan and nationalists like Bourassa were not far apart in certain aspects of their attitude to the United States. The *Montreal Star*, suffering an attack of "yellow fever" and disturbed by a nightmare about the German menace, alleged that articles by Bourassa pointing out the danger of absorption by the United States were calls for annexation. Cahan came to the defence of Bourassa, who was, he said, of all Canadians, the "most antagonistic to those regrettable tendencies which so frequently find expression in the social, political, and commercial life of the United States."[68]

Yet even those who had long feared American strength were beginning to accept the idea that military confrontation was unlikely. George T. Denison's autobiographical study, *The Struggle for Imperial Unity*, published in 1909, declared that few Canadians now favoured Continental union but that "the lesson taught by this period of danger is clear. We must never forget that with a powerful neighbour alongside of Canada, speaking the same language, and with necessarily intimate commercial intercourse, an agitation for closer relations, leading to ultimate absorption, is easy to kindle, and being so plausible, might spread with dangerous rapidity."[69] One of Canada's most persistent advocates of military preparedness, Denison feared peaceful absorption but apparently no longer expected American aggression or believed in the need for Canadian defences against the United States.

Maj.-Gen. Charles W. Robinson's *Canada and Canadian Defence*, published in London and Toronto a year later, took a quite different stand. Robinson, a son of Sir John Beverley Robinson, chief justice of Canada, had served in the British Army from 1857 until his retirement in 1898. He had continued to live in England. In his well-known book, Robinson analysed the War of 1812 and later developments and claimed that the danger to Canada was now greater than it had ever been because of developments in technology, communications, and territorial expansion across the continent. "Defence must be thoroughly up-to-date. . . . It is only the system, not the necessity of the defence posts, which has changed." Robinson argued that Canada could not afford to neglect the defence of her southern border or allow control of the Great Lakes to be lost.[70] His book, ornamented on the front board cover with a sword, maple leaf, and union jack, is so often found today, in libraries and second-hand book catalogues, that it is probable that it had a very wide circulation in its time. But Robinson was out of touch with informed opinion in Canada.

Warnings about an American threat to Canada in this period also arose from fear that the United States would directly challenge Britain for hegemony. An article in a British periodical, allegedly written by an American citizen with the unlikely name of Arthur Wellesley Kipling, said that Canada was safe from aggression for two reasons, her intense national spirit and protection by the Monroe Doctrine which was a stern "hands off" to foreign nations. Kipling asserted that it was unfortunate that some Americans linked protection by the Monroe Doctrine with a feeling of material ownership. He said that the greatest possible source of external threat to the existence of the British Empire was the United States. American mercantile marine expansion, high tariffs, and a big navy could deal a heavy blow at British prestige and retaliation was now impossible. One reason for this was that Canada would be invaded. With tongue in cheek, Kipling concluded that if ultimate union came about "it is more probable that Canada would annex the United States as such a course would spare the feelings of the smaller nation." Alternatively an Anglo-American offensive and defensive alliance could be mutually beneficial and "the greatest stride the world has seen towards the Christian ideal of peace on earth and good will towards men." [71]

A retired British officer also warned Canadians against a deliberate American quest for world power. Referring in 1911 to steps taken by the United States to become mistress of the seas, Maj. William Cyprian Bridge, an obscure relative of the famous admiral, who had retired in 1901 from the South Staffordshire Regiment after two decades of service, said that to allow the German menace to absorb all Britain's attention was very dangerous. If it could be proved that the Americans were going to strive for world power, "we ought surely to shake off our complaisance and false sense of security before it is too late." Bridge said that exclusive control of the Panama Canal would give the United States a new advantage and make the defence of Canada more difficult. In his opinion the latest example of American unfriendliness was "the attempted arrangement over our heads of a comprehensive trade agreement with one of our chief overseas possessions, Canada." Bridge suggested that the flow of American immigrants to Canada might bring a cry for annexation. He asked, "Are we going to tamely submit, or are we going to resist by force of arms?" The only way to get respect from a people like the Americans was to stand up for one's rights. American friendship went no further than words and lasted only as long as Britain tamely submitted. Moral cowardice would only encourage American ambitions. [72]

Warnings about a possible American contest with Great Britain for world power, and about the resultant continuing danger on the Canadian-American border, came mainly from British sources, or from Canadians who had been anglicized in the British army or by settlement in England. But they were occasionally echoed by members of the Canadian parliamentary opposition. By and large unofficial military thought in Canada, if the *Canadian Military Gazette* and Denison can be taken as typical, was no longer directed toward the United States. Those concerned about the military defence of Canada's interests now believed that Canada should arm against the German menace to the Empire.

This view was, however, rejected on unusual grounds in an appeal to Canadians which incidentally revived discussion of the question of defence against the United States. The debate about whether Canada should prepare to help Britain against Germany or should look to her own defences on the border was examined on the eve of the First World War by an author who called himself "Christopher West." West had previously published *Canada and Sea Power* which was not, as is sometimes assumed, a treatise on the lines of Mahan, but was a call for

Canada to give the lead in promoting moral international relations on lines advocated by Norman Angell. West was critical of both the Liberals' proposal for a Canadian navy and the Conservatives' gift of battle-cruisers to the Royal Navy.[73]

West followed his book on sea power with a shorter study on the defence of Canada in which he praised Sir John A. Macdonald for rejecting militarism, for refusing to create a standing army, and for relying on citizen soldiers for the safety of Canadian soil. West said that it was a clear corollary of this policy that Canada should not "interfere by force outside her own territory or be made responsible for imperial policy over which the Dominion has no control." He believed that the current state of amicable relations between Britain and the United States was partly a consequence of this Canadian approach to the problem of defence.[74] In the guise of internationalism, West thus bridged the gap between the isolationism in nineteenth-century Canada and that which was to appear in the 1920s.

His views were also a foretaste of 1918, when Wilsonian idealism assumed that peace could be maintained by moral pressure alone, and of the 1920s when Mackenzie King feared lest Canada be dragged again into European wars. However, West's pacifism, although swamped by the Canadian response to Britain's danger in 1914, may be seen as conforming in some degree with the development of Canadian attitudes towards the United States before the First World War. Despite growing rejection of many aspects of American life, Laurier had shied away from any military measures directed against the United States and Canadians had begun to tackle the problem of dealing with Americans by peaceful means without the backing of military strength or British military aid.

West's desire for peaceful international relations was frustrated in 1914 by Canada's acceptance of responsibility for aiding Britain in the struggle with Germany. Since the Militia Act of 1904, Canada had undertaken significant reforms which, although far from adequate to meet the challenge of the coming war, completed the strategic revolution in North America. Once military autonomy was well established in Canada, there was much less suspicion of British motives. Beginning with the measures taken as a result of the Venezuela crisis in 1895–96, the Canadian militia had been reorganized, reequipped, and expanded to a degree "beyond anyone's dreams." By 1909 the militia budget, which had been fixed in 1865 at $1,000,000 but had often fallen below that amount, had reached $6,500,000. Despite threatened cuts in 1908, expansion had continued.[75]

Sir Frederick Borden's willingness to accept British aid as long as

Canadian political control was assured had been demonstrated by his appointment of a British general, Colin Mackenzie, to succeed the first Canadian chief of the General Staff in 1910. Stimulated by cooperation with the British army through the educational system of the Imperial General Staff, Canada had begun to standardize her organization and equipment with that of the British army (except for the unfortunate exception of the Ross Rifle) and to train officers for command and staff appointments. Progress was slow and the Canadian Expeditionary Force would depend heavily throughout the war on staff officers from the British army; but autonomy had made possible more effective cooperation on lines that were to be developed in the postwar Commonwealth.[76]

These military changes were clearly not directed towards Canadian defence against an American danger. A few reminders of the ancient fear of the United States remained, but they were now relics of a bygone age. In 1908 a reporter of the *New York Herald* falsely accused the Canadian chief of the General Staff, Otter, of having stated that it would take the United States at least twenty-five years to conquer Canada. Canadian newspapers in Winnipeg and Vancouver were shocked by this example of sensational journalism.[77] In 1910, when Gen. Sir John French, future commander-in-chief of the British Expeditionary Force in France, inspected the Canadian militia, he talked of the need for defence against a land attack.[78] Even as late as 1914 Brig.-Gen. François Louis Lessard, a veteran of the Canadian militia, was convinced that it would be necessary to defend Toronto against a Fenian raid.[79] But in fact the Canadian militia was now designed for quite different purposes. Until 1911 its mobilization plans had been based on the Leach Commission's report which had stressed the defence of Montreal against the United States.[80] In 1910, on April 1 (an ironical date), a memorandum stated, "The Montreal Field Force is intended for the active defence of Montreal where it would concentrate."[81] But in 1911 a British officer who had served previously in Canada was authorized to devise mobilization plans. Col. W. G. Gwatkin's mobilization orders were directed towards general mobilization in Canada for unspecified purposes and for a special force for overseas. They made no reference to mobilization for defence against the United States.[82] The former purpose was clearly designed for the militia's historic role, but the second objective was now the more important.

A strategic revolution had been completed. It had been brought about as much by events outside the continent as by developments in North America. Both Canada and the United States had developed their military forces because of increasing tensions in Europe. Close similarities in their point of view on developments abroad helped to assuage their fears of friction nearer home. American intervention in Mexico in 1916, a result of American political instability, and of President Wilson's unwise attempt to push the Mexicans towards constitutional government, drove the European war headlines for a time from the American press.[83] But this only served to demonstrate the very different attitude of the United States to Canada. In 1914 the Toronto *Saturday Night* had spoken of Mexican instability and the need to counter it by protective forces, and had contrasted this with Canada's lack of fear of the United States.[84]

Canada was now more concerned with ensuring that the United States would take a stand against Germany than with fear of an American invasion. Stephen Leacock, the Canadian economist, humorist, and imperialist, said of the American appeal for reciprocity of good feeling, and of their moral support, which "with true American humour they called neutrality," that Canadians owed them much for these things. He suggested that the United States could be repaid if ever they were threatened by Mexico or by a raid from the Galapagos Islands. "I for one am in favor of marching the entire McGill University Battalion, professors and all, to their support." He went on to say that it was a pity the support of the great bulk of the American press was not better known in Canada. "When this war is over let us invite our friends from Washington to Ottawa and then to the music of the footmarch of our regiments returning from the war that America has helped us win, we will frame a compact of peace, of amity, that shall last as long as a common speech and a common freedom unite the people of England and America."[85]

A special relationship between Canada and the United States had been fostered by the similarity of their ideals and interests and by mutual fear of external dangers. Canada's fear of America's potential military might had given way to thankfulness that it existed to support and protect vital natural interests. After the British military withdrawal the Canadian government had begun to learn to live within the shadow of the American colossus. Henceforward the danger of peaceful assimilation would have to be resisted by peaceful means.

On her part the United States had come to prefer Canada to be a contented independent neighbour rather than a rebellious vassal, partly because of more distant responsibilities, but chiefly because the instinctive American world mission, to spread the benefits of Anglo-Saxon freedoms, was inapplicable north of the border. In the course of time the belief that shared ideals would lead to political union had declined. Americans had come to realize, if only vaguely, that the similarities between the two countries concealed basic differences that would make political bonds insecure, especially when they were strained by world pressures and responsibilities. Strangely, this revolution in the American outlook had been accomplished at a time when professional military planning in the United States, designed for training and for contingencies, had matured into an accepted consensus of the way in which Canada could be conquered if war came. The dichotomy between political reality and military planning, derived from the constitutional concept of the subordination of the military to the civil authorities, had made possible an attitude of tolerance and forbearance that suited well with Canada's cautious quest for the preservation of national identity by peaceful means. Refinement and expansion of the technique of military planning had not led to increased danger. It may indeed have worked in the opposite direction. Although much was done in secret, unofficial discussion had revealed to both sides the uncertainties of military ventures, especially when political support might lack unanimity. At a time when military dominance of the continent and its neighbouring waters had passed conclusively to the United States, worldwide complications had made Canada neither a hostage nor a pawn, but a potential ally.

8

From War Planning to Alliance (post–1919)

The First World War's shattering impact, and public revulsion against further involvement in Europe, brought a strengthening of isolationist and anti-imperialist sentiment in North America. These things helped to confirm the prewar belief held by many that disputes between Canada and the United States should and could be settled peacefully. Yet not until the next great major conflagration and the ensuing Cold War did Canadian-American relations consolidate into a military alliance that presumably precludes the need for defensive counter-planning. Meanwhile, in the interwar period, the continuance of war planning by the military had paradoxically demonstrated by its growing unreality the strength of the informal popular entente in North America. It had also incidentally provided some insight into the somewhat ephemeral relationship between war planning and political decision-making in both Canada and the United States.

Before the United States entered the war in 1917, its proclamation of neutrality thwarted Canadian recruiting below the border; but thousands of Americans crossed into Canada to enlist. Despite this evidence of cordial relations on the part of some of their neighbours, Canadian "Home Guards" in the Niagara peninsula, who were militia too old for active service, drilled enthusiastically against a renewal of the Fenian raids. The chief of the General Staff had to call a halt. He told the militia that times had changed since 1866.[1] Meanwhile the neutrality proclamation had not outlawed trade in arms and American industrial production had helped to meet Canada's wartime needs. In return the expanded Canadian aviation industry was able to fill orders for American war requirements in 1917. Earlier, Canadian pilots had trained in the United States and this also was reciprocated when the United States entered the war. Part of the American Expeditionary Force sailed for Europe from Halifax.

But Canadian and American association in the war against Germany included little bilateral cooperation. Canada was still only partially autonomous, both politically and militarily.[2] When arrangements for the training and commitment of American troops were discussed, the Americans negotiated with Britain and France, but not with Canada. Gen. Arthur Currie, the Canadian commander of the CEF, showed a greater understanding of the problems involved in working with the Americans than did Field-Marshal Haig who wanted to absorb them into allied formations. Currie advised his minister that placing American troops under Canadian command would become a sensitive issue in the United States and would only "invite" disaster.[3] Perhaps in consequence of his opinion, American divisions trained with British and Australian Corps, as well as with the French;[4] but not on any substantial scale with the CEF. Active service in France thus brought no close military cooperation in training or operations for the two North American armies. Both expeditionary bodies were parts of the "Allied" force; but there was no formal Canadian-American military alliance in the German war. Canadian and American units did serve together more intimately in the mixed Allied forces that fought the Bolsheviks in Murmansk and Archangel in 1918;[5] and a year later detachments of the 16th Canadian Field Artillery Brigade gave support to another Allied force in North Russia that included the 339th American Infantry Regiment.[6] These instances of somewhat closer operational integration were, however, small-scale; and furthermore they were still part of multilateral rather than of bilateral arrangements.

After the Armistice and the Peace of Versailles, when the peoples and politicians in North America shared a determination not to get embroiled again in Europe's troubles, and hope based on the new League of Nations and on the spread of pacifism flourished in some circles, professional soldiers were sceptical. Lacking adequate political direction, working with tight budgets, and struggling against the prevailing pacifist philosophy, they strove to keep alive the rudiments of military preparedness. Inevitably, for want of other cogent reasons, in both countries some of them looked back to the historic justification for maintaining armed forces in North America, the defence of the Canadian-American border.

In Canada, although the Permanent Force had been established at 10,000 by statute in 1919, it numbered less than 4,000 all ranks in some subsequent years; and the number trained in the Non-Permanent Active Militia, much below a new increased postwar establishment, was actually considerably less than before the war.[7] These figures show the weak state of Canada's defences and the failure of government and people to take the country's defence needs seriously. Many Canadian soldiers had now had personal experience of fighting a modern war, but little was done to organize an effective force on their return. In 1922 one reform was undertaken, the concentration of administration of all three branches of the armed services, including the new Royal Canadian Air Force, under a Department of National Defence, but this was mainly for purposes of economy. The arrangement was intended to serve the military needs of a small country with a limited defence budget.[8] However, there was at first no joint general staff committee, and the reorganization did not include a modern general staff committee, and the reorganization did not include a modern general staff for war planning and operations. Furthermore, Canada had no representation overseas or other means of gathering the necessary military and political intelligence. Finally there was no Canadian staff college. Canadian officers had to go to Britain for staff training.

In the early 1920s a single officer, Col. J. ("Buster") Sutherland-Brown, director of military operations and intelligence, was solely responsible for the formulation of strategic plans in Canada. Born in Simcoe, Ontario, of Scottish descent, he had served with distinction with the CEF in France, ending the war as AA and QMG of the First Division. In 1920 Sutherland-Brown noted that the Imperial General Staff in London had anticipated four possible sources of danger to the Empire, a European combination, the United States, Japan, or a combination of these, and that it had placed them in that order of priority. He reasoned that only the second and fourth of these dangers, and to a lesser extent the third, would put Canada in such immediate danger of invasion as to require a general mobilization. He therefore decided that his duty was to draw up defence plans for three possibilities, for defence against the United States, for defence against Japan, and for the organization of an expeditionary force to help the Empire in the event of either a hostile European combination or a minor crisis.[9]

Between December 1920 and April 1921, working with a small staff of NCO clerks, Sutherland-Brown prepared the Defence Scheme Number 1, a 200-page plan for war with the United States. The basis of his plan was an expectation of invasion by American flying columns at the outset of a war. He proposed the mobilization of the Canadian Militia in order to capture key American invasion bases at Spokane, Seattle, Minneapolis and St. Paul, Albany, part of Maine, as well as bridgeheads on the Great Lakes frontier from the Niagara to the St. Mary's rivers.[10] Sutherland-Brown's rationale for drawing up this plan was that, having studied the United States and its citizens since his youth, he believed that he knew them well. Although some people assumed a war with the U.S. was "unthinkable," Brown argued that all that had so far prevented an Anglo-American war was that Britain had patiently endured American insults. He believed that growing national feeling in Canada, if backed by a military force that could not be taken lightly and by Empire support, would make the Americans stop to think before they attempted anything. Furthermore he urged that a defence scheme that covered the borders could be turned to meet any other eventuality,[11] a point that has often been overlooked by his critics.

Sutherland-Brown's Defence Scheme Number 1 did not conform with advice which Lord Jellicoe had given the Canadian government in 1919, that the possibility of a war between Britain and the United States was so small that it should not affect Canadian planning; nor did it fit with the ideas of either the Department of External Affairs or the high command of the new Royal Canadian Air Force;[12] but after the Washington conference of 1921–22 had seemed to decrease the danger from Japan, and after the Chanak incident in Turkey (1922) had fed Prime Minister Mackenzie King's suspicions of British imperialism, the production of Defence Plans Numbers 2 and 3 was delayed. Brown's Defence Scheme Number 1 therefore remained the only extant Canadian army war plan until he was moved to another appointment in 1927.[13]

Defence Scheme Number 1 should not be attributed solely to Sutherland-Brown's obsessive, archaic, and seemingly pathological concern about an American danger to Canada. When the Canadian Joint Staff Committee was established in 1927, the chief of the General Staff, Maj.-Gen. H. C. Thacker, approved Brown's agenda for the first meeting despite the fact that it gave priority to the problem of defending Canada against the United States; and Commodore Walter Hose, director of the Naval Service, by detailing at that first meeting the navy's plans for mobilization on the Great Lakes, seemed to give Sutherland-Brown's ideas tacit approval.[14]

But two years later Hose told Vice-Admiral Sir C. T. M. Fuller, the British commander-in-chief of the America and West Indies station who was then visiting Canada, that the possibility of an American war was not seriously considered in any Canadian defence plan.[15] As Defence Scheme Number 1 was still Canada's only extant plan, this was inaccurate. However, the retiring chief of the General Staff, General Thacker, had in fact already instructed Sutherland-Brown to prepare Defence Plan Number 3 for the dispatch of an expeditionary force overseas in the event of a major war. This new plan was completed by one of Sutherland-Brown's successors, H. H. Mathews, but not until 1932. Meanwhile, the notorious Number 1 was withdrawn in May 1931. In October General McNaughton ordered Military District commanders to burn it.[16]

Sutherland-Brown's war planning has been the subject of considerable ridicule;[17] but it is not entirely clear whether this is because he is considered to have been out of touch with political reality or because any Canadian defence against the United States would have been militarily hopeless. Undoubtedly Sutherland-Brown reflected archaic Canadian fears rather than current opinion; and although he guessed accurately what American soldiers were already planning, he had probably incorrectly assessed the reaction of the American public and politicians in the event of troubled relations with Canada. But at a time when the need for the maintenance of armed forces in Canada could be premised on little else than the abstract concept that every national state needs self-defence forces, for Brown and others to respond to historic fears was not unnatural, especially when the only other apparent alternative for advocating military preparation, a major overseas commitment, was politically unattractive.

Sutherland-Brown's activities seem less bizarre today than they did a few years ago. For it is now known that his professional counterparts in the United States had anticipated him and were very much more active in studying plans for war in North America. In 1919, in acknowledgement of the value of the General Staff's contribution (without which, as Secretary of War Newton D. Baker said, the war could not have been won),[18] the president and Congress had reconstituted the Army War College which had been closed during hostilities. The college was charged to identify "possible enemies of the future, and the probability of war with them as indicated by our present relationships and by such future relations as can be determined."[19] As before the war, when the War College had been the United States Army's only planning staff, the students prepared war plans and, acting as operations sections of a General Staff, wrote the appropriate staff directions. Each spring, towards the end of the annual course, this theoretical work was tested in war games.[20]

In that same year, 1919, the Joint Board of the army and navy, which had been dormant for the past ten years, was also revived. Moreover, it was now given a planning staff in the form of a Joint Planning Committee with at least three representatives from each of the services.[21] In March 1920, Gen. Peyton C. March, chief of staff of the army, recommended to the Joint Board that the Navy and Army War Colleges should study the same strategic problems.[22] Finally, by the National Defense Act of 1920, Congress provided the army's General Staff with an adequate complement of officers and authorized it to undertake broad duties of a general planning nature. Pershing, appointed chief of staff in July 1921, organized the army's General Staff on the lines of his wartime headquarters. He also gave it a War Plans Division to handle strategic plans and related preparations for war.[23]

These measures effectively relieved the War Colleges of the sole responsibility for war planning. The army's War Plans Division at first worked also on mobilization plans;[24] but in 1923 that duty was transferred to G-3 of the General Staff. Thereafter planning for operations in a future war was one of the chief functions of the War Plans Division of the army as also of that of the navy.[25] Members of these divisions of the two services served on the Joint Board's War Planning Committee. Much of the Joint Board's work was concerned with voluminous studies for use in international disarmament conferences. It drew up and distributed contingency plans for defence construction at, and the employment of military and naval forces in defence of, particular localities in hypothetical situations. But it also coordinated the war plans of the two services.

The classic theory of staff planning developed from supposed Prussian practice in the nineteenth century was that peacetime staffs should prepare plans for every conceivable eventuality. This entailed assessments of the possibility of war. Even if war with a particular state was considered quite unlikely, it was assumed in theory that the military should be prepared. Plans drafted by the American army and navy and approved by the Joint Board would be ready for use when the president needed them for any emergency.[26] The major hypothetical war plans were known for security reasons by colours, the device invented by Gen. Adna R. Chafee, chief of staff, 1904–1906. One undated postwar list included twenty such colours, most of them representing war with a single nation. The White Plan was for internal disturbances, Grey was for war with a combination of Caribbean countries, and Rainbow at that time represented action under the auspices of the League of Nations.[27]

Among these plans the one that entailed most technical staff work by the army was Blue which planned a state of national readiness against any possible combination of powers. Blue was in effect a master plan for general mobilization. Orange (Japan), was primarily a naval plan, always seen as the one most relevant to foreseeable developments in foreign relations.[28] It occupied most of the attention of American planners between the wars. It was the most comprehensive of the plans, continually kept up-to-date, revised, and expanded. In addition to Blue, only two other colour plans called for national mobilization. These were Red (Britain), and Red-Orange.[29]

The drafting of a colour plan did not signify anticipation of war with the country concerned. The colour plans were contingency plans to meet either probable or improbable situations. An official U.S. military history has stated that *in all cases* they were "simply outlines of missions to be accomplished" and, except for Orange, were "meaningless because they had so little relation to contemporary international and political and military alignments. . . . They were valuable . . . as abstract exercises in the technical process of detailed military planning, providing useful training for the officers who drew them up."[30] It should be added that the results of these plans affected the direction of much of the other work of the War Plans Divisions, their detailed recommendations for construction and development for the defence of ports and of other localities including American island territories, and also their ideas about mobilization.

Perhaps because of the dislike of the American public for another involvement in Europe that would take large numbers of troops overseas, the U.S. Army's planning was virtually restricted to the defence of American territory. Hence there was little or no work on Army Plan Black for war with Germany;[31] and when the Navy War College studied Plan Black in 1927 in connection with the security of the Caribbean and a possible German invasion of the United States from bases there, there was severe criticism in the newspapers.[32] So, although the system of colour planning conformed with the idea of being prepared for any emergency, complications of foreign policy and domestic politics coupled with popular sentiment prevented it from being comprehensive. As previously noted, it was in some ways easier to study war plans with an unlikely enemy than with a likely one, especially with one that had a considerable constituency in the United States. Furthermore, planning for the most difficult war, rather than the most likely one, had attractions for training and also perhaps for claiming larger budget appropriations.

The Army War College had no organic connection with the army's planners after its commandant ceased to wear two hats in 1920;[33] yet, although no longer the sole planning agencies and now restricted to their ostensible function, training, the War Colleges were still closely tied in with the War Plans Divisions. Until 1925–26 the war planning part of the Army War College's course continued to be called "Army War Plans Division: General Staff Division"; and it obtained files from the Military Intelligence Division. Members of the War Plans Division gave lectures at the college. Its first course had a head start on the Plans Division, because that body took some time to organize itself.

In 1919–20, Committee Number One of the first postwar War College course, among other exercises, studied Canada.[34] Intelligence was obtained from the chief of the Engineers about the Canadian army and about the geography of the border, including railroads, and roads in the vicinity.[35] The General Staff also produced a "Naval Plan for the Great Lakes" that dealt with the defence of cities on the lakes, the dimensions of canal locks, and identification of areas to be occupied by the army in order to ensure the possibility of naval control within fifteen days.[36] The Military Intelligence Division produced an intelligence summary of the "Estimate of the Situation in Canada"[37] and also furnished information about the ordnance and aircraft brought to Canada from France by the CEF, and about the organization of Canadian field batteries.[38]

Students on this and succeeding War College courses prepared plans for an invasion of Canada in the event of a hostile British-Japanese coalition. They took into account the new air factor and the location of radio stations. These training exercises discussed Canada's characteristics and probable course of action.[39] One committee reported that Canada was a "self-governing dependency, having more points in resemblance to Blue than to Red," that Canadians were "unmilitary in character but . . . bold, courageous, vigorous, and . . . excellent soldiers when trained." The report went on to say that "Red has dealt generously with her and she will certainly join Red-Orange combination against Blue with her full strength notwithstanding her dislike for Orange and friendship for Blue." The plans presented by that committee followed the traditional lines of strategy for invasion to sever Canada's contact with Britain by seizing the St. Lawrence River.[40]

The orientation lecture in the War Plans Division course given in 1923–24 outlined the functions of the new higher-level Planning Division. It revealed that it had been set up to formulate plans for use in the theatre of war and, in the event of mobilization, to furnish personnel for the nucleus of general staffs for each division and for the General Headquarters in the field. Additional personnel for these general staffs were to be obtained from the War College.[41] A conference on March 22, 1924, had determined what war plans were to be prepared. It said, "Conflict is possible with Japan and with Great Britain, but more probably with Japan. The abrogation of the Anglo-Japanese Alliance has greatly reduced the probability of a coalition of those powers against the United States." In conclusion it ranked the danger of war with Mexico or Cuba first because of their instability, then with Japan over the Monroe Doctrine or "her possible disregard for treaty obligations as to the status quo of fortifications and the open door in China." Finally it said, "with Great Britain there is possibility of conflict under the Monroe Doctrine and with our special interest in the Caribbean and also due to commercial competition."

Dealing especially with Britain the division answered that war with Britain was improbable and that at present trade was a source only of "friendly rivalry"; but it went on to add that "one of Great Britain's worries at the present time is the possibility of American sea supremacy. They do not wish us to have a large merchant fleet and will try every way to prevent the United States from having a ship subsidy." The division then set down the degree of urgency (and therefore the order of planning) for preparation for war as follows: 1. Mexico; 2. Cuba; 3. Japan; 4. Insurrection in the Philippines; 5. Great Britain; 6. Great Britain and Japan, assuming that Japan would declare war against the United States after Great Britain and the United States had become engaged.[42]

An appendix to Army Strategic Plan Red detailed the transportation that would be required to supply the armies that undertook the occupation of Canada. An accompanying operations map showed that this campaign was expected to require four armies, one operating in the Maritime Provinces, a second in Quebec, a third in Ontario, and the fourth in the rest of Canada west of the Great Lakes. This plan also laid down the policy to be followed after Canada was occupied. It said, "Blue intentions are to hold in perpetuity all Crimson and Red territory gained. The policy will be to prepare the provinces and territories of Crimson and Red to become states and territories of the Blue Union upon the declaration of peace. The Dominion government will be abolished. . . ."[43]

In the following years the Army War Plans Division worked on the perfecting of what was still called "tentative Plan Red." Toward the end of 1925 the Operations Division of the General Staff was instructed to prepare a Situation Estimate for a war with Britain that might be caused by that country's loss of a favorable balance of trade. The instructions assumed that Britain would attempt to control the Western Atlantic by using Halifax as a principal base and Quebec as an auxiliary base. She would then attempt to invade the United States, aiming at Pittsburgh through "friendly territory," that is to say through Canada. In the following year this tentative plan "from the Army Point of view" was sent for the approval of the army chief of staff for submission to the Joint Staff Board. The plan assumed that Britain would seek to retain the initiative in land operations in North America and that Canada could not oppose the United States without British aid. The plan also emphasized the strategic importance of the Maritime Provinces.[44] An air member of the Army War Plans Division submitted a minority report. He argued that Britain's power in the air could be asserted through the "part of the Royal Air Force now stationed in Canada (the Canadian Air Force) [which] had been underestimated."[45] This was a ludicrous argument.

A year later, after a G-2 officer on the General Staff had contended that Canada could hold Halifax until reinforcements arrived from Britain and that that port should therefore not be an initial strategic objective for the American land attack,[46] and after the Supply Division of G-4 had set out to produce detailed supply estimates for mobilization for the Red Plan, the Army War Plans Division began to work once more on the Red-Orange Colour Plan.[47] Within a year it was being assumed that Canada's first war mission would be to destroy the Sault Ste. Marie locks in order to cut off the supply of iron ore to the United States, and that the Canadian Air Force would then bomb invasion routes in the vicinity of Montreal and Quebec. After the destruction of the Great Lakes transportation system the air force would turn to the Eastern theatre to prevent demonstrations against Halifax and would bomb Boston, New York, Philadelphia, Baltimore, and Washington.[48]

Even if it may be assumed that the function of war planners should be to prepare for the worst possible situation, this was carrying things to absurd lengths. If Canada's weakness in the air was not already known in the United States, it must have become known three years later when a U.S. naval attaché reported that he had been informed by a RCAF officer that Canadian air force units were not distributed to military districts, that they were not organized into functional fighting organizations, that their "so-called squadrons" included planes of several different types, and that they existed for training purposes only. "In as much as Canada had no idea of trouble with any other country it was not considered necessary to maintain a proper air force."[49] Furthermore, if the idea was that the Royal Air Force would send significant reinforcements, that was unrealistic to say the least. The U.S. Army Air Force's contentions sound like special pleading to bolster its quest for support.

By 1928, however, the tentative Army Strategic Plan Red was completed. It included speculation about the unity of the British Empire and whether Canada would remain neutral in the event of war.[50] This question had been the subject of a special War College study in 1926. Several officers had been assigned the task of recommending means of ensuring the neutrality, or the active assistance, of Canada and Australia in case of a war with Britain and Japan. The terms of reference for the study emphasized that the word "ensure" was to be taken in the sense of "secure" rather than "make sure." The studies that were produced stressed those facts that pointed to Canadian and Australian good-will towards the United States—economic ties and dislike for oriental immigration; and they recommended that the friendship of these countries should be cultivated. But they said it should be made quite clear to Canada that in a war she would suffer grievously.[51] One infantry major's study introduced a new thought. He noted in passing that it had sometimes been suggested that Canadian neutrality might not be desirable for the United States from a military point of view. "Our interests would demand that we compel her to come out squarely or as an ally."[52] More was to be heard of this idea later.

Meanwhile the Army War College continued to study the details of possible operations against Canada. Faculty and students were now ordered "not to cross the border during the Quebec reconnaissance"[53]—on-site reconnaissance of that kind would attract attention. But preparation of the Joint Board's War Plan Red had been delayed because the naval planners had been concentrating on their Japan plans. Hence, when on February 12, 1929, the Joint Army and Navy Basic War Plan Red was approved by the secretary of the navy, it was only provisionally, "as a basis for further study," because the naval members of the Joint Planning Committee had not yet been able to give sufficient time to it. The plan was given tentative approval at that time because the War Department needed it for mobilization planning. The Joint Board assumed that whatever modifications the navy would request would not seriously alter its main lines.[54]

The navy's Basic Plan Red was completed and approved by the secretary of the navy and the acting secretary of war on May 10, 1930. It assumed that Canada, and especially Halifax, could be used by Britain to concentrate forces to attack the United States. It stressed the geographic, strategic, and economic importance of the "Ontario [Niagara]

Peninsula" and of the Welland Canal, use of which was necessary for Britain but not for the United States. It called Winnipeg a "bottleneck" for the delivery of western wheat via the Hudson Bay route and noted that the city was particularly vulnerable to an American attack. It noted that the three possible routes for invading Canada in the Montreal-Quebec area each possessed a railroad and a primary highway.

The navy planners considered the possibility that, because of her ties with the United States or to avoid becoming a battleground, Canada might stay neutral and would thereupon secede from the Empire. Her neutrality would free Britain from the moral responsibility of defending her, and would thus permit greater concentration on a British attack on American shipping. Canada's neutrality would deprive Britain of a base for attacking the United States. But the navy planners believed that it would be to American advantage for Canada to be allied with Britain so that the United States could employ its superior manpower to overrun the Dominion in order to offset losses that might be suffered elsewhere. Canadian neutrality would in their opinion be of little advantage to the United States, especially since its duration would be in doubt. Neutrality might merely be a cloak to protect the Dominion while it was weakest and to enable it to grow stronger. From the beginning of a war with Britain the United States would have to maintain forces ready to move into Canada on need.

The navy planners said that it seemed certain that Canada would not ally herself with the United States. She was more likely to remain loyal to Britain. They believed that the decision to go to war would have to be approved "by the Empire as a whole," but that once it had been made Britain would secretly begin to build up forces in the Western hemisphere. Britain's object would be to eliminate the United States as an important economic and commercial rival in international trade. They concluded that the American plan ought to be to defend the Panama canal, to seize and hold the Great Lakes waterways system, especially at its narrows, to launch an offensive at Winnipeg to isolate Western forces, to secure Halifax "provided the situation at the outbreak of war justifies such an operation," to make a major offensive against the Quebec-Montreal area, and eventually to invade other parts of Canada to destroy all British forces.[55]

The Army General Staff now called for a list of the support troops that would be needed for operations to carry out such campaigns.[56] On January 2, 1931, five months before Sutherland-Brown's Defence Scheme Number 1 was withdrawn in Canada, American army officers began to work on a special mobilization plan for invasion of the Dominion.[57] But the U.S. Air Force component of the General Staff continued to express doubt about Plan Red. It said, "our slower mass standardized production methods would not begin to work to our advantage until after the seventh month."[58]

In March 1935 a suggestion made at the hearings of the Federal Aviation Committee that the United States might be bombed from tenders on the coast of Labrador and in Hudson Bay led to a proposal to send American officers there on secret reconnaissance missions. This was ruled out because they could probably not avoid detection, because their effort would be useless, and because it would jeopardize the defenceless state of the land frontier between Canada and the United States which had been for a hundred years a symbol of outstanding friendliness and an ideal for other nations to follow.[59] However, in testimony given secretly to the Military Committee of the House of Representatives, information about a related project leaked out. It was revealed that, as part of the American defence program, a "camouflaged air base" was being built near the Canadian border. As a result there was considerable public concern and the committee's chairman had to calm this by declaring that the air base was not designed against Canada. He said that such precautions were like the French fortifications on the Belgian border, "not against Belgium but against what might come through Belgium."[60] (It was not known at the time that the Maginot line was not in fact extended along the Franco-Belgian border to the sea.)

American planning for war with Canada had been completed, although only in outline, just about the time that General McNaughton ordered the destruction of the Defence Plan Number 1. Four years later, after the Japanese invasion of Manchuria and after Italy's invasion of Albania, the Joint Planning Board in the United States had come to believe that, if a Japanese-American war occurred, Britain might stay neutral and might even ally itself eventually with Blue.[61] Nevertheless, in 1935–36 Committee Number 8 of the Army War College prepared a current estimate of the British Commonwealth which included a "critical" atlas of Canada and the approaches thereto, with a map showing the distribution of Canada's militia strength and units by districts;[62] and in 1937–38 students prepared a War Plan for Blue versus Red (Britain), Gold (France), and Crimson (Canada). The army's mission in this plan would be to seize the lower bank of the St. Lawrence River to prevent the use of that waterway by the forces of the coalition.[63]

In 1937 the army's Red Plan was declared obsolete. Copies were ordered to be destroyed by burning.[64] War College courses then prepared another survey of the British Commonwealth "from the theater point of view" in 1938–39, a plan for war with Red, Crimson, and Gold, and also a counter plan.[65] To accompany this study the Army War College obtained a Naval War College Operational Problem entitled "Overseas Expeditionary Force to capture Halifax from Red-Crimson coalition."[66] With the growing certainty of a war in Europe and the increasing likelihood of Britain and France being drawn into it, it seems possible that this plan was a contingency exercise designed to prepare for a very different situation, that is if events in Europe went awry and the Canadian port was in danger of falling into hostile hands.

That American plans for war with Britain were more than mere exercises is suggested by the fact that on May 25, 1939, when Admiral William D. Leahy, chief of naval operations, declared that re-study had shown that the navy's Red Plan was now "wholly inapplicable to present conditions," he added that some of its directions could be adapted for use in a major war in the Atlantic. Although no further planning should be done on the plan, it should be retained until such time as a Joint War Plan requiring major effort in the Atlantic became available.[67] Nothing more effectively illustrates the general nature of all this contingency planning than the fact that the plan for a war with Britain on the high seas was now to be adapted to cope with a possible German threat if the Nazis triumphed in Europe, and for other aspects of a resulting war in the Atlantic.

Canadian and American planning between the wars differed because the former country did not have more than the rudiments of a professional defence force; but Sutherland-Brown's ideas were similar in nature to those developed by the military staffs in the United States and he had guessed correctly what their thinking would be. The American military bureaucracy, being more ponderous, worked more slowly. The implication of a preponderance of American power for the military relations of the two countries had become clear first in Canada, possibly because the hopelessness of defence was understood and accepted there, and therefore the need for realism was appreciated earlier. Meanwhile American planners did what they were employed to do, that is, to study the strategy of defending the United States against any possible foreign aggression. Lacking adequate political direction, they responded, but belatedly, to the changing international scene, first to prepare plans for a possible, although unlikely, British attack with or without the support of Japan, and then to scrap those plans in view of a greater danger from Germany as well as Japan. In neither Canada nor the United States was sufficient armed force available to cope with all possible situations; in both countries the supremacy of the civil powers was unquestioned; in both, professional soldiers had to plan with inadequate support, inadequate direction, and inadequate understanding of political realities. Defence problems had not yet become so technical that they could be monopolized by military professionals or academic strategists.

As war in Europe drew nearer in the late 1930s, Canada had begun reluctantly to rearm. Colonel Stacey has shown that this process was carried out with one eye on the United States, but that this was because it was assumed that unless Canada took steps to protect itself if attacked by another power, the United States would feel constrained to move in.[68]

Planning for war in North America between the wars seems to us today to have been an anachronism. But without the planning that had been carried on earlier both Canada and the United States might have been even less prepared when need arose elsewhere. Even with such planning they were caught by surprise when it was decided to commit Canadian troops to the European conflict and when the United States in 1941 was forced by Pearl Harbor to go to war. So, although planning for war in North America had not reflected what is now known to have been the drift of international relations, it had served however inadequately a limited military purpose.

In the two decades between the World Wars, planning for wars in North America had not only been unrelated to the political reality of current international relations, it was also unimportant domestically. Governments and people in both the United States and Canada, after first pinning their hopes on international disarmament and collective security, had found themselves fighting the Great Depression that further reduced their willingness to spend money on preparation for war. Civilian administrators had therefore given little thought to defence problems, except to cut appropriations for them. Furthermore, within the military establishments, General Staffs were so concerned about the continued existence of armed forces that war planners were without influence. Planning staffs were always kept small. The Joint Board of the army and navy in the United States seemed to be an impressive advance over the prewar years, but it had all the weakness of a coordinating committee and little power. Its best work was connected with details of army and navy cooperation in defence installations, in ports, and in navigable home waters. From the beginning it was ignored, and even snubbed by the State Department. As a result no real attempt was made to relate its planning to foreign policy, except for the significant priority given to Plan Orange.

War planning in the United States included exploration of strategy for a war with Britain—and so with Canada—which was an anachronistic vestige of older concerns. At about the time that the Japanese invasion of Manchuria in 1931 was reducing the possibility of British collaboration with Japan against the United States to its lowest point, the war planning machinery in the United States finally cranked out its most developed plan for war with Britain.

If such a war was then a remote possibility, the question of Canadian neutrality or involvement was crucial. But the strategic plans Red and Crimson had been drawn up without any very thorough consideration of that important question. American professional war planners thus showed very little more political discrimination than "Buster" Brown. American planning for war with Canada was, however, inconsequential in the early 1930s. At the same time O. D. Skelton, an influential adviser of the Canadian prime minister, believed that the military's task was to "submit military plans" *after* the civil arm of the government had laid down "the scheme of policy and liabilities."[69] If this order of business had been strictly followed there would have been no planning at all, for Canadian governments did not give that much attention to preparation for defence.

What was not realized at the time in either country was that the Canadian-American relationship was moving towards military alliance. Two recent historians have stated their belief that when Sir Robert Borden and his colleagues in the Canadian cabinet during the First World War turned to the United States for much needed investment and trade, they took a revolutionary step that had far greater consequences than they expected. Canada was thus moved towards dependence on the United States rather than on Britain.[70] But Canadian military authorities were wary of becoming involved in an American war with Japan. They therefore opposed fly-over rights for American planes between the United States mainland and Alaska. On this they had to be overruled by the government.[71]

What eventually changed their attitude towards the United States was the darkening situation in Europe which led them to urge that Canada should seek an understanding that would make American military supplies available. Now it was the turn of the Department of External Affairs to drag its feet.[72] However, the ice was broken as a consequence of the personal friendship that developed between Mackenzie King and Franklin Roosevelt. Declarations by the president at Chautauqua in 1936 and at Kingston in 1938, that the United States would not allow an enemy to overcome Canada, were followed by the prime minister's statement that Canada would not permit an enemy to use its soil as a base for attacking the United States. The American chiefs of staff remained more concerned about their southern neighbours than about the north; but Roosevelt personally reconnoitred the sea approaches to Canada and the United States on the West and East.[73] King was of the opinion that the Americans had always exaggerated the Japanese danger, but he agreed to secret American-Canadian staff talks in Washington. The American chiefs, although apparently unaware that the initiative for these talks had come from their own president, talked cordially with their Canadian opposite numbers.[74]

After Britain declared war on Germany, it was in this atmosphere of amiable cooperation that Roosevelt overruled the State Department and accepted Mackenzie King's interpretation that Canada was still "neutral" until her Parliament decided otherwise. The amount of war material that crossed to Canada during the short period when the neutrality legislation was not applied is not known,[75] but it may have been considerable. Thereafter the purchase of American weapons, munitions, and other material that was clearly for war purposes ceased until the legislation was amended in June 1940. However, despite American neutrality, the ties between the two countries became very close and the number of agencies that operated across the border proliferated astonishingly.[76]

Long before the United States entered the war, there was virtually a state of alliance with belligerent Canada. Nevertheless, during the "phony war" period, the U.S. service chiefs examined the problem of defending neighbouring Canadian territory, but made no arrangements for defence cooperation with Canada. The American service chiefs continued to be more concerned about Central America. Canadian attempts to purchase non-military material for war purposes in the United States had at first been blocked, though some buying took place through private deals.[77] But after the fall of France, when there was fear of a threat to North America, traditional isolationism was muted. By the Ogdensburg Agreement of August 18, 1940, Roosevelt and King jointly declared a new policy of cooperation for defence. The Permanent Joint Board for Defence, created by politicians without consulting the defence departments, was designed to give Canada a voice in the defence of North America and to facilitate American use of Canadian bases for mutual security. Later, at Hyde Park on April 20, 1941, the two heads of state also agreed to mesh the resources and industrial capacity of their countries for war purposes even though the United States was still technically neutral. On September 13, 1941, when the United States was still not at war, U.S. naval vessels took over convoy duties in the American sector of the North Atlantic and seventy-five Canadian war vessels engaged in that duty came under American command.[78]

The approach of war had thus brought about an informal military alliance between Canada and the United States. After Pearl Harbor the Americans, unwilling to leave in the hands of another power contiguous areas essential for their safety, pressed for unified commands in various Canadian regions.[79] But Canadian service chiefs invariably resisted this right through the war. Only one such command, for the protection of overseas shipping off Newfoundland, was created; and it was set up by Roosevelt and Churchill without consulting Canada.[80] Air routes across Canada for ferrying short-range aircraft to Greenland and on to the United Kingdom brought American servicemen to work in Eastern Canada under the direction of the United States War Department. Ironically, this project was code-named "Crimson,"[81] the code for prewar invasion plans. One aspect of the War College's planning had thus been carried out bloodlessly, but in an entirely different context and manner from what was anticipated. Similar American intrusion on Canadian soil in the West to establish an air staging route and a highway to Alaska seemed to many Canadians to be much too independent of Canadian control. American military commanders often acted there as if they worked in areas under American jurisdiction. As a result Western Canadians talked of "the American occupation." The Canadian government had to send a retired major-general, W. W. Foster, with the sonorous but empty title of "Special Commissioner for Defence Projects in North-West Canada," to assert the Canadian presence in Canada. Foster, travelling in an old Lysander, was graciously received by American commanders who were often unable to understand the need for his presence.[82]

A recent article by the historian of the Canadian armed forces has stated that "Washington had an even greater tendency than Whitehall to take Canada's war effort for granted."[83] At the level of the troops who were engaged on operational tasks, apart from occasional lapses of discipline, fraternal association was usually marked by a spirit of good-will.[84] Nevertheless, the official American history of the cooperation admits that it brought American demands for command of Canadian forces in Canada and for other arrangements that were unacceptable to the host country. The smaller state was, however, free to take a divergent stand because it was secure in the knowledge that the U.S. would not resort to force to get its way. Provided it could stand up to the political, economic, and psychological pressures that the Americans, with their vastly greater number, wealth, and power, could bring to bear, Canada could prevail. But when she sought to gain particular objectives or gain important interests, her relative weakness placed her at a great disadvantage. This became even more obvious after the United States entered the war. Canada then found that the two principal partners in the alliance preferred to run the war on their own, without consulting Ottawa. The Second World War thus provided Canada with extremely important lessons for any future military alliance with the United States.[85]

During the war some Canadians had expressed the belief that the Canadian-American alliance should be terminated when the war ended because it would irritate the USSR.[86] Instead Soviet aggression in Eastern Europe, the advent of nuclear weapons, and the expectation of intercontinental missiles to deliver them, brought a more formal alliance.

The two North American countries joined the multinational NATO Treaty for the defence of Western Europe and then, for the defence of the North American continent, joined bilaterally in the NORAD agreement. At first the main threat came primarily from trans-Arctic bombers and early warning stations in Northern Canada were needed. Canada was careful to insist that agreements made with the Americans about construction and the deployment of troops should protect Canadian sovereign rights. But the heavy cost of the defence systems set up in Canada, and American monopoly of the all-important strategic nuclear deterrent, meant that the United States bore by far the greater share of the burden. Canada therefore accepted heavy moral obligations to the United States for her defence. To the military in both countries, and to many civilian defence strategists, especially Americans, the new alliance was an inevitable consequence of geographic proximity and modern technology;[87] but a perceptive British scholar has shown that it was the result of a Canadian political decision and that Canada can exercise a degree of independent choice in defence priorities.[88]

Canada's achievements in the Second World War, and other factors, led to the growth of a new national spirit in Canada that found the American alliance irksome. Since it coincided with a great increase in the weight and extent of American economic domination through investment and the control of Canadian resources and Canadian industry, and with growing cultural pressure through the mass media that seemed to thwart a more urgent quest for a clear Canadian identity, many Canadians came to regard the military alliance as a triumph of "continentalism" likely to bring about the peaceful conquest of the country.[89] This seemed to promise consummation of the objectives of the secret American military planning undertaken between the wars.

Since Canadians found many American policies objectionable, nationalists regarded the American alliance as a bond that tied them to a new imperialism. Canada's attempt to assert a new international image by leadership in peacekeeping operations and by contact with Third World countries was not enough to offset their fears that their country was rapidly being absorbed. An American scholar has acknowledged that the United States is indeed a national security risk to Canada.[90] Disenchantment with American policy in Korea,[91] dissociation from that policy in South-East Asia, disputes about sovereignty in Arctic waters,[92] and about the dangers of pollution and the use of natural resources, intensified Canadian feeling about the American relationship. To offset this development, Prime Minister Trudeau issued White Papers on foreign policy and defence, and the secretary of state for external affairs spoke of Canada making a deliberate choice that would steer a middle course between unproductive obstruction of American policies and the drift to continentalism.[93]

The American menace thus no longer takes the form of planning for a military invasion on the ground, and Canada's defence against it has similarly changed its shape. With the rise of military professionalism in the United States and the creation of the National Security Council in 1947 the Americans at last have defence planning capacity that can take political considerations into account. But it is unlikely that American studies now take the form of the traditional ground attacks to cut the St. Lawrence and the prairie railways. Many other agencies, in the White House and in such organizations as the CIA, have also become engaged in planning for various emergencies or even in covert operations, sometimes in illegal ways. Canadian affairs, for instance the separatist movement in Quebec, have come within the purview of one or more of such agencies. But American planning must now necessarily be more subtle and sophisticated than the crude strategic operation moves that were developed for Plan Red and Plan Crimson. If any go as far as to call for the use of overt force, which is far from certain, they would be centred upon the seizure of air fields and telecommunications systems.[94] Military action would be more likely to take the form of support for sympathetic Canadian national opposition groups that sought to resist a Communist take-over or to oppose a weakening of the joint defence system.

However, although some of the irresponsible and semi-criminal elements that produced Watergate and similar horrors in the United States may have included Canada in their planning in some such way, there was probably no need for consideration of either overt or covert direct action. The enormous pressures that the United States can bring to bear through its financial and economic strength, through congressional action, and through the media will probably serve American purposes effectively in any dispute with Canada about foreign or domestic policies.[95] It has been suggested that even if Canada were to subscribe to the Warsaw Pact, which is an extreme that is hardly worth considering, the United States might not be driven to military invasion or occupation.[96] But it would certainly bring into play subtle but powerful weapons that Canada would find it very hard to resist. The future independence of Canada may continue to rest ultimately on American forbearance.

NOTES

ABBREVIATIONS

AWC   Army War College (U.S.)
BM   British Museum
CAB   Cabinet Papers
CDC   Colonial Defence Committee
CID   Committee of Imperial Defence
CO   Colonial Office
FO   Foreign Office
OCMH   Office of the Chief of Military History (U.S.)
PRO   Public Record Office
SNA   Scottish National Archives
USMHC United States Military History Collection, Carlisle Barracks,
          Pa.
USNA   United States National Archives
WCD   War College Division, U.S. General Staff
WD   War Department
WO   War Office
WPD   War Plans Division, U.S. General Staff

INTRODUCTION

1. This theme is elaborated in D. Stairs, "The Military as an Instrument of Canadian Foreign Policy," in H.J. Massey, ed., *The Canadian Military: A Profile* (Toronto: Copp Clark, 1972), especially pp. 86–92.

2. Ibid., p. 113.

3. *Kingston Whig-Standard*, June 8, 1971.

4. In a letter to the present writer, Sept. 9, 1971.

5. C.S. Mackinnon, "The Imperial Fortresses in Canada: Halifax and Esquimalt, 1871–1907," 2 vols. (Ph.D. diss., University of Toronto, 1965), II, 459–60; J.A.S. Grenville, *Lord Salisbury and Foreign Policy* (London: Athens Press, 1964), pp. 389, 422.

6. Stanley W. Dziuban, *Military Relations between the United States and Canada, 1939–1945* (Washington, D.C.: Office of the Chief of Military History, 1959), p. 18n.

7. One of the main themes of Prime Minister Pierre Trudeau's revision of foreign and defence policy was greater provision for the assertion of Canadian sovereignty by "surveillance" and "control" by Canada's armed forces. See Office of the Prime Minister, press release, April 3, 1969; Donald S. Macdonald, *Defence in the Seventies: White Paper on Defence* (Ottawa: Information Canada, 1971), pp. 17–24; Douglas M. Johnston, "Canada's Marine Environment: Problems of Legal Protection," Behind the Headlines, XXIX (Toronto: Canadian Institute of International Affairs, 1970), pp. 1–7. Roger F. Swanson, "The United States as a National Security Threat to Canada," ibid.,

pp. 9–16; Mitchell Sharp, *Foreign Policy for Canadians* (Ottawa: Information Canada, 1970), p. 15.

8. Charles P. Stacey, *Canada and the British Army, 1846–1871: A Study in the Practice of Responsible Government* (London: Longmans, Green, 1936; rev. ed., University of Toronto Press, 1968); J. Mackay Hitsman, *Safeguarding Canada: 1763–1871* (Toronto: University of Toronto Press, 1968); Robin Winks, *Canada and the United States: The Civil War Years* (Baltimore: The Johns Hopkins Press, 1960); Kenneth Bourne, *Britain and the Balance of Power in North America* (London: Longmans, Green, 1967).

9. Bourne, *Britain and the Balance of Power*, pp. 313–18.

10. Desmond Morton, *Ministers and Generals: Politics and the Canadian Militia, 1868–1904* (Toronto: University of Toronto Press, 1970).

11. James Eayrs, *In Defence of Canada*, I, *From the Great War to the Great Depression* (Toronto: University of Toronto Press, 1964); idem, II, *Appeasement and Rearmament* (Toronto: University of Toronto Press, 1965).

CHAPTER 1

1. The population of the United States was ten times that of British North America in 1812, nearly ten times in 1851, and over fourteen times in 1900. Kenneth Bourne, *Britain and the Balance of Power in North America, 1815–1908* (London: Longmans, Green, 1967), pp. 58–59, citing Helen I. Cowan, *British Emigration to British North America* (Toronto: University of Toronto Press, 1961), H.C. Allen, *Great Britain and the United States* (New York: St. Martin's, 1955), and J.B. Brebner, *North Atlantic Triangle* (New Haven: Yale, 1945).

2. J. Mackay Hitsman, *Safeguarding Canada, 1763–1871* (Toronto: University of Toronto Press, 1968), p. vii; Bourne, *Britain and the Balance of Power*.

3. Albert K. Weinberg, *Manifest Destiny* (Baltimore: Johns Hopkins University Press, 1935).

4. S.F. Wise and Robert Craig Brown, *Canada Views the United States: Nineteenth Century Political Attitudes* (Seattle: University of Washington Press), p. 108.

5. E.g., Henri Bourassa, *Great Britain and Canada* (Montreal: Beauchemin, [1901]), p. 7.

6. Wellington, "Memorandum [on the defence of Canada], March 3, 1841," PRO, WO 1/537, pp. 71–106.

7. W.L. Morton, *The Canadian Identity* (Madison: University of Wisconsin Press, 1961), p. 86.

8. James M. Callahan, *American Foreign Policy in Canadian Relations* (New York: Macmillan, 1937), p. 300.

9. Brian Bond, *The Victorian Army and Staff College, 1815–1914* (London: Eyre Methuen, 1972), pp. 33–34; Richard Glover, *Peninsular Preparation:*

the Reform of the British Army, 1795–1809 (Cambridge University Press, 1963), p. 22; Russell F. Weigley, *History of the United States Army* (New York: Macmillan, 1967), pp. 134–39.

10. For a chronological and detailed study of the strategic problems of the defence of Canada in the first three-quarters of the nineteenth century see the books by Hitsman and Bourne cited above.

11. Wellington, memorandum, March 31, 1841, PRO, WO 1/537, pp. 71–106. In response to a discussion of the strategic effect of the improvement of American communications shortly before the construction of the British St. Lawrence canals, Wellington concluded that difficulties caused by geography would persist.

12. C.P. Stacey, "The Backbone of Canada," Canadian Historical Association, *Report . . . . 1953*, pp. 1–13.

13. C.P. Stacey, "Another Look at the Battle of Erie," *Canadian Historical Review*, XXXIX (1958), 51.

14. Alvin C. Gluek, *Minnesota and the Manifest Destiny of the Canadian Northwest: a Study in Canadian–American Relations* (Toronto: University of Toronto Press, 1965), pp. 220–21.

15. Capt. A.T. Mahan, *Sea Power in its Relation to the War of 1812* (London: Sampson Low, 1945), I, v–vi.

16. Comm. E.W.C.R. Owen to John Wilson Croker, June 30, 1815, PRO, WO 80/11; C.P. Stacey, "An American plan for a Canadian campaign: Secretary James Monroe to Major-General Jacob Brown, Feb. 1815," *American Historical Review*, XLVI (1940–41), 348–58.

17. Wellington to Bathurst, March 1, 1919, PRO, WO 80/11.

18. Metcalfe to Stanley, July 11, 1845, PRO, WO 1/552, ff. 136–59.

19. Hitsman, *Safeguarding Canada*, p. 108.

20. Bourne, *Britain and the Balance of Power*, pp. 13–14.

21. Callahan, *American Foreign Policy*, p. 94.

22. Bourne, *Britain and the Balance of Power*, pp. 33–34.

23. Wellington to Bathurst, March 1, 1919, PRO, WO 80/11.

24. Ibid.

25. Hitsman, *Safeguarding Canada*, pp. 117–18.

26. Ibid., pp. 120–22.

27. Aberdeen to Sir George Murray, Sept. 29, 1841, PRO, WO 80/11; G.C. Mundy, Inspectorate of Fortifications, to Under-secretary for the Colonies, July 2, 1856, PRO, WO 6/90, pp. 497–99.

28. Hitsman, *Safeguarding Canada*, pp. 125–29.

29. G.F.G. Stanley, *Canada's Soldiers: The Military History of an Unmilitary People* (Toronto: Macmillan, 1960), p. 209.

30. Stanley to Sir George Murray, Sept. 29, 1841, PRO, WO 80/11; Sir George Arthur, confidential memorandum on the defence of Canada. "Summary of 1841," WO 80/11.

31. James T. Riccalton to Comdr. W.N. Fowell, RN, April 16, 1844, PRO, WO 1/537; Metcalfe to Stanley, April 18, 1844, PRO, WO 1/540, p. 8.

32. G. Murray to Gladstone, May 11, 1846, PRO, WO 1/555, pp. 453-64; [Murray?], memorandum, undated, PRO, WO 80/11.

33. [Four] Reports of Col. Holloway and Capt. Edward Boxer, RN [1845-46], PRO, WO 1/555, pp. 219-36.

34. Capt. Edward Boxer, RN, Jan. 4, 1845, PRO, WO 1/552; Cathcart to Lord Stanley, Dec. 11, 1845, PRO, WO 1/552; Bourne, *Britain and the Balance of Power*, pp. 155-58.

35. [Stanley] to Cathcart, Feb. 3, 1846, [draft], "Administration, etc.," PRO, WO 1/552.

36. Cathcart to Gladstone, March 26, 1846, PRO, WO 1/554, pp. 123-33.

37. Callahan, *American Foreign Policy*, pp. 172-80.

38. Ibid., pp. 227-28.

39. E.g., Lt. M.F. Maury, Aug. 1851, U.S., Congress, 37 Cong., 2nd sess., *House Exec. Docs.*, Report 86 in 1145, pp. 476-77. Maury was making a case for naval preparedness and anticipatory action.

40. Emmanuel R. Lewis, *Sea-coast Fortifications of the United States* (Washington: Smithsonian Institute Press, 1970), pp. 37-61.

41. *Report of General J.G. Totten, Chief Engineer, on the Subject of National Defences* (Washington: Printed by A. Boyd Hamilton, 1851), p. 81.

42. Ibid., pp. 83, 85.

43. Metcalfe to Stanley, July 4, 1845, PRO, WO 1/552, ff. 136-95.

44. Bourne, *Britain and the Balance of Power*, p. 153.

45. Metcalfe to Stanley, confidential, July 4, 1845, PRO, WO 1/552, ff. 136-59.

46. C.P. Stacey, *Canada and the British Army, 1846-1871: a Study in the Practice of Responsible Government*, rev. ed. (Toronto: University of Toronto Press, 1963), *passim*.

47. The implications of responsible government for Canadian defence were discussed by Grey and Elgin in a well-known exchange of correspondence. This is summarized in Stacey, *Canada and the British Army*, pp. 65-73.

48. Ibid., pp. 72-74, 104.

49. E. Hammond, FO, to H. Merivale, June 2, 1857, PRO, CO 42/611.

50. Head, confidential, Nov. 26, 1856, PRO, CO 42/605; FO to CO Aug. 30, 1858, PRO, CO 42/615.

51. Lt.-Gen. Sir William Eyre to CO, July 10, 1857, PRO, CO 42/610.

52. Lord Seaton to Lord John Russell, Dec. 30, 1839, "Papers Relating to the Fortification and Defence of Canada. Printed solely for the use of the Cabinet," PRO, [n.d.], WO 80/11.

53. Murray to Henry Goulburn, Sept. 3, 1945, PRO, WO 80/11.

54. Wellington, memorandum, 1841, PRO, WO 1/537.

55. Robin Winks, *Canada and the United States* (Baltimore: Johns Hopkins, 1960), p. 375.

56. Stacey, *Canada and the British Army*, p. 112.

57. Winks, *Canada and the United States*, p. 375.

58. Ibid., p. 376.

59. Weigley, *History of the U.S. Army*, p. 200.

60. Stacey, *Canada and the British Army*, p. 118.

61. Anon., "The Eastern Provinces of North America," *Colburn's United Service Magazine* (March 1862), pp. 398–408.

62. Head, confidential, Sept. 9, 1861 to Newcastle, PRO, CO 42/627.

63. Newcastle to Monck, Dec. 14, 1861, PAC, RG 7, G21, vol. 74, no. 165, vol. I.

64. FO to CO, May 16, May 22, May 24, 1861, PRO, CO 42/629.

65. Stacey, *Canada and the British Army*, p. 119.

66. Anon., "Forts versus ships, also defence of the Canadian Lakes. By an Officer," *Colburn's United Service Magazine* (October 1862), p. 269; "W.S.G." to the Editor, ibid., pp. 274–77; Hitsman, *Safeguarding Canada*, p. 165.

67. Anon., "Memo. Halifax and Quebec Railroad," [n.d.], National Library of Wales, Harpton Court Mss, 2957.

68. Newcastle to Monck, Dec. 21, 1861, Nottingham University, Newcastle Papers, NeC 1120/5.

69. Col. Wetherall to Newcastle, June 10, 1862, Harpton Court Mss, 2989.

70. Monck to Newcastle, Nov. 30, 1861, Newcastle Papers, NeC 11, 389; Monck 23, Dec. 9, 1861, PRO, CO 42/428.

71. Hitsman, *Safeguarding Canada*, p. 172.

72. Monck, 4, Jan. 7, 1862, PRO, CO 42/632.

73. W. Morton, *The Critical Years* (Toronto: McClelland and Stewart, 1964), p. 102.

74. Winks, *Canada and the United States*, p. 103.

75. T.F.Elliot, minute on Monck 147, Oct. 30, 1862, PRO, CO 42/635.

76. FO to CO, May 1, 1863, 1863, PRO, CO 42/639.

77. FO to CO, Nov. 13, Dec. 10, 28, 30, 1863, PRO, CO 42/639.

78. Stacey, *Canada and the British Army*, pp. 163–66.

79. *Globe*, Nov. 22, 1864, quoting *London Examiner*.

80. Monck, confidential, Feb. 4, 1865, PRO, CO 42/648; "Report of a Committee of the Executive Council," March 27, 1865, PAC, RG 7, G21, vol. 75, no. 165, vol. II; Monck, 38, March 28, 1865, PRO, CO 42/648.

81. Capt. W.S. Moorsom to Capt. Charles Moorsom, Nov. 30, 1861, India Office Library, Mss EUR. E, 299/14, Litt. 14/4.

82. Gen. John F. Burgoyne, "Thoughts on war with the United States, as regards operations by land forces," 1861, Harpton Court Mss, 2984.

83. Capt. Wm. Hatt Noble, RE, "Naval Considerations [in a war with the United States]," Nov. 2, 1861, appended to Collinson, "Canada Lakes, Memoranda. . . .," Devon County Record Office, Seymour Papers, 1392, M/PPP, 10 (Box 21).

84. Burgoyne, "Thoughts on War," 1861.

85. "Memorandum by Sir John Burgoyne on the Defence of Canada, February 1862," in "Report of the Commissioners appointed to consider the defences of Canada, 1862," app. no. 2, PRO, WO 33/11, x.i. 2219.

86. Capt. Richard Collinson, "Memoranda on the Assistance which can be

rendered to the Province of Canada by Her Majesty's Navy in the event of War with the United States," Sept. 2, 1861, Seymour Papers, 1392 M/PPP, 10 (Box 21).

87. W.E.G[ladstone], "Defence of Canada," Palmerston (Broadlands) Papers, Historical Manuscripts Commission.

88. Palmerston to Cardwell, "Defence of Canada," May 21, 1865, Palmerston (Broadlands) Papers, GC/CA/414).

89. WO to CO, Aug. 10, 1860, PRO, CO 42/625; CO to WO, Jan. 17, 1861, ibid.; Edward Lugard, WO, to T.F. Elliot, CO, Jan. 17, 1861, PRO, CO 42/630.

90. Collinson, "Memoranda."

91. J.M. Hitsman, "Please send us a garrison," Ontario History, L (Autumn 1958), 189–92.

92. Monck to Williams, Aug. 19, 1862, Palmerston (Broadlands) Papers, MM CA1.

93. Williams to Monck, Aug. 21, 1862, Palmerston (Broadlands) Papers, MM/CA; Monck to Cardwell, Nov. 16, 1864, Gladstone Papers, BM Add. Mss. 44600, f. 68.

94. Cardwell to Palmerston, Sept. 24, 1864, Palmerston (Broadlands) Papers, GC/CA/394–414.

95. Monck, 121, Aug. 21, 1864, PRO, CO 42/642; Monck, 123, Exec. Council Report, Aug. 26, 1864, CO 42/642; Monck, 128, Sept. 1, 1864, CO 42/642.

96. Gen. J.G. Totten, "Report," Jan. 18, 1861, U.S., Congress, 36th Cong., 2nd sess., House Exec. Docs., vol. II, 85 (in 1105), p. 28.

97. E.g., U.S., Congress, House, Congressional Globe, 37th Cong., 2nd sess., Jan. 17, 1862, pp. 380–84.

98. E.g., U.S., Congress, House, Congressional Globe, 37th Cong., 3rd sess., Feb. 7, 1863, pp. 808–809.

99. Capt. C.J. Moorsom to Capt. W.S. Moorsom, [Nov.] 1861, India Office Library, Mss. EUR., E299.

100. "Report of the Secretary of War," Dec. 5, 1863, U.S., Congress, 38th Cong., 1st sess., House Exec. Docs., 1 (in 1184), p. 11.

101. Bourne, Britain and the Balance of Power, p. 273.

102. Monck to Newcastle, Jan. 23, 1862, Newcastle Papers, NeC 11, 394a.

103. "Report of the Commissioners appointed to consider the Defence of Canada, 1862, Montreal, Sept. 1, 1862," PAC, RG 8, II, 18 (also in PRO, WO 33/11).

104. Secretary of War to T.F. Elliot, Aug. 26, 1864, PRO, CO 42/630.

105. Lt.-Col. W.F.D. Jervois, Report on the Defence of Canada and the British Naval Stations in the Atlantic . . . Feb. 1864 (London: [War Office], 1864).

106. [Col. H.F.C. Fletcher?], "Colonel Jervois's Memo," PAC, Dufferin Papers, Canadian Letters, vol. II, no. 48, reel A412, film 1145.

107. Cambridge to Earl de Grey, Jan. 7, 1865, PRO, CO 42/651.

108. Wm. McDougall, Secretary, Executive Council, to Jervois, Oct. 18, 1864, PAC, RG 8, II, 32, p. 10.

109. Copies of Jervois's maps of proposed temporary defences for Kingston, Toronto, Hamilton etc., which are not in the Public Archives of Canada, were discovered in the Seymour Papers in the Devon County Record Office.

110. [Jervois], *Report on the Defence of Canada made to the Provincial Government on the 10th November, and of the British Naval Stations in the North Atlantic: Together with Observations on the Defence of New Brunswick* (London: [War Office], 1865).

111. Macdonald to Col. Gray, March 29, 1865, PAC, MG 2, 6 A, 1 (e), vol. 511, pp. 5–6.

112. Gladstone, confidential, "Defence of Canada," July 12, 1864, Palmerston (Broadlands) Papers.

113. Richard Cartwright, *Remarks on the Militia of Canada* (Kingston: Daily News Office, 1864).

114. W. Howard Russell, *Canada: Its Defences, Conditions, and Resources being a Second and Concluding Volume of "My Diary, North and South"* (Boston, 1865), pp. 4–5, 61.

115. This view was expressed in a Privy Council minute, Monck, 147, Oct. 30, 1867, PRO, CO 42/635.

116. Stacey, *Canada and the British Army*, p. 148.

117. Ibid., p. 146.

118. Monck, secret [1862] 162, PRO, CO 42/635 (by Newcastle).

119. Wm. H. Lee, Clerk of the Executive Council [1865?], confidential [Report of a Committee of Council], Devon County Record Office, 1392 IM/PPP, 10 (Box 21), also in Monck, confidential, Feb. 4, 1865, PRO, CO 42/648.

120. Twenty years later the traditional fear was still strong. See Sir E.W. Watkin, *Canada and the United States* (London, New York: Ward, Lock, 1887), pp. 16–17.

121. Cardwell to Palmerston, April 27, 1865, Palmerston (Broadlands) Papers, GC/CA 373–409/2.

122. E. Cardwell to [Monck], Jan. 21, 1865, Province of Canada, *Papers relating to the Conferences . . . on the . . . Defence of the Province*, 1865, p. 1.

123. Privy Council Minute on the defence of the Provinces. Monck, confidential, Feb. 4, 1865, PRO, CO 42/648.

124. WO to CO, Feb. 12, 1867, PRO, CO 42/666.

125. Stacey, *Canada and the British Army*, pp. 165–88; Hitsman, *Safeguarding Canada*, pp. 190–200.

126. Palmerston to Cardwell, May 21, 1865, Palmerston (Broadlands) Papers, GC/CA/414.

127. Bourne, *Britain and the Balance of Power*, pp. 265–68, 278–79, 283–89; Stacey, *Canada and the British Army*, pp. 124–25, 171; Hitsman, *Safeguarding Canada*, pp. 195–96.

128. Hitsman, *Safeguarding Canada*, p. 197; Stacey, *Canada and the British Army*, pp. 201–203.

129. W.E. Gladstone, memorandum, May 10, 1865, BM Add. Mss, 44603, f.17.

130. Bourne, *Britain and the Balance of Power*, pp. 273–83.

131. Monck, 38, March 28, 1865, PRO, CO 42/648.

132. Monck to Newcastle, March 26, 1865, PAC, RG7, G21, vol. 75, no. 165, vol. 2; and Monck, 38, March 28, 1865, PRO, CO 42/648.

133. Monck, 38, March 28, 1865, PRO, CO 42/648.

134. Weigley, *History of U.S. Army*, pp. 266–67, 567.

135. *Globe*, Oct. 21, 1864. There is a clipping in the Gladstone Papers, BM Add.Mss. 44600, f.1.

136. *Globe*, Dec. 21, 1864. Jan. 21, 1866.

137. Michel, memorandum, forwarded with Monck, 44, June 2, 1866, PRO, CO 42/655.

138. Macdonald to Angus Morrison, Sept. 29, 1866, PAC, MG 26, AI (e), vol. 513, p. 185.

139. C.P. Stacey, "The Fenian Troubles and Canadian Military Development, 1863–1870," *Canadian Defence Quarterly*, XIII, no. 3 (April 1936), 270–79.

140. Monck, 148, Sept. 26, 1866, PRO, CO 42/656; WO to CO, April 30, Aug. 21, Sept. 9, Dec. 12, 1867, CO 42/666.

141. Andrew Robb, "The Toronto *Globe* and the Defence of Canada, 1861–66," *Ontario History*, LXIV, no. 2 (June 1972), 65–77.

142. *Globe*, Jan. 16, 1866.

143. Clarendon to Sir Edward Thornton, Feb. 19, 1870, Christ Church College, Oxford, Clarendon Papers, C476.

144. Desmond Morton, *The Canadian General: Sir William Otter* (Toronto: Hakkert, 1974), pp. 3–37.

145. *Globe*, Dec. 3, 1864; Col. Walker Powell, quoted in John Castell Hopkins, *Canada: an Encyclopaedia*, 6 vols. (Toronto: Lippincott, 1898–1900), IV, 419.

146. *Globe*, Jan. 10, 1867.

147. *Globe*, Jan. 22, 1867.

148. Callahan, *American Foreign Policy*, pp. 299–325; Bourne, *Britain and the Balance of Power*, p. 301.

149. *Globe*, July 1, 1867.

150. John Boyd, *Sir George Etienne Cartier Bart: His Life and Times: A Political History of Canada from 1814 until 1873* (Toronto: Macmillan, 1914), p. 291.

151. Morton, *Ministers and Generals*, p. 6.

152. Ibid., pp. 9–10.

153. "Memorandum respecting Fortifications in Canada . . .," May 6, 1869, Bright Papers, BM Add. Mss. 44392.

154. C.P. Stacey, "The withdrawal of the Imperial Garrisons from Newfoundland, 1870," *Canadian Historical Review*, XVII (1936), 147.

155. Sir John Michel to Macdonald, Aug. 14, 1867, PAC, MG 26, A 1(a), vol. 100, no. 39512.

156. [P. MacDougall], "Canada: The Fenian Raid and the Colonial Office," *Blackwood's Edinburgh Magazine* 108 (Oct. 1870), 497.

157. Cardwell to Gladstone, Jan. 9, 1869, Cardwell Papers, PRO, 30/48/2/6.

158. WO to CO, June 23, 1869, PRO, CO 42/682.

159. Granville to Cardwell, Dec. 17, 1868, Cardwell Papers, PRO, 30/48/5/28.

160. WO to CO, Jan. 12, 1867, PRO, CO 42/666, extracts Sir John Michel's Report, Dec. 19, 1866, quoting Gen. Fenwick Williams.

161. Cambridge to Cardwell, Aug. 3, 1869, Cardwell Papers, PRO, 30/48/3/11.

162. Cardwell to Granville, Dec. 5, 1869, Cardwell Papers, PRO, 30/48/5/28.

163. Cardwell to Col. Hamilton, RE, Aug. 31, 1870, Cardwell Papers, PRO, 30/48/5/31.

164. Kimberley to Gladstone, Dec. 9, 1870, Cardwell Papers, PRO, 30/48/5/31.

165. Cambridge to Cardwell, Aug. 3, 1869, PRO, 30/48/3/12.

166. Cambridge to Cardwell, Dec. 19, 1868, PRO, 30/48/3/11.

167. Macdonald to Sir John Young, Oct. 21, 1869, PAC, MG 26, A I(e), p. 297.

168. Allan Pinkerton to General Pope, Jan. 13, 1869, USNA, AGO, 44A/1869, Feb. 2, 1820, AGO, 39C/1870; Meade to Sherman, May 27, 1870, AGO, 370A/1870.

169. Macdonald to Cartier, July 24, 1869, PAC, MG 26, A I(e), vol. 516, pt. I, p. 24.

CHAPTER 2

1. *Army and Navy Journal*, IX, (Feb. 24, 1872), 333.

2. "The death of Cartier and the fall of the Macdonald government put the brake upon defence preparations in Canada." (G.F.G. Stanley, *Canada's Soldiers: The Military History of an Unmilitary People* [Toronto: Macmillan, 1960], p. 243.)

3. Granville to Sir John Young, April 14, 1869, Canada, Parliament, *Sessional Papers*, 1871, no. 46, pp. 2–4.

4. Thomas Wolley to Under-Secretary, May 31, 1870, ibid., p. 17.

5. Lester B. Shippee, *Canadian-American Relations, 1849–1874* (New Haven: Yale, 1939), pp. 180f.

6. Allan Nevins, *Hamilton Fish: The Inner History of the Grant Administration* (New York: Dodd, Mead, 1936), p. 416.

7. Donald F. Warner, *The Idea of Continental Union: Agitation for the Annexation of Canada to the United States, 1849–1893* ([Lexington, Ky.]: University of Kentucky Press, 1960), p. 91.

8. C.P. Stacey, "The Fenian Troubles and Canadian Military Development,

1865–1871," *Canadian Defence Quarterly*, XIII (April 1936), 276; idem, "Fenianism and the Rise of National Feeling in Canada at the Time of Confederation," *Canadian Historical Review*, XI (Sept. 1931), 238–61.

9. *Annual Report on the State of the Militia for 1870*, Canada, *Sessional Papers*, 1871, no. 7, pp. 5–8.

10. Stacey, "Fenian Troubles," p. 277.

11. D.G. Creighton, *John A. Macdonald: The Old Chieftain* (Toronto: Macmillan, 1955), pp. 41–43; G.F.G. Stanley, *The Birth of Western Canada: A History of the Riel Rebellions* (Toronto: University of Toronto Press, 1960), p. 75.

12. Nevins, *Fish*, pp. 298–99, 386, 395; Alvin C. Gluek, *Minnesota and the Manifest Destinies of the Canadian North-West: a study in Canadian-American Relations* (Toronto: University of Toronto Press, 1956), pp. 196ff.

13. Belknap, memorandum, April 12, 1870, USNA, RG 94, 257 A 70, Microfilm 619/773.

14. Sherman to Meade, April 13, 1870, telegram to Meade, May 4, 1870, Meade to Sherman, May 11, 1870, Meade to Adjutant-General, May 31, 1870, ibid.

15. Sherman to Meade, May 11, 1870, Cooke to Meade, May 19, Capt. A.H. Offley, Fort Brady, May 11, 28, 1870, ibid.

16. [Wolseley], "Narrative of the Red River Expedition," pt. II, *Blackwood's Magazine*, CIX (January 1871), p. 49.

17. C.P. Stacey, "The Military Aspect of Canada's Winning of the West, 1870–1885," *Canadian Historical Review*, XXI (March 1940), 1–24.

18. Sherman to Meade, May 17, 1870, USNA, RG 94, 247, Microfilm 619/773.

19. J. Mackay Hitsman, *Safeguarding Canada, 1763–1871* (Toronto: University of Toronto Press, 1968), pp. 213, 218–19.

20. *Thoughts on Defence from a Canadian Point of View By a Canadian* (Montreal: John Lovell, 1870), pp. 4–5.

21. A. Campbell to Sir John Young, Sept. 10, 1870, Canada, *Sessional Papers*, 1871, no. 46, p. 27.

22. Nevins, *Fish*, p. 422.

23. "The Royal Commission on the Defence of British Possessions and Commerce Abroad, 29 July, 1880," in Alice Stewart, "Sir John A. Macdonald and the Imperial Defence Commission of 1879," *Canadian Historical Review*, XXXV (June 1954), 123.

24. W.F.D. Jervois, "Considerations on the Military Position of Great Britain with respect to the United States," p. 2, in BM Add. Mss. 43892, Bright Papers.

25. Capt. Lindesay Brine, RN, "Memorandum upon the Attacking and Defensive Resources of the United States, 12 April, 1871," PRO, ADM 1/6203, XI, 2248. Brine (1834–1906) entered the navy in 1847, served in the Black and Baltic Seas during the Crimean War, in the Far East, off Africa, and on missions to Burma and Aden, and commanded the *Invincible* at the occupation of Cy-

prus. He won a prize in 1852 for an essay, "On the best means of Providing an Efficient Force of Officers and Men for the Navy, including the Reserves," *Journal of the Royal United Service Institution*, XXVI (1882), 115. He published *The Taiping Rebellion in China* (London: John Murray, 1862) and *Travels amongst American Indians* (London: Sampson Lowe, 1894).

26. A Colonist, "The Colonies," *Times*, Jan. 18, 19, 20, 1870.

27. *Thoughts on Defence*, pp. 9–10.

28. Ibid., p. 49.

29. Capt. Francis Duncan, *Canada in 1871; or our Empire in the West* (Lecture at the Russell Institution, Jan. 22, [18]72: London/Woolwich, 1872), pp. 16–18. Duncan was also the author of *A History of the Royal Artillery*, 2 vols. (London: John Murray, 1872).

30. *Thoughts on Defence*, p. 8.

31. Jervois, "Considerations," [p. 1].

32. Brine, memorandum, Minutes, May 3, [1871], PRO, ADM 1/6203, XI, 2248.

33. Goldwin Smith, *The Treaty of Washington: A Study in Imperial History* (Ithaca, New York: Cornell University Press, 1941), p. 88.

34. Memorandum by Lord Tenterden, "Relations with the United States (Nov. 21, 1870)," PRO, FO 881/1828. Confidential.

35. Hitsman, *Safeguarding Canada*, pp. 220–21, quoting Cardwell Papers, PRO, Box 5/31, Kimberley to Gladstone, Dec. 9, 1870.

36. Hitsman, *Safeguarding Canada*, p. 221.

37. Goldwin Smith, *Treaty of Washington*, pp. 72–90. The Americans retained possession of San Juan, seemingly a strategic advance, but the island was actually of marginal value. Barry M. Gough, *The Royal Navy and the North-West Coast of North America, 1810–1914* (Vancouver: University of British Columbia Press, 1971), pp. 151–68.

38. Macdonald to Charles Julyan, Oct. 10, 1871, PAC, MG 26, A 1 (e), vol. 603.

39. Macdonald to Hugh Richardson, Oct. 30, 1871, PAC, MG 26, A 1 (e), vol. 519, 2, p. 394.

40. Stacey, "Military Aspect of Canada's winning of the West," *Canadian Historical Review*, XXI, 13–14.

41. Capt. Lloyd Wheaton to Assistant Adjutant-General, Oct. 5, 1871, USNA, RG 94, 3248/AGO/1871, microfilm 66/31; PRO, CO 42/700, Lisgar 1 83, Nov. 8, 1871.

42. Wheaton to AAG, Dec. 4, 1871, USNA, RG 94, 3248/AGO/1871, Microfilm 666/31.

43. Macdonald to Col. C.S. Gzowski, Jan. 23, 1873, PAC, MG 26, A 1 (e), vol. 522, pt. 3.

44. *Militia Report*, 1887, p. xxiv.

45. Macdonald to Sir John Rose, Jan. 19, 1872, PAC, MG 26, A 1 (e), vol. 17, pt. 1, p. 98.

46. Cartier to Macdonald, Oct. 17, Nov. 23, Dec. 5, 1872, PAC, MG 26, A 1 (b), vol. 202; Macdonald to Cartier, Dec. 11, Dec. 23, 1872, ibid.; Dufferin 115, April 30, 1874, PRO, CO 42/727.

47. Col. Robertson Ross, "Report of a Reconnaissance of the North-West Provinces and Indian Territories of the Dominion of Canada, and Narratives of Journey [sic] across the Continent through Canadian Territory to British Columbia and Vancouver Island," *Journal of the Royal United Service Institution*, XVII (1873), pp. 543–67. Also published in Canada, *Sessional Papers*, 1873.

48. Roderick C. Macleod, "The North-West Mounted Police, 1873–1905: Law Enforcement and Social Order in the Canadian North-West" (Ph.D. diss., Duke University, 1971).

49. Macdonald to Gzowski, Jan. 23, 1873, PAC, MG 26, A 1 (e), vol. 522, pt. 3.

50. Warner, *Idea of Continental Union*, p. 95.

51. Albert K. Weinberg, *Manifest Destiny: A Study of Nationalist Expansionism in American History* (Baltimore: Johns Hopkins Press, 1935), chap. VIII.

52. Russell F. Weigley, *History of the United States Army* (New York: Macmillan, 1967), p. 285.

53. Weigley, *History of the U.S. Army*, pp. 265–67, 567; "Report of the Secretary of War," 1870, U.S., Congress, 41st Cong., 3rd sess., *House Exec. Docs.*, 1 (in 1446), pp. 44–45. Brig.-Gen. Cooke listed Fort Wayne, Fort Brady, Fort Mackinac, Fort Gratiot, Fort Wilkins, Fort Porter, Fort Niagara, Fort Ontario, and Madison Barracks, in the Department of the Lakes.

54. E.R. Lewis, *Sea-coast Fortifications of the United States: an Introductory History* (Washington: Smithsonian Institute Press, 1970), pp. 68–69; E. Griffin, *Our Sea-Coast Defences* (New York & London: Putnams, 1885), pp. 8–9, indicates that the ordnance revolution began during the Crimean War, not the Civil War.

55. Griffin, *Our Sea-Coast Defences*, pp. 8–9.

56. U.S. Grant, Message to Congress, Jan. 20, 1875, "Armament for Sea-Coast Defense," U.S., Congress, 43rd Cong., 2nd sess., *House Exec. Docs.*, 126 (in 1648).

57. E.g., "Report of the Chief of Engineers," 1872, on Fort Porter, Black Rock, Buffalo, U.S., Congress, 42nd Cong., 3rd sess., 1872–73, *House Exec. Docs.*, 1, pt. 2, vol. II (in 1559), p. 3.

58. E.g., J.F. Farnsworth of Illinois, U.S., Congress, House, *Congressional Globe*, 41st Cong., 3rd sess., Feb. 23, 1871, p. 1536. Some opponents wanted the money for railroads.

59. "Report of Gen. Geo. G. Meade," Oct. 27, 1870, U.S., Congress, 41st Cong., 3rd sess., *House Exec. Docs.*, 1 (in 1446), pp. 44–45.

60. Ibid., p. 46.

61. "Report of the Chief of Engineers," 1873, U.S., Congress, 43rd Cong., 1st sess., *House Exec. Docs.*, 1, pt. 2 (in 1598), p. 4.

62. Ibid., *passim*.

63. "Report of Maj.-Gen. W.S. Hancock," Sept. 30, 1873, U.S., Congress, 43rd Cong., 1st sess., *House Exec. Docs.*, 1, pt. 2, (in 1598), p. 53.

64. "Report of Brig.-Gen. Cooke," Oct. 7, 1871, U.S., Congress, 42nd Cong., 2nd sess., *House Exec. Docs.*, 1, pt. 2 (in 1503), p. 58.

65. Stanley, *Canada's Soldiers*, p. 250; Barry Gough, *The Royal Navy and the Northwest Coast of North America, 1810–1914: A Study of British Maritime Ascendancy* (Vancouver: University of British Columbia Press, 1970), pp. 220–22; PRO, CO 42/745, *passim*; Dufferin to Carnarvon, Dec. 7, 1877, PRO, 30/6/31.

66. Dufferin to Carnarvon, March 26, 1874, PRO, 30/6/26, pp. 65–74.

67. WO to CO, March 18, 1874, PRO, CO 42/731.

68. Desmond Morton, *Ministers and Generals: Politics and the Canadian Militia, 1868–1904* (Toronto: University of Toronto Press, 1970), pp. 33–36.

69. Sir C. Adderley, 1871, Notice of Questions in the Commons, March 9, 10, 1871, PRO, CO 42/701, March 8, 1871; Major Arbuthnot, question of July 18, 1872, PRO, CO 42/710, July 5, 1872; Lord Oranmore and Browne, question in the House of Lords, PRO, CO 42/710, June 29, 1872; see *Hansard's Parliamentary Debates*, 3rd ser. (1871), 1673, 1773; (1872), 420–21, 1364–65.

70. Dufferin to CO, secret, June 1, 1874, PRO, CO 42/728.

71. E.g., editorial, *The Nation* (Toronto), I, no. 2 (April 9, 1874).

72. Miles Emeritus, *Canada Defended by Her Militia* ([Military Institute], n.d.), p. 1.

73. Miles, "Our Militia," *Canadian Monthly*, V, no. 3 (March 1874), 185–91.

74. Fidelis, "Historical Sketch of the War of 1812," *Canadian Monthly*, VI (July 1874), 1–24; William Norris Ingersoll, "Canadian Nationality and its Opponents," ibid., VIII (1875), 237–43.

75. John Mathew, "The Political Future of Canada," *Canadian Monthly*, VIII (1875), 54–61, 89–98.

76. Dufferin to Carnarvon, April 30, 1874, PRO, 30/6/26, 148–57. *Globe*, April 29, 1874; C.W. de Kiewiet and F.H. Underhill, *Dufferin-Carnarvon Correspondence, 1874–75* (Toronto: Champlain Society, 1955), p. 40.

77. Maj. H.S. de Hubertus d'Etraigne, "Defence of North America in the Event of War," in WO to CO, Nov. 23, 1876, PRO, CO 42/746.

78. Carl Berger, *The Sense of Power: Studies in the Ideas of Canadian Imperialism, 1867–1914* (Toronto: University of Toronto Press, 1970), pp. 49–77.

79. Goldwin Smith, "The Political Destiny of Canada," *Canadian Monthly*, XI (January 1877), 596–615.

80. Macdonald to Lisgar, Feb. 17, 1871, PRO, CO 537/102, pp. 45–48.

81. Dufferin to Carnarvon, March 26, 1874, PRO, 30/6/26, pp. 65–74.

82. Pierre Berton, *The Impossible Railway: The Building of the Canadian Pacific* (New York: Knopf, 1972), p. 114; Dale C. Thomson, *Alexander Mackenzie: Clear Grit* (Toronto: Macmillan, 1960), pp. 174–76.

83. H.C. Fletcher, *Memorandum on the Militia System of Canada* ([Ottawa], 1873), pp. 6–9.

84. H.C. Fletcher, *The Defence of Canada: a lecture delivered at the Literary and Scientific Institute* (Ottawa: February 1875).

85. H.C. Fletcher, "A Volunteer Force, British and Colonial in the event of war," *Journal of the Royal United Services Institution*, XXI (1877), 643.

86. Gen. Hastings Doyle to Cambridge, May 18, 1875, Royal Archives, Windsor, Cambridge Papers.

87. Walker Powell to Minister of Militia, Jan. 1874, *Militia Report*, 1873, p. x.

88. *Militia Report*, 1887, p. xxiv; *Militia Report*, 1874, pp. xii–xiii.

89. Richard A. Preston, *Canada's RMC* (Toronto: University of Toronto Press, 1969), pp. 25–26; WO to CO, March 18, Nov. 1874, PRO, CO 42/731; Dufferin 205, July 25, 1874, CO 42/728; Carnarvon to Dufferin, April 30, 1874, PRO, 30/6/26, pp. 146, 148.

90. Selby Smyth to Cambridge, June 2, 1876, Royal Archives, Windsor, Cambridge Papers.

91. Dufferin to Mackenzie, n.d., PAC, Dufferin Papers, Reel A 409, pp. 14–16; Reel A 406, Letter Books, vol. I, 250–52.

92. Dufferin to Carnarvon, April 30, 1874, PRO, Northern Ireland, Dufferin Papers, p. 180.

93. Selby Smyth to Minister, Nov. 17, 1875, in *Militia Report*, 1875, pp. i–ii, xxiii–xlvii; Thornton to Fish, July 10, 1875, USNA, RG 94, 3837/AGO/75 Microfilm 666/223; FO to CO, Aug. 11, 1875, PRO, CO 42/739.

94. FO to CO, June 14, 1876, PRO, CO 42/746.

95. Dufferin, secret, May 7, 1873, PRO, CO 42/717.

96. Dufferin 157, June 11, 1877, PRO, CO 42/749; FO to CO, Aug. 30, 1877, CO 42/750.

97. Shippee, *Canadian-American Relations*, pp. 472–75.

98. FO to CO, Jan. 11, 1876, PRO, CO 42/746.

99. Dufferin to Carnarvon, April 25, 1874, PRO, 30/6/26, p. 105.

100. FO to CO May 6, 1875, PRO, CO 42/739.

101. Warner, *Idea of Continental Union*, pp. 152–54.

102. *Militia Report*, 1887, p. xxiv.

103. *Militia Report*, 1871, tip-in facing p. 66.

104. FO to CO, Sept. 11, 1876, PRO, CO 42/746.

105. Morton, *Ministers and Generals*, pp. 31–51.

106. *Militia Report*, 1877, p. xi; ibid., 1878, pp. xiii–xiv.

107. *Colburn's United Service Magazine* (October 1875), pt. III, pp. 155–64.

108. *Army and Navy Journal*, XI (Aug. 16, 1873), 8.

109. Ibid., XII (April 3, 1875), 537.

110. Ibid., XIII (Jan. 15, 1876), 374.

111. Ibid., XV (May 11, 1878), 645.

112. Ibid. (April 6, 1878), 562.

113. Mackenzie to Dufferin, Aug. 5, 1878, PAC, Dufferin Papers, microfilm Reel A 411 (also in PRO, Northern Ireland).

CHAPTER 3

1. Gen. Selby Smyth, GOC of the Canadian militia, described the Fenians as "communistic" in his *Annual Report on the State of the Militia for 1878*, p. xiv (in Canada, *Sessional Papers*, 1879), and also in his report to the minister, May 29, 1878, PRO, CO 537/117, no. 167, p. 75.

2. Dufferin to Hicks Beach, May 27, 1878, Gloucester County Archives, Hicks Beach Papers, PCC/92.

3. *Speeches of the Earl of Dufferin, 1872–78* (Toronto: Ross Robertson, 1878), pp. 107–109; *Militia Report*, 1878, p. xiii.

4. *Militia Report*, 1879, pp. x–xi.

5. Leonid I. Strakhovsky, "Russian privateering projects of 1878," *Journal of Modern History*, VII (March 1935), 22–40.

6. Dufferin, secret, May 30, 1878, PRO, CO 537/177, no. 167.

7. Lt.-Col. Sir George Sydenham Clark, ed., *The Defence of the Empire: A Selection from the Letters and Speeches of Henry Howard Molyneux Herbert, Fourth Earl of Carnarvon* (London: John Murray, 1897), p. x.

8. "On a Colonial Naval Volunteer Force," *Journal of the Royal United Service Institution*, XXII (1878), 641–60.

9. H.C. Fletcher, *Memorandum on the Militia System of Canada* ([Ottawa], 1873).

10. "The Protection of our Naval Base in the North Pacific," *Journal of the Royal United Service Institution*, XXVII (1883), pp. 367–81.

11. *Journal of the Royal United Service Institution*, XXIII (1879), pp. 101f.

12. See Richard A. Preston, *Canada and 'Imperial Defense': The Origins of the British Commonwealth's Defense Organization, 1867–1919* (Durham, N.C.: Duke University Press, 1967).

13. T.C. Scoble, "The Utilization of Colonial Forces in Imperial Defence," *Journal of the Royal United Service Institution*, XXIII (1879), no. 103, 1056–66; Centurion, "The Militia System of Canada," in *Rose-Belford's Canadian Monthly and National Review* (formerly *Canadian Monthly and National Review*), IV (1880), 293–301.

14. Maj. and Brevet Lt.-Col. Salter M. Jarvis, "Imperial Federation and Canadian Defences," *Rose-Belford's Canadian Monthly*, V, (May 1880), 449–59. See also the speech on the militia estimates by Fred Strange, MP, the surgeon of his regiment (Canada, *Commons' Debates*, 1880, III, 1359–61).

15. Machaon [pseud.], "Amateur Soldiers and Permanent Protectors," *Rose-Belford's Canadian Monthly*, VII (July 1881), 40–46.

16. Walker Powell to Macdonald, May 11, 1882, PAC, MG 26, A 1 (a), vol. 100.

17. Macdonald to Lorne, Aug. 8, 1882, PAC, MG 26, A 1 (c), vol. 82, p. 166.

18. Macdonald to Northcote, May 1, 1878, Joseph Pope, ed., *The Correspondence of Sir John Macdonald* (Garden City, N.Y., and Toronto: Doubleday, Page, 1921), pp. 239–42.

19. *Militia Report*, 1884, pp. 183–90.

20. Luard to Cambridge, Dec. 8, 1880, and April 21, 1883, Royal Archives, Windsor, Cambridge Papers.

21. Desmond Morton, *Ministers and Generals: Politics and the Canadian Militia, 1868–1904* (Toronto: University of Toronto Press, 1970), pp. 47–48.

22. *Militia Report*, 1879, p. lxi.

23. *Journal of the Royal United Service Institution*, XXIII (1879), 102ff; also in Royal United Service Institution, *Papers on Defence, 1876–79*; and in *Militia Report*, 1879, app. 7, pp. 269–301.

24. "Gunner Centennial," *Canadian Army Journal*, IX, no. 2 (April 1955), pp. 109–26; Obituary, *Canadian Defence Quarterly*, III, no. 1 (October 1925), pp. 6–7.

25. (London: Macqueen, 1894).

26. Colin Campbell, memorandum, Oct. 23, 1884, PAC, Minto Papers, Microfilm reel A 130; Defence Committee, first meeting, Dec. 28, 1884, ibid.

27. Hincks to Dr. J.S. Drennan, July 31, 1878, PRO, Northern Ireland, Dufferin papers, DOD 729/39.

28. G.M. Grant, "Imperial Federalism from a Canadian Point of View," published in the *Critic* of Halifax, N.S., and reprinted in *Imperial Federalism*, April 1, 1886.

29. FO to CO, Jan. 29, 1880, PRO, CO 42/765.

30. *British Whig*, Jan. 8, 1880.

31. Ibid., Nov. 10, 1879.

32. Lorne, 78, March 20, 1879, PRO, CO 42/756; FO to CO, April 18, 1879, PRO, CO 42/758.

33. Lt.-Col. W. Osborne Smith to Adjutant-General, April 4, 1878, *The Defences of Canada*, Jan. 1, 1886 (Ottawa: Maclean, Robec, 1886), pp. 24–25.

34. FO to CO, April 18, 1879, memorandum of conversation, Lorne and Evarts, PRO, CO 42/758; Lorne, confidential, April 23, 1879, PRO, CO 42/756; Lorne, confidential, May 12, 1879, PRO, CO 42/757; memorandum of conversation, Lorne and Evarts, Sept. 18, 1879, Hicks Beach Papers, PC/PP 62/4.

35. MacDougall, 5, Dec. 27, 1882, PRO, CO 42/744; Lorne, 207, Aug. 2, 1883, ibid.; Lorne, 212, Aug. 6, 1883, ibid.; FO to CO, Jan. 13, 1883, PRO, CO 42/776.

36. FO to CO, Aug. 23, 1883, PRO, CO 42/776.

37. Lorne, 96, May 7, 1883, PRO, CO 42/744.

38. Admiralty to CO, March 14, 1883, PRO, CO 42/775.

39. Lansdowne, 82, 132, 147, April 29, June 8, July 17, 1884, PRO, CO 42/777.

40. Lansdowne, 42, Nov. 16, 1883, PRO, CO 42/775.

41. "History of the Intelligence Branch, Quarter Master General's Department, Horse Guards," PRO, WO 33/32, X, 1, 2219, pp. 2–12.

42. Carnarvon Commission Report, app. IX, p. 548, WO Library.

43. FO, Confidential Report 4690, "United States Coast Defences (Atlantic Coast), 1882. Reports of William Arthur, R.N., C.B.," Jan. 13, 1882, no. 113 and Feb. 17, 1882, no. 120.

44. "Information re. Naval Coast Defences of the United States," July 6, 1882, Canadian Defence Commission, vol. VI, quoted in *Defences of Canada*, 1886, pp. 56–57.

45. G.S. Clarke, "The Defences of Halifax, Confidential," Feb. 20, 1884, PRO, CAB 11/28.

46. Col. Crossman, RE, "Defence of Esquimalt Harbour, B.C.," WO to CO, Oct. 10, 1881, PRO, CO 42/770.

47. Report of the Privy Council, March 16, 1879, PAC, MG 26, A 1 (a) vol. 100; memorandum, "Defence of Canada, April 21, 1880," PAC, RG, 7, G 21, no. 165, vol. 4 (e); Hicks Beach to Lorne, July 3, 1879, PAC, RG 7, G. 21; WO to CO, June 15, 1881, ibid., vol. 4 (c).

48. "Report of Colonel Nugent, R.E. on the defence of Esquimalt, October 8, 1880," *Defences of Canada*, 1886, pp. 54–55.

49. Russell F. Weigley, *History of the United States Army* (New York: Macmillan, 1967), p. 286.

50. Albert K. Weinberg, *Manifest Destiny: A Study of Nationalist Expansionism in American History* (Baltimore: John Hopkins Press, 1935), pp. 365–65; U.S., Congress, House, *Congressional Record*, 46th Cong., 2nd sess., pp. 13–14.

51. By W. Dorsheimer of New York, U.S., Congress, House, *Congressional Record*, 48th Cong., 1st sess., June 30, 1884, pp. 5820–21.

52. Fort Appropriation Bill, 1880, U.S., Congress, Senate, *Congressional Record*, 45th Cong., 3rd sess., H.R. 5231, Dec. 12, 1878, p.112; ibid., 46th Cong., 2nd sess., H.R. 2787, March 12, 1880, pp. 1505–7.

53. U.S., Congress, House, *Congressional Record*, 48th Cong., 1st sess., June 30, 1884, pp. 5816–18.

54. Message from the President, April 11, 1884, ibid., pp. 2886–87; Fort Appropriation Bill, July 1, 1884, ibid., p. 5869.

55. *Report of Secretary of War*, 1880, U.S., Congress, 46th Cong., 3rd sess., *House Exec. Docs.*, 1, pt. 2 (in 1952), p. 164.

56. Ibid., 1879, U.S., Congress, 46th Cong., 2nd sess., *House Exec. Docs.*, 1, pt. 2 (in 1903), pp. xv–xvi, 120.

57. Gen. W.S. Hancock, "Military Posts on the Northern Lakes," Feb. 5, 1880, U.S., Congress, 46th Cong., 2nd sess., *House Exec. Docs.*, 45 (in 1922), pp. 2–4; Secretary of War, "Condition of Fortifications," Dec. 6, 1881, U.S., Congress, 47th Cong., 1st sess., *Senate Exec. Docs.*, 3 (in 1986), pp. 19–22.

58. *Army and Navy Journal*, XVII (Aug. 23, 1879), 22, 45, 57, quoting the *Oswego Times*.

59. Ibid., XXI (July 19, 1884), 1038; Ibid., XXII (Sept. 13, 1884), 123; "Report of the General of the Army," 1882, U.S., Congress, 47th Cong., 2nd sess., *House Exec. Docs.*, 1, pt. 2 (in 2091), p. 8.

60. General Sherman to Secretary Lincoln, Oct. 16, 1882, ibid., p. 10.

61. Secretary of War, "Condition of the Fortifications," Dec. 6, 1881, U.S., Congress, 47th Cong., 1st sess., *Senate Exec. Docs.*, 3 (in 1986), p. 22.

62. Gen. W.T. Sherman, "Estimates for Building at Military Posts," Oct.

16, 1882, U.S., Congress, 47th Cong., 2nd sess., *House Exec. Docs.*, 1, pt. 2, vol. I (in 2091), p. 10.

63. *Army and Navy Journal*, XIX (Jan. 28, 1882), 563.

64. Ibid., XXII (Sept. 13, 1884), 123.

65. Ibid., XXI (Nov. 24, 1883), 331.

66. "Report of the Adjutant-General," Oct. 00 [*sic*], 1883, U.S., Congress, 48th Cong., 1st sess., *House Exec. Docs.*, 1, pt. 2 (in 2182), pp. 50–51.

67. Weigley, *History of the U.S. Army*, pp. 288, 290.

68. Ibid., pp. 273–74.

69. Anon., "The United States' Navy and Army," *The Army and Navy Magazine*, II (May–October 1881), pp. 857–58.

70. Capt. Alexander Kirchhammer, "The Military Impotence of Great Britain," *United Service*, IV (June 1881), 708–41.

71. *Army and Navy Journal*, XVI (May 31, 1879), 772.

72. Ibid., XVII (March 13, 1880), 658.

73. Ibid., p. 694. There is no record of a Lewis Holton as a member of the Dominion Parliament. Luther Holton, MP, was born in South Wales.

74. Ibid., XXI (Dec. 29, 1883), 443.

75. Ibid., XX (June 30, 1883), 1090.

76. M. Waters Kirwan, "The Soldiers of Canada," *United Service*, XI (July 1884), 523–29; *Army and Navy Journal*, XXII (Oct. 18, 1884), 221.

77. *Army and Navy Journal*, XXII (May 2, 1885), 798.

78. Anon., "The United States Navy and Army," *Army and Navy Magazine*, II (May–October 1881), 857–62.

79. Brevet-Maj. Wm. H. Powell, "The National Guard and the necessity for its adoption by the General Government," *United Service*, II (January 1885), 19–31.

80. Brig.-Gen. George R. Snowdry, "The Battalion System for the National Guard," *United Service*, XII (March 1885), 294–99.

81. General Order, no. 64, HQ, AGO, Washington, Aug. 25, 1880, OCMH.

82. AGO Letter Book, vol. 28, pp. 238–39, USNA.

83. Army Regulations, 1881, vol. I, para. 89, OCMH.

84. General Order, no. 130, Nov. 28, 1884, OCMH.

85. Army War College, index card, "Canada," USNA, 3076.

86. Ibid., 3100.

87. Ibid., 3077.

CHAPTER 4

1. Colin Campbell to Melgund, Oct. 23, 1884, PAC, Minto Papers, Microfilm Reel A-130.

2. Richard A. Preston, *Canada and 'Imperial Defense': A Study of The*

Origins of the British Commonwealth's Defense Organization, 1867–1919 (Durham, N.C.: Duke University Press, 1967), pp. 157–60.

3. *The Defences of Canada* (Ottawa: Maclean, Robec, 1886).

4. Preston, *Canada and 'Imperial Defense'*, pp. 180–82.

5. Admiralty to CO, confidential, April 25, 1885, PRO, CO 42/782.

6. Lansdowne, secret, Nov. 12, 1885, PRO, CO 42/781.

7. *Canadian Militia Gazette*, vol. I, no. 3 (May 26, 1885).

8. Stanley, confidential, Dec. 18, 1890, PRO, CO 42/803; Minute by Director of Artillery for Secretary of State for War, Jan. 1, 1891, WO 32/500/57, Gen. No. 1482.

9. *Canadian Militia Gazette*, XIV, no. 30 (Aug. 1, 1889).

10. The order of priority in the Report of the Board on Fortifications published in 1886 rated Portland only 18th out of some twenty places that needed defence works. (U.S., Congress, 49th Cong., 1st sess., *House Exec. Docs.*, 49 (in 2395).)

11. Kenneth Bourne and Carl Byrd, "Captain Mahan's 'War' with Great Britain," *Proceedings of the United States Naval Institute*, XCIV, no. 7 (July 1968), 71–78.

12. U.S., Congress, 51st Cong., 1st sess., *Senate Exec. Docs.*, 1530 (in 2712), p. 2 (July 21, 1890).

13. Barry Gough, *The Royal Navy and the North-west Coast of North America 1810–1914* (Vancouver: University of British Columbia Press, 1971), p. 234n.

14. "The United States Navy" [editorial], *Broad Arrow and Military Gazette*, XLVI, no. 1090 (May 18, 1889), 606–607; H. Lawrence Swinbourne, "The Growth of the United States Navy as a naval power," *United Service Magazine*, n.s., VII (September 1899), 1308–20.

15. "Report of Brig. Gen. William P. Carlin, Department of Columbia," Aug. 18, 1893, U.S., Congress, 53rd Cong., 2nd sess., *House Exec. Docs.*, 1. pt. 2 (in 1198), p. 149.

16. Gough, *The Royal Navy*, p. 234.

17. Preston, *Canada and 'Imperial Defense'*, pp. 195–97.

18. C.S. Mackinnon, "The Imperial Fortresses in Canada: Halifax and Esquimalt, 1871–1906," (Ph.D. diss., University of Toronto, 1965), pp. 201–202; Lt.-Col. C.H. Fairfax, RA, and Lt.-Col. G. Barker, RE, "Report of the Defence of Halifax, N.S. (Nov. 23, 1886)," PRO, CAB/18/17/2; "Defences of Halifax (1882–94)," CAB 11/28; CDC Minutes, no. 31R (April 8, 1889), CAB 11/27; CDC Minutes, memorandum no. 88R, Minute 13.3.98; WO to CO, Feb. 6, 10, Nov. 18, 1892, PRO, CO 42/813.

19. John Buchan, *Lord Minto* (London: Nelson, 1924), pp. 77–78; Melgund, "Preparation to resist a Fenian raid on Winnipeg," PAC, MG 27, II B1 (c) (2), Reel A 130.

20. Desmond Morton, *The Last War Drum* (Toronto: Hakkert, 1972).

21. "Report of the Secretary of War," U.S., Congress, 49th Cong., 1st

sess., *House Exec. Docs.*, 1 (in 2369); USNA, RG 165, AGO 1744/1885, Microfilm M 689, Reel 350.

22. E.g., C. McKibbin, commanding Fort Pembina, to AAG, April 4, 1885, USNA, RG 165, AGO 1881/1885, and other papers in microfilm M 689, Reel 350.

23. Sackville-West to Bayard, April 9, 1885, USNA, M 689/R 349, M 50, Microfilm R-111, "A Canadian Girl" to Cleveland, April 3, 1885, USNA, M 666/R349, M 50.

24. *Canadian Militia Gazette*, I (Feb. 9, 1886), 314.

25. Ibid. (Feb. 23, 1886), 329.

26. Ibid. (March 16, 1886), 353.

27. Ibid., III (Nov. 10, 1887), 148.

28. *The Week*, I (Jan. 24, 1884), 114.

29. Ibid. (Feb. 28, 1884), 194.

30. Ibid. (Feb. 7, 1884), 146.

31. *Canadian Militia Gazette*, III (Nov. 3, 1887), 142, quoting Maj. C.E. Mayne, RE, to *Toronto Mail*; reply by correspondent of *Canadian Militia Gazette*, III (Nov. 10, 1887), 149.

32. "Memorandum on the Canadian Pacific Railway from an Imperial Point of View compiled at the Intelligence Department of the War Office by Captain L. Darwin, R. E. with a note on the commercial advantages of this route as compared with that by the United States by Lieutenant E.F.G. Law," March 1886, FO 88/5207.

33. Raymond McFarland, *A History of New England Fisheries* (New York: Appleton, 1911), pp. 329–30.

34. *Army and Navy Journal*, XIV (May 24, 1879), 72.

35. C.C. Tansill, *Canadian-American Relations, 1875–1911* (New Haven: Yale University Press, 1943), chaps. I–IV.

36. *Army and Navy Journal*, XXIII (June 5, 1886), 922–23.

37. Chamberlain to Salisbury, Nov. 18, 1887, Birmingham University, Chamberlain Papers, JC 3/1.2.

38. Lansdowne, confidential, March 3, 16, 25, 1886, PRO, CO 42/784; Admiralty to CO, April 13, 1886, CO 42/786; Lansdowne, 88, March 30, 1886, PRO, CO 42/784.

39. *Army and Navy Journal*, XXVI (Sept. 1, 1888), 10–11.

40. John B. Babcock, AAG, to AG, U.S. Army, Sept. 1893, USNA, WCD 639–94, p. 4.

41. James M. Callahan, *American Foreign Policy in Canadian Relations* (New York: Macmillan, 1937), p. 397, quoting *New York Tribune*, May 14, 1888, and "State Department Pamphs. G. B. Political Relations, I"; "Testimony of Joseph Nimmo, Jr., before the Select Committee on Relations with Canada, July 21, 1890," U.S., Congress, 51st Cong., 1st sess., *Senate Exec. Docs.*, 1530 (in 2712), pp. 893–94.

42. Lt. T.M. Woodruff, "Our Northern Frontier," *Journal of the Military Service Institution of the United States*, IX (March 1888), 1–32.

43. Addison Browne, "The Future of Canada," *The Week*, III, no. 7 (Jan. 14, 1886), 99.

44. Goldwin Smith, "The Fisheries Question and the crisis in England," *The Week*, III, no. 28 (June 10, 1886), 443–44.

45. Addison Browne, "The Future of Canada," p. 99.

46. E.g., J. Castell Hopkins, "Canadian hostility to annexation," *Forum*, XVI (November 1893), pp. 325–35.

47. G.H.M., "Canada's Future," *The Week*, IV, no. 49 (Nov. 3, 1887), pp. 783–84.

48. "The Canadian Militia—Its Future," *Canadian Militia Gazette*, II (Dec. 9, 1886), 578–79.

49. Denison to Macdonald, Feb. 6, 1890, PAC, MG 26, A 1 (c), pp. 210–11, 213–16; Denison's comments in *Toronto Empire*, July 9, 1890, ibid., p. 220; maps from *New York Daily Graphic*, Dec. 13, 1888, *New York World* (1888), and illustrations in *Once a Week*, March 16, 1889, PAC, Denison Papers, MG 29, F 13, vol. 19, pp. 102–104.

50. Watson Griffin, "Our True Independence," *Dominion Illustrated* I, no. 12 (Sept. 22, 1888), 182–83.

51. Benj[amin] F. Butler, "Defenseless Canada," *North American Review*, CXLVII (October 1888), 440–62.

52. E.g., Justin S. Morrill (of Vermont), "Is Union with Canada desirable?", *Forum*, XXVII (January 1899), 457–464.

53. B., "The American Side of Annexation," *The Week*, III, no. 1 (Dec. 3, 1885), 10.

54. J.G. Bourinot, "Why Canadians do not favor Annexation," *Forum*, XIX (May 1895), 276–88.

55. *Army and Navy Journal*, XXIV (May 21, 1887), 860.

56. "Mobilization and Concentration of the Canadian Militia for the Defense of the Frontier," *Journal of the Military Service Institution*, VIII (June and July 1887), 88–93, 159–68.

57. Arthur L. Wagner, "The Military Geography of Canada," *Journal of the Military Service Institition*, XIII (March 1893), pp. 429–65.

58. Terrae Filius, "The Canadian Question: A Military Glance at it," *The United Service*, II, n.s. (October and November 1889), 334–46.

59. Anon., "Canada and the United States: Belligerent Views of an American Writer," *United States Gazette*, no. 2973 (December 1889), 1036.

60. Peter Karsten, *The Naval Aristocracy: The Golden Age of Annapolis and the Emergence of Modern American Navalism* (New York: Free Press, 1972), pp. 299–333.

61. "Origization [*sic*] of the Military Information Division, 1885" (1891), USNA, RG, 165, DWC 639–2 and 3.

62. Bruce W. Bidwell, "History of the Military Intelligence Division, Department of the Army General Staff, Part One Preliminary Development, 1775–1917" (M.A. thesis, Georgetown University, 1959–61), p. 102, quoting

memorandum, AG to Lt.-Gen. Commanding the Army, March 17, 1902, AWC 639–14, Records of WDGS.

63. USNA, RG 165, Army War College Index, "Canada."

64. Lt. Andrew Rowan, "Report on the Canadian Pacific Railway, 1890," USNA, RG 165, WCD 3071-d, File Box 8, 1890.

65. USNA, RG 165, War College Index, "Canada."

66. Lt. A.D. Schenck, "Our Northern Frontier," *Journal of the Military Service Institution*, XI (November 1890), 869–913.

67. Joseph B. Batchelor, Jr., "A United States Army: Graduating thesis of the United States Infantry and Cavalry School," *Journal of the Military Service Institution*, XIII (March 1892), 54–74.

68. Capt. Arthur L. Wagner, "The Military Geography of Canada" in *Military Geography: Lectures in the Department of Military Art Delivered before the Class of Officers at the United States Infantry and Cavalry School, Fort Leavenworth, Kansas, 1893–1895*, pp. 5–6. This is a reprint of the paper with the same title cited above (n. 57) except for the omission of one footnote.

69. Wagner, "Military Geography of Canada," *passim*.

70. Samuel F. Bemis, *A Diplomatic History of the United States* (New York: Henry Holt, 1950), p. 789; Thomas A. Bailey, *A Diplomatic History of the American People* (New York: Appleton-Century-Crofts, 1958), p. 445.

71. Lt. William R. Hamilton, "If attacked could the United States Army carry on an offensive war?", *The United Service*, XIV (November 1895), 395–405.

72. Walter R. Herrick, *The American Naval Revolution* (Baton Rouge: Louisiana State University Press, 1966), pp. 23, 29.

73. Quoted in Anon., "Fortifying the Border," in *Canadian Militia Gazette*, IV (May 1, 1893), 143.

74. U.S., Congress, House, *Congressional Record*, 49th Cong., 1st sess., July 17, 1886, XVII, pt. 7, p. 7099.

75. *Report of the Board of Fortifications or other defences, House Executive Document no. 49, 49th Congress, 1st Session* (Washington: Government Printing Office, in 1886), no. 2359.

76. "Report of Major-General Howard, Department of the East," U.S., Congress, 52nd Cong., 1st sess., *House Exec. Docs.*, 1, pt. 2 (in 2921).

77. "Report of the Secretary of War, 1890," U.S., Congress, 51st Cong., 2nd sess., *House Exec. Docs.*, 1, pt. 2 (in 2831), pp. 5–9, 44.

78. *Army and Navy Journal*, XVIII (Sept. 17, 1890), 71.

79. Ibid., XXVIII (Nov. 29, 1890), 225; XXIX (Nov. 7, 1891), 189.

80. Ibid., XXIX (Oct. 10, 1891), 117, XXX (June 30, 1894), 776.

81. Ibid., XXIX (Sept. 26, 1891), 74 (Oct. 24, 1891), 143.

82. Quoted in ibid. (Feb. 6, 1892), 423.

83. Ibid.

84. Ibid., XXX (October 1893), 119; "Report of Major-General Howard, Department of the East," U.S., Congress, 52nd Cong., 1st sess., *House Exec.*

Docs., 1, pt. 2 (in 2921); "Report of Secretary of War" (1893), ibid., 1, pts. 2–6 (in 3198); U.S., Congress, Senate, *Congressional Record*, 51st Cong., 2nd sess., Feb. 2, 1891, pp. 2053, 2056, 2083; 52nd Cong., 1st sess., pp. 3582–86.

85. Russell F. Weigley, *History of the United States Army* (New York: Macmillan, 1967), p. 281.

86. Lansdowne, confidential, March 29, 1888, PRO, CO 42/795.

87. "Selection of Correspondence re. seizure of Canadian Vessels," PRO, CAB 37/27, vol. 27, nos. 24, 34, 35; CAB 37/28, vol. 28, no. 42; CAB 37/30, no. 28.

88. FO to CO, Jan. 21, 1891, PRO, CO 42/808.

89. *New York Sun*, Jan. 7, 1891.

90. C.A. Spring-Rice to Chamberlain, April 21, 1891, Chamberlain Papers, JC 7/4/2/1.

91. Lord Stanley to Salisbury, Oct. 11, 1891, Christ Church College, Oxford, Salisbury Papers, vol. 78, no. 98.

92. *Washington Post*, Jan. 7, 1891; FO to CO, Jan. 26, 29, 1891, PRO, CO 42/808.

93. Admiralty to CO, Oct. 19, 1892, PRO, CO 42/812.

94. Pauncefote to Salisbury, Nov. 8, 1895, Salisbury Papers, vol. 138, no. 3.

95. Callahan, *American Foreign Policy*, pp. 411–13.

96. High Commissioner to CO, January 1892, PRO, CO 42/813.

97. U.S., Congress, Senate, *Congressional Record*, 52 Cong., 1st sess., XXIII, pt. 4, p. 3095.

98. FO to CO, 22 July 1892, PRO, CO 42/815.

99. Admiralty to CO, March 5, 1895, PRO, CO 42/456; Admiralty to CO, June 20, 1895, CO 42/456.

100. High Commissioner to CO, Jan. 1892, PRO, CO 42/813; FO to CO, July 22, 1892, CO 42/815; FO to CO, Jan. 31, 1893, CO 42/820; FO to CO May 11, 1892, CO 42/814; FO to CO May 14, 1892, CO 42/814; Admiralty to CO June 25, 1892, CO 42/812; Stanley, confidential, July 7, 1892, CO 42/812.

101. FO to CO, Jan. 8, 1891, PRO, CO 42/808, referred to in CO 35/838, Jan. 15, 1881.

102. FO to CO, Jan. 7, 1895, PRO, CO 42/833.

103. Maj. C. Barter, "Confidential. The Military Aspects of the Northern Frontier of the United States . . .," PRO, WO 33/55 (A336); also to be found in FO 881/6626. Due to "unforeseen circumstances" Barter's report was not printed for circulation until March 1895.

104. D.M. Taylor, Capt. of Ordnance, "Report of a Journey of Observation," U.S. Naval War College Archives. The report is undated. It may have been produced while he was in charge of the Military Information Division, 1890–92. However, it is more likely that it was made earlier, in 1886 (cf. p. 110 above) and that Daniel Taylor was the most persistent of American officers concerned about the possibility of war with Canada, a subject on which he was to lecture at the Naval War College as late as 1900. George W. Cullum, *Bio-*

graphical Register of the Officers and Graduates of the U.S. Military Academy at West Point, New York . . . Supplement V, 1900–1910 (Saginaw, Mich.: Sieman and Peters, 1910), p. 156.

105. Maj.-Gen. Nelson A. Miles to the Adjutant-General, Feb. 27, 1883, Colonel Huggins Mss, in private possession (made available by courtesy of Richard A. Pierce, Queen's University, and John Weaver, McMaster University).

106. USNA, Army War College Record Card, 3083-1. The document has been destroyed and details are not available.

107. Preston, *Canada and 'Imperial Defense'*, pp. 188–202.

108. Aberdeen, 12, Jan. 11, 1894, PRO, CO 42/822.

109. Desmond Morton, *Ministers and Generals: Politics and the Canadian Militia, 1868–1904* (Toronto: University of Toronto Press, 1970), pp. 103, 108, 110; "Report of the General Officer Commanding the Militia, 1894," *Canada Sessional Papers*, 1895, XXXVIII, no. 10, S.P. no. 19, p. iv; Aberdeen, telegram, May 17, 1894, PRO, CO 42/844.

110. Deputy Governor General Strong, 311, Oct. 25, 1894, PRO, CO 42/824.

111. FO to CO, Aug. 29, 1895, PRO, CO 42/835 and ADM 1/7263.

CHAPTER 5

1. Chamberlain to Selborne, Dec. 20, 1895, Birmingham University, Chamberlain Papers, 7/5/1B/4.

2. *Broad Arrow*, LVI, no. 1436 (Jan. 14, 1896), 17; ibid., no. 1438 (Jan. 18, 1896), p. 67; *United Service Gazette and Organ of Imperial Federation*, no. 3390 (Jan. 1, 1898), 1043; "Professional Notes," *Journal of the United States Cavalry Association*, IX (March 1896), 76–86, quoting *The Army and Navy Gazette, The Broad Arrow*, and *The Admiralty and Horse Guards Gazette*.

3. *The Week*, XIII (Feb. 28, 1896), 321.

4. Gascoigne to Adjutant-General, Feb. 5, 1896, PRO, WO 32/275A/266/Canada.

5. Desmond Morton, *Ministers and Generals: Politics and the Canadian Militia, 1868–1904* (Toronto: University of Toronto Press, 1970), p. 115.

6. *Canadian Military [sic] Gazette*, V (Jan. 1, 1896), 6–10.

7. C.F.H., "A Militia System," *Canadian Military Gazette*, XIII (Nov. 15, 1898), 1.

8. Hamilton, "Defence, 1812–1912," in A. Shortt and A.G. Doughty, eds., *Canada and Its Provinces* (Toronto: Brook and Co., 1914), VI, 429.

9. Richard A. Preston, *Canada's R.M.C.: A History of the Royal Military College* (Toronto: University of Toronto Press, 1969), p. 126.

10. Morton, *Ministers and Generals*, p. 115.

11. Capt. A.H. Lee, memorandum, n.d., PRO, CAB 18/17/3; see also WO 32/275A/266.

12. Richard A. Preston, *Canada and 'Imperial Defence': A Study of the British Commonwealth's Defense Organization* (Durham, N.C.: Duke University Press, 1967), p. 235.

13. CDC memorandum, "Canada, the Navy League and Canadian Defence," secret, no. 60M, March 31, 1896, PRO, CAB 11/27.

14. Van Horne to Lee, Nov. 21, 1896, Chamberlain Papers, JC 15/11.

15. Chamberlain to Selborne, Dec. 20, 1895, Chamberlain Papers, JC 7/5/1B/4.

16. H.O. Arnold-Forster to H.F. Wilson, Dec. 20, 1895, Chamberlain Papers, JC 7/5/1B/5.

17. Chamberlain to Selborne, Dec. 20, 1895, Chamberlain Papers, 7/5/1B/4.

18. Chamberlain [to Salisbury], Jan. 9, 1896, Chamberlain Papers, JC 7/5/1B/14.

19. PRO, CAB 18/17/3, No. 2.

20. CDC minutes, secret, 59M, "Defence of the Dominion," March 27, 1896, PRO, CAB 11/27.

21. Ibid., March 31, 1896.

22. March 28, 1896, PRO, WO 106/40 B/1/5.

23. The Foster Reports of 1895 and 1896 are not extant. Under the heading "Confidential Report by Major Foster, July 1895," in War Office Library A Papers, no. 300, and PRO, WO 33/56, is the endorsement "Copy not available for binding." Maj. W.R. Robertson gave some details from Foster's reports in 1901 in his "Memorandum on the Defence of Canada." March 15, 1901, PRO, WO 106/40/B1/7.

24. Joint Naval and Military Committee on Defence, "Defence of Canada," April 23, 1896, PRO, WO 106/40, B/1/5; also in CAB 18/17/3, no. 7.

25. Foster produced a "Report on the Land Forces of the United States, 1896" which is referred to in PRO, WO 33/56, p. 257. The report is wanting and the place in the War Office Library Collections endorsed "Copy not available for binding."

26. Sir John Ardagh to St. John Brodrick, June 13, 1896, PRO, WO 106/40; Sir John Ardagh, "Comment on the Leach plan for the defence of Montreal," WO 32/275A/266/Canada/2057/1992.

27. Sir John Ardagh, "Comments on the Leach Plan for the defence of Montreal [revised version], March 10, 1897," PRO, WO 32/275A/266, Canada 2058/1992.

28. Arthur Haliburton, WO, to Undersecretary, CO, March 25, 1897, Chamberlain Papers, JC 15/7.

29. "Notes and comments," *Canadian Military Gazette*, XI (Jan. 15, 1896), 9–12.

30. *Army and Navy Journal*, XXXIII (Feb. 8, 1896), 414.

31. Ibid., p. 403.

32. FO to Admiralty, "Naval Preparations in the United States, Feb. 13, 1896," ADM 1/7302.

33. USNA, Record Card 2128, "Canada Before May 1, 1911, correspondence

between W[ar] C[ollege] D[ivision] and the Department of Militia and Defence concerning maps, pubs, etc." ["Destroyed"], USNA, Record Card 3066, "Document Destroyed"; N. Penlington, *Canada and Imperialism* (Toronto: University of Toronto Press, 1965), p. 37.

34. USNA, Record Card 3066, "Document Destroyed."

35. Aberdeen 17, Jan. 16, 1896, PRO, CO 42/838.

36. *New York Tribune*, March 1, 1897, in PRO, CO 42/851, 401.

37. M. Rees Davies, "The American Navy," *United Service Magazine*, n.s., XII (January 1896), 335–348; Capt. William Jacques, late U.S.N., "The Production of War Material in the United States," *Journal of the Royal United Services Institution*, XL (February 1896), 106–117.

38. M. Rees Davies, "The American Land Forces," *United Service Magazine*, n.s., XIII (April 1896), 173–80.

39. L.A. Kimberley to Capt. H.C. Taylor, May 3 and 13, 1895, Library of Congress, Taylor Papers.

40. Herbert to Gridley, Jan. 23, 1896, USNA, Naval Records, OL 1896. These papers are erroneously cited by Grenville and Young, *Politics, Strategy and American Diplomacy*, as "VI file, Venezuela crisis," and by Bourne, *Britain and the Balance of Power*, p. 324n, as "Subject file OX Box I, Venezuela incident."

41. Robert J. Macdonald, "Captain Gridley and the German Gas Buoy," *Inland Seas*, XV (1959), 288–90.

42. *Dictionary of American Biography*, VII, 610.

43. Herbert to Gridley, Jan. 24, 1896, USNA, Naval Records, OL 1896.

44. George Washington Cullum, *Biographical Register of Officers and Graduates of the U.S. Military Academy at West Point . . .*, IV, *Supplement, 1890–1900* (Cambridge: Riverside Press, 1901), 186–87. It is interesting to note that Henry Taylor's son went to live in Canada and that Henry died when visiting him there in 1904.

45. H.C. Taylor, memorandum for Comdr. V. Gridley, Jan. 25, 1896, USNA, Naval Records, OL1896.

46. Gridley to Taylor, Feb. 10, 1896, ibid.; Gridley's report, 1896, p. 70v, ibid.

47. Gridley to Taylor, Feb. 13, 1896, ibid.

48. Ibid.

49. Gridley's report, pp. 101–107, ibid.

50. Taylor to Gridley, March 13, 1896, ibid.

51. Gridley's report, p. 108, ibid.

52. Ibid., pp. 112–15.

53. Gridley to Taylor, April 1, 1896, ibid.

54. Gridley to Taylor, March 28, 1896, ibid.

55. Capt. H.C. Taylor, USN, "A Memorandum of an examination of important points on the Canadian Frontier. Made during July 1896," U.S. Naval War College Archives.

56. Herbert to Gridley, Jan. 23, 1896, ibid.

57. Comdr. Charles H. Stockholm, U.S. Navy, *Preparations for War: A Discussion of some of the various elements to be considered in the formation of plans and operations in the study of campaigns.* Delivered at the opening of the course in the Naval War College, R.I., May 31, 1899 (Washington: Government Printing Office, 1899), p. 13.

58. Chamberlain to Aberdeen, Oct. 20, 1896, PAC, RG 7, G 21, vol. 77, no. 165, vol. 6 (c).

59. "Colonial Defence: Public Statement by the Chairman of the Defence Committee . . . 23rd Dec. 1896," PRO, CAB 5/1/9C. On the relations between professional Joint Military and Naval committee and the Colonial Defence Committee see Zara Shakow, "The Defence Committee: A Forerunner of the Committee of Imperial Defence," *Canadian Historical Review*, XXXVI (March 1955), 6–44.

60. "Memorandum on the Defence of Canada, forwarded with approval by R. Grant, Inspector General of Fortifications," 1.3.97, PRO, WO 32/275A/266, Canada 2058/1992; Memorandum by R. Grant, IGF, 14.4.97, ibid.; Ardagh to COC, Militia, 23.6.97, ibid.

61. Lieut.-Colonel Turnbull, Late Commandant of the Royal School of Cavalry, "Canadian Defence," *Canadian Military Gazette*, XII (April 1, 1897), 18.

62. J. Ardagh to Chamberlain, July 10, 1897, Chamberlain Papers, 9/2/IC/I; memorandum by Ardagh, 10.7.97., JC 9/2/IC/2.

63. Capt. Thomas Maxwell to Laurier, Nov. 25, 1896, PAC, Laurier Papers, 9066–107.

64. R. Lanigan to Laurier, May 18, 1897, Laurier Papers 14881–2.

65. *Canadian Military Gazette*, XI (March 15, 1897), 7.

66. Wilfrid Laurier to Chamberlain, July 16, 1897, Chamberlain Papers, JC/9/2/IK/1.

67. FO to CO, March 17, 1897, PRO, CO 42/851; FO to CO, Feb. 2, 1898, CO 42/861; WO to CO, March 14, 1898, CO 42/865; Aberdeen, secret, Dec. 30, 1897, CO 42/848; Aberdeen, telegram, April 23, 1898, CO 42/857; CDC memorandum 128M, "Canada: Canal Communication to the Great Lakes in relation to war" [March 15, 1895], CAB 11/27; "Preliminary Examination for a ship canal from the Great Lakes . . . to the Hudson River," July 15, 1847, U.S., Congress, 55th Cong., 1st sess., *House Exec. Docs.*, 86 (in 3571).

68. Aberdeen, 30, Feb. 5, 1898, PRO, CO 42/856; CDC memorandum 133M, Nathan, "Canada: Survey by U.S. Engineers in Canadian Territory," March 15, 1898; Admiralty to CO, March 21, 1898, CO 42/859; Aberdeen, telegram, April 29, 1898, CO 42/857; FO to CO, May 23, 1898, CO 42/862.

69. CDC minute, Oct. 29, 1897, PRO, CAB 11/27.

70. E.F. Wurtele, Nov. 3, 1897, PRO, CO 537/475.

71. Lt. J.B. Murdoch, USN, to the President, Naval War College, Dec. 1, 1897, U.S. Naval War College Archives; Murdoch, "Report of Data collected

on a visit to St. Lawrence Region with Naval Militia of New York" (1897), ibid.

72. WO to CO, March 25, 1898, PRO, CO 537/481.

73. Aberdeen, telegram, April 23, 1893, PRO, CO 42/837.

74. FO to CO, July 26, 1898, PRO, CO 42/863. *La Patrie*, Montreal, April 26, 1898.

75. CDC memorandum 127M, Nathan, "Canada: American Warships on the Great Lakes," March 8, 1898, PRO, CAB 11/27.

76. WO to CO, March 25, 1898, PRO, CO 537/481.

77. Aberdeen, telegrams, April 23, 26, 29, 1898, PRO, CO 42/857; Aberdeen 121, 124, 128, May 2, 6, 10, 1898, ibid.

78. CDC memorandum 127M, CO Canada 753, secret, March 8, 1898, "Canada: American Warships on the Great Lakes," PRO, CAB 11/17/3.

79. Aberdeen, telegram, April 23, 1898, PRO, CO 42/857.

80. CDC minute, 18.3.97, "Amount for Defence of Montreal, Kingston, and Quebec," PRO, CAB 11/27; CDC memorandum 132 M, CO, Canada 764, CAB 18/17/3.

81. CDC memorandum 132M, Nathan, "Canada: Armaments of Montreal, Quebec, and Kingston," March 15, 1898, PRO, CAB 11/22; WO to CO, May 20, 1898, CO 42/865; WO to CO June 16, 1898, ibid.; High Commissioner to Colonial Secretary, June 3, 1898, CO 42/860; WO 106/40 B/1/6, "Defence of the Canadian Frontier," 1897.

82. Aberdeen, secret, Dec. 16, 1897, CO 42/848.

83. *Canadian Military Gazette*, XII, no. 16 (Aug. 18, 1897).

84. CDC memorandum 141R, "Halifax Defence Scheme Revised to Jan. 1896", PRO, CAB 11/27; CDC no. 166R, May 9, 1897, and General A. Montgomery Moore, Jan. 17, 1898, in "Halifax, Defence Scheme Revised to Jan. 1898," PRO, CAB 11/28/Part 9.

85. WO to CO, April 6, 1898, PRO, CO 42/865.

86. The Russian fleet in the Pacific expanded from two cruisers in 1877–87 to a battleship and six armoured cruisers in 1896. The American Pacific fleet grew from two coastal defence ships and six cruisers in 1887 to one battleship, three monitors, and eight cruisers in 1896 with another battleship under construction. Misc 405, Naval Intelligence Dept. "Memorandum on the Defence of Esquimalt," Dec. 11, 1896, PRO, CAB 1/2.

87. WO to CO, Oct. 29, 1897 (enclosing CDC memorandum no. 19M) and CO to WO, Dec. 15, 1897, in PRO, WO 32/275/266, Canada 33, Esquimalt. Estimates.

88. CDC memorandum 183R, Nathan, March 15, 1898, Esquimalt, PRO CAB 11/27.

89. Lt. Andrew S. Rowan to O/C Military Information Division, AGO, War Dept., from Seattle, 1897, USMHC, F 1089, V3, R 78.

90. Lt. D.F. Skelters, USN, Intelligence Office, to Chief of Bureau of Navigation for C.N.I., Port Esquimalt, June 20, 1900, ibid.

91. Pauncefote to Chamberlain, Jan. 21, 1898, Chamberlain Papers, JC/7/4/213.

92. Aberdeen, telegram, April 7, 1898, PRO, CO 42/857; Chamberlain to Aberdeen, secret, April 21, 1898, Chamberlain Papers, JC 15/18; Pauncefote to Salisbury, May 26, 1898, Christ Church College, Oxford, Salisbury Papers, vol. 139, no. 72.

93. Ms notes of an article, "Recent Developments and Policy in the United States and their relation to an Anglo-American Alliance" (1898), Chamberlain Papers, JC 4/3/1.

94. Hutton to Minto, Sept. 3, 1898, SNA, Minto Papers, Box 205, no. 375.

95. Minto to Prince of Wales, Jan. 1, 1899, SNA, Minto Papers, M 748, I, 22.

96. Minto to Chamberlain, Jan. 6, 1899, SNA, Minto Papers, I, 25.

97. Minto to Peter [Eliot], Feb. 26, 1899, PAC, Minto Papers, MG 27, II, B 1, p. 15.

98. Denison to Laurier, July 23, 1898, PAC, Laurier Papers, 224948-9.

99. Denison to Laurier, Dec. 8, 1898, PAC, Laurier Papers, 225086-9; Capt. R.N. Custance, "Naval Defence of the Canadian Frontier, 1894, Revised and Brought up to date by Capt. W.G. White, RN," 1899, PRO, CAB 18/18/3; E.C.A. Altham to Hutton, May 24, 1899, PAC, Hutton Mss, MG 21, pp. 558–61.

100. *Daily Graphic*, Dec. 27, 1898, SNA, Minto Papers, press cuttings, M 754; Denison to Laurier, April 8, 1899, PAC, Laurier Papers, 32199-32202; "Our Lake Defences," *Canadian Military Gazette*, XV, no. 5 (March 6, 1900), 10.

101. Montgomery-Moore to Laurier, Jan. 7, 1898, PAC, Laurier Papers, 10719-22.

102. Militia Department, PAC, RG9, II B 2 (71) vol. 32, docket 16461.

103. Aberdeen to Laurier, Feb. 15, 1898, PAC, Laurier Papers, 20391-2; Aberdeen, secret, Feb. 26, 1898, PRO, CO 537/479; Aberdeen, telegram, Feb. 28, 1898, CO 537/477.

104. Chamberlain to Aberdeen, April 13, June 22, 1898, PAC, RG7, G 21, vol. 77, no. 165, vol. 7; F. Borden to Minto, June 28, 1898, RG9, II A 2, 18, 16, 861; Adm. to CO, July 27, 1898, PRO, CO 42/859.

105. Hutton to Ardagh, June 12, 1898, PAC, Hutton Papers, IV, 364.

106. Chamberlain [to Minto], July 29, 1898, Chamberlain Papers, JC 15/80; CDC Minutes, no. 47M, secret, PRO, CAB 11/27.

107. "Instructions to Committee on Military Matters," PAC, RG7, G 21, vol. 77, no. 165, vol. 7; also in PRO, CAB 11/27 No. 147M, secret.

108. Intelligence Division, War Office, "Schedule of Papers collected for the use of officers selected to assist the Canadian government in drawing up a scheme of defence. No.1. Memorandum by E.F. Chapman, July 11, 1898," PRO, CAB 18/17/3.

109. "Defence Committee, Canada, Report No. 1, 1898, Copy No. 3," PAC, CEF Section; also in PRO, CAB 18/8.

110. Memorandum to Chamberlain, April 5, 1899, PAC, RG 7 G 21, vol. 77, no. 165, vol. 7.

111. Leach to Hutton, Oct. 13, 1899, PAC, Hutton Papers, MG 21, pp. 576–77.

112. Hutton to Sir Richard Harrison, July 17, 1899, PAC, Hutton Papers, MG 21, pp. 1034–37.

113. Hutton to Lord Seymour, Jan. 15, 1899, PAC, Hutton Papers, MG 21, vol. 695.

114. Hutton to Minto, March 30, 1899, PAC, Minto Papers, MG 27, II, B 1, XV, 15; Hutton to Sir Richard Harrison, n.d., Hutton Papers, MG 21, 1041–2; Hutton Mss, "Narrative," p. 1731.

115. E.P. Leach to Hutton, Oct. 13, 1898, PAC, Hutton Papers, MG 21, 576–77.

116. Chamberlain to Hutton, March 14, 1899, PAC, Hutton Papers, MG 21, VII, 974.

117. Hutton to Borden, May 30, 1899, PAC, Hutton Papers, MG 21, pp. 1021–1027.

118. FO to CO, June 27, July 3, Aug. 1, 1900, PRO, CO 42/878.

119. Hutton to Seymour, Jan. 4, 1900, PAC, Hutton Papers, MG 21, pp. 196–97, Hutton to Seymour, Jan. 20, 1900, ibid., p. 71.

120. Laurier to Minto, Jan. 5, 1900, PAC, Minto Papers, MG 27, II, B 1, V, 36; Minto to Pauncefote, Jan. 7, 1900, SNA, Minto Papers, M 748, I, 289; Hutton to Seymour 1900, PAC, Hutton Papers, MG 21, pp. 196–97.

121. Lee to Hutton, April 6, 1899, PAC, Hutton Papers, MG 21, pp. 481–83.

122. "Report of Major-General Commanding U.S. Army," 1898, U.S., Congress, 55th Cong., 3rd sess., *House Exec. Docs.*, 2 (in 3745), pp. 190–92.

123. Army War College index cards have four reports on Canada in 1896, three in 1897, and no more thereafter until 1903.

124. U.S., Congress, *Congressional Record*, House, 55th Cong., 2nd sess., Feb. 3, 1898, XXI, pt. 2, p. 1422.

125. Denison to Laurier, Nov. 3, 1899, PAC, Laurier Papers, 225412-5; T.A. Bull to Laurier, Dec. 5, 1899, ibid., 225437-40.

126. Minto to Pauncefote, Aug. 25, 1900, SNA, Minto Papers, M 478, II, 96; Lee to Hutton, March 28, 1899, PAC, Hutton Papers, MG 21, pp. 479–80; Lee to Hutton, May 2, 1899, ibid., pp. 484–86.

127. *Canadian Military Gazette*, XIV, no. 14 (July 14, 1899), 11.

128. Lee to Hutton, March 8, 1899, PAC, Hutton Papers, MG 21, pp. 477–78.

129. *Morning Herald*, Sept. 2, 1899, Minto Papers, Press Cuttings, SNA, M 754, p. 112.

130. *Times*, June 12, 1900, SNA, Minto Papers, Press Cuttings, M 755, p. 35.

131. Hutton, "Narrative," PAC, Hutton Papers, MG 21.

132. Robert Craig Brown's *Canada's National Policy, 1883–1900; A Study in Canadian-American Relations* (Princeton, N.J.: Princeton University Press, 1964) significantly makes no reference to the military or defence factor.

CHAPTER 6

1. A.E. Campbell, *Great Britain and the United States 1895–1903* (London: Longmans, 1960), pp. 86–98; Charles S. Campbell, *Anglo-American Understanding* (Baltimore: Johns Hopkins, 1957), p. 346; Kenneth Bourne, *Britain and the Balance of Power in North America* (Berkeley and Los Angeles: University of California Press, 1967), pp. 346–51; idem, *Foreign Policy of Victorian England* (Oxford: Clarendon, 1967), pp. 173–75; R.G. Neale, *Great Britain and United States Expansionism* ([Lansing, Mich.]: Michigan State University Press, 1966), pp. 211–15.

2. "Reports of Exploration in the Territory of Alaska. . . .," AG's Office, War Dept., no. XXV [1898], USMHC; *Explorations in Alaska for an All-American Overland Route from Cooke Inlet, Pacific Ocean, to the Yukon* (Washington, Government Printing Office, 1901), ibid., no. XXXI.

3. Campbell, *Anglo-American Understanding*, pp. 184–185.

4. F. Newton to Joseph Chamberlain, Nov. 27, 1901, Chamberlain Mss, JC 15/300, in PAC, Minto Papers, "Klondike Reign of Terror," unsigned typescript dated [1901?], ibid.; Minto to Lansdowne, June 4, 1902, SNA, Minto Papers, M 750, III, 219–21.

5. AG to Cmdg. General, District of Columbia, Nov. 29, 1901, USNA, AGO 412889; Capt. H.W. Hovey, Skagway, to AG District of Columbia, Dec. 4, 21, 1901, ibid.

6. Pauncefote to Hay, Feb. 8, 1902, USNA, microfilm T 136.

7. AG to Brig.-Gen. G.M. Randall, March 29, 1902, USNA, RG 165, 412889; Capt. W.P. Richardson to AG, April 18, 1902, AGO 412889/N.

8. "Defence of Canada: Operations in a War with the United States," including Levita to Altham, Nov. 1, 1898, and Lake to Levita, Oct. 4, 1898, PRO, WO 106/40, B1/7.

9. "War with the United States, 1901, Defence of Canada. Secret. Not to be Registered," PRO, WO 106/40, B1/7.

10. Lt.-Col. C.V. Townshend. "Reconnaissance reports on certain portions of the Canadian frontier," Intelligence Department, PRO, WO 1902, A764; CAB 18/17, no. 4.

11. Capt. A. Haldane, "Memorandum on policy to be adopted in a war with the United States. Revised March 12, 1902. Revised Jan. 15, 1903, Comments by E.A. Altham, DAAG," PRO, WO 106/40, B1/1.

12. Franklyn Johnson, *Defence by Committee* (London: Oxford University Press, 1960); Richard A. Preston, *Canada and 'Imperial Defense': A Study of the British Commonwealth's Defense Organization, 1867–1919* (Durham, N.C.: Duke University Press, 1967), pp. 307–11.

13. "Halifax Defence Scheme. Revised Jan. 1901," PRO, CAB 11/28, pt. 2; "Correspondence with the Admiralty on the Strategic Position of Halifax in the event of war with the United States," WO 106/40, B1/2; WO Intelligence Dept., "Memorandum on the Standards for the Naval Defence of Halifax . . .," Sept. 17, 1903, CAB 5/1/3, and WO 106/40, B1/17; Admiralty In-

telligence Dept., "Strategic Position of British Naval Bases in the Western Atlantic," Nov. 24, 1903, CAB 5/1/5C; WO Intelligence Dept., "The Adequacy of Existing Defences of Halifax . . .," Dec. 11, 1903, CAB 5/1/7C; "Halifax Defence Scheme. Revised to Jan. 1904," CAB 11/29, pt. 2; CID Minutes, 48th meeting, July 8, 1904, CAB 2/1; Sir G. Clarke to Sir M. Ommanney, Aug. 12, 1904, CO 537/492; "Withdrawal of Infantry Battalion from Halifax," WO 32/816/058/2848; CID Minutes, 61st meeting, Dec. 9, 1904, CAB 2/1; "Halifax. Practicability of a Cruiser Raid upon" [and other papers about the withdrawal of the garrison, 1904–1906], CAB 17/41.

14. Clarke to Minto, Aug. 15, 1904, SNA, Minto Papers, Box 210/3.

15. Thomas Raddall, *Warden of the North* (Toronto: McClelland and Stewart, 1971), pp. 243–44.

16. H.A. Lawrence, DAQMG, "Canada: Standard of Defence, Esquimalt," March 1, 1902, PRO, WO 32/275B/266; Admiralty to WO, April 19, 1902, ibid.

17. Col. A.M. Murray, *Imperial Outposts: From a strategical and commercial aspect, with special reference to the Japanese alliance* (London: John Murray, 1907), p. 171.

18. Samuel F. Wells, Jr., "British Strategic withdrawal from the Western Hemisphere, 1904–1906," *Canadian Historical Review*, XLIX (December 1968), 335–56.

19. "Canada. Remarks on the Defence of Canada, May 4, 1903," PRO, CO 42/895.

20. Desmond Morton, *Ministers and Generals: Politics and the Canadian Militia, 1868–1904* (Toronto: University of Toronto Press, 1970), pp. 174–76.

21. "Memorandum from the Military Members of the Militia Council to the Minister of Militia and Defence . . .," June 14, 1905, Canada, *Sessional Papers*, 1905, no. 130, p. 1.

22. "Canada. Remarks on the Defence of Canada. Secret. May 4, 1903," minute, Sir John Anderson to Sir Michael Ommanney, PRO, CO 42/895, 173.

23. Richard A. Preston, *Canadian Defence Policy and the Development of the Canadian Nation, 1867–1917*, Canadian Historical Association Booklets, no. 25 (Ottawa, 1970), p. 16.

24. Minto to Clarke, April 25, 1904, SNA, Minto Papers, Box 210/3.

25. Lt.-Col. G.M. Kirkpatrick, "A Study of Strategical Conditions existing on the Canadian Frontier 1904," in PRO, CAB 18/17, 424; also in CAB 18/17/6 and WO 32/320.

26. Charles E. Callwell, "The Defence of Canada in a War with the United States, Dec. 2, 1903," submitted Oct. 3, 1904, PRO, WO 106/40, B1/3.

27. Dundonald to Field-Marshal the Hon. Earl Roberts, April 27, 1903, Queen's University Archives, Dundonald Papers.

28. Colonel Hughes, "Paper on Canadian Defence, 1904," PRO, WO 32/275/266, Canada 205.

29. Lt.-Col. H.J. Foster, RE, "A Study of the Strategic Considerations Affecting the Invasion of Canada by the United States," July 1904, PRO, WO 104/40, B1/8.

30. General Staff, "The Defence of Canada," Dec. 13, 1904, referring to CID memorandum 15C, PRO, WO 106/40, B1/9.

31. Col. W.R. Robertson, GS to DMO, March 17, 1905, "Military Resources of the United States," PRO, WO 106/40, B1/16.

32. CID minutes, 75th meeting, July 13, 1904, PRO, CAB 2/1; "Canada, Defences of: Decisions of the C.I.D., 1905," WO 106/40, B1/4; "Memorandum by the General Staff on Admiralty Memorandum," no. 21/C, March 1905, ibid., B1/10; "Defence of Canada, Questions submitted by the General Staff," ibid., B1/11; "Military Resources of Canada," 1905, ibid., B1/13.

33. Lt.-Col. Kirkpatrick, "Memorandum on Canadian Military Policy," Dec. 29, 1905, PRO, WO 106/40, B1/12.

34. N.G. Lyttelton, "Canada and the United States: Defence and Military Resources," January 1906, and C.E. Callwell, "The Defence of Canada," Feb. 7, 1906, PRO, WO 106/40, B1/14.

35. J.A.S. Grenville, *Lord Salisbury and Foreign Policy: The Close of the Nineteenth Century* (London: Athlone Press, 1964), p. 389; C.S. Mackinnon, "The Imperial Fortresses in Canada: Halifax and Esquimalt, 1871–1906," 2 vols. (Ph.D. thesis, University of Toronto, 1965), pp. 459–60.

36. "Military Report on the Northern Frontier of the United States," pts. I–IV, Foreign Office, Confidential Papers, 8753, 9646–8.

37. Sir H.M. Durand, "Report on the United States for the year 1906," confidential, FO 881/8834.

38. Anon., Secret, "Memorandum Respecting Relations between Great Britain and the United States," February 1908, FO 881/9156.

39. John Buchan, *Lord Minto* (London: Nelson, 1924), p. 124.

40. George Pappas, *Prudens Futuri: The United States Army War College* (Carlisle Barracks, Pa.: Alumni Association of the Army War College, 1967), pp. 22, 37, 41; Louis Matloff, *American Military History* (Washington: OCMH, 1969), p. 348.

41. "Plan of General Wood—Invasion of Canada," confidential, March 24, 1903, USNA, RG 165, AWC Index, 1757.

42. Ibid., 2128, 783n.

43. Ibid., 3d, p. 86.

44. Ibid., 1757.

45. Ibid., 2128, 783n.

46. Ibid., S 69.

47. John W. Masland and Lawrence I. Radway, *Soldiers and Statesmen: Military Education and National Policy* (Princeton: Princeton University Press, 1957), p. 84.

48. C. Joseph Bernardo and Eugene H. Bacon, *American Military Policy: Its Development since 1775* (Harrisburg, Penna.: Military Service Publishing Company, 1955, p. 293.

49. Russell F. Weigley, *History of the United States Army* (New York: Macmillan, 1967), pp. 323–25; Pappas, *Prudens Futuri*, p. 16.

50. Weigley, *History of the U.S. Army*, p. 333.

51. Lt. John B. Hatterdorf, "Technology and Strategy: A study in the professional thought of the U.S. Navy, 1900–1916," *Naval War College Review*, XXIV, no. 3 (November 1971), 25–48; Rear-Adm. Bradley A. Fiske, *From Midshipman to Rear-Admiral* (London: T. Werner Laurie, 1919), pp. 477–89.

52. Richard Challener, *Admirals, Generals, and American Foreign Policy, 1898–1914* (Princeton: Princeton University Press, 1973), pp. 10, 26–29, 401–406.

53. Dundonald to Minto, Aug. 25, 1902, PAC, Minto Papers, MG 27, II, B1, vol. XXI, 12–14, and SNA, Minto Papers, Box 213.

54. "Report of Major-General Samuel Young, Dept. of the Columbia," Aug. 26, 1901, U.S., Congress, 57th Cong., 1st sess., *House Exec. Docs.*, 2 (in 4271), p. 275; "Report of the Secretary of War, 1902," ibid., 2nd sess., 2 (in 4443), pp. 21, 24; *Sites for Military Posts*, referred to Committee on Military Affairs, May 10, 1902, 57th Cong., 1st sess., 618 (in 4379), *passim*, and Brig.-Gen. E.S. Otis, Dept. of the Columbia, to AG, Nov. 6, 1894, Seattle Chamber of Commerce to Brig.-Gen. G.M. Randall, n.d., and idem to the Board on Army Posts, Jan. 8, 1902, pp. 561–67.

55. Albert K. Weinberg, *Manifest Destiny: A Study in National Expansionism in American History* (Baltimore: Johns Hopkins Press, 1935), pp. 355–70.

56. Kitson to Minto, March 26, 1902, SNA, Minto Papers, Box 213.

57. Kitson to Minto, May 24, 1902, PAC, Minto Papers, MG 27, II B1, XXI, 204–209.

58. *Saturday Night*, Feb. 22, 1902.

59. A Canadian (pseud.), "America: the Great Delusion," *Saturday Review*, May 17, 1902, SNA, Minto Papers, M 756, Press cuttings, p. 34.

60. *Montreal Gazette*, Jan. 23, 1903, SNA, Minto Papers, M 756, Press cuttings, pp. 229–31.

61. *Morning Post*, Dec. 11 and 26, 1902; *Review of Reviews* (December 1902), and *The Week's Survey* (Jan. 31, 1903), in SNA, Minto Papers, M 756, Press cuttings, pp. 175, 184.

62. "For annexation," *Montreal Star*, March 29, 1902, SNA, Minto Papers, M 755, Press cuttings, p. 318.

63. R.C. Jebb, "Mr. Bourassa on Canadian Imperialism: in the Monthly Review, September and October, 1902," *McGill University Magazine*, II (April 1903), 26–37.

64. Minto to Hon. C. Fitzpatrick, Feb. 9, 1902, SNA, Minto Papers, M 750, III, 212–22.

65. Minto to Hon. Arthur Elliot, MP, Oct. 18, 1903, SNA, Minto Papers, M 751, pp. 194–97.

66. Minto to Chamberlain, March 2, 1903, Chamberlain Papers, JC 18/4/14; O.D. Skelton, *Life and Letters of Sir Wilfrid Laurier* (Toronto: Oxford University Press, 1921), II, 125n, 139; J.S. Willison, *Sir Wilfrid Laurier and the Liberal Party: A Political History* (Toronto: Morang and Co., 1903), II, 164–66.

67. *Canadian Annual Review, 1903*, p. 312; Edward Farrer, "The New Imperialism," *Contemporary Review*, LXXXIV (December 1903), pp. 761–74; Minto to Sir Mortimer Durand, Jan. 12, 1904, SNA, Minto Papers, M 751, III, 276–78.

68. Minto to Earl of Onslow, March 28, 1902, SNA, Minto Papers, M 750, III, 153–54.

69. *Globe*, Oct. 30, 1902, in Minto Papers, PAC, MG 27, II, B1, XXXVI, 258–59.

70. *Globe*, June 30, 1902, SNA, Minto Papers, M 756, p. 41.

71. *Globe*, Oct. 30, 1902, PAC, Minto Papers, MG 27, II, B1, XXXVI, 258–59.

72. Minto to Sir Michael Herbert, Oct. 21, 1902, SNA, Minto Papers, M 750, pp. 271–75.

73. Minto to Sir Arthur Bigge, March 29, 1902, SNA, Minto Papers, M 750, III, 159–60.

74. Kitson to Minto, March 26, 1902, SNA, Minto Papers, Box 213.

75. Campbell, *Anglo-American Understanding*, pp. 257–58.

76. Minto to Sir Michael Herbert, Oct. 21, 1903, SNA, Minto Papers, M 750, pp. 271–75.

77. Minto to Alverstone, Dec. 8, 1903, SNA, Minto Papers, M 751, IV, 235–41; George P. de T. Glazebrook, in *A History of Canadian External Relations* (London: Oxford University Press, 1950), maintains that the Canadian Commission's Jetté and Aylesworth showed "a dignified restraint in comments on the award" (p. 247).

78. Glazebrook, *Canadian External Relations*, pp. 248–49.

79. Dundonald to Borden, March 8, 1904, PAC, Minto Papers, MG 27, B1, XXI, 53–54; Dundonald to Minto [December 1903], March 11, 1904, ibid., pp. 48–49, 52; Foster to Minto, July 22, 1903, SNA, Minto Papers, Box 205; Minto to Dundonald, March 14, 1904, ibid., M 751, IV, 318–39; Campbell, *Anglo-American Understanding*, p. 342n.

80. *Canadian Military Gazette*, XVIII (Nov. 3, Dec. 22, 1903).

81. G.R. Stevens, *The Canadian National Railway* (Toronto: Clarke Irwin, 1972), II, 174–75.

82. Minto to CO, Dec. 3, 1903, enclosed in Minto, secret, to Lyttelton, Dec. 8, 1903, PAC, Minto Papers, MG 27, II, B1, II, 55–60; Minto, secret, Dec. 13, 1903, ibid., pp. 661–69; Minto to Lyttelton, Jan. 9, 1904, ibid., III, 71–75.

83. Conversations with Laurier, Dec. 13, 1903, SNA, Minto Papers, Box 212/2.

84. *Army and Navy Journal*, XL (Nov. 7, 1903), 236.

85. Ibid., XLI (March 19, 1904), 748.

86. Ibid. (May 21, 1904), p. 992.

87. Ibid. (June 4, 1904), p. 1048.

88. Ibid. (Aug. 27, 1904), p. 1343.

89. Ibid., XLII (Dec. 10, 1904), 359.

90. Minto to Marquis of Lansdowne, Dec. 29, 1903, SNA, Minto Papers, M 751, IV, 265–69.

91. Henry J. Morgan to Laurier, May 14, 1902, PAC, Laurier Papers, pp. 65137–38.

92. *Canadian Military Gazette*, XVIII (July 21, 1903).

93. *Montreal Daily Herald*, Jan. 27, 1906, Chamberlain Papers, JC 20/2/11.

94. *Canadian Annual Review of Public Affairs, 1905* (Toronto: Canadian Review, 1906), p. 523.

95. Ibid., p. 525.

96. Sir A. Douglas to Minto, June 6, 1904, SNA, Minto Papers, Box 213.

97. Quoted in *Canadian Military Gazette*, XIX, no. 23 (Dec. 13, 1904), p. 9.

98. *Reports of the Annual Meetings of the Lake Mohonk Conferences, 1895–1917* (Lake Mohonk Arbitration Conference, 1895, *et seq.*).

99. Ibid., *1905*, p. 52.

100. Ibid., *1906*, p. 86.

101. Ibid., *1907*, p. 114.

102. Ibid., *1908*, p. 115.

103. Ibid., *1909*, p. 91.

104. Ibid., pp. 63–65, 111.

105. Ibid., *1910*, pp. 3, 10, 58, 108–12, 127–28; *1911*, p. 133; *1912*, pp. 60–63.

106. Ibid., *1910*, pp. 105–107; *1912*, pp. 75–84; *1913*, p. 59.

107. The secretary of the Canadian Peace and Arbitration Society was Rev. C.S. Eby of Toronto. The secretary of the Canadian Peace Century Committee was E.H. Scammell of Ottawa. As the First World War had broken out in Europe before the celebrations were held, the anniversary was observed quietly in the United States, Britain, and Canada. (Ibid., *1915*, p. 281; *Review of Reviews*, *1915*, pp. 51–54.)

CHAPTER 7

1. Kenneth Bourne, *Britain and the Balance of Power in North America* (Berkeley and Los Angeles: University of California Press, 1967), pp. 402–408. For a contrary interpretation, see John Gooch, "Great Britain and the Defence of Canada, 1896–1914," *Journal of Imperial and Commonwealth History*, III (May 1975), 369–85. Writing almost exclusively from the War Office and CID sources, Dr. Gooch argued that the defence of Canada continued to be a problem for the military, and an embarrassment for the politicians.

2. C.P. Stacey, *The Military Problems of Canada* (Toronto: Ryerson, 1940), pp. 48–69, especially p. 68.

3. Maj. A. Grant, "Remarks on the Halifax Defence Scheme" (May 14, 1908), PRO, WO 106/40, B1/19.

4. CID, "Halifax Defence Scheme," pt. 5 (January 1908), PRO, CAB 11/29.

5. CID, "Halifax Defence Scheme, 1909," pt. 6, PRO, CAB 11/39.

6. CID, "Halifax Defence Scheme, 1910," pt. 7, PRO, CAB 11/19.

7. Stacey, *Military Problems of Canada*, pp. 69–70.

8. CID, "Halifax Defence Scheme, 1912," PRO, CAB 11/30.

9. WO to CO, April 29, 1913, PRO, CO 537/497, no. 14600.

10. CID minutes, 73rd meeting, June 28, 1905, PRO, CAB 2/1.

11. CDC memorandum no. 430M, April 24, 1911, in Grey, confidential, Jan. 11, 1910, PRO, CO 437/493.

12. CID minutes, 108th meeting, Jan. 26, 1911, PRO, CAB 2/2/2.

13. Maj. Grant Duff, "Conditions of a war between the British Empire and the United States" (Jan. 23, 1908), PRO, WO 106/40, B1/20.

14. "Summary of the Proceedings of the Committee of Imperial Defence in regard to the defence of Canada," May 14, 1908, PRO, CAB 17/44.

15. Bryce to Grey, May 1, 1911, PRO, CO 537/494, no. 16244.

16. H.C. Lowther to Lionel Earle, Feb. 16, 1912, PRO, CO 537/496, no. 7123; Earle to Lowther, March 6, 1912, ibid.

17. Capt. S.C. Vestal, lecture notes, Fort Leavenworth, Feb. 1, 1906, USNA, RG 165, 5268–1.

18. Lt. F.E. Wilson, "The Defence of the Northern Border of the United States against Invasion," April 22, 1909, USNA, RG 165, AG 1517645.

19. Maj. R.H. Van Deenen, "Historical Sketch of the steps taken by the War Department for the collection, classification, and distribution of military information in the Army" (Office of the Chief of Military History), p. 17; Josiah Bernardo and Eugene H. Bacon, *American Military Policy: its Development since 1775* (Harrisburg, Pa.: Military Service Publishing Co., 1955), p. 322; Russell F. Weigley, *History of the United States Army* (New York: Macmillan, 1967), p. 333.

20. Army War College, Session 1909–10, "Outline of Course of Instruction," p. 10, USMHC.

21. Army War College, Session 1909–10, XIII, 25, USMHC.

22. Ibid., pp. 145–56.

23. Capt. Richard A. McMaster, "The military geography of our northern frontier" (submitted May 19, 1910), USNA, RG 165, WCD 6908–1.

24. Army War College, Session 1910–11, "Outline of Course of Instruction," p. [12], USMHC.

25. Army War College, Session 1910–11, III, "Problems and Exercises," 327–31, USMHC.

26. Army War College, Session 1911–12, IV (January–March 1912), USMHC.

27. Army War College, Session 1912–13, III (December 1912) (Canadian), 202–334, USMHC.

28. Lt.-Col. Thomas B. Dugan, "Military Geography of the Provinces of Ontario and Quebec, to include a study of an attack on those provinces by the United States," Army War College, Session 1912–13, USNA, WCD 8364–2.

29. Dugan, "Reconnaissance of the Crossing of the St. Lawrence," Jan. 10, 1913, USNA, WCD 7524–1; Maj. de Rosey Cabell, 11th Infantry, and Maj. William H. Hay, 10th Cavalry, "Invasion of Canada (Canadian War Plans): Concentration of Troops to meet attack by Red," Army War College, Session 1912–13, USNA, WCD.

30. Maj. B.A. Poore, General Staff, "General Plan. Red *vs* Blue, with brief details of such movements as are not studied by the Army War College Class," lecture, Sept. 14, 1913, Army War College, Session 1913–14, "Problems and Exercises," I, OCMH.

31. Lt. Col. B.H. Fuller, USMC, "Military Geography of Eastern Canada and a study of the invasion thereof by United States forces," Jan. 29, 1914, USNA, WCD 8364–3.

32. Col. Abner Pickering, "Military Geography of Western Canada including a study of an invasion by United States Forces," January 1914, USNA, WCD 3864–3.

33. Brig.-Gen. M.M. Macomb to Chief of Staff, March 18, 1915, USNA, RG 165, AWC 7524–4.

34. Brig.-Gen. M.M. Macomb, memorandum for Chief of Staff, June 1915, USNA, RG 165, AWC 9053–40.

35. "Plans for a campaign [against Canada] and details of plan of attack" with "Alleged plan [map] for invasion of Canada," endorsed "rec'd Mar 21, 1916," USNA, RG 165, WCD 8805–2. I am indebted to Dr. Howard Moon for drawing my attention to these papers.

36. Frederick Palmer, *Newton D. Baker: America at War*, 2 vols. (New York: Dodd Mead, 1921), II, 40–41.

37. *Army and Navy Journal*, XLV (March 2, 1908), 908; ibid., XLVI (Sept. 25, 1909), 96; XLVII (June 25, 1910), 1395; XLIX (Sept. 30, 1911), 121.

38. Ibid., XLVIII (Oct. 15, 1910), 185.

39. Maj. J.M. Phillips, "The Canadian Militia," *Infantry Journal*, X (May–June 1914), 896–903.

40. Weigley, *United States Army*, pp. 312–41.

41. U.S., Congress, House, *Congressional Record*, 61st Cong., 3rd sess., p. 1006 (Jan. 17, 1911).

42. U.S., War Department, *Report of the Secretary of War*, 1912, I, app. B, 168.

43. Albert K. Weinberg, *Manifest Destiny: a Study of Nationalist Expansionism in American History* (Baltimore: Johns Hopkins Press, 1935), pp. 372–78.

44. S.F. Wise, "The Annexation Movement and Canadian Opinion," in Wise and Brown, *Canada views the United States* (Seattle and London: University of Washington Press, 1967), p. 94.

45. R.C. Brown, "Canadian Opinion after Confederation," ibid., pp. 113–14.

46. David Potter, "Commentary," ibid., p. 128.

47. Carl Berger, *The Sense of Power: Studies in the Ideas of Canadian Imperialism* (Toronto: University of Toronto Press, 1970), p. 259 and *passim*.

48. Elizabeth Wallace, *Goldwin Smith: Victorian Liberal* (Toronto: University of Toronto Press, 1957), pp. 53–54.

49. Alvin C. Gluek, "The Passamaquoddy Bay Treaty, 1910," *Canadian Historical Review*, XLVII (March 1966), 7.

50. Grey to Stead, March 9, 1909, PAC, Grey Papers, 178, file 17.

51. John S. Galbraith, *Canadian Diplomatic Status at Washington* (Berkeley and Los Angeles: University of California Press, 1951), p. 5. For a fuller discussion see Peter Neary, "Grey, Bryce, and the Settlement of Canadian-American differences, 1905–1911," *Canadian Historical Review*, XLIX (December 1968), 357–80.

52. James Eayrs, *The Art of the Possible* (Toronto: University of Toronto Press, 1965), p. 29; Mary Elizabeth Hallet, "The Fourth Earl Grey as Governor-General of Canada, 1904–1911" (Ph.D. diss., University of London, 1969), p. 216.

53. Canada, Department of External Affairs, *Documents on Foreign Relations*, I, *1908–1919* (Ottawa: Queen's Printer, 1967), pp. 3–4, 5–6, 12; James Eayrs, "The Origins of Canada's Department of External Affairs," in Hugh L. Keenleyside *et al.*, *The Growth of Canadian Policies in External Affairs* (Durham, N.C.: Duke University Press, 1960), pp. 14–32.

54. Gaddis Smith, "External Affairs during World War I," in Keenleyside, p. 34.

55. George W. Brown, *The Growth of Peaceful Settlement between Canada and the United States* (Toronto: Ryerson, 1948), pp. 25–26.

56. Donald F. Warner, *The Idea of Continental Union: Agitation for the Annexation of Canada to the United States, 1849–1893* (Lexington, Ky.: University of Kentucky Press, 1960), p.v.

57. Grey to Sifton, Dec. 7, 1908, University of Durham, Grey Papers, Canadian Letters 1908–09, no. 176, file 5.

58. Denison to Chamberlain, Aug. 4, 1910, Chamberlain Papers, JC 15/132.

59. D.C. Masters, *Reciprocity, 1846–1911* (Ottawa: Canadian Historical Association, 1961), p. 17.

60. G.E. Foster, "Reciprocity with the United States," *University Magazine*, VIII (1909), 550–62.

61. Olivar Asselin, *A Quebec View of Canadian Nationalism: an essay by a dyed in the wool French-Canadian on the best means of ensuring the Greatness of the Canadian Fatherland* (Montreal: Guertin Printing Co., 1909), p. 19.

62. Henri Bourassa, "Imperialism and Nationalism," in *Addresses Delivered before the Canadian Club of Ottawa, 1912–1913* (Ottawa: [n.p.], 1913), pp. 85–86.

63. *Ottawa Citizen*, Oct. 2, 1905, University of Durham, Grey Papers, 172, Clipping file.

64. Foresight (pseud.) to the Editor, *Canadian Military Gazette*, XXIV (May 11, 1909).

65. *Canadian Military Gazette*, XXIV (Aug. 24, 1919), p. 5.

66. Lt.-Col. Hugh Clark, "Imperial Defence," in *Addresses delivered before the Canadian Club of Toronto, Season 1908–1909* (Toronto: Warwick Bros. and Rivers, 1909), pp. 144–51.

67. C.H. Cahan, "Colonial Responsibilities," in Gerald H. Brown, ed., *Ad-*

dresses delivered before the Canadian Club of Ottawa, 1903–1909 (Ottawa, 1910), pp. 38–44.

68. Henri Bourassa, *The Spectre of Annexation and the Real Danger of National Disintegration with two letters from C.H. Cahan, K.C.* (Montreal: *Le Devoir* Printing, 1912).

69. Col. George T. Denison, *The Struggle for Imperial Unity: Recollections and Experiences* (London, New York: Macmillan, 1909), p. 369.

70. Maj. Gen. C.W. Robinson, *Canada and Canadian Defence: The Defensive Policy of the Dominion in relation to the character of her frontier, the events of the war of 1812–14, and her position today* (Toronto: Musson, 1910), pp. 139, 142.

71. Arthur Wellesley, "The Downfall of the British Empire," *National Defence*, IV (1910), 484–99.

72. Maj. W. Cyprian Bridge, "The Race for Hegemony: Great Britain versus the United States," [British] *United Service Magazine*, n.s. XLIII (July 1911), pp. 383–91.

73. Christopher West, *Canada and Sea Power* (Toronto: McClelland and Goodchild, 1913; London, 1914). As the author's name appears in the *Canadian Annual Review*, 1913, p. 12, in quotation marks, it may be presumed to be a pseudonym. Cf. J.L. Granatstein and Paul Stevens, *Canada since 1867: A Bibliographical Guide* (Toronto: Hakkert, 1974), p. 40, where *Canada and Sea Power* is described as "essentially a religio-militarist tract calling on Canadians to support the imperial fleet." "Christopher West" was probably Emerson Bristol Biggar (1853–1921), a Toronto journalist (information from Thomas A. LaRue; see also *Canadian Notes & Queries*, no. 18 [1976], 3).

74. West, *The Defence of Canada: in the light of Canadian History* (London and Toronto: J.M. Dent & Sons, 1914), pp. 11–12.

75. Desmond Morton, *The Canadian General: Sir William Otter* (Toronto: Hakkert, 1974), p. 295.

76. Richard A. Preston, *Canada and 'Imperial Defense': A Study of the British Commonwealth Defense Organization* (Durham, N.C.: Duke University Press, 1967), pp. 401–14.

77. Morton, *Canadian General*, p. 299.

78. Gen. Sir John French, *Report on his Inspection of the Canadian Militia*, in Canada, *Sessional Papers*, XLV, 1911, vol. 21, no. 35a.

79. Morton, *Canadian General*, p. 331.

80. "Mobilization of the Field Army," 1906, PAC, RG 24, vol. 2431, HQ C 484, vol. I.

81. Ibid., April 1, 1910.

82. Canadian General Staff, *Mobilization Regulations* (Ottawa: Government Printing Bureau, 1912), PAC, RG 24, S/016, HQW 125–1.

83. Weigley, *United States Army*, pp. 347–48.

84. Morton, *Canadian General*, p. 321.

85. Stephen Leacock, "The American Attitude," *University Magazine*, XIII (1914), 595–97.

CHAPTER 8

1. Col. A. Fortescue Duguid, *Official History of the Canadian Forces in the Great War, 1914–1919* (Ottawa: King's Printer, 1938), I, pt. 1, 111–12.

2. Col. Stanley W. Dziuban, *Military Relations between the United States and Canada, 1939–1945* (Washington: Office of the Chief of Military History, 1959), pp. 1–2.

3. A.J.M. Hyatt, "The Military Career of Sir Arthur Currie" (Ph.D. diss., Duke University, 1964), p. 178.

4. *The United States Army in the World War, 1917–1919: Training and Use of American Units with the British and French* (Washington: Historical Division of the Army, 1948), pp. 1, 98.

5. Col. G.W.L. Nicholson, *C.E.F.: The Canadian Expeditionary Force, 1914–1919* (Ottawa: Queen's Printer, 1962), p. 513.

6. L.F.B. Reed, "The American Expeditionary Force, North Russia: Genesis to Dissolution" (M.A. thesis, Duke University, 1966), pp. 78–80.

7. Col. C.P. Stacey, *The Military Problems of Canada: A Survey of Defence Policies and Strategic Conditions, Past and Present* (Toronto: Ryerson, 1940), p. 89.

8. Ibid., pp. 86–87.

9. James Eayrs, *In Defence of Canada*, I, *From the Great War to the Depression* (Toronto: University of Toronto Press, 1964), 70–73.

10. "Extracts from Defence Scheme No. 1, April 12, 1921," ibid., 323–28, app.

11. Brown to the CGS, Nov. 11, 1927, Queen's University Archives, Sutherland-Brown Papers.

12. Eayrs, *In Defence of Canada*, I, 70.

13. Ibid., pp. 75, 85.

14. Agenda for Joint Staff Committee, Sept. 28, 1927, Minutes of the First Meeting of the Joint Staff Committee, Oct. 31, 1927, Chiefs of Staff Committee Minutes, 1927–1939, I, 22–24, 27, 28, Armed Forces Historical Section, Ottawa.

15. Joint Staff Committee, Aug. 8, 1929, ibid., I, 59–61.

16. Eayrs, *In Defence of Canada*, I, 77.

17. Notably by Dr. Eayrs, ibid., pp. 70–78, 323–28.

18. Russell F. Weigley, *History of the United States Army* (New York: Macmillan, 1967), p. 403.

19. George S. Pappas, *Prudens Futuri: The U.S. Army War College, 1901–67* (Carlisle Barracks: Alumni Association, 1967), p. 90.

20. Ibid., pp. 84, 105.

21. Joint Army and Navy Board Files, USNA, RG 225–301, p.3, July 24, 1919.

22. Pappas, *Prudens*, 102; Fred Greene, "The Military View of American National Policy, 1904–1940," *American Historical Review*, LXVI (January 1961), 354n.

23. Maurice Matloff, ed., *American Military History* (Washington: OCMH, 1969), pp. 408–409.

24. Weigley, *History of the U.S. Army*, p. 406.

25. Ray S. Cline, *Washington Command Post: The Operations Division* (Washington: Office of the Chief of Military History, 1951), pp. 34–35.

26. Ibid., p. 35.

27. "[List of] War Plan Colors" [n.d.], USMHC, 111–56, M. Later Rainbow was used for war with the Axis powers. Cline, *Washington Command Post*, p. 36.

28. Louis Morton, "War Plan Orange: Evolution of a Strategy," *World Politics*, XI (1959), 221–250; Lt.-Comm. Thomas B. Buell, "Admiral Raymond Spruance and the Naval War College," *Naval War College Review*, XXIII (March 1971), 30–31.

29. Cline, *Washington Command Post*, pp. 35–36.

30. Ibid., p. 35.

31. M. Matloff, "The American Approach to War," in M. Howard, *Theory and Practice of War: Essays Presented to B.H. Liddell Hart on his Seventieth Birthday* (New York: Praeger, 1965), p. 219.

32. Buell, "Admiral Spruance," p. 37.

33. Pappas, *Prudens*, p. 95.

34. War Plans Course, 1919–20, Committee No. 1, USMHC, Army War Plans Division, General Staff College, Intelligence. Plans for operations with Canada were also studied elsewhere. An "inch-thick stack of blue prints, charts and letters," dating from 1919 and discovered in the Federal Records Center in Kansas City in September 1945 by Dr. Lawrence H. Larsen of the University of Missouri at Kansas City, outlined plans for the defence of Dakota and Montana against an invasion from Saskatchewan using cavalry, tanks, and heavy guns mounted on flat cars. This material was apparently prepared by officers of the Corps of Engineers, who obtained maps by writing to the Canadian topographical survey. Their studies were blocked when the Army Air Force and the Corps of Engineers disagreed about who should pay for cameras for photo-reconnaissance. This local planning was probably inspired by the enquiries instituted by the new Army War College course (*Washington Post*, Oct. 8, 1975).

35. Chief of Engineers, Sept. 30, [19]19, USMHC, AWC 35–3.

36. GSC, Dec. 17, [19]19, ibid., AWC 111–1.

37. GSC, Sept. 10, [19]19, ibid., AWC Int. S7–1.

38. MID, Feb. 5, [19]19, ibid., AWC 89–9/1.

39. Details are given in Richard A. Preston, "Buster Brown Was Not Alone: American Plans for the Invasion of Canada, 1919–1939," *Canadian Defence Quarterly*, III, no. 4 (Spring 1974), 48.

40. War Plans Course, 1921–22, V, 203, USMHC, AWC, Army War Plans Division, General Staff College, Intelligence.

41. Col. H.B. Crosby, "Orientation," Feb. 28, 1924, Army War College,

Session 1923–24, USMHC, WPD Docs., nos. 1–21, VIII, "Lectures, Studies, Summaries."

42. "Determination of War Plans to be prepared, Conference March 22, 1924," 3, ibid.

43. "Appendix to Army Strategic Plan, War Plan Red," 5, ibid.; App. no. 4, "Army Strategic Plan Red," ibid.

44. USNA, RG 167, WD General Staff, Red Plan, 2444–4, 2444–5, 8069.

45. Maj. H.A. Darque, Air Service, War Plans Representative, memorandum for Maj. John L. Jenkins, General Staff, May 25, 1927, USNA, RG 165, WD General Staff, Red 2444–4.

46. Col. Stanley H. Ford, "The Halifax Expedition," Nov. 22, 1927, USNA, RG 165, WPD, no. 10, Red 3069.

47. USNA, RG 165, WD General Staff 2963, Red-Orange, May 16, 19, 1927.

48. "Estimate of Blue-Red Plan" [of July 15, 1927], [Role of the Air Force], USNA, RG 165, WD General Staff, Red 2444–6.

49. U.S. Naval Intelligence Dept. Attaché's Report, Royal Canadian Air Force, Dec. 20, 1930, U.S. Naval War College Records, ser. no. 863.

50. Brig.-Gen. George S. Simonds, for Chief of Staff, Feb. 18, 1928, USNA, RG 165, WD General Staff, Red 2444–8.

51. Memorandum for the Director, G-2 Division, Army War College, "A Study of the possible means for ensuring the neutrality or active assistance of (a) Canada, and (b) Australia in case of a war with Red-Orange, Feb. 6, 1926," USMHC, Army War College, Session 1925–26.

52. Maj. A.C. Cron, Infantry, D.O.L., ibid.

53. May 24, [19]19, USMHC, AWC 28–71.

54. Simonds, memorandum for Chief of Staff, USNA, RG 165, WD General Staff, Red 2444–13.

55. "Navy Basic Plan (Red)," U.S. Navy Records, WPL22, vol. I.

56. Memorandum to Depts., "Subject War Plan Red," Sept. 18, 1930, USNA, RG 165, WD General Staff, Red 2444–18.

57. Memorandum for Chief of Staff, Aug. 22, 1932, USNA, RG 165, WD General Staff, 2444–20.

58. Memorandum for Chief of Staff, "Subject GHQ Air Force," April 25, 1932, USNA, RG 165, WD General Staff, Red 2444–23.

59. Brig.-Gen. C.E. Kilbourne, memorandum for Assistant Chief of Staff, G-2, "Military Reconnaissance," Feb. 4, 1935, USNA, RG 165, WD General Staff, Red 3818.

60. Stacey, *Military Problems of Canada*, pp. 30–31.

61. DNI to D. WPD, June 27, 1935, USNA, RG 165, WD General Staff, 3203–5.

62. Army War College, Dec. 18, 1935, USMHC, AWC 2–1936–8, G2, no. 19A.

63. Army War College, Session 1937–38, War Plans Docs., no. 30, vol. VII, "Student Blue War Plan versus Red-Gold-Crimson coalition," USMHC, AWC 5–1933–1911.

64. Obsolete War Plans, March 3, 1937, USNA, RG 165, WD General Staff, Red 2444–37; Certificates of Destruction, June 15, 1937, ibid., 2444–38; Lt.-Col. L.T. Girow, GS, to Executive WPD, March 22, 1938, ibid., WD General Staff, 2444–39.

65. Army War College, Jan. 28, 1938, Committee No. 8, USMHC, AWC 2–1938–8.

66. Oper. Probl. VI (TAC 1939–SR), also called simply, "Force to Capture Halifax," USMHC, NWC 2–1939.

67. Admiral William Leahy, CNO, to Joint Board, May 25, 1939, USNA, Joint Board, no. 325, ser. 643.

68. Stacey, *Military Problems of Canada*, pp. 35–36.

69. James Eayrs, *In Defence of Canada*, II, *Appeasement and Rearmament* (Toronto: University of Toronto Press, 1965), 82.

70. R.D. Cuff and J.L. Granatstein, *Canadian-American Relations in Wartime: From the Great War to the Cold War* (Toronto: Hakkert, 1975), p. 22.

71. Eayrs, *In Defence of Canada*, II, 177.

72. C.P. Stacey, *Arms, Men, and Governments: The War Policies of Canada, 1939–1945* (Ottawa: Queen's Printer, 1970), pp. 75–76.

73. Ibid., 96–97; Eayrs, *In Defence of Canada*, II, 179, 184.

74. Eayrs, *In Defence of Canada*, II, 176–184; Stacey, *Arms, Men, and Governments*, pp. 95–99; Dziuban, *Military Relations*, p. 3.

75. Eayrs, *In Defence of Canada*, II, 184–86.

76. Harold G. Skilling, *Canadian Representation Abroad, From Agency to Embassy* (Toronto: Ryerson, 1945), p. 304.

77. Dziuban, *Military Relations*, pp. 6–7.

78. Ibid., pp. 22–24, 79–80, 90–94, 123–24.

79. Ibid., pp. 109–10.

80. Ibid., pp. 112–13, 122–26.

81. Ibid., p. 130.

82. Ibid., p. 340; A.D.P. Heeney, *The Things That Are Caesar's: Memoirs of a Canadian Public Servant* (Toronto: University of Toronto Press, 1972), p. 74.

83. Alec Douglas, "Why Does Canada Have Armed Forces?", *International Journal*, XXX (Spring 1975), 270–71.

84. Dziuban, *Military Relations*, pp. 126, 340.

85. Ibid., pp. 339–45.

86. Grant Dexter, *Canada and the Building of Peace* (Toronto: Canadian Institute of International Affairs, 1944), pp. 165–67.

87. Charles Foulkes, *Canadian Defence Policy in the Nuclear Age*, Behind the Headlines, XXI, no. 1 (Toronto: Canadian Institute of International Affairs, 1961), p.1; John B. McLin, *Canada's Changing Defense Policy 1957–1963: The Problems of a Middle Power in Alliance* (Baltimore: Johns Hopkins, 1967), p. 9; Melvin Conant, *The Long Polar Watch: Canada and the Defense of North America* (Westport, Conn.: Greenwood Press, 1974), pp. 21–22.

88. Colin S. Gray, *Canadian Defence Priorities: A Question of Relevance* (Toronto: Clarke, Irwin, 1972), p. 19.

89. Ibid., pp. 14–38, 158–68; Stephen Clarkson, ed., *An Independent Foreign Policy for Canada?* (Toronto: McClelland and Stewart, 1968), pp. 260–63; Andrew Brewin, *Stand on Guard: The Search for a Canadian Defence Policy* (Toronto: McClelland and Stewart, 1965), p. 8; John Warnock, *Partner to Behemoth: The Military Policy of a Satellite Canada* (Toronto: New Press, 1970), pp. 296–317.

90. Roger Swanson, *The United States as a National Security Risk to Canada*, Behind the Headlines, XXIX, nos. 5–6 (Toronto: Canadian Institute of International Affairs, 1970), p. 9.

91. Denis Stairs, *The Diplomacy of Constraint: Canada, the Korean War, and the United States* (Toronto: University of Toronto Press, 1974), pp. 92–140.

92. Gray, *Canadian Defence Priorities*, pp. 125, 121–55.

93. Donald S. Macdonald, *Defence in the Seventies: White Paper on Defence* (Ottawa: Information Canada, 1971); *Foreign Policy for Canadians* (Ottawa: Queen's Printer, 1970), p. 15; Mitchell Sharp, "Canada-U.S. Relations: Options for the Future," *International Perspectives* (Autumn 1972), *passim*.

94. This form of attack is dealt with in rather fanciful form in the novels by Richard H. Rohmer, *Ultimatum* (Toronto: Clarke, Irwin, 1973) and *Exxoneration* (Toronto: McClelland and Stewart, 1974).

95. John Holmes, *The Better Part of Valour: Essays on Canadian Diplomacy* (Toronto: McClelland and Stewart, 1970), p. 145.

96. Gray, *Canadian Defence Priorities*, pp. 18–19.

NOTE ON SOURCES

Few secondary works have dealt with the problems of the defence of Canada after Confederation, or with American military policies with respect to the northern border of the United States after the Civil War. One reason for this is that historians accept the primacy of other aspects of Canadian-American relations and have stressed the lack of public concern about military factors. The brief historiographical outline in the Introduction to this book suggested that the hiatus in our knowledge is only partially explained by the nature of the subject. The likely course of military operations in North America, if war should come, and plans to anticipate it and shape its results, always posed conundrums that were as fascinating as they were complex. The development of professional opinion on this subject, and the failure to find answers that were convincing, were most probably a contributory factor in helping to promote eventual reliance on peaceful solutions for the settlement of disputes between Canada and the United States. But in both countries the politicians, soldiers, and others who turned their attention to the problem were usually secondary figures. Although war was frequently discussed at a higher level in Britain, a strong inclination to avoid entanglement made the question somewhat academic. Furthermore, in all three countries such discussions were usually confidential for both military and political reasons. Hence the sources for the study of the strategies of defence and attack in North America are scattered and hard to come by.

The chief British source for such a study is the Colonial Office papers in the British Public Record Office, both for the period before Confederation and for that which followed the withdrawal of the British garrison in 1870–71. Britain's guarantee to Canada in 1865, and again in 1869–70, induced British political and military leaders to keep in mind the implications of, and therefore the method of conducting, a war in North America. These are to be found in the correspondence between the governor general and the Colonial Office and in attached papers in the CO 42 series and the confidential defence series CO 537. Intelligence reports and strategic analyses concerning Canada are to be found in the War Office papers, mainly in WO 32 and WO 106, but also in WO 1, WO 6, WO 33, and WO 80. These War Office and Colonial Office papers can be consulted on microfilm in the Public Archives of Canada.

Admiralty papers are less fruitful despite the paramount importance of the imperial naval base at Halifax and of the control of the Great Lakes, but reference should be made to papers in ADM 1.

The important Tenterden memorandum on military relations with the United States is in the Foreign Office papers, FO 881/1828; and confidential reports on US coast defences are in FO Confidential Report 4690.

For the study of the early twentieth century the papers of the Committee of Imperial Defence are filed in the Public Record Office under a cabinet (CAB) reference, and the series also includes earlier papers of the Colonial Defence Committee. These are a most important source but the microfilmed copy of CAB 38, which purports to cover all the basic material, is not exhaustive. It should be supplemented by reference to other numbers in the series.

The Jervois Reports of 1864 and 1865 were printed and published; but the three volumes of the Report of the Carnarvon Commission on Imperial Defence were restricted in circulation. They can now be seen in the War Office Library.

Various private collections of papers include military material about North America. The papers of the duke of Cambridge, the general officer commanding in chief and later the commander-in-chief, are now in the Royal Archives, Windsor, where they were examined by gracious permission of Her Majesty the Queen. Useful information about the British garrison during the Civil War can be found in the letters of Captain Moorsom in the India Office Library or on microfilm in the Massey Library of the Royal Military College of Canada. The papers of two GOCs of the Canadian militia are also invaluable. Gen. E. T. H. Hutton's papers are in the British Museum and in transcript in the Public Archives of Canada; and Lord Dundonald's papers are on microfilm in the Douglas Library at Queen's University, Kingston.

Papers of Edward Cardwell as secretary of the colonies and as secretary of state for war are in the Public Record Office with copies in the Canadian archives. The earl of Carnarvon's correspondence with the marquis of Dufferin, also in the Public Record Office, was not published in its entirety in the Champlain Society volume edited by Frank Underhill and C. W. De Kieweit. The earl of Clarendon's papers are in Christ Church College, Oxford; and Lord Palmerston's papers housed at Broadlands were seen at the offices of the Historical Manuscripts Commission. The marquis of Dufferin's papers are in the Public Record Office of Northern Ireland and the earl of Minto's in the Scottish National Archives in Edinburgh. The papers of Sir George Cornewall Lewis, an undersecretary for war, are in the Harpton Court Collection in the National Library of Wales, Aberystwyth. Sir Michael Hicks Beach's papers are in the Earl St. Aldwyn collection in the Gloucester Record Office. The Seymour Papers in the Devon County Record Office, Exeter, contain maps of Canadian defence plans not found elsewhere.

Articles that reveal contemporary British professional opinion on the problem of defending Canada can be found in newspapers and periodicals such as the *Times, Blackwood's Magazine,* and *Nineteenth Century;* but the best source for military opinion is the service press. The *Journal of the Royal United Services Institution, Broad Arrow,* the *United Service Magazine, National Defence,* and the *United Service Gazette and Organ of Imperial Federation* contain scattered articles.

Official papers in Canada are less rewarding than those in Britain but an essential source is the *Annual Report* of the Department of Militia published in the *Sessional Papers.* Of particular significance is an appendix to the Report of 1879, an article by Lt.-Col. (later Maj.-Gen.) T. B. Strange. The papers of the Militia Department (RG 9), of British Military and Naval Records (RG 8), and of the governor general (RG 7) are the chief sources in the Public Archives of Canada. A calendar, *The Defences of Canada,* prepared by a secretary of a Canadian Defence Committee appointed a few years earlier and published in 1886, is a useful guide up to that date. The report of the Leach Commission of 1898 which is among the RG 9 series is especially important.

Prime ministers' papers contain a few items of interest but Macdonald, Mackenzie, and Laurier apparently gave little personal attention to defence matters, especially vis-à-vis the United States. The ministerial papers of the ministers of militia, Sir Adolphe Caron, in the Public Archives, and Sir Frederick Borden in the Nova Scotia Archives, deal with administrative, political, and patronage questions rather than with strategy.

Valuable information about the attitudes of interested and informed Canadians, especially of militia officers and of serving and retired British regular officers may be found in books, pamphlets, and articles in periodicals. In addition to Strange's seminal article mentioned above, of particular significance are

Col. H. C. Fletcher's *Memorandum on the Militia System* (1873), Richard Cartwright's *Remarks on the Militia of Canada*, and the anonymous *Thoughts on Defence from a Canadian Point of View* (1870). For a later period Christopher West's *Canada and Sea Power* and also his *Defence of Canada* should be read to offset the much better known contemporary book, Gen. C. W. Robinson's *Canada and Canadian Defence* (1910), which takes a very different stand.

Writing on this subject is, of course, coloured by the subjective approach of the author and this is particularly true for articles on defence in the military press. One of the best sources for brief expressions of opinion is the *Canadian Militia Gazette*, called significantly in later periods the *Canadian Military Gazette*. The Directorate of History of the Canadian Armed Forces has a complete run of this periodical. Among nonprofessional periodicals, the *Canadian Monthly and National Review*, later called *Rose-Belford's Canadian Monthly*, and Col. G. T. Denison's *The Week*, paid particular attention to defence questions. Occasional articles or opinions can be found in the *Nation*, *Saturday Night*, the *Dominion Illustrated*, the *Forum*, as well as in newspapers like the *Globe*, and the *British Whig*. By and large such articles add little to the debate on the technical problems of war on the Canadian-American border but they serve to indicate the attitudes of certain sections of the Canadian public on the question of war with the United States.

The starting point for the study of American military thought about the problem of defending the northern border, or of operations there in the event of war with Britain, is the vast collection of Executive Documents submitted to Congress. These are especially informative on the question of defence construction or planning for construction in the nineteenth century. Especially to be noted are the reports of Gen. T. G. Totten (1851) and of the Board of Fortifications (1866).

A most useful preliminary guide to manuscript materials in some American archives was a report in the archives of the Directorate of History of the Canadian Armed Forces prepared by Lt. J. L. Granatstein for the Director of History of the Canadian Army in 1965. The most valuable source he located was the collection of Records of the Adjutant-General's Office in the United States National Archives (RG 165). Granatstein covered the period down to 1919, providing detailed reference guides to a series of border incidents. He noted the existence of the files of the Joint Board of the Army and Navy and correctly stated that they did not mention Canada down to 1914. And he examined the index cards of the Army War College which refer to many documents that have been destroyed. General Staff plans down to 1915 were declassified for him to see; but the Army Color Plans for a later period were restricted until 1973.

The conclusion of Granatstein's report, that "material available in the American Archives . . . is very limited," is, however, now quite misleading. Lieutenant Granatstein found an index card in the National Archive for a memorandum about the invasion of Canada prepared by Assistant Adjutant-General T. M. Vincent at the time of the Venezuela crisis and reported that the document itself had been destroyed, but he missed the longer series of documents in the naval records on the same subject, USNA (OL). He noted that the Army War College Archives at Carlisle Barracks (USMHC) might contain more material; but he was not able to go there and so he did not see the whole range of suggestive material in the course records. The Army Color Plans are now available at the National Archives but the papers referring to Canada are not extensive. The navy's plans are in the Naval Records Center at the Washington Navy Yard. Some useful papers were received from the U.S. Naval War College but the records there are disappointing.

Lieutenant Granatstein suggested that American military periodicals would be a useful source of information about opinion but he made reference only to one, the *United States Infantry Journal* founded in 1904, which did not mention Canada until 1914 when it published an article on the Canadian militia. Much more rewarding for a study of the defence of the northern border are the *Army and Navy Journal*, the *United Service*, the *Journal of the Military Service Institution of the United States*, the *Army and Navy Magazine*, the *United Service Gazette*, and the *Naval War College Review*.

Index